Upper Grijalva River Basin Survey

Largartero, Tr-99, located during Upper Grijalva River Basin Survey.

PAPERS

of the

NEW WORLD ARCHAEOLOGICAL FOUNDATION

NUMBER SEVENTY-NINE

Upper Grijalva River Basin Survey

by

Michael Blake, Thomas A. Lee Jr., Mary E. Pye and John E. Clark

with contributions by

Barbara Voorhies, James M. White

VOLUME EDITOR

Mary E. Pye

New World Archaeological Foundation
Brigham Young University Press
Provo, Utah
2016

ACKNOWLEDGMENTS

Editors

A multi-year project of this scale and scope requires the efforts of many individuals to be successful, and the Upper Grijalva River Basin Project was the beneficiary of significant support, both institutional and individual. However, given that the work took place over 40 years ago, memories have faded, and the field director of the project has passed away, therefore, we apologize for any omissions in our gratitude.

We thank the NWAF personnel who participated in this project in surveying, map creation, test-pitting, documentation, and analysis, including Pierre Agrinier, Susanna Ekholm, Gareth Lowe, Ronnie Lowe, Eduardo Martínez, Jorge Acuña Nuricumbo, Vicente Pérez, Alejandro Sánchez, and Artemio Villatoro, colleagues including Sydney Markman and Barbara Voorhies, as well as the many students who participated, David Bathgate, Doug Bryant, Fausto Ceja, Deanne Gurr-Matheny, Don Miller, Glenna Nielson, Maricruz Paillés, Sonia Rivero, James White, Nicole Boucher White. Others were essential in photography and illustration, including Susan Blake, D'Arcy Blake, Kristi Butterwick, Ralph Hilt, Victoria Jefferies, Kornelia Kurbjuhn, Elizabeth Ross, and Mario Vega.

We acknowledge the professionalism and long-term institutional collaboration from the personnel of INAH over the lifetime of this project, including the Directors of the Departamento de Monumentos Prehispánicos, Ángel García Cook, Joaquín García-Barcena, Ignacio Marquina; the Presidents of the Consejo de Arqueología, Ignacio Bernal, Joaquín García-Barcena, José Luis Lorenzo, and Eduardo Matos M., as well as the Regional Directors of the Centro-INAH Chiapas, Norberto González Crespo, Jordi Gussinyer, and Enrique Méndez Martínez. We further thank the many local municipal and ejidal authorities and landowners who granted us permission to walk the lands and document the sites.

Publishing the archaeological efforts of this project was also labor of several years; particularly noteworthy were the Indesign skills and management of student artists by Arlene Colman. Many students worked on the figures, improving and digitizing them. We thank them all for their assistance in finishing this work.

Finally, we acknowledge and thank the many individuals and institutional support provided by Brigham Young University throughout the life of this project.

Barbara Voorhies

Several people participated significantly in this project and their contributions are very much appreciated. I am particularly grateful to my "socio," Alejandro Sánchez, for sharing his knowledge and his joie de vivre during the fieldwork. I am also grateful to the late Dennis Breedlove for identifying the plants and for reading several versions of this paper. His advice saved me from several embarrassments. James Nations also read a draft and I am appreciative of his assistance.

Financial support for the field research was provided by the New World Archaeological Foundation, Brigham Young University. My salary was provided by the University of California during a sabbatical leave in the Winter Quarter of 1977. The preparation of the map was facilitated by a General Research Grant from the University of California Academic Senate, which allowed me to employ several able assistants. I wish to thank Joan Chavez, Janine Gasco, and Diane Plante for their contribution in finalizing the map. The late Paul E. Heuston photographed the field sheets of vegetation zones and reduced them for the base map. In addition, he lettered the final reduced map and prepared the photographs. I am very grateful for his help.

CONTENTS

FIGURES

TABLES

CHAPTER 1

INTRODUCTION

Mary E. Pye, John E. Clark, and Michael Blake

This publication presents the results of a reconnaissance in the upper Grijalva River Basin (Figure 1.1). Beginning in 1973, and continuing through 1982, personnel working for the New World Archaeological Foundation (NWAF) recorded more than 300 archaeological sites in this region of southeastern Chiapas. The data recovered and recorded here provided the basis for several large-scale excavation projects that are currently in the process of being published (e.g., Blake 2010; Bryant 2008; Byrant et al. 2005; Miller 2014). The reconnaissance data allowed for more than simply a selection of sites for excavation, however, it also permitted an assessment of the changing organization of the societies which occupied this region over the past three millennia. Although the survey was by no means a systematic one, and parts of the study area remain to be reconnoitered, the information obtained tells us a great deal about the evolution of complex societies in this part of Mesoamerica. The settlement data presented here, together with the data recovered during the excavations undertaken in the region, contributes to a clearer understanding of the prehistory of the upper tributaries region.

The upper tributaries of the Grijalva River drain a huge inland valley bounded by the Sierra Madre Mountains to the south, the Cuchumatan Mountains in Guatemala to the east, and the central plateau of Chiapas to the north. The region was occupied (and quite densely at certain moments) more or less continuously from the end of the Archaic Period at least by 2200 BC (Lee and Clark 1988). While there was initial hope of uncovering large centers comparable with Lowland Maya cities (i.e., Palenque), no such monumental sites were found. Nonetheless, large centers and densely populated zones were documented throughout the region. Here, we provide the basic information on those sites uncovered, including maps, chronological assessments,

and other data, all from a region that was generally unknown in the 1970s when the project began. The publication of the findings from the NWAF's work in the upper Grijalva River Basin region has been ongoing since 2005 and, with this volume, we are near the halfway point in publishing excavations. The NWAF investigations represent the collective work of dozens of individuals in fieldwork, analyses, and dissemination, not all of whom are listed here as co-authors of chapters. Tables 1.1 and 1.2 present updated versions of tables first published in the *Ceramic Sequence of the Upper Grijalva Region* volumes (Bryant et al. 2005) and provide further information as to the participants and publications related to this project. The individuals directly involved in reconnaissance work included: Thomas A. Lee Jr., director of the research project in the region, and (in alphabetical order) Michael Blake, John Clark, Deanne Gurr, Ronald Lowe, Eduardo Martínez, Alejandro Sánchez, Sonia Rivero Torres, Barbara Voorhies, James White, and Nicole Boucher White.

THE GENESIS OF THE "UPPER GRIJALVA MAYA RESEARCH PROJECT"

The idea for this upper tributaries project arose from discussions around Tom Lee's desire to pursue doctoral studies at the Universidad Nacional Autónoma de México (UNAM) while in the employ of the NWAF. To enter a postgraduate program in the Mexican system requires the presentation of a formulated research problem and project which would then develop into a thesis. Hence, in 1972, he was ruminating on what project to pursue that would interest him but also make sense in terms of NWAF interests, which had generally focused on Preclassic occupations of Chiapas (e.g., Izapa) or salvage projects undertaken with the Instituto Nacional de Antropología e Historia

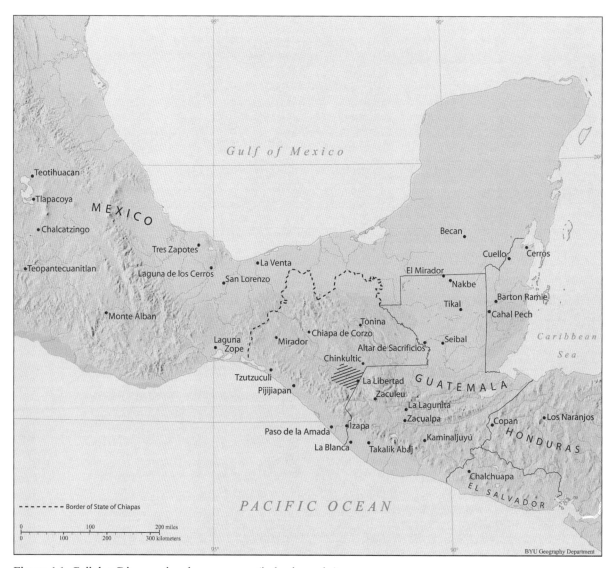

Figure 1.1. Grijalva River regional survey area (in hash marks).

(INAH) (e.g., Malpaso Dam). Correspondence between Lee and Gareth Lowe, Field Director of the NWAF at the time, reveals an insightful dynamic involving new theory ("New Archaeology"), logistical realities, complete voids of archaeological information for large swaths of Chiapas, and a bit of generational conflict (Lowe was 17 years older than Lee). All these played out in the process of developing this project—a project that would also significantly evolve from its original premises.

In somewhat graduate student style, Lee expressed to Lowe his concerns as to the lack of new theoretical approaches exhibited in work done by the NWAF up to that point:

> We, however, with Longacre, Binford and the rest on the loose are skating on thin ice if we don't try and shape our efforts up into a modern format. I agree with you many do less, but they are beginning to be picked off by "new archaeologists" and we are long overdue…Perhaps I cannot do what I want to due to a lack of capacity but I feel I must try and do something more than simple presentation of the facts. [The] Carnegie [group] was able to arrive at that

Table 1.1. Surveys in the upper Grijalva River Basin under the auspices of the NWAF.

Region	Nos.	Yrs	Primary Investigators	References
Bella Vista	BV 1-8	1974	White, Lee	White 1976
Chicomuselo[1]	Ch 1-66	1974	Lee, White	White 1976
Comalapa	Co 1-69	1974	Lee, White	White 1976
La Trinitaria	Tr 1-206	1973-74	Bryant, Clark, Lee, Rivero, White	Lee & Clark 1988
Morelos*	Tr 207-252	1980	Clark, R. Lowe	Bryant & Clark 1983, Clark & R. Lowe 1980
Rosario Valley		1973-74	Agrinier, Lee	Agrinier 1979a, 1984, n.d.
Upper Grijalva		1955-58	Lowe	Lowe 1959, Shook 1956

*results from this survey will be published in the forthcoming monograph on the excavations of El Cerrito.

level and did a good job, but 20 to 30 years later can we rest there? (Lee 3/24/1972).

In response, Lowe offered some possible field projects that the NWAF could undertake and be incorporated into Lee's dissertation plans. The first suggestion was survey and testpits on the west bank of the La Venta River Canyon between the Pan-American Highway and the Oaxaca border and/or the Mal Paso Lake, building on work done by the joint INAH-NWAF Malpaso Dam salvage project in 1965-66 (Lee et al. 2015) and by Frederick Peterson's 1958-59 surveys in western Chiapas (Peterson 2014). The other Lowe suggestion was for Lee to scout the area around the Jatate River and Lacanja drainage or along the road to the Maya site of Bonampak (Figure 1.2). In his letter of April 7, 1972, Lowe further offered that: "If you find static too great about the Bonampak Road, then I would seriously propose the upper Grijalva tributary region, i.e., Comitan to the [Guatemalan] border and south to the Sierra Madre. To me this is a delightful region and as rich archaeologically as any other...I frankly think this is a lovely alternative to the hot humid lowlands with its devastating rainfall,

communications problems, Maya complications, and generally competitive situation. Think about it."

Apparently also not in agreement with Lee's assessment of a dearth of theory exhibited in NWAF work, Lowe then states:

> There are some other problems for us to discuss. You note your slow progress with Md 4 SI [San Isidro] discussion and a need to do something more profound than has been done in some of our other papers. Well and good. But you cannot incorporate "new archaeology" after the fact of digging, or for that matter in the complex situation within Mound 4. As Bruce [Warren] says, the new archaeology only works with one-period sites! (4/7/1972)

Lowe was waiting on Lee to finish writing up the excavations of Mound 4 at San Isidro (see Lee 1974b) and Lowe ended his comments with:

> You can't say much about function and culture let alone process because of the limited "research design" governing your brief salvage efforts. No one can expect it. As for Sanders' criticism of Agrinier, this is all very well, but what did Sanders

---

[1] This is the modern spelling of the name, but it also appears as Chicomucelo, particularly in older publications and when referring to the native language.

Table 1.2. Excavations in the upper Grijalva River Basin under the auspices of the NWAF.

Site	No.	Years	Primary Investigators	Primary Occupation(s)	References
Camcum	Tr-183	1979-80	Clark, Lee	Archaic-Modern	Lee & Clark 1988
Canajasté	Tr-69	1981-82	Blake	Early Postclassic, Late Postclassic	Blake 1986, 2010
El Cerrito	Tr-42	1980	Clark, R. Lowe	Protoclassic	Clark & Lowe 1980
Los Cimientos	Tr-29	1977	Rivero	Late Classic	Rivero 1978, 1987
Coapa	Tr-162	1978, 1980	Bryant, Lee	Colonial	Lee 1979a, 1979b, 1996; Lee & Bryant 1988
Coneta	Tr-95	1975-76	Lee, Markman	Late Postclassic, Colonial	Lee & Markman 1977, 1979; Markman 1984
Los Encuentros	Tr-94	1977	Bryant, Lee	Early Postclassic, Late Postclassic	Lee & Bryant n.d., 1996
Entre Ríos	Tr-109	1977	Lee, Lowe, Miller	Early Preclassic, Middle Preclassic	Miller & Lowe 2014
Guajilar	Tr-59	1976, 1978	Bryant, Clark, Lee	Late Classic, Early Postclassic	Lee 1994; Wells 2015
Lagartero	Tr-99	1975-77	Blake, Ekholm, Gurr-Matheny, Rivero, et al.	Late Classic	Ekholm 1979b, 1990; Ekholm & Martínez 1983; see Rivero, Tenorio
La Libertad	Tr-157	1975-76	Lee, Lowe, Miller, Nielsen	Middle Preclassic	Clark 1988; Miller 2014
Mango Amate	Tr-105	1976	Paillés, Ávila	Protoclassic	Paillés & Ávila López 1987
Ojo de Agua	Tr-152	1976, 1980	Bryant, Ceja, Lowe	Protoclassic, Early Classic	Bryant 1984, 2008
Portrero Mango	Tr-172	1977, 1980	Lee, Lowe, Miller	Early Preclassic, Late Preclassic	Miller and Lowe 2014; Lee 1980
El Rosario	Tr-142	1979	Agrinier, de Montmollin	Late Classic	Agrinier 1979a; de Montmollin 1979
Santa Marta Rosario	Tr-19	1979	Bathgate	Early Preclassic, Middle Preclassic	Bathgate 1980
Tenam Rosario	Tr-9	1975	Agrinier	Early Classic, Late Classic	Agrinier n.d., 1979a, 1979b, 1983, 1984, 1993; de Montmollin 1988, 1989c

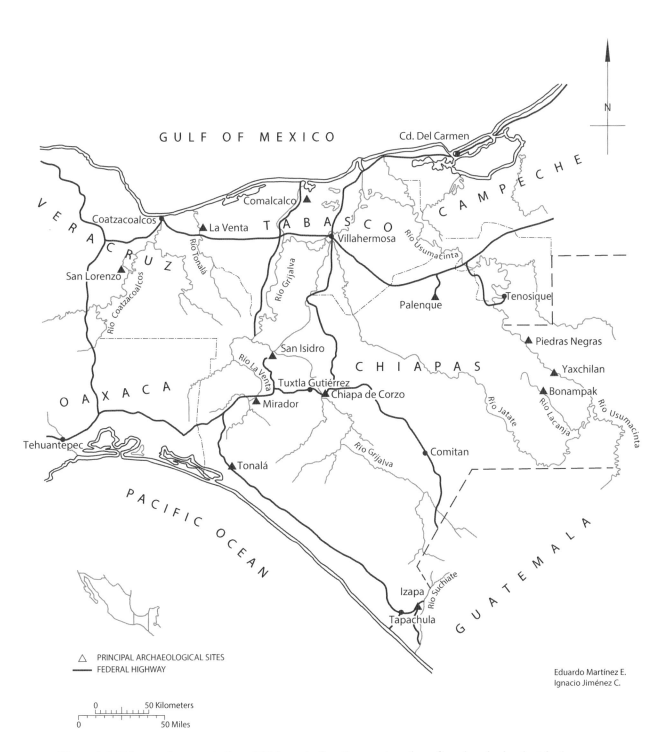

Figure 1.2. Primary rivers and sites of Chiapas before the construction of modern hydroelectric dams.

himself have to say about anything after digging directly in domestic structures, supposedly at Santa Cruz? Nothing at all. He never got beyond ceramics, chronology, and comparisons [Sanders 1961]. It isn't so easy. People who make profound statements at the end of excavations are usually those who had profound problems formulated before they began (and rarely fail to fulfill them), even when, as in Binford's case they never get the time to actually study and report the artifacts. Bull. (Lowe 4/7/1972)

It seems that Lowe continued to be irked by this charge and in a subsequent letter, he stated:

I have given considerable thought to your obviously thought-provoking charge that the Foundation has had no [theoretical] problem. I realize that you did not mean just that, but that we have had no apparent problem orientation. The situation appears to be that we lost sight of our problem, or rather of emphasizing our problem or problems, in dealing with the workaday material.

Our approach in Chiapas was regional, and I have emphasized that from the beginning, and thus arranged for a large number of site studies by a variety of people, first in the central depression and then on the coast. What we have been after are the culture history and lifeways of two major regions. If you have not realized that, it is for lack of concern, on the one hand, and for my own failure to be constantly driving it home on the other. (Lowe 1/4/1973)

In the end, the upper Grijalva tributary area became the new focus of research for the NWAF, with the project titled "The Upper Grijalva Maya Research Project," and the scope was both regional and long-term, with the idea of understanding human occupation from its earliest moments to the Spanish Colonial incursions in the 16th century.

THE GOALS OF THE UPPER GRIJALVA MAYA RESEARCH PROJECT

The proximate inspiration of the Upper Grijalva Maya Research Project was the genetic model of Maya origins as summarized by Evon Vogt (1964). The basic proposition was that Maya languages (and thus biological groups and cultures) originated in the western highlands of Guatemala (the Cuchumatan Mountains) by 1800 BC and diffused or migrated from there to the four winds until Maya peoples came to occupy all the places in which they were found at the time of the Spanish Conquest, as well as places they continue to occupy today.

In 1973, Lee designed a major project for the NWAF that combined the genetic model with an ecological and evolutionary approach to culture history. He proposed to study Maya adaptation to three different but contiguous environmental zones in eastern Chiapas along the Guatemala border. The project was to spend the first five years in the headwater tributary region of the Grijalva River in the eastern end of the Central Depression, the central valley that runs the length of Chiapas. This is semi-arid hot country. The next five years were to be spent to the north on the Comitan Plateau, a more temperate climate; the final five years were to move even more to the north and investigate the lowland jungles known as the Lacandon Forest, the well-known environment of the Classic period Lowland Maya. If original Maya peoples migrated into these zones from highland Guatemala, how did basic environmental parameters influence their subsequent development in these regions?

The research was meant to combine survey and excavation for each of the three contiguous ecological zones. As fate would have it, the first zone was so complicated that the project never progressed to the next region. Lee's approach and hypothesis basically amounts to adaptive radiation, but he did not have that specific model in mind or use that language. The primary assumption was that the Maya came into the area early and gradually adapted to the local conditions. The Grijalva Valley is one of the regions immediately adjacent to the Cuchumatan Mountains, so it was a very likely place to look for early Maya. Prior to 1973, no significant excavations of an archaeological site had been conducted in this region, and it was only known from a few surveys (Lowe 1959; Piña Chan 1961; Shook 1956). Lengthy citation of the original intent of the NWAF project is appropriate because it was published in a place most investigators cannot access, a paper presented in 1973 at the Thirteenth Mesa Redonda of the Sociedad Mexicana de Antropología at Xalapa, Veracruz. The following is taken from Lee (1975:35-36):

> A major goal of the new long range program planned by the BYU-New World Archaeological Foundation will be to test an alternative hypothesis for part of the development of Lowland Maya culture and society. Previous archaeological work in the Central Depression of Chiapas has established the cultural precocity of this dry tropical intermontane valley. Many and diverse characteristic attributes of early Maya society such as polished waxy ceramics, punched-eye figurines, ballcourts and ceremonial plazas, terraced pyramids and even calendrics appear earlier in the intermediate Chiapas highlands than they do in either the Maya Lowlands or in the northern Guatemala Highlands, according to present data.

The propinquity of the Chiapas Central Depression and the Cuchumatan Mountains of Guatemala, in which the major headwaters of the Grijalva River lie, is self-evident. What is not so clear, or at least has never been emphasized, as far as I know, is the proximity of the southern or upper end of the Central Depression to the point of origin of the Maya languages in the Cuchumatanes [sic] Mountains suggested by linguistic evidence (Kaufman 1971; McQuown 1971). Nor have many investigators taken into consideration the linguistic complexity of the margins of the upper end of the Central Depression itself. Besides Tzeltal and Tzotzil, there are still Tojolabal, Chuj, Jacalteca, Mam, Motzintleca, Teco and perhaps even other Maya languages spoken in this area today.

The McQuown-Kaufman linguistic hypothesis of Maya dispersal from the postulated Cuchumatanes homeland would have the various languages migrating out to the north and to the south about 1800

B.C. onward. What this hypothesis does not explain is the impetus for the many Maya migrations. It is hardly likely that the Maya or another language group would over a long period of time produce such a series of migrations by some internal generative force alone. If this migration idea is correct, then a search for its causes and mechanisms is as imperative as is its history. Eastern Chiapas presents the ideal opportunity for investigation of these problems…

> The new long range program of research … will encompass the Intermediate Highland Maya regions of Eastcentral [sic] Chiapas, next to the present-day western border between Mexico and Guatemala. A proposed 15-year program will be divided into three five-year segments during which efforts will be directed to the recovery and synthesis of the local cultural developments in three major ecological zones. The project will move in sequence from south to north up out of the hot and relative dry low-forested Central Depression, through a natural saddle in the cool humid pine-oak zone around Comitan in the Highlands, and down into the intermediate Southern Lacandon tropical forest … This program should allow us to observe the development of prehispanic Maya culture over a long but ecologically varied continuum, region by region. It will also permit the testing of a general hypothesis of certain Lowland Maya Civilization origins from the southwest.

PROJECT DEVELOPMENT INTO THE "UPPER GRIJALVA RIVER BASIN PROJECT"

By 1975, Lee was able to report the results of two years of reconnaissance and the discovery of hundreds of sites and their chronology in the upper Grijalva region. The next six years were taken up with test excavations at 15 sites (Figure 1.3).

The Upper Grijalva Maya Project was the first program undertaken by the New World Archaeological Foundation (NWAF)

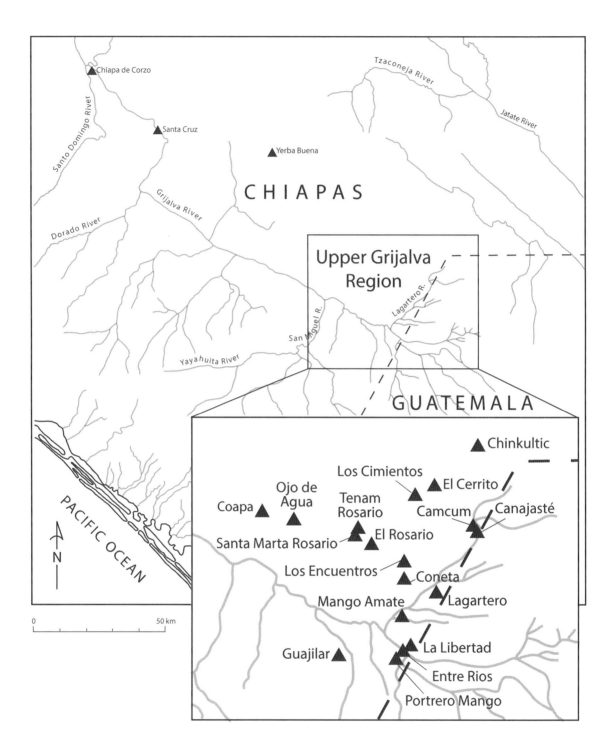

Figure 1.3. Excavated sites in the upper Grijalva River region.

in which the entire sequence of human occupation of a large region, from the Archaic through Colonial periods, was taken into consideration. One of our goals was to understand cultural evolution over the course of all prehistory and trailing into the Colonial era and, if possible, to trace different ethnic and linguistic identities through time and space… The inclusion of Colonial Indian villages in the research design brought our coverage into recorded history and amplified our understanding of the transformation or mestizaje of Maya society after the Spanish Conquest, a process typical of all Latin America but one not previously addressed for Maya communities in Chiapas (Lee 1984a:195-205). Early in our research we realized that the earliest cultures in the upper Grijalva region were not Maya, thus we changed the name of the project to the more appropriate Upper Grijalva River Basin Project (UGRB), the term we use throughout this study. (Clark et al. 2005:1)

From 1975-1977, excavations were undertaken at Tenam Rosario, La Libertad, Entre Ríos, Lagartero, Potrero Mango, Mango Amate, Coneta, Los Encuentros, Ojo de Agua, and Guajilar. In 1978, Coapa and the large Classic center of Guajilar, located on the left bank of the Santo Domingo River, were the focus. Santa Marta Rosario and El Rosario were excavated in 1979. The first two months of 1980 saw the excavations of the rockshelter of Camcum, the only site found in the region with both Archaic and Early Preclassic period occupation. Excavation at El Cerrito followed directly on the heels of this research, while in 1980, Ojo de Agua was again examined, and finally in 1981-82, excavations were undertaken at Canajasté. The site excavations were planned to provide information on each major time period and in each part of the study region. Some gaps still exist but, even so, the coverage is reasonably complete. Table 1.2 lists primary occupations of the sites that have been excavated to at least some extent, along with principal investigator(s) and references to information of the investigations.

Given the wealth of data recovered, and the passage of time, by 1979 the question being researched was no longer how the early Maya had acclimated and accommodated themselves to the semi-dry eastern valleys of the Grijalva River but rather to the question of when they had actually arrived. The ceramic evidence from the project was taken as sufficient warrant that the earliest ceramic-using villagers in eastern Chiapas, including the Central Depression, were not Maya. In 1977, Gareth Lowe published his well-known article on Maya-Zoque relations, a paper he labored over for years before it was published. By the late 1980s, the project title needed to better reflect this new complexity, and so it became "The Upper Grijalva River Basin Project" (UGRB).

One thing that Lee left out of his 1975 summary project objectives and findings was the then current notion that the Maya had a truncated history compared to some of their neighbors. This was clear in his original project proposal submitted to the NWAF board of directors in 1973.

By whatever means the Maya groups arrived in the Chiapas Highlands and Cuchumatan Mountains, the fact is that by the time of the Conquest there were at least ten Maya groups located in the headwaters of the Grijalva River in Mexico and Guatemala. These groups include in rough order, west to east, the Tzotzil, Tzeltal, Tojolabal, Chicomuceltec, Mototzentlec, Coxoh, Chuj, Jacalteca, Kanjobal, Teco and Mam. With the exception of Chicomuceltec and Coxoh, now extinct, all of these linguistic groups are still represented in the upper Grijalva River Basin.

Although we know little about the origin of Maya culture in general, we do know that up to the present there is no evidence for the beginning of lowland Maya culture prior to the Middle Preclassic period. The earliest evidence of occupation in the area is found at Altar de Sacrificios (Willey 1973:22-27) and Seibal (Willey 1970:315-355) in the Real Xe ceramic sphere which does not date prior to 900 B.C. This fact has always been more than a little surprising in view of the relatively high development in ceramics and ceremonial architecture and settled village life based on agriculture that both imply in the areas surrounding the Maya lowlands at an earlier date. The presence of this well-developed life-style in the general Tabasco-Veracruz Isthmus area, the Chiapas Central Depression and the Pacific Coast of Chiapas and Guatemala during the Early Preclassic can be dated to at least 1500 B.C. Recent work in the eastern end of the Guatemala Highlands of Alta and Baja Verapaz by [David] Sedat and [Robert] Sharer [Sharer and Sedat 1987] suggests that this area too participated in this earlier development. (Lowe and Lee 1973:5-7)

This discussion is followed by the logical proposal that the early Maya could have come from, or have been influenced by, the cultures in these surrounding areas, coming from the south, east, or north. Each of these possible homelands could be tested by gathering archaeological data on early occupations and comparing the artifacts from each of the regions in question.

Vogt (1964:19-20) recognized in his original study the need to know the material content of the highland areas on the early time level in order to establish those "diagnostic Maya traits" which could be used to prove, disprove or change the linguistic-based cultural history of the Maya genetic unit. This search, however, limited as it is to almost the very beginnings of settled village life, well before the distinctive characteristically Maya systemic patterns have developed is committed to failure before it starts. Only by returning in time to a point where the Classic period Maya patterns are clear can one progressively work backward in time tracing the roots of material cultural patterns via logical and direct typological and modal antecedents with any level of probability of their relationships portraying their true history.

The specific linguistic affiliation of even the Classic period lowland Maya cannot be surely known except through a direct

historical approach program of research. Although this is theoretically possible through pure linguistic analysis and comparison of modern languages and glyphic corpus of Classic written Maya, the problems involved suggest that this level of understanding is far away in the future.

The new long range research program planned ... will be concerned with not only the origin and dispersal of those cultural elements basic to the development of lowland Maya culture, but will also test the general linguistic hypothesis of origin and migration from the Cuchumatan Mountains ... Considerable emphasis will be placed on the identification of historic systemic patterns and specific cultural attributes identifiable with specific Maya languages in an attempt to trace the linguistic affiliation of earlier archaeological complexes. Considerable aid will be required in the field of ethnohistory in order to establish the Conquest period base line from which the earlier roots may be traced. (Lowe and Lee 1973:9-11)

Just a few years after this program of research of the early lowland Maya was started, spectacular but misinterpreted finds at Cuello, Belize, were to accord the Maya a very deep antiquity, a millennium deeper than any of their neighbors (Hammond et al. 1977). Although these claims were tempered over the ensuing two decades (Andrews and Hammond 1990), never again would the Maya be seen as late-arrivals on the Mesoamerican scene.

Testing linguistic theories of Maya origins, or for any people, with potsherds and other artifacts has always been a dicey business subject to frequent derision, and matters remain little changed today. Identity issues now have the protective cover of ethnic studies, ethnicity being a slightly more flexible construct than language because it is arguably a deliberate cultural choice with deliberate manifestations and material signals that can be recovered archaeologically. In the NWAF project, Lee meant to address Vogt's suggestion that the material markers of Mayaness should be traced in time and space. Ironically, research in western

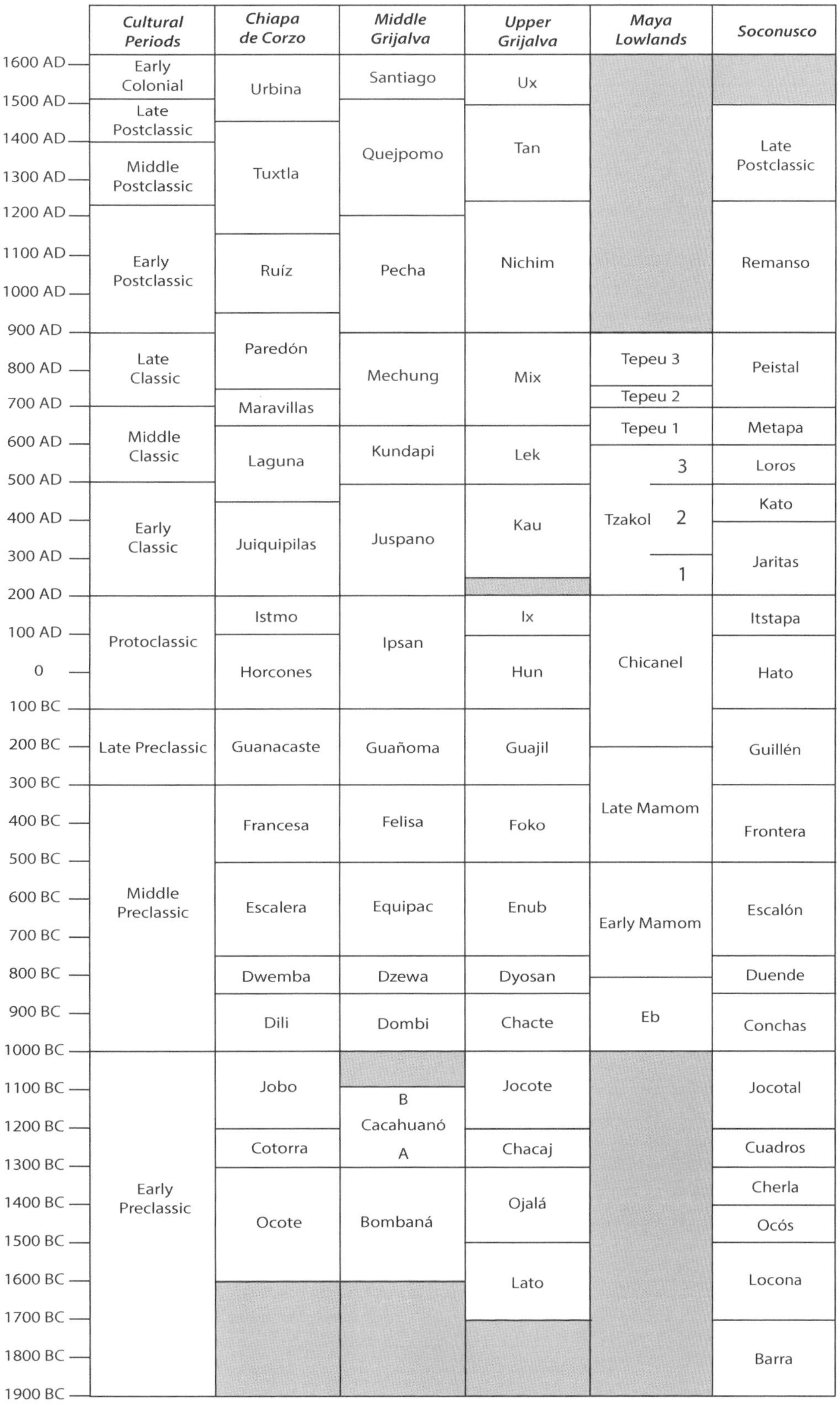

	Cultural Periods	Chiapa de Corzo	Middle Grijalva	Upper Grijalva	Maya Lowlands	Soconusco
1600 AD	Early Colonial	Urbina	Santiago	Ux		
1500 AD	Late Postclassic		Quejpomo	Tan		Late Postclassic
1400 AD	Middle Postclassic	Tuxtla				
1300 AD						
1200 AD				Nichim		
1100 AD	Early Postclassic	Ruíz	Pecha			Remanso
1000 AD						
900 AD		Paredón				
800 AD	Late Classic		Mechung	Mix	Tepeu 3	Peistal
700 AD		Maravillas			Tepeu 2	
600 AD	Middle Classic		Kundapi	Lek	Tepeu 1	Metapa
500 AD		Laguna			3	Loros
400 AD	Early Classic	Juiquipilas	Juspano	Kau	Tzakol 2	Kato
300 AD					1	Jaritas
200 AD						
100 AD	Protoclassic	Istmo	Ipsan	Ix	Chicanel	Itstapa
0		Horcones		Hun		Hato
100 BC						
200 BC	Late Preclassic	Guanacaste	Guañoma	Guajil		Guillén
300 BC						
400 BC		Francesa	Felisa	Foko	Late Mamom	Frontera
500 BC						
600 BC	Middle Preclassic	Escalera	Equipac	Enub	Early Mamom	Escalón
700 BC						
800 BC		Dwemba	Dzewa	Dyosan		Duende
900 BC		Dili	Dombi	Chacte	Eb	Conchas
1000 BC						
1100 BC		Jobo	B Cacahuanó	Jocote		Jocotal
1200 BC		Cotorra	A	Chacaj		Cuadros
1300 BC	Early Preclassic					Cherla
1400 BC		Ocote	Bombaná	Ojalá		Ocós
1500 BC						
1600 BC				Lato		Locona
1700 BC						
1800 BC						Barra
1900 BC						

Figure 1.4. Chronologies of Chiapas and central Maya Lowlands.

Guatemala still has not produced evidence of early villagers there, as postulated by language theorists.

As evident in the preceding quotation, the real target of the UGRB project was the Maya of the tropical lowlands, the region to be investigated in the final stage of the project. The clear material markers of Maya culture from the Classic period were to be traced backwards to find their origins. As noted, in 1973 there was nothing known in the Maya Lowlands like the Early Preclassic materials described for various regions of Chiapas. Moreover, the Middle and Late Preclassic materials were also significantly different. The earliest clear Lowland Maya ceramics found at sites in the Grijalva Basin date to the Chiapa V phase, what is known in Chiapas as the Late Preclassic period, 300-100 BC (Bryant and Clark 1983). These Chicanel era ceramics are rare and appear to be trade wares. This trade influence marked by imported ceramic vessels was discovered in Chiapa de Corzo by NWAF in their work there in the 1950s. The earliest bona fide Maya pattern found en masse along the Grijalva dates to the following Chiapa VI period, or what is called the Protoclassic period in Chiapas (it is known as the Terminal Preclassic period in the Maya Lowlands, so temporal comparisons are confusing) (Figure 1.4). This is also contemporaneous with the Chicanel period in the Maya Lowlands.

PHYSICAL CHARACTERISTICS OF THE STUDY REGION

The upper Grijalva River Basin is located in the southeastern section of the Central Depression of Chiapas (Figure 1.5). The zone is marked by higher elevations on three sides. To the southeast, just over the international border between Mexico and Guatemala, are the Cuchumatan Mountains. On the north lies the Comitan Plateau and the Central Highlands, while the foothills of the steep Sierra Madre Mountains are found on the southern side. The tectonic down-faulted Central Depression begins in Chiapas and continues eastward through the Motagua Valley, Guatemala, and then into the Cayman Trench of the Caribbean Sea (West 1964:65). The Central Depression

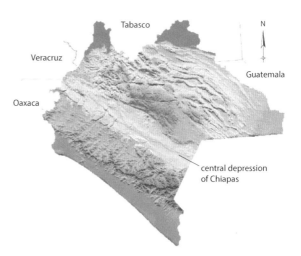

Figure 1.5. Relief map of the region. INEGI map: http://www.cuentame.inegi.org.mx

consists of many layers of limestone dating to the early Cretaceous period that are slightly sloped to the northeast. Along the base of the Central Highlands to the north is a wide band of sediments; these highlands are karstic with high mesas and low relief ridges. To the south of the depression, the interior side of the Sierra Madre is different; although the interior slope is less dramatic than its Pacific Coast side, the processes of erosion have nonetheless created isolated "islands" and mountain ridges, some 2000 m in height, which loom above the flat depression (Helbig 1964:31). To illustrate, White (1976:8) noted in his survey of the municipality of Chicomuselo a "microzone" along the valley bottoms, where water is abundant and dependable; however, the rivers have down-cut into the alluvium so that the water surface can be found anywhere from 5 to 30 m below the level of the valley floor, rendering it difficult to access.

The surface contours and hydrology of this region present a complex mosaic of environments. Helbig (1964:117) notes that while the Grijalva River system runs through this Central Depression it is not exactly a river valley, highlighting that "the river does not possess a legitimate valley of its own, but rather searches for its route with penetrating branches through hills and running through the rest of its rocky beds so deeply carved that one cannot speak of flooding nor irrigation. And not only this, a great stretch along this riverbed, running over almost naked rock—and in no way over humid or fertile soils—immediately sees the same sparse and dry vegetation that one sees far from the riverbanks that dominates most of the region."

The waters of the Grijalva River system (with its many names) begin in Guatemala in the Cuchumatan Mountains at altitudes over 3800 m, and include the rivers Selegua, Azul, and Nentón (Plascencia et al. 2014:35). Flowing west, these waters ultimately converge and form the Lagartero River and swampy land where the site of Lagatero is located. Farther west, the Lagartero becomes the San Gregorio River. The northern escarpments of the Comitan Plateau and the slopes of the Sierra Madre to the south drain precipitation into this system; the waters then flow into the Angostura lake, created by the dam of the same name in 1974.

The climate of the upper Grijalva River region is classified as temperate highland with considerable cooling as the elevation rises around the depression. This intertropical region receives solar warming throughout the year and also lies in something of a rainfall shadow, given the highlands to the north and the Sierra Madres to the south, with average annual rainfall of 1000 to 1200 mm in the upper tributaries and lessening rainfall totals as one moves west (Plasencia et al. 2014:41). The Central Depression has a number "micro-climates" depending on topography, hydrography, and soils. The area north of the depression, as well as the area south, enjoys a cooler climate, with increasing humidity and rainfall as one climbs further in elevation up from the river. In contrast, the Central Depression proper has a marked and reduced dry-rainy season with intense heat and aridity in the dry season. In Chapter 2, Barbara Voorhies reviews more of the micro-climates and vegetation of this region.

SURVEY SPECIFICS & METHODS

There had been some limited survey of the upper basin of the Grijalva River prior to the 1970s (Lowe 1959; Piña Chán 1961; Shook 1956). Salvage reconnaissance and excavations had been conducted for the central Grijalva River region beginning in the late 1950s (Lowe

1959). The flooding of the Angostura Reservoir just to the northwest of the upper basin prompted a large scale salvage project in the late 1960s (García Cook et al. 1970; Gussinyer 1972; Lowe 2007). Dozens of sites were recorded and some were test excavated. In 1967, A small team of linguists, ethnographers, and archaeologists undertook a survey in the Sierra Madre area south of the municipalities of Chicomuselo and Frontera Comalapa (shortened to Comalapa) toward Motozintla (Navarrete 1978b). There had also been work done in the neighboring region of highland Guatemala (e.g., Borhegyi 1965; Dutton 1943; Woodbury 1953). To the north, the highlands of Chiapas had been surveyed by a team from by the University of Chicago. That project resulted in the location of large numbers of sites and the establishment of a chronology of occupation corresponding well with that of neighboring Maya areas (Adams 1961). As a result, in the 1970s the upper tributaries region was perhaps the least known and explored area along the Grijalva River in Chiapas. From the start, the main goal of the reconnaissance segment of the UGRB Project was to provide the groundwork for future investigations. It was not intended to recover information about every site in the region.

The survey area was bounded by the town of La Trinitaria to the north, the Mexico-Guatemala border to the east, the town of Chicomuselo at the foot of the Sierra Madre to the south, and the Angostura Reservoir to the west. Since this whole area was essentially unknown archaeologically it was necessary to first conduct a general and rapid reconnaissance. In this way the project uncovered the general outlines of settlement for the entire 250 km^2 region, even though no one sub-region was covered as thoroughly as possible. Nonetheless, the advantage in covering the whole region at least partially was that it allowed important sites to be selected for excavation and critical sub-regions to be surveyed in their entirety.

The reconnaissance was only the initial part of the overall project. By far, the majority of resources were devoted to the excavations and mapping of sites discovered during survey. Both arms of the project—reconnaissance and excavation—allowed a continuing reinterpretation of each other in light of the data that were independently provided by the two types of archaeological research. For example, during the initial stages of the research, the ceramic chronology was not very well established because there had been so little previous work in the region. In fact, it was essentially dependent upon known sequences for neighboring regions. The ceramics collected during reconnaissance were provisionally typed to establish tentative chronological placements for each site (see for example, White 1976). After a number of sites were excavated, the ceramics were re-evaluated over the years to fine-tune the original chronological designations; the most recent assessment for the entire Upper Grijalva ceramic sequence was published in 2005 (Bryant et al. 2005; Clark and Cheetham 2005). Clark took another look at the survey materials in the summer of 2014 in light of the refined ceramic sequence, and his findings are reflected in the designated chronological assignments here.

The study of Canajasté (Tr-69) provides a good example of the interplay between survey and excavation. Canajasté was originally located in 1973, and a small sample of ceramics was collected. Not enough was known at the time to give it a definite chronological placement; although it was tentatively called a Late Postclassic site, based on its layout and defensive wall. In 1980 a detailed topographic map of the site was made. In analyzing the settlement layout, it was apparent that the site lacked many of the structures common to Late Classic period sites. A re-examination of the surface collections made during mapping confirmed that the site was in fact Late Postclassic since it had many of the diagnostics of late sites excavated in the upper tributaries region, as well as exhibiting ceramics common in neighboring highland Guatemala. Finally, the site was intensively excavated in 1981-82 by Michael Blake, and both an Early and a Late Postclassic occupation were uncovered. Albeit dating to late in the Nichim phase, the Early Postclassic ceramics and several other artifacts, such as spindle whorls, eventually provided a series of diagnostics that were used to more accurately date some of the survey sites found almost a decade earlier.

For the site data presented here, the chronological assessments were entirely based on the ceramics recovered from the survey and/or excavations at each site. There is often commentary in the site descriptions on the likely dating of a site based on architectural features or layouts—these assessments are included for insight for the readers, but they are not reflected in the actual phase designations. In addition, determinations as to whether a site was habitational or ceremonial in nature often came down to the interpretation of the archaeologist undertaking the survey.

As for the survey methodology, it should be remembered that the area was unexplored and many individuals participated in the reconnaissance over a period of years. Hence, the information on any given site is typically limited to: 1) location (identified in an era without GPS or INEGI 1:50,000 scale maps); 2) name of the farm and/or owner of land or ejido on which the site was noted; 3) assessment of the vegetation, terrain, and water resources in the site area; 4) assessment of site function (habitation and/or ceremonial use); 5) sketch map of site; 6) artifacts collected, where available; 7) and site location plotted on aerial photos, where available. The overall fieldwork strategy was to address municipalities: Chicomuselo, Frontera Comalapa, and La Trinitaria, and subregions in the case of La Trinitaria, the largest and most accessible of this group.

Tom Lee, Director of the UGRB project, began survey in February through April of 1973 in the northern half of the municipality of La Trinitaria, around the San Lucas and Santa Inés Rivers. According to site survey forms, Lee managed to survey a wide swath of land from Santa Inés west to the border with Guatemala (see Figure 1.7). In the following year, survey began again in Feburary, with the addition of James White and his wife, Nicole Boucher White. During this month, Lee, White, and Boucher White, surveyed the area around Lagartero and produced a pace and compass map of the site (Figure 5.166).

In March and April of 1974, White, Boucher White and NWAF foreman Alejandro Sánchez moved southwest to the Chicomuselo municipality, including a small segment of the Bella Vista municipality just south of the Chicomuselo border. Sections of this municipality had minimal or no road access, so the group often used trails along the bottoms of the Yayahuita and Tachinula Rivers (Figure 1.6). James White, a graduate student at Simon Fraser University, ultimately wrote a master's thesis (1976) on this segment of the survey, and so we have more detailed specifics from his writing on this area.

In late April, the Chicomuselo team moved north and east into the Frontera Comalapa municipality, surveying along the Tierra Blanca and Santo Domingo Rivers (Figure 1.6). Meanwhile, Lee had surveyed south of Largartero into the border area between the municipalities of La Trinitaria and Comalapa.

The focus for the survey teams was on locating all major and minor sites, in particular for the Archaic to Colonial periods. There were areas in the survey region in the early 1970s that were accessible only during the dry season or completely inaccessible by road. The permission of land owners, both individuals and ejidos, was also crucial, but not always granted, and trespassing on lands in rural Mexico was and continues to be an unsafe proposition. In addition, depending on the time of year in the agricultural cycle, a given area might be completely covered in corn or burned off and tilled in preparation for planting—creating two very different scenarios for recovering artifacts. Lee had expressed the hope of applying "New Archaeology" principles (such as sampling programs) in this project, as did other participants, but given the logistics, this was not realistic. James White, who walked large swaths of the survey zone, best summarized the situation:

> …a preliminary reconnaissance was conducted in a virtually unknown area with the purpose of locating the archaeological resources and providing an outline culture history for the Early Preclassic to Hispanic periods. The information is to be used in the planning of further research. Field work was hindered by scant topographic information, poor access, vegetation covered sites, the difficulty of finding landlords to get permission to explore their lands, and some public suspicion of our intentions. The reconnaissance succeeded in building a detailed catalogue of archaeological information for the Municipality, but the limitations of the data merit consideration. (White 1976:17)

In should be noted that many surveys have been conducted since the NWAF work in the 1970s, focusing on more detailed reconnaissance in specific subregions, such as the Morelos Valley around the site of El Cerrito (Clark and Lowe 1980) and the Rosario Valley (de Montmollin 1989a, 1989c, 1995). Where it was possible to reference site descriptions from the original survey, such as the municipality of Chicomuselo (White 1976), or easily cross-reference previous or subsequent NWAF survey findings those citations are noted in the "References" line after the site description.

OUTLINE OF THE BOOK

Given the many individuals involved in the final publishing of this work, it should be said that, even with editing, the coverage and presentation of this survey project is uneven. There have been losses of information over time, and the text reflects the distinct voices of the survey leaders, Tom Lee and James White, as well as our attempts to reconcile and edit their presentations. The data we present were collected between 30-35 years ago, and we have not brought it up to date with the significant work that has been done in the decades since. Extensive regional projects and excavations have taken place and continue in the Rosario (de Montmollin 1989c, 1995, 2014) and San Gregorio Valleys (Rivero 1983, 1990), and at site zones including Lagartero (Rivero 1994, 1999, 2001, 2007b), north of the town of La Trinitaria at Las Margaritas (Álvarez Asomoza 2000; Lowe and Álvarez Asomoza 2007), west of La Trinitaria at Chinkultic (Navarrete 1975, 1976, 1984, 2001, 2007; Navarrete and Hernández 2002), not to mention work on the Guatemalan side of the border (e.g., Borgstede 2004; Clark et al. 2001; Tejada et al. 2000).

While not perfect, this survey information is critical for understanding this key area of Mesoamerica at a point when archaeological sites and data are disappearing daily in the upper Grijalva. It provides the long-term history of the region and the context for the sites excavated within it.

Chapter 2 offers more detailed environmental descriptions focusing on the vegetation or "Formations" in the survey area, which essentially describe eco-zones, some small and some large. The work for this study was undertaken in 1977 by Barbara Voorhies and Alejandro Sánchez, the NWAF foreman who had participated in much of the site survey done previously. The two walked the survey zone and collected plant specimens. Sánchez identified these specimens by their local names, while Dennis Breedlove, botanist and specialist on Chiapas flora, provided formal identifications. Voorhies prepared a manuscript of this work originally slated for publication in an edited volume on the Upper Grijalva River Basin Project; unfortunately, that volume did not come to fruition, and Voorhies's manuscript became an oft-cited unpublished work on the environment of the upper tributaries region of the Central Depression. The manuscript has been edited and is included here.

Chapters 3 through 6 are organized by municipalities and present site data, which include individual site information and maps, where available. Chapter 3 presents the sites uncovered in the municipality of Chicomuselo

(abbreviation: Ch); Chapter 4 describes sites in the municipality of Frontera Comalapa (Co); and Chapters 5 and 6 present sites in the municipality of La Trinitaria (Tr). Over 200 sites were recorded in La Trinitaria, hence, the natural chapter was split into two for convenience of data presentation and easier map consultation. Each of these four chapters begins with maps locating the sites. Given the density of sites in some subregions, and the format size of these volumes, the map of the site locations consists of the primary map, with one inset or close-up view (see Figures 1.7 and 1.8), which includes sites from the northeast corner of the survey area. Figure 1.6 shows the primary map with the locations of key towns and settlements in the survey region. These have been placed on a separate map to avoid the inevitable crowding of information. Figures 1.7 and 1.8 give the location of all the sites discussed in this book.

A brief concluding chapter reviews the findings. Given the many sites recorded during the reconnaissance, it has been possible to discern marked changes in the prehistoric settlement patterns. Although there are significant gaps in the survey, it is likely that some representatives of different site types were found throughout the region (small hamlet versus rockshelter). A limitation is that we cannot construct maps of the regional settlement hierarchies because we do not know what kinds of sites are present in unsurveyed zones. Still, we can use the information we do have to make initial estimates of the range and numbers of sites that are likely to be found in the region as a whole.

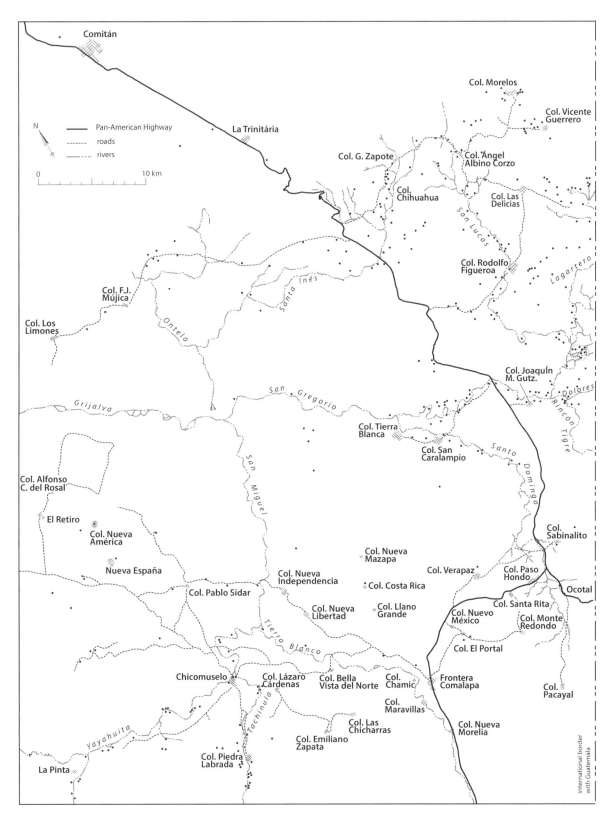

Figure 1.6. Locations of key modern towns and settlements in the survey region. Archaeological sites are not shown.

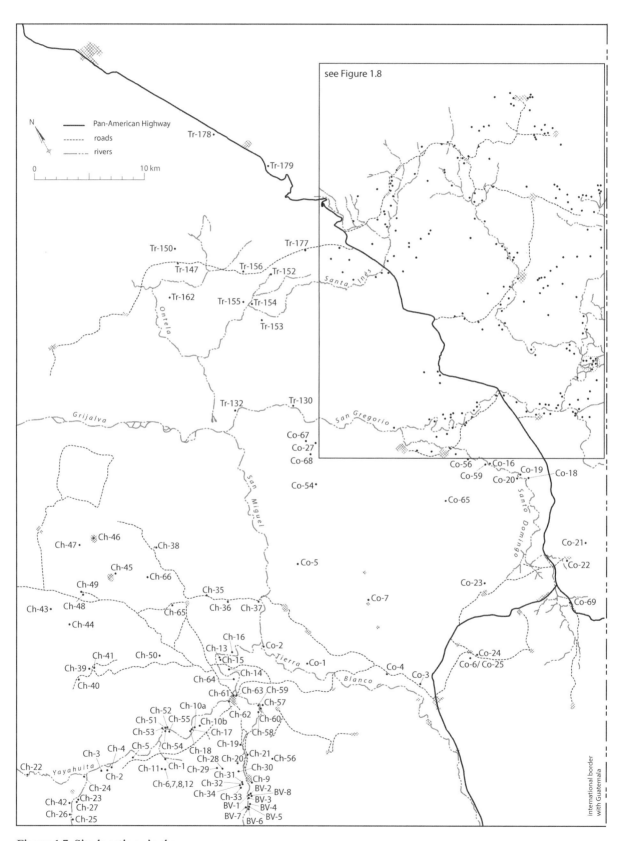

Figure 1.7. Site locations in the survey area.

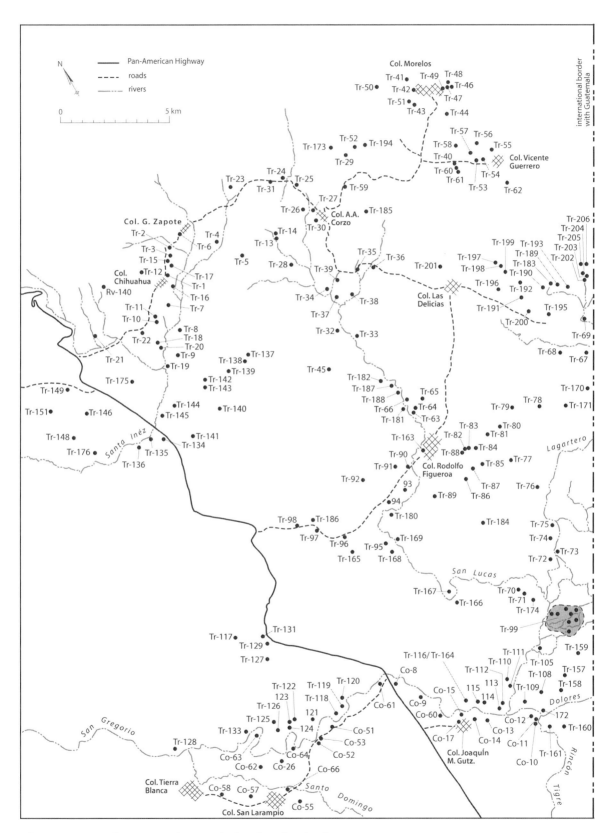

Figure 1.8. Inset from map (Figure 1.7) showing sites in close-up.

CHAPTER 2

VEGETATION FORMATIONS OF THE UPPER GRIJALVA BASIN, CHIAPAS, MEXICO

Barbara Voorhies

OBJECTIVES

The purpose of this chapter is to identify the major vegetation communities within the upper Grijalva Basin and to determine their individual distributions. The report is based on field observations that were carried out with the express purpose of producing phytogeographic information that could be compared with ancient human settlement data for the same area. Accordingly, the principal objective of the vegetation study was to produce a vegetation map of the upper Grijalva Basin.

Before discussing the study, however, it is useful to consider the reasoning behind my conviction that it can be heuristically valuable to compare the distribution of present-day vegetation zones with distribution patterns of ancient human settlements. At its foundation, this conviction rests on the assumption that human populations, like other biotic populations, must adapt to specific biophysical environments. Consequently, ancient human groups in the upper Grijalva Basin must have made specific choices concerning preferred settlement locations. These choices would have been governed, in part, by the nature of the environments that these groups encountered. Plant life, an important component of the biophysical environment, would have been a significant factor in habitat selection. Moreover, since the distribution of plants is controlled by both edaphic and climatic factors, if we are able to identify the presence of a particular community of plants, then we are often able to infer additional information about the biophysical environment.

The obvious question that arises, however, is how representative is the present-day distribution of plant communities of the ancient environments to which early inhabitants of the upper Grijalva Basin were adapting? The answer, of course, is that we do not really know at the present time. To determine this would require extensive regional study of paleoenvironments in the upper Grijalva Basin. Such a study is not presently available, and cannot be achieved either quickly or economically. Therefore, until such a time when paleoecological data are in hand, other less precise ways of determining the paleoenvironments of the study area must be sought.

My reasoning is that when we consider the upper Grijalva Basin in its entirety (that is, by employing a macroscale level of analysis), and consider the length of time of human occupation of this region (which is short by geologic standards), it is reasonable to assume that the major plant communities manifested spatial continuity through time. That is, I argue that the same types of plant communities manifested spatial continuity through time. Further, I argue that the same types of plant communities that are found today within the study area were also present at least during the last few millennia and that in a general way, the present-day and ancient zonal boundaries are somewhat isomorphic. This assumption is based on the idea that the major controlling factors of plant communities, such as topography, soils, radiant energy, and water availability, have not changed radically within the time span of the known archaeological record for the area.

I wish to emphasize that I am not proposing that the environment of the upper Grijalva Basin has remained totally unchanged during the course of human occupation. It most certainly has not. Specifically, I do not believe that within any particular plant community there has been unwavering floristic continuity through time. Humans, as well as other agents, have unquestionably altered the makeup of communities through the application of various forces of selection. My argument is simply that whatever specific changes have occurred, they have not been so great as to make the plant communities totally unrecognizable. I also hope to avoid the misunderstanding that specific zonal boundaries are believed by me to have remained absolutely fixed through time. As I discuss below, there is evidence that such was not the case, although at present we can only guess at the nature of specific changes. Nonetheless, the evidence does indicate that it is logical to assume the expansion of some plant communities at the expense of others during the time under consideration.

This study then has been predicated on the assumption that the identification of current plant communities of the upper Grijalva Basin provides some insight into the past environment of the same region. This knowledge, although imperfect, can aid the archaeologist in the interpretation of settlement pattern data.

PREVIOUS RESEARCH

A number of investigators have discussed the vegetative types of Chiapas, but the amount of detail in their coverage is varied. Some researchers, such as Goldman (1951), Goldman and Moore (1946), Gómez-Pompa (1965), Gonzales Quintero (1974), Leopold (1950), Miranda and Hernández (1963), Pennington and Sarukhan (1968), and Wagner (1964) discuss vegetation types for all of Mexico or even larger territories. Not surprisingly, the treatment of Chiapaneca vegetation is necessarily superficial and the vegetation of the upper Grijalva Basin is not distinguished. Maps accompanying these studies are too small to be adequate for my purposes.

Both Breedlove (1973) and Miranda (1952, 1975) focus exclusively on the vegetation of Chiapas, and therefore these studies have been particularly valuable as aids in this research. Both authors discuss the phytogeography of the state, although they employ different systems for classifying vegetation. Miranda, in addition, provides a wealth of ecological and ethnobotanic information on individual plant species.

Miranda (1975:14) has produced a vegetation map of the entire state of Chiapas,

Figure 2.1. Map of Chiapas with physiographic regions outlined (after Mülleried 1957). Location of study area is shown by shading. Transect A-B shows location of profile in Figure 2.2.

but it is too generalized to permit a useful comparison with the archaeological map of the upper Grijalva Basin. Thus, the most detailed existing map of vegetation zones is insufficient for our purposes.

DEFINITION OF THE STUDY AREA

The study area is located in the southwestern part of the state, adjacent to the Guatemalan border and is defined by the limits of the municipalities of La Trinitaria, Chicomucelo, and Comalapa (Figure 2.1). This is the area in which the New World Archaeological Foundation has conducted a settlement survey and subsurface investigation at selected sites. The region is approximately 2700 km² in area.

Physiographically, the study area includes a broad, flat basin that forms the eastern portion of the Central Depression of Chiapas. This NW-SE trending basin is occupied by the uppermost portion of the Grijalva River. The northeastern side of the valley ascends toward the Central Plateau in a series of terraces, the lowest of which are included within the study area. The southwestern side of the valley rises sharply to

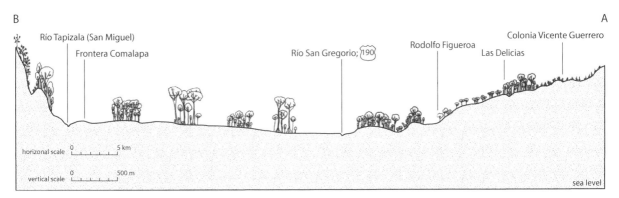

Figure 2.2. Profile section of upper Grijalva Basin along Transect A-B. Vegetation formations are indicated by sketches that are not to scale.

form the Sierra Madre of Chiapas. The lower slopes of this mountain range are also included in the region of study. Figure 2.2 shows a profile section of the valley taken along the transect A-B. A detailed description of the geography of the region has been written by Helbig (1964).

The altitudinal variations, combined with extreme variations in the availability of water, produce a situation in which the diversity of vegetation formations is high. Within the region, contrasts in vegetation abound; swamp formations are found not far from parched thorn thickets, and cool climate pine forests are near the hot climate evergreen tropical forests. Before describing the vegetation formations in detail I will discuss the methods of investigation.

METHODS

The investigation was carried out by Alejandro Sánchez and me during two short field seasons in 1977. The first fieldwork took place from mid-February through March during the height of the dry season (November through May). The second period of investigation was in September during the wet season (June through October). The six month separation between the two phases of the study permitted us to investigate the vegetation during each of the two major seasons of the annual cycle.

Our method of studying the vegetation consisted of: 1) describing the local vegetation and collecting herbarium specimens at particular sites; and 2) making observations on vegetation type and plotting these on aerial photographs.

The sites where detailed descriptions were made were chosen in such a way that the major vegetation classes would each be sampled (but no formal method of site survey was employed). At these locations I filled out a field data sheet with entries for the edaphic features of the site and the structure and floristic composition of the vegetation. Photographs in both black-and-white and color frequently were taken. The locations of sites where botanic field sheets were filled out, or in a few cases where only photographs were taken, are shown by the numbers in the accompanying map (Figure 2.3), and are identified in Table 2.2 (see end of Chapter 2). A few numbers were accidentally skipped in the field and consequently do not appear on the map.

The identification of plants in the field was done by Alejandro Sánchez, who as a native Chiapaneco with an interest in local flora, was able to identify many dominant species by local names. Sánchez's home is Chiapa de Corzo, a town located outside the study area and inhabited predominantly by Spanish-speaking people of Chiapanec descent (Navarrete 1966). Sánchez is himself a descendant of Chiapanec speakers so that his linguistic labeling of plants presumably reflects this heritage. In addition to this procedure, whenever possible we would waylay local individuals and query them about the names of plants, but informants were not used either systematically or frequently. This is because we rarely encountered knowledgeable and cooperative passersby when working at a station because we tended to work at locations that were somewhat distant from villages. These

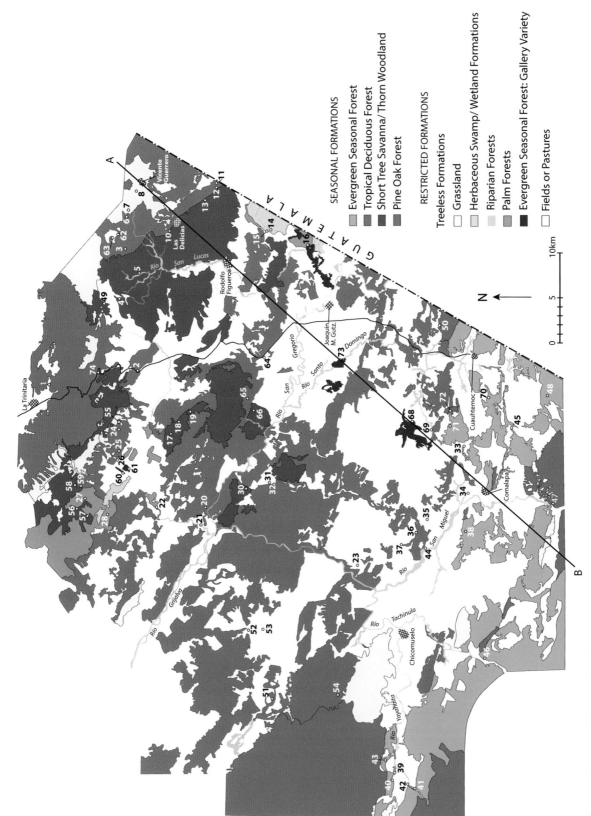

Figure 2.3. Map of vegetation formations in the upper Grijalva Basin. Numbers refer to study stations (see Table 2.2).

relatively remote locations are where vegetation appeared to be less disturbed compared with areas closer to population centers. In short, we did not attempt to produce a systematic ethnobotanic study.

We also collected herbarium specimens that were numbered by location and named by Sánchez wherever possible. These specimens were sent to Dennis E. Breedlove of the California Academy of Sciences for identification and curation. The results of Breedlove's work are reported in Table 2.1 at the end of the chapter.

Mapping was carried out continuously as we traversed the area by truck. Observations of vegetation type were plotted onto transparent sheets covering air photo mosaics. The mosaics are at a scale of approximately 1:20,000. They were constructed of aerial photographs taken by Méxicana Aerofoto, an aerial photography company based in Mexico City. In general, the scale of the photo mosaics and their quality were adequate for my objectives. The principal difficulty in using these photographs as base maps was that some of the roads that we traveled had been constructed since the photographs were taken, and because of this, it was sometimes difficult to accurately determine ground location on the photographs.

The major vegetation units that have been mapped are FORMATIONS[1] as defined by Beard (1944). As Breedlove (1973:149) has previously stated, Beard's classification system of vegetational formations is remarkably adequate for Chiapas. As defined by Beard, a formation consists of climax communities that are similar in structure and life form. For example, the formation that Beard (1944:136) considers optimum within the American tropics is the Rain Forest. The characteristic feature of this formation is the arrangement of the forest into three or four tree strata. Additional characteristics of the Rain Forest formation is the long clean boles of the dominant trees, the lack of lianas, and the accumulation of epiphytes in the upper rather than the lower strata. Thus, the defining characteristics of particular formations concern their physiognomies, rather than their floristic composition or other characteristics. The relationships of these and other formations are diagrammatically shown in Figure 2.4.

In this section, I describe each of the formations that has been identified within the study area. In addition, I discuss the spatial distribution of each formation that is graphically displayed in Figure 2.3.

OPTIMUM FORMATIONS

No optimum formations (Beard 1944) are located within the study area. The reason for this is that the climate of the upper Grijalva Basin is sufficiently dry to prevent the development of either Tropical Rain Forest or Lower Montane Rain Forest (cf. Figure 2.4): the optimal formations expected on the basis of altitude. However, the seasonal formation Evergreen Seasonal Forest, which in many ways resembles Tropical Rain Forest, is present and will be discussed in the following section.

---

[1] Beard (1944) has proposed a taxonomic system for classification of tropical vegetation in the Americas and the "Formation" constitutes one taxon within this scheme. Formations are subsumed under the taxon named FORMATION-SERIES, a more inclusive taxon that classes habitats. In Beard's (1944:133) view, Formation-series are ecologically controlled most significantly by moisture relations. Accordingly, Formations are combined to form FORMATION-SERIES on the basis of similar moisture conditions. However, I have not attempted this classification in the present study.

Formations are composed of plant communities that are floristically uniform, and these are known in Beard's system as ASSOCIATIONS. An association is defined as the maximum community that is floristically uniform and is often named for one of the principal dominants in the community. The association is a taxon in Beard's classification that is subordinate to the Formation taxon. I have collected some data on the associations within the field area. However, these data were not systematically collected for the study area and boundaries of associations were never determined. They are not reported here.

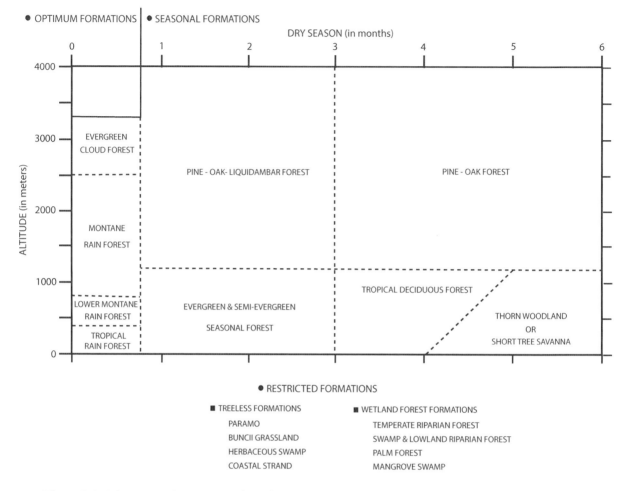

Figure 2.4. Diagrammatic representation of the vegetational formations of Chiapas (from Breedlove 1973:154).

SEASONAL FORMATION SERIES

Evergreen Season Forest, altitude 0-1200 m

Superficially this formation is similar to the Rain Forest formation, but it differs in having fewer distinct tree strata. According to Breedlove (1973:158) there may be only one tree layer, although two layers are probably more characteristic. The canopy is closed and reaches a height of 14-30 m, which is lower than the closed Rain Forest canopy (Beard 1944:138). Occasional large trees with diameters of 3 m or more may emerge above the closed canopy to a height of 35 m.

During the marked dry season, the forest floor becomes dry and there is great seasonal variation in the low story of herbaceous plants.

In addition, during the dry season some or all of the trees of the upper stratum may experience leaf-loss. These trees are facultatively deciduous in that the degree of leaf-fall varies with drought intensity (Beard 1944:139). Lianas and epiphytes are usually quite abundant and the flora is fairly rich, with 50-80 tree species per association (Beard 1944:139).

Beard (1944) distinguishes between the Evergreen Seasonal Forest and a Semi-evergreen Seasonal Forest, but Breedlove (1973:158) considers this split meaningless because in Chiapas these communities intergrade in large zones. I have not attempted to separate the two types of forests but have followed Breedlove in utilizing only a single category. Nonetheless, I do distinguish two forms: 1) a gallery variety

Figure 2.5. Evergreen Seasonal Forest formation. Site 16 at Lagartero.

proximate to water courses on the bottom of the Central Depression; and 2) a second variety found on the limestone foothills of the southern part of the study area.

The present distribution of the gallery variety of Evergreen Seasonal Forest formation within the study area consists of several widely separated stands, each of which is restricted in extent. These forests are shown by the red areas on the accompanying Figure 2.3. They occur generally in the tributary drainages of the uppermost Grijalva system. The stands are found only in protected areas where the water table is high, often in association with surface water as in the case of the Lagartero forest (Site 16; see Figure 2.5), which is near a swamp,

or the Guajilar forest (Site 73) that fringes the banks of the Río Santo Domingo. Miranda (1975:73), in discussing these forests of the Central Depression, mentions that they are also found on deep soils.

At present, these patches of Evergreen Seasonal Forests provide hardwoods for use by the local population. The stands are too small to support a major export lumber industry. Miranda (1975:73-74; see also Wagner 1964:248) believes that in general this class of forests in Chiapas has been subjected to unyielding interference by the human population. In his opinion much of this forest has been removed for agricultural purposes because it is found on deep, fertile soils in areas that are comparatively

Figure 2.6. A relic stand of *ramon* (*Brosimum alicastrum*) in middle ground at Site 39. This is an example of Evergreen Seasonal Forest. In the foreground is a recently cleared area, whereas Tropical Deciduous Forest covers the hills in the background.

healthy (compared to Rain Forest) given the presence of a distinct dry season. The former extensions of these forests are indicated by the presence of occasional *guanacaste* trees (*Enterolobium cyclocarpum*) and ceiba trees that have been selectively left standing in otherwise cleared fields. Such isolated trees are encountered within the study area and provide clues to the climax vegetation that has been otherwise totally removed.

Another type of Evergreen Seasonal Forest is located in the middle elevations of the mountains that lie in the southern portion of the study area (Figure 2.6). This formation is shown in light green on the accompanying map (Figure 2.3). The forest is ecotonal and intergrades with oak forest within the study area (Breedlove, personal communication). It forms over limestone bedrock especially on hills in the southeast portion of the study area that have the characteristic form of haystacks. In the case of the Evergreen Seasonal Forest of the middle elevations, it is the abundant rainfall, rather than a high water table (as in the gallery variety),

Figure 2.7. Tropical Deciduous Forest at Site 19 during the dry season.

which determines its presence. In many places the native vegetation has been partially removed in order to grow coffee.

Tropical Deciduous Forest, altitude 0-1200 m

This two-storied formation normally attains a height of 10-20 m and exhibits a dense thicket-like understory. In some riparian situations the trees reach a height of 40-50 m and have straight trunks. The understory is sparse (Breedlove 1973:159). The formation is floristically diverse, with 30-50 species of trees per association. Lianas and epiphytes are present but less abundant compared with the Evergreen Seasonal Forest formation. During the long and severe

dry season the majority of trees lose their leaves as do many of the understory plants (Figure 2.7). Many trees flower at this time (Breedlove 1973:159). During the rainy season the forest becomes verdant; a dense stand of herbaceous plants reaches a height of 1-2 m. Beard (1944) refers to this formation as Deciduous Seasonal Forest, whereas Miranda (1975) uses the term Selva Baja Decidua.

Tropical Deciduous Forest is the most widespread formation within the study area. It is the characteristic vegetation over most of the broad basin of the upper Grijalva Depression as is shown by the purple zones in the accompanying map (Figure 2.3). It is the

Figure 2.8. Short Tree Savanna at Site 8.

climatic climax vegetation of the basin forming on rocky or shallow soils (Miranda 1975:84). Consequently, its local absence is due either to removal for cultivation or pasture, or because of the presence of hydrologic or edaphic features that favor other formations within a restricted area. It is also found on the lowest slopes of both the southern escarpment of the Chiapas Plateau and the northern escarpment of the Sierra Madre.

Short Tree Savanna, altitude 0-1200 m

This formation consists of widely spaced, low trees and may have a grass understory (Figure 2.8). It is commonly found on deep, poorly drained soils on gradually sloping plains or flat bottomlands (Breedlove 1973:159). During the rainy season savanna soils tend to be waterlogged because of their poor drainage, whereas they are very dry in the dry season (Miranda 1975:94). The trees are gnarled in appearance and rarely attain a height over 20 m (Breedlove 1973:160).

The trees of this formation are not floristically diverse, and there is a tendency for stands to be monospecific. In Chiapas (Miranda

1975:95-98) the most common short tree savannas have one of the following species as the dominant:

1. Brazil (*Haematoxylon brasiletto*) (Figure 2.9)
2. Espino (*Acacia pennatula*)
3. Gorojo or Siete Pellejos (*Ateleia pterocarpa*)
4. Hojaman or Cacaito (*Curatella americana*) (Figure 2.10)
5. Morro or Jícara (*Crescentia cujete* and *Crescentia alata*) (Figure 2.11)
6. Nanche (*Byrsonima crassifolia*)
7. Quebracho (*Acacia milleriana*)

It is not known whether Short Tree Savanna is an edaphic climax formation or whether it is a disclimax due to human activities. Miranda (1975:95-96) discusses the problem of origins of this formation. He observes that these savannas are periodically burned by local farmers and that occasionally islands of Tropical Deciduous Forest are found within the savannas on identical soils. These observations lead him to the conclusion that a large part of the present-day savannas were once vegetated by Tropical Deciduous Forest (Miranda 1975:95).

Figure 2.9. Short Tree Savanna formation at Site 18. Dominant tree is brazil (*Haematoxylon brasiletto*). Note the extremely rocky soils upon which this formation is commonly found.

Figure 2.10. Hojaman Short Tree Savanna near El Ocote. Pines are on ridge in the background.

Figure 2.11. Short Tree Savanna formation. The dominant tree is bottle gourd (*Crescentia* sp.).

The distribution of Short Tree Savanna within the study area is indicated by brown zones (Figure 2.3). It occurs on the first terrace of the Chiapas Plateau southwest of La Trinitaria, and over a wide area in the vicinity of Colonia Las Delicias. This latter region is a highly dissected zone that is intensively grazed and farmed. The underlying white soils appear to me to be very infertile.

Pine-Oak Forest

This formation usually consists of mixed stands of pine and oak but pure stands (Figure 2.12) of either can occur under special edaphic conditions (Breedlove 1973:161). Tree height ranges from 15-40 m. Epiphytes are sparse to common but heavy only in canyon situations. The understory is herbaceous with occasional shrubs and low grassy patches between the trees (Breedlove 1973:161). This formation is predominant in Chiapas between 1300 and 2500 m; occasionally, the formation is found as low as 1000 m.

Within the study area Pine-Oak Forest occurs on both escarpments fronting the Central Depression. It is shown in turquoise on the accompanying map (Figure 2.3). The lower slopes of the Central Plateau included within the study area are vegetated with a scrub oak association rather than with tall oak or pines. Tall trees do occur on the same slope at higher elevations than have been included on the map. On the northeastern slopes of the Sierra Madre, the Pine-Oak Forest is fully developed within the study area and the scrub oak association is not present (Figure 2.13).

WET-LAND FORMATION SERIES

Palm Forest

This restricted formation contains palms as the predominant tree and has a sparse understory. The height of the palms ranges from 24 to 40 m, and individuals can be closely spaced. The formation occurs on sandy, alluvial flats and terraces on poorly drained soils (Breedlove 1973:162). The soils tend to be deep, and they become waterlogged during the rainy season (Miranda 1975:98). Within the study area the *palmares* are dominated usually by the *palma real* (*Sabal mexicana*) (Figure 2.14) but sometimes by *coyol* (*Acrocomia mexicana*) (Figure 2.15).

Figure 2.12. Pine-oak Forest formation. Homogenous stand of oaks at Site 50.

Figure 2.13. Pine-oak Forest formation. Taken at Site 47 near Tapizala. A *fresno* tree (*Tabebubia pentaphylla*) is in the right foreground. The lower boundary of Pine-oak Forest formation is in the center of the photograph.

Figure 2.14. Palm Forest formation at Site 17. Dominant tree is *palma real* (*Sabal mexicana*).

Figure 2.15. Palm Forest formation near Site 51. Shows cultivated grass and *coyol* palms (*Acrocomia mexicana*).

Figure 2.16. Temperate Riparian Forest formation at Site 41. The Río Yayhuita is fringed by *alamos* (*Populus arizonica*) in the vicinity of Nueva Morelia.

The distribution of the Palm Forest within the study area is indicated by orange on the accompanying map (Figure 2.3). Most of these forests are located north of the Río Grijalva at the base of the Central Plateau.

Miranda (1975:98) discusses the similarity between the conditions producing Short Tree Savanna and Palm Forests and the fact that the two formations can occur as a mixed formation. In addition, Miranda points out that the Palm Forest species are resistant to repeated dry season burnings.

Riparian Formations

All riparian formations are shown in light blue in the accompanying map (Figure 2.3). In the higher elevations of the Central Plateau and Sierra Madre a Temperate Riparian Forest formation occurs above 1500 m (Breedlove 1973:162). Trees range between 10-25 m in height and very pure stands can sometimes be found. In the study area the predominant tree is locally known as *alamo* (*Populus arizonica*) (Figure 2.16). The understory is dense and thicket-like.

At lower elevations within the study area, giant bald cypress (*Taxodium mucronatum*) stand in the beds of perennial streams (Figure 2.17). Miranda (1975:135) writes that these trees can occur between 500-1200 m. An understory of willow thickets is present (Wagner 1964:263). At the same elevations a variety of Evergreen Seasonal Forest can fringe watercourses that contain intermittent streams.

TREELESS FORMATION SERIES

Herbaceous Marsh

Herbaceous Marsh is a restricted formation that consists of an herbaceous cover on shallow standing water. Within the study area the associated species are characteristic of temperate marshes. Breedlove (personal communication) lists the following species as generally typical:

> *Cladium jamaicense*
> *Cyperus* sp.
> *Ludwigia peruviana*
> *Lythrum vulneraria*
> *Rhynchospora* sp.
> *Typha latifolia*

Figure 2.17. Tropical Riparian Forest formation. Río Rincón Tigre with *sabinos* (*Taxodium mucronatum*) lining the river.

Figure 2.18. Herbaceous Marsh formation at Site 15. Marsh has rushes that have been partially cleared for cultivation (center of photograph). *Sabinos* fringe the marsh at center left and on the horizon. The Cuchumatan Mountains are in the background.

Figure 2.19. Grassland formation. View is of the hills on the north side of the Río Yayahuita.

Herbaceous marsh occurs only in two patches within the study area at the eastern end of the Central Depression. The formation is shown in pink on the accompanying map. The northernmost location is a bog that is seasonally farmed (Figure 2.18). In the south, the marsh is associated with open water and is perpetually wet. Using Beard's criteria (1944:148), at this location the formation is more accurately described as swamp, as he prefers to use the term marsh for situations where inundation is seasonal.

Grassland

A grassland formation occurs on both the western portion of the escarpment of the Central Plateau and the northern escarpment of the Sierra Madre (Figure 2.19). It is shown on the map (Figure 2.3) by yellow. These grasslands occur at the same elevation as Pine-Oak Forest (2000-4000 m) and may be due to frequent burning (Miranda 1975:136).

CONCLUSIONS

I have identified eight vegetation formations within the upper Grijalva Basin study area following the criteria established by Beard (1944). Within the basin bottomlands, the most widespread formation is Tropical Deciduous Forest, a type of hot country forest that is found where a definite and fairly long dry season occurs. Within the basin this predominant formation is locally replaced by any one of the five different formations as a result of either differences in soil nutrients or water availability. For example, the local availability of water produces the linear riparian formation that fringes the major water courses. This factor is also responsible for the Evergreen Season Forest formation that occurs in zones in well-watered and well-drained bottomlands. Abundant water but poor drainage are significant ecological factors responsible for the local presence of both Palm Forest and Herbaceous Marsh. Since these limiting conditions do not occur widely in the study area, each of the two formations is restricted in extent. Poor drainage is responsible also for the development of the Short Tree Savanna, but additionally I suspect that relatively infertile soils are implicated in producing this formation.

On the slopes of the escarpment of the Central Plateau scrub oak gradually gives way at higher elevations to a fully developed Pine-Oak Forest. In places the Pine-Oak forest is interrupted by zones of grassland, which may be the result of human interference with the climax vegetation but also could be the local climax vegetation.

The lower and middle elevations of the escarpment of the Sierra Madre de Chiapas and the Cuchumatan Mountains are vegetated with Evergreen Seasonal Forest, giving way at higher elevations to Pine-Oak Formations. Grasslands are present also in some locations similar to those across the valley.

The current distribution of vegetation formations may not be absolutely identical to those encountered by the earliest human occupants of the basin. In particular, it is possible that the effect of millennia of human interference with native vegetation has reduced the extent of the gallery variety of Evergreen Seasonal Forest and has extended the areas covered by both Grassland and Short Tree Savanna. The possibility of these changes must be considered in the evaluation of the prehistoric human settlement patterns of the area.

The potential economic importance of each of the identified vegetation zones is difficult to evaluate. In the first place I have not collected and reported botanical specimens for a large number of species. Second, the economic potential of plants varies for human populations at different stages of economic development. For example, preferred locations for mobile foraging groups might be places that combine water availability with maximum accessibility to multiple habitats. Accordingly, foragers might prefer locations that maximize access to multiple zones when all other factors are equal. Agricultural communities, in contrast, might seek out locations where a single set of factors combine to produce favorable farming conditions as well as availability of water. Consequently, such peoples would prefer to locate within certain zones favorable for farming, rather than toward zone peripheries. Still, agricultural communities might tend also to maximize habitat diversity wherever feasible, because of the necessity of certain critical products such as palm or grass for thatch, lumber for construction, etc.

These considerations lead me to predict that the earliest and largest farming communities within the study area should occur along the major drainages, especially where Evergreen Seasonal Forest, gallery variety or Tropical Deciduous Forest are present, since these zones appear to have high potential for farming. Early farming communities may have avoided certain locations for habitation both because of the absence of water and apparent low agricultural potential. These zones may well have been economically exploited but on an occasional rather than continual basis. Palm Marsh might also be a less preferred habitation habitat because of annual flooding, but access to Palm Marsh could have been selected for because of the economic importance of palms (for thatch, baskets, mats, etc.). Herbaceous Marsh would be a low preference for direct human habitation particularly where there is abundant dry land for the situation of houses. However, the marsh environment provides water, as well as plants and animals of potential economic importance so that habitation near to the Herbaceous Marsh would be readily explicable.

Table 2.1. Identification of upper Grijalva River Basin floral specimens collected by Barbara Voorhies and Alejandro Sánchez; compiled by Dennis E. Breedlove.[2]

Station 1

1-1	*Quercus* sp.
1-2	*Psychotria erythrocarpa*
1-3	*Rhus* sp.
1-4	*Quercus* sp.
1-5	*Tillandsia* sp.
1-6	legume (sterile)
1-7	*Quercus* sp.
1-8	missing
1-9	*Pistacia mexicana*
1-10	*Vernonia* sp.
1-11	*Carex polystachya*

Station 2

2-1	*Acacia pennatula*
2-2	*Ceiba aesculifolia*
2-3	missing
2-4	*Alvaradoa amorphoides*
2-5	*Pithecoctenium crucigerum*
2-6	*Phoradendron* sp.
2-7	*Swietenia humilis* Zucc.
2-8	sterile shrub
2-9	*Tecoma stans*

Station 3

3-1	*Rhus schiedeana*
3-2	*Tecoma stans*
3-3	*Alvaradoa amorphoides*
3-4	*Acacia cornigera*
3-5	*Brysonima crassifolia*
3-6	*Daphnopsis americana*
3-7	*Clusia rosea*
3-8	*Pistacia mexicana*
3-9	*Jacquinia aurantiaca*
3-10	*Myrcianthes fragrans*
3-11	*Styrax argenteus*
3-12	*Lysiloma auritum*
3-13	*Pisonia*?
3-14	missing

3-15	*Ficus cookii*
3-16	*Thevetia ovata*
3-17	*Bursera bipinnatifida*
3-18	*Fraxinus purpusii*

Station 4

4-1	*Fraxinus purpusii*
4-2	*Furcraea* sp.
4-3	*Calea trichotoma*?
4-4	*Elaeodendron trichotomum*
4-5	*Fraxinus purpusii*
4-6	*Lippia controversa*
4-7	?
4-8	*Bursera simaruba*
4-9	*Bromelia* sp.
4-10	grass
4-11	sterile grass

Station 5

5-1	*Exothea paniculata*
5-2	?
5-3	*Styrax argenteus*
5-4	*Myrcianthes fragans*
5-5	*Annona* sp.
5-6	*Elaeodendron trichotomum*
5-7	?
5-8	*Bakeridisia* sp.
5-9	*Ficus glabrata*
5-10	*Leucaena* sp.
5-11	*Spondias mombin*
5-12	*Godmania aesculifolia*
5-13	*Guazuma ulmifolia*
5-14	*Mastichodendron capiri* var. *tempisque*
5-15	*Croton guatemalensis*
5-16	*Xylosma albidum*
5-17	*Exothea paniculata*
5-18	*Psidium* sp.
5-19	*Machaerium riparium*
5-20	*Xanthosoma robustum*

[2] Retained botanical specimens are stored at the California Academy of Sciences, San Francisco.

Station 8

8-2	sterile grass
8-11	sterile grass

Station 12

12-1	*Combretum fruticosum*

Station 14

14-X	*Coccoloba barbadensis*
14-Y	*Justicia spicigera*
14-Z	*Brosimum alicastrum*
14-1	*Sapindus saponaria*
14-2	*Ruellia inundata*
14-3	*Pithecellobium dulce*
14-4	Araceae family
14-5	*Salix humboldtiana*
14-6	*Typha* sp.
14-7	*Taxodium mucronatum*
14-8	*Lasiacis* sp. (sterile)
14-9	*Hydrocotyle* sp.
14-10	*Gomphrena decumbens*
14-11	*Bumelia* sp.
14-12	*Asclepias curassavica*
14-13	*Mandevilla* sp.
14-14	*Syngonium* sp.
14-15	*Godmania aesculifolia*
14-16	*Calathea* sp. or *Canna* sp.
14-17	legume

Station 15

15-1	*Lonchocarpus rugosus*
15-2	*Bauhinia schlechtendaliana*
15-3	sterile grass
15-4	*Bumelia* sp.
15-5	bamboo
15-6	*Spondias mombin*
15-7	*Inga* sp.
15-8	*Solanum erianthum*? sterile
15-9	sterile grass
15-10	*Pithecolobium sp.*
15-11	*Paullinia tomentosa*
15-12	*Simsia foetida*

Station 16

16-1	*Brosimum alicastrum*
16-2	*Manikara achras*
16-3	sterile
16-4	Annonaceae family (sterile)
16-5	sterile
16-6	*Adiantum* sp.
16-7	*Eupatorium* sp.
16-8	*Piper* sp.
16-9	*Styrax argenteus*
16-10	*Urera* sp.
16-11	sterile
16-12	sterile
16-13	sterile grass
16-14	*Cladium jamaicense*
16-15	sterile lily
16-16	*Citrus* sp.
16-17	*Brosimum alicastrum*
16-18	*Barleria micans*
16-19	*Piper* sp.
16-20	*Neurolaena lobata*
16-21	*Trichilia* sp.
16-22	*Senecio kermesianus*
16-23	*Cecopia* sp.

Station 17

17-1	*Gliricidia sepium*
17-2	*Haematoxylon brasiletto*

Station 18

18-1	*Curatella americana*
18-2	missing
18-3	*Karwinskia calderoni*

Station 22

22-1	*Ceasalpinia* sp.
22-2	*Ceasalpinia eriostachys*

Station 24

24-1	*Swietenia humilis*

Station 27

27-1	*Sabal mexicana*

Station 28

28-1	*Capparis lundellii*
28-2	*Hippacratea*?
28-3	Acanthaceae family
28-4	missing
28-5	*Petrea volubilis*

Station 30

30-1	*Amaranthus scariosus*
30-2	*Piptadenia biuncifera*

Station 31

31-1	*Brosimum alicastrum*
31-2	?
31-3	sterile

Station 32

32-1	*Astronium*?
32-2	?
32-3	*Randia aculeata*
32-4	sterile sticks

Station 33

33-1	*Platymiscium* sp.
33-2	*Eugenia* sp.
33-3	?
33-4	sterile Rubiaceae
33-5	*Cestrum lanatum*
33-6	missing
33-7	*Plumeria rubra*
33-8	*Pilea*?
33-9	?
33-10	*Cissus* sp.
33-11	*Cucurbita* sp.
33-12	*Calonyction aculeatum*
33-13	*Epiphyllum* sp.

Station 34

34-1	*Cochlospermum vitifolium*

Station 36

36-1	*Lafoensia punicifolia*
36-2	*Genipa caruto*

Station 38

38-4	*Solanum hernandesii*
38-5	*Piper* sp.
38-6	*Fraxinus uhdei*?
38-7	*Muntingia calabura*

Station 39

39-1	bamboo
39-2	*Cassia emarginata*

Station 40

40-1	*Pinus oocarpa*
40-2	*Curatella americana*
40-3	*Quercus sapotaefolia*
40-4	*Byrsonima crassifolia*
40-5	*Conostegia xalapensis*

Station 41

41-1	*Populus mexicana*
41-2	*Stemmadenia obovata*

Station 43

43-1	*Quercus* sp.

Station 44

44-1	*Pithecolobium dulce*
44-2	*Astianthus viminalis*

Station 54

54-1	*Pinus* sp.

Station 56

56-1	*Wimmeria pubescens*
56-2	*Alvaradoa amorphoides*
56-3	*Acacia* sp.
56-4	legume
56-5	*Leucaena* sp.
56-6	*Mimosa* sp.
56-7	*Croton ciliato-glandulosus*
56-8	*Melampodium* sp.
56-9	*Heliotropium* sp.
56-10	Malvaceae family
56-11	*Salvia* sp.
56-12	*Selaginella pallescens*

56-13	missing		59-12	*Bauhinia* sp.
56-14	*Phoradendron* sp.		59-13	*Heliocarpus donnell-smithii*
56-15	*Cordia globosa*		59-14	*Colubrina triflora*
56-16	*Krameria revoluta*			

Station 57

57-1	*Ximenia americana*
57-2	*Colubrina elliptica?*

Station 61

61-1	sterile
61-2	sterile
61-3	sterile
61-4	*Annona* sp.
61-5	sterile
61-6	*Annona* sp.
61-7	sterile
61-8	?
61-9	sterile
61-10	sterile
61-11	sterile
61-12	*Capsicum annuum var. minimum*
61-13	*Hamelia patens*
61-14	*Randia aculeata*
61-15	sterile
61-16	grass
61-17	sterile
61-18a	*Acalypha* sp.
61-18b	*Acalypha* sp.
61-18c	*Acalypha* sp.
61-19	*Priva lappulacea*
61-20	*Elvira biflora*
61-21	*Commelina* sp.
61-22	*Dorstenia contrajerva*
61-23	sterile grass
61-24	missing
61-25	*Saracha* sp.
61-26	*Oxypetalum cordifolium*
61-27	*Rivina humilis*
61-28	Araceae family
61-29	Araceae family
61-30	*Desmodium* sp.
61-31	*Serjania* sp.
61-32	Asclepiadaceae family or Apocynaceae family

Station 58

58-1	*Neopringlea viscosa*
58-2	*Bucida buceras*
58-3	*Beaucarnea goldmanii*
58-4	*Bursera excelsa*
58-5	sterile legume?
58-6	missing
58-7	missing
58-8	*Bursera simaruba*
58-9	*Karwinskia calderoni*
58-10	missing
58-11	*Ayenia* sp.
58-12	sterile
58-13	*Capparis lundellii*
58-14	*Bourreria andrieuxi*
58-15	sterile legume, not *Poeppigia procera*
58-16	*Colubrina?*
58-17	*Bumelia* sp.

Station 59

59-1	*Cordia globosa*
59-2	*Randia* sp.
59-3	*Cordia* sp.
59-4	*Thevatia ovata*
59-5	*Croton guatemalensis*
59-6	sterile legume
59-7	*Bourreria andrieuxii*
59-8a	*Croton* sp.
59-8b	legume
59-9	*Acacia pennatula?*
59-10	*Celtis iguanaea*
59-11	*Croton* sp.

Stations 63

63-1	*Bursera bipinnata*
63-2	*Byrsonima crassifolia*
63-3	*Croton ciliato-glandulosus*
63-4	sterile
63-5	*Stylosanthes* sp.
63-6	*Calea* sp.
63-7	*Peperomia humilis*
63-8	sterile
63-9	*Notholaena aurea*
63-10	*Ardisia escallonioides*
63-11	*Paspalum* sp.
63-12	sterile grass
63-13	*Bletia* sp.
63-14	*Paullinia*?
63-15	legume
63-16	*Xylosma* sp.
63-17	mixed sterile
63-18	sterile
63-19	*Chaptalia nutans*
63-20	sterile
63-21	*Juniperus comitana*
63-22	*Psychotria erythrocarpa*

Station 64

64-1	*Cordia* sp.
64-2	*Sclerocarpus uniserialis* var. *frutescens*
64-3	*Lantana achyranthifolia*
64-4	*Cassia uniflora*
64-5	*Parthenium hysterophorus*
64-6	*Bouchea prismatica*
64-7	*Sida acuta*
64-8	*Croton* sp.
64-9	*Lantana camara*
64-10	*Malvaviscus arboreus*
64-11	*Martynia annua*
64-12	*Croton* sp.
64-13	*Ruellia* sp.

Station 68

68-1	*Elaeodendron trichotomum*
68-2	*Urera caracasana*
68-3	sterile Rubiaceae
68-4	?
68-5	*Celtis iguanaea*
68-6	legume
68-7	*Cucurbit* sp.
68-8	*Petiveria alliacea*
68-9	legume
68-10	sterile?
68-11	sterile
68-12	*Serjania* sp.
68-13	sterile
68-14	*Maranta arundinacea*
68-15	sterile
68-16	sterile legume
68-17	sterile
68-18	*Scleria* sp.
68-19	*Selaginella* sp.
68-20	*Eugenia* sp.
68-21	*Randia aculeata*
68-22	*Daphnopsis americana*
68-23	*Cassia* sp.

Station 69

69-1	*Piptadenia* sp.

Station 70

70-1	*Brosimum alicastrum*
70-2	*Myriocarpa* sp.
70-3	sterile?
70-4	missing
70-5	sterile
70-6	sterile?
70-7	sterile
70-8	*Ardisia* sp.
70-9	sterile?
70-10	sterile
70-11	*Cnidoscolus* sp. or *Jatropha* sp.
70-12	*Lasiacis* sp.
70-13	sterile
70-14	*Barleria micaus*
70-15	?
70-16	*Adiantopsis* sp.
70-17	*Olyra latifolia*

70-18	Acanthadeae family
70-19	*Schaefferia* sp.
70-20	*Dorstenia contrajerva*
70-21	composite (*Zexmenia*?)
70-22	sterile legume
70-23	*Syngonium* sp.
70-24	Gesneriaceae family
70-25	*Peperomia* sp.
70-26	*Polypodium* sp.
70-27	sterile?
70-28	*Polypodium* sp.

Station 71

71-1	*Spondias mombin*
71-2	*Eugenia* sp.
71-3	*Guazuma ulmifolia*
71-4	sterile
71-5	sterile
71-6	*Annona* sp.
71-7	*Casearia* sp.
71-8	*Cordia alliodera*?
71-9	*Casearia* sp.
71-10	*Acalypha unibracteata*
71-11	sterile
71-12	sterile
71-13	*Paullinia* sp.
71-14	sterile
71-15	legume (sterile)
71-16	missing
71-17	*Pseuderanthemum* sp.
71-18	*Smilacina* sp.
71-19	*Dorstenia contrajerva*
71-20	*Pedilanthus* sp.
71-21	sterile legume
71-22	*Lycianthes lenta*
71-23	*Cissus* sp.
71-24	*Peperomia* sp.
71-25	*Gonolobus* sp.
71-26	*Tabernaemontana* sp.
71-27	*Vitis bourgaeana*
71-28	*Verbesina*?

71-29	sterile
71-30	*Bauhinia* sp.
71-31	*Pseuderanthemum* sp.
71-32	sterile
71-33	sterile
71-34	Orchidaceae family

Station 72

72-1	*Quercus* sp.
72-2	*Calliandra houstoniana*
72-3	sterile
72-4	sterile legume
72-5	*Vernonia*?
72-6	sterile legume
72-7	*Croton* sp.
72-8	missing
72-9	*Calea vitifolia*
72-10	sterile legume
72-11	*Dalea* sp.
72-12	*Mimosa albida*
72-13	missing
72-14	*Maranta arundinacea*
72-15	*Cassia* sp.
72-16	*Pithecoctenium echinatum*
72-17	*Desmodium* sp.
72-18	*Scleria* sp.
72-19	grass (sterile)
72-20	*Acalypha* sp.
72-21	sterile composite
72-22	*Byrsonima*?
72-23	*Croton* sp.
72-24	legume
72-24a	*Apaeyn.* (sic) *or Asclepias* sp.
72-25	*Sida acuta*
72-26	*Zexmenia* sp.
72-27	missing
72-28	*Desmodium* sp.
72-29	*Aphelandra deppeana*
72-30	legume
72-31	*Phaseolus* sp.

Table 2.2. Location of botanical collection stations, upper Grijalva River Basin.

Station #	Description
1	Southeast of La Trinitaria along road to Pemex oil well. Station is approximately 1.5 km east of Mex 190.
2	On the east side of Mex 190, approximately 18 km south of La Trinitaria.
3	Approximately 0.5 km east of Col. Angel Albino Corzo on the road to Col. Morelos.
4	Approximately 3.25 km east of Chihuahua on south side of road to Col. Albino Corzo.
5	Approximately 2.75 km west of Col. Albino Corzo on south side of road to Chihuahua.
6	Approximately 3.5 km west of Col. Morelos, 0.5 km north of road to Col. Albino Corzo.
7	Approximately 2.66 km west of Col. Morelos on south side of road to Col. Albino Corzo.
8	Approximately 1 km west of Col. Vicente Guerrero on north side of road to Col. Morelos.
9	N. A.
10	Approximately 0.875 km west of Col. Las Delicias on north side of road to San Lucas.
11	Approximately 6 km southeast of Las Delicias on north side or road that departs from the southeast corner of Las Delicias and proceeds toward the Guatemala border.
12	Approximately 5.25 km southeast of Las Delicias on north side of road that departs from the southeast corner of Las Delicias and proceeds toward the Guatemala border.
13	Approximately 3.5 km southeast of Las Delicias on south side of road which departs from the southeast corner of Las Delicias and proceeds toward the Guatemala border.
14	Approximately 6.75 km southeast of Col. Rodolfo Figueroa, 0.25 km east of road departing from southeast corner of Col. Rodolfo Figueroa and proceeding in a wide arc to an intersection with Mex 190 near Río San Gregario.
15	Approximately 6.25 km southeast of Col. Rodolfo Figueroa on east side of road departing from southeast corner of Col. Rodolfo Figueroa and proceeding in a wide arc to an intersection with Mex 190 near Río San Gregorio.
16	Approximately 10.5 km on road that departs from southeast corner of Col. Rodolfo Figueroa and proceeds in a wide arc to an intersection with Mex 190 near Río San Gregorio. There is a turnoff to the south about 0.125 km before Río Joaquín. This new road stops about 1 km after leaving main road. Station 16 is another 1 km farther south-southeast of end of turn-out road.
17	General vicinity of San Joaquín. Location is not precise—samples collected along the road.
18	Approximately 0.25 km north of San Joaquín on road to Boquerón.
19	Approximately 1.5 km southeast of San Joaquín on west side of road departing from southeast corner San Joaquín.
20	Approximately 6 km from intersection near El Salvador on north side of road to San Felipe.

Station #	Description
21	Approximately 5 km north of the end of the road that proceeds north 0.5 km from San Felipe.
22	Approximately 1.75 km as crow flies northeast of San Caralampio.
23	Approximately 1 km northwest of Nueva Independencia.
24	At turnoff to Ojo de Agua archaeological site, approximately 2 km west of Santa Ana on road to La Florida (site located on south side of road).
25	Approximately 1 m east of La Florida on north side of road to Santa Ana.
26	At La Florida.
27	Approximately 1.5 km west of Santa Rosa on north side of road to Tres Amores.
28	At Coapa archaeological site, approximately 3.5 km south (as crow flies) of Tres Amores.
29	N. A.
30	Approximately 1 km west of Sinaloa on west side of road that departs from north corner of settlement and proceeds in a northeast direction.
31	Approximately 1.25 km south of Sinaloa on east side or road that leaves south corner of Sinaloa and proceeds due south.
32	Approximately 1.5 km south of Sinaloa on west side of road leaving south corner of Sinaloa and proceeding due south.
33	At El Portal.
34	Approximately 2 km north of Comalapa on east side of road to Guadalupe Grijalva.
35	Approximately 6 km south of Nueva Libertad on east side of road to Guadalupe Grijlava.
36	Approximately 4 km south of Nueva Libertad on east side of road to Guadalupe Grijlava.
37	Approximately 1.5 km south of Nueva Libertad on east side of road to Guadalupe Grijlava.
38	Approximately 6 km southeast of Reforma on north side of road to Col. Chamic.
39	Approximately 1.25 km west of San Nicolas Yayahuita, 0.25 km south of road proceeding west from San Nicolas Yayahuita.
40	Approximately 2.5 km west of San Nicolas Yayahuita on south side of road proceeding west from San Nicolas Yayahuita.
41	Approximately 1 km north of Nueva Morelia on west side of road to La Pinta.
42	Approximately 0.33 km south of La Pinta on east side or road to Nueva Morelia.
43	Approximately 1.25 km northeast of San Nicolas Yayahuita.
44	On east bank of Río San Miguel approximately 1 km west of Rosarito.

Station #	Description
45-49	N. A.
50	Approximately 1.25 east of Sabinalito on south side of road to Llano Grande.
51	Approximately 0.66 km southwest of Santa Monica on east side of main road that runs from Chicomucelo northwest to La Llanada.
52	Approximately 7 km as crow flies due north of Col. Pablo Sidar.
53	Approximately 5 km as crow flies due north of Col. Pablo Sidar.
54	Approximately 0.75 km northwest of San Antonio Ocotal on south side of road that proceeds northwest from San Antonio Ocotal.
55	Approximately 1 km west of Santa Ana on south side of road to La Florida.
56	Approximately 0.25 km west of Tres Amores on north side of road to Col. Francisco J. Mújica.
57	Across the road from #56.
58	Approximately 1 km northeast of El Naranjo on south side of road that proceeds northeast from El Naranjo.
59	At Corral de Piedra.
60	Approximately 2 km as crow flies due south of Esperanza.
61	Approximately 1.25 km south of La Florida, 0.25 km south of road that proceeds south then west of La Florida.
62	Approximately 3 km east of Col. Albino Corzo on north side of road to Col. Morelos.
63	Approximately 2.5 km as crow flies due west of Col. Morelos.
64	At Santa Elena.
65	Approximately 5.5 km east of Santa Elena on north side of road to El Salvador.
66	Approximately 4.5 km east of Chilar on north side of road to El Salvador.
67	N. A.
68	Approximately 2.75 km northwest of Col. Vera Paz, and 0.25 km west of road that proceeds northwest from Col. Vera Paz.
69	At Finca Tres Cruces.
70	Approximately 0.66 km as crow flies east of Col. Monte Redondo.
71	Approximately 2.66 km as crow flies east of Col. Nuevo Mexico.
72	Approximately 2.25 km as crow flies due south of Col. Vera Paz.
73	At the archaeological site of Guajilar.

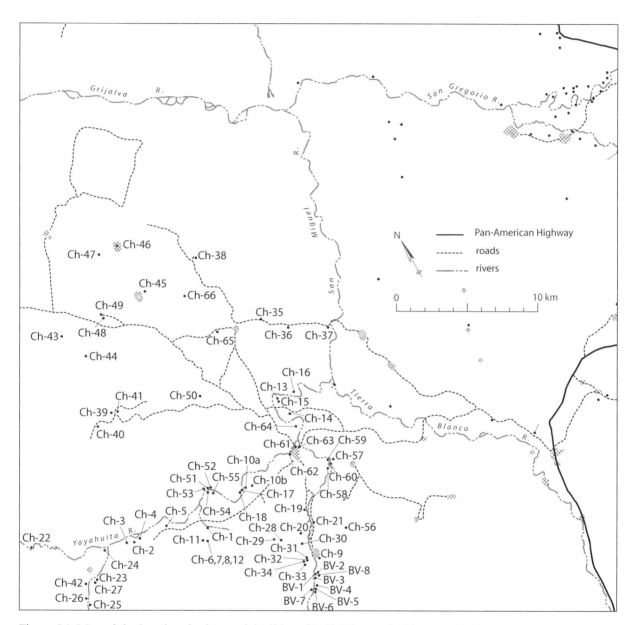

Figure 3.1. Map of site locations in the municipalities of Bella Vista and Chicomuselo (close up of map in Figure 1.7).

CHAPTER 3

SITE DESCRIPTIONS: MUNICIPIOS BELLA VISTA AND CHICOMUCELO

James M. White, Michael Blake, Thomas A. Lee Jr., John E. Clark, and Mary E. Pye

MUNICIPIO BELLA VISTA

BV-1 (no map)

Site Type: Habitational

Occupation: Protoclassic, Late Classic, Late Postclassic

Location and Setting: BV-1 is on the east side of the Río Tachinula, 1.5 km south of Colonia Piedra Labrada. It is in the river valley 100 m from the river's edge. The site zone is used as milpa.

Environmental Stratum: Riparian Forest

Description: Only two small mounds are present at this site that was probably a single house group. One mound is 5 m by 3 m and 0.25 m high. The other, 10 m to the northeast, is even smaller. Significant ceramics were noted over the site surface, but no other mounds were plotted.

References: White 1976:45

BV-2 (Figure 3.2)

Site Type: Habitational

Location and Setting: BV-2 is 1.5 km south of Colonia Piedra Labrada and only 80 m east of BV-1 on the east side of the Río Tachinula. It is in the valley bottom in an area used as pasturage.

Environmental Stratum: Evergreen Seasonal Forest-Riparian Forest

Description: The largest mound is 2 m high and, although quite high for a house mound, is only 10 m by 10 m on a side. Next to it is a much smaller mound, only 0.5 m high. Both may have formed a single house group in some way related to the large site Ch-9 (Piedra Labrada) just downstream.

References: White 1976:46

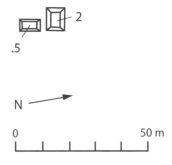

Figure 3.2. Site sketch of BV-2.

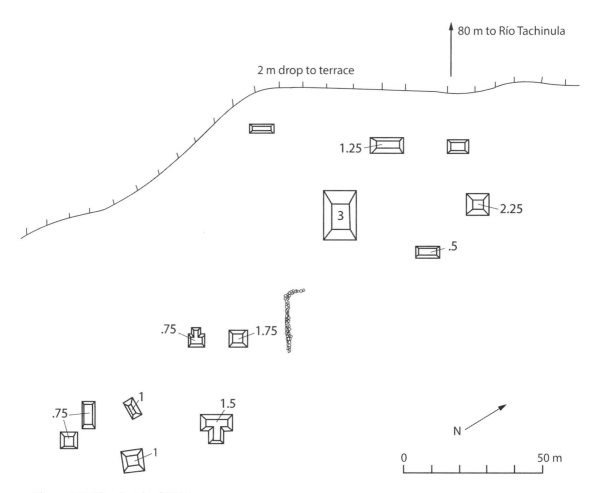

Figure 3.3. Site sketch of BV-3.

BV-3 (Figure 3.3)

Site Type: Ceremonial and habitational

Occupation: Late Middle Preclassic, Protoclassic, Early Classic, Late Classic, Postclassic

Location and Setting: BV-3 is 1.5 km south of Colonia Piedra Labrada on the east side of the Río Tachinula. It is on a river terrace approximately 5 m above the floodplain and 80 m from the river's edge. The site area is used as milpa.

Environmental Stratum: Riparian Forest

Description: The single ceremonial plaza consists of five mounds arranged around a plaza area. The largest mound is 3 m high. It faces a 2.25 m mound across the plaza. Three other smaller mounds define the northwest and southeast sides. All are faced with river cobbles. South of the main buildings are several smaller mounds that may have been house groups. Some are quite tall and (1.5 to 1.75 m) so could be elite residences. They are fairly tightly aggregated and could have formed a series of contemporaneously occupied houses. Between the residential area and the main plaza is an L-shaped cobble wall over 20 m long.

References: White 1976:46

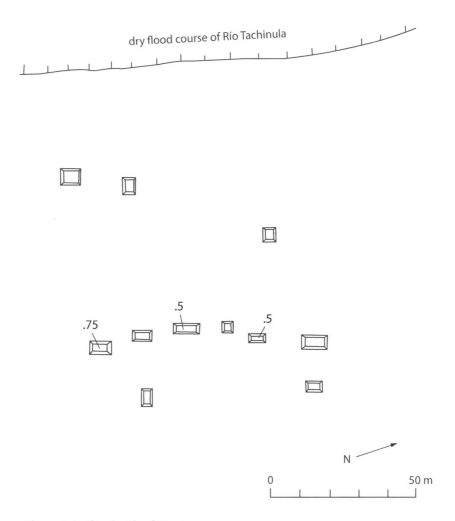

Figure 3.4. Site sketch of BV-4.

BV-4 (Figure 3.4)

Site Type: Habitational

Occupation: Late Postclassic

Location and Setting: This site is 2 km south of Colonia Piedra Labrada on the east side of the Río Tachinula. It is approximately 180 m from the river in an area used as milpa.

Environmental Stratum: Riparian Forest

Description: There are 11 house mounds distributed over an area of about 80 m by 90 m. None of the houses form clear house groups. Some of the platforms are as high as 0.5 to 0.75 m, but the majority of them are lower.

References: White 1976:46-47

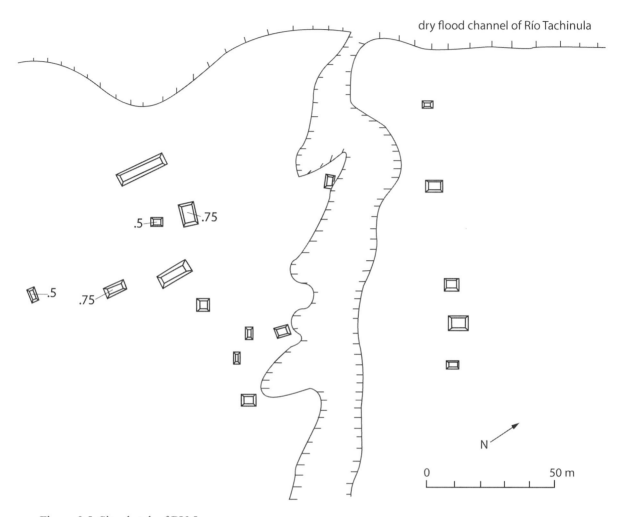

Figure 3.5. Site sketch of BV-5.

BV-5 (Figure 3.5)

Site Type: Habitational

Occupation: Late Classic, Postclassic

Location and Setting: BV-5 is a little over 23 km south of Colonia Piedra Labrada on the east side of the Río Tachinula. It sits on the river terrace overlooking the floodplain. At present, the land is used as milpa.

Environmental Stratum: Riparian Forest

Description: The site is cut by an arroyo that may actually have removed several houses. On the south side there is a plaza group of three fairly large platforms with a smaller central mound. The longest mound is 20 m by 5 m. Its length is reminiscent of the Late Postclassic style of house mound construction in other parts of the study area. Few of the platforms show any clear arrangement that would suggest house groupings.

References: White 1976:47

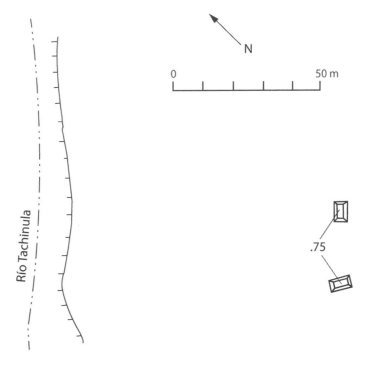

Figure 3.6. Site sketch of BV-6.

BV-6 (Figure 3.6)

Site Type: Habitational

Occupation: Late Classic, Late Postclassic

Location and Setting: This site is a few hundred meters south of BV-5 and 2.5 km south of Colonia Piedra Labrada. It is on the east side of the Río Tachinula, only 100 m from and 6 m above the river. It is in the yard of a modern house.

Environmental Stratum: Riparian Forest

Description: This site consists of only two house mounds 15 m apart from each other. They are both 7 m by 4 m and roughly 0.75 high. Both may have been partly destroyed by modern construction activity.

References: White 1976:47

BV-7 (no map)

Site Type: Sherd scatter

Occupation: Late Classic, Late Postclassic

Location and Setting: This site is directly across the river from BV-6 on the west bank of the Río Tachinula, 2.5 km downstream from Colonia Piedra Labrada. The land is used as a milpa.

Environmental Stratum: Riparian Forest

Description: This scatter of sherds covers approximately 1500 m^2. It is in the only habitable area on this side of the river. There were probably perishable houses built directly on the ground surface.

References: White 1976:47

BV-8 (Figure 3.7)

Site Type: Habitational

Occupation: Late Classic, Late Postclassic, including one Chinautla Polychrome sherd

Location and Setting: BV-8 is 1.5 km south of Colonia Piedra Labrada on the east side of the Río Tachinula. It sits on a low hill approximately 300 m from the river. The land is used as a milpa.

Environmental Stratum: Evergreen Seasonal Forest-Riparian Forest

Description: The nine low platforms at this site are tightly clustered on the top of the hill. Their orientation conforms more to the hill's topography than to any regularized layout. They do not form readily definable house groups.

References: White 1976:47

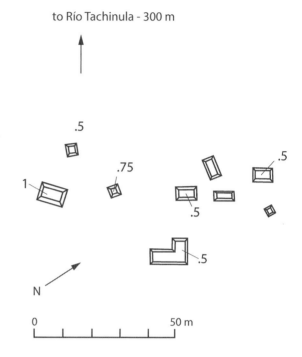

to Río Tachinula - 300 m

Figure 3.7. Site sketch of BV-8.

MUNICIPIO CHICOMUSELO
CH-1 (no map)

Site Type: Historic-industrial

Occupation: possible Colonial, post-Colonial

Location and Setting: On a side tributary of Río Yayahuita, 1.5 km from its confluence and 8 km west of Chicomuselo. The site lies on a hillslope and is used as pasture and milpa.

Environmental Stratum: Evergreen Seasonal Forest

Description: White (1976:25) describes this structure as follows: "This stone structure with true arches, tunnels and an aqueduct is the remains of a colonial industrial building of unknown use. Water was evidently drawn from the adjacent mountain slope down a cemented sluice on top of the structure, from there being let into low arched chambers….the low partially underground tunnels seemed to be roofed in the corbelled arch fashion—[a] possible combination of Maya and European architectural elements." It may have functioned as a foundry; lead mines are reported in the vicinity.

References: White 1976:25

CH-2 POTRERO TERRENAL 1
(Figure 3.8)

Site Type: Ceremonial and habitation

Location and Setting: Potrero Terrenal 1 is located on the south bank of Río Yayahuita, 12 km upriver from Chicomuselo. The site sits on the river valley bottom on a small terrace 200 m from the river. Another small stream passes it 10 m to the west on its way to the Yayahuita. The vegetation on the site is mainly dense grass and is used as pasture.

Environmental Stratum: Evergreen Seasonal Forest-Riparian Forest

Description: This site is a small ceremonial center with two large mounds and three smaller platforms surrounding a small plaza. The tallest mound was 2.5 m high. One small mound, possibly an altar located on the east side of the plaza, overlooks a steep terrace drop. Potrero Terrenal 1 is within 300 m of Ch-3 and could be another part of that large site—it is likely contemporary with it.

References: White 1976:25-26

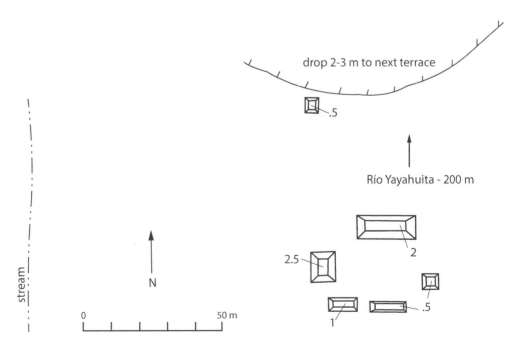

Figure 3.8. Site sketch of Ch-2, Potrero Terrenal 1.

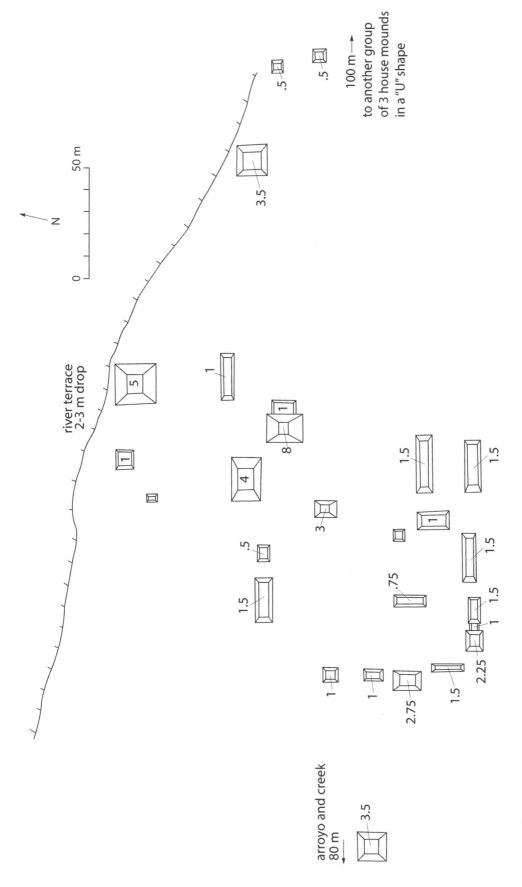

Figure 3.9. Site sketch of Ch-3, Potrero Terrenal 2.

CH-3 POTRERO TERRENAL 2
(Figure 3.9)

Site Type: Ceremonial and habitation

Occupation: Late Classic?

Location and Setting: Potrero Terrenal 2 is situated on the south bank of Río Yayahuita, 12.5 km upriver from the modern settlement of Chicomuselo. It is roughly 300 m west of Ch-2. The site is in the valley bottom approximately 5 m above the level of the Yayahuita and 200 m south of it. Vegetation on the site is primarily grassland used for pasturage at the time of the survey.

Environmental Stratum: Evergreen Seasonal Forest-Riparian Forest

Description: This site consists primarily of a large ceremonial center with perhaps some elite residential structures near the main plaza. There are two main types of structures in the center. At the north end of the site are three large mounds between 4 m and 8 m in height. The 5 m mound is on a 2-3 m high natural terrace overlooking the Río Yayahuita floodplain. The two other large mounds together form the northeast corner of the plaza. To the south of them, forming another corner of the plaza, are two long parallel mounds that may have formed a ballcourt, although they are rather widely spaced. The southwest and north sides of the plaza are comprised of eight low mounds, some of which could have been residential platforms. In the interior of the plaza area is an additional low platform. To both the west and east of the plaza are two large square mounds, each 3.5 m high. They appear to mark the bounds of the site center.

Additional low residential structures may have been located in the area surrounding the main plaza, but the grass was too dense at the time of the survey to observe more than just a few. For example, 100 m east of the easternmost house mound was a small house group comprised of three houses around a patio.

The layout of this site suggests at least two phases of construction. The group of tall mounds may have been begun during the Middle Preclassic[1] since they have a layout similar to such sites in the region. The main plaza to the south of these mounds has many more low buildings, rectangular in shape, and arranged so as to close off the plaza area. This is more Terminal Classic style and so probably represents a later addition.

References: White 1976:26

CH-4 POTRERO TERRENAL 3
(Figure 3.10)

Site Type: Habitation

Occupation: Late Classic

Figure 3.10. Site sketch of Ch-4, Potrero Terrenal 3.

---

1 Editorial note– At the time of White's thesis, it was believed that large mound construction began in the Late Preclassic. Excavations at sites in the upper Grijalva since survey was undertaken revealed that large mound construction actually began in the Middle Preclassic (e.g., La Libertad [Miller 2014]). The text has been updated here and elsewhere to reflect this finding. Unfortunately, in this case, no Preclassic sherds were recovered during survey hence the possible Late Classic date.

Location and Setting: This site is located on the south side of Río Yayahuita, 11.5 km west of Chicomuselo. It sits on a natural terrace 200 m south of the river channel. Vegetation on the site is mainly dense grass used as pasturage, but there are large riparian trees nearby.

Environmental Stratum: Riparian Forest

Description: Only three mounds were noted at this site. They appear to be part of two different house groups approximately 12 m apart. One at the east part of the site has two low mounds that form a patio group. The west mound is an isolated platform approximately 1 m high. This layout is typical of Late Classic sites in the region.

References: White 1976:26

CH-5 (Figure 3.11)

Site Type: Ceremonial

Occupation: Late Classic

Location and Setting: Ch-5 is located on top of a low hilltop 300 m south of Río Yayahuita

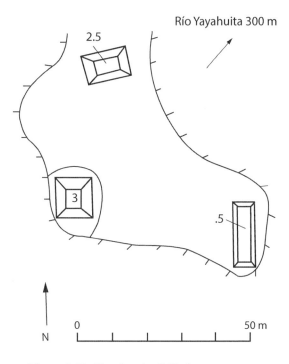

Río Yayahuita 300 m

2.5

3

.5

0   50 m
N

Figure 3.11. Site sketch of Ch-5.

and 9.5 km west of the modern settlement of Chicomuselo. The site is covered with grass and small shrubs and is presently used as pasturage.

Environmental Stratum: Fields or Pastures

Description: The three mounds recorded at this site sit on a well-defined and more or less level hilltop. They are located near the edge of the hill-drop and face onto a small plaza area. The largest mound is 3 m high but sits on a 3 m high natural rise increasing its prominence. It is surfaced with river cobbles. The north side of the plaza is bounded by a 2.5 m high platform while the southwest side is defined by a long rectangular mound that sits 0.5 m high. This latter structure could have been a residential platform. Its relative length suggests a Postclassic date and could have postdated the other two structures that appear more like Late Classic ceremonial mounds in the region.

References: White 1976:26

CH-6 PORTRERO DEL CERRO (CAVE 1)
(no map)

Site Type: Ceremonial cave

Location and Setting: This cave site is located 8 km west of Chicomuselo and 2 km south of Río Yayahuita. It is nearby the ceremonial and residential site of Ch-11 and three other cave sites (Ch-7, Ch- 8, and Ch-12). The caves are at the base of a steep rocky cliff face that begins its ascent just south of Ch-11.

Environmental Stratum: Evergreen Seasonal Forest

Description: No map was made of the cave. It has a narrow mouth that opens into a small chamber. Inside were several sherds and a fragment of human skull. A portion of a pig skull was also noted.

References: White 1976:26-27

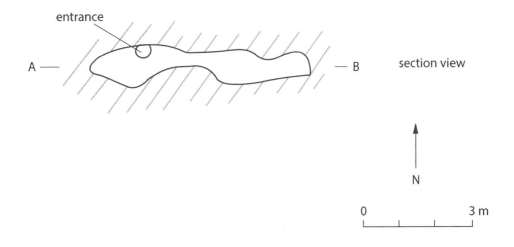

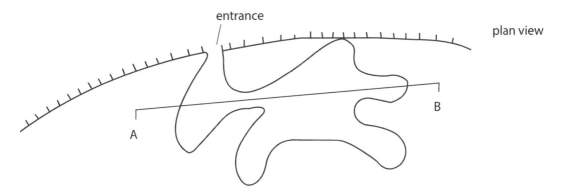

Figure 3.12. Site sketch of Ch-7, Portrero del Cerro (Cave 2).

CH-7 PORTRERO DEL CERRO (CAVE 2)
(Figure 3.12)

Site Type: Ceremonial cave

Occupation: possible Late Preclassic, Late Classic

Location and Setting: This cave is 50 m west of Ch-6 at the base of the same cliff that faces north towards Río Yayahuita, 2 km away. The site is 8 km west of Chicomuselo.

Environmental Stratum: Evergreen Seasonal Forest

Description: There is a chamber about 6 m wide and 3 m deep that can be entered by way of an extremely narrow mouth. Once inside, the chamber it is only about 1 m in height. Several sherds were found on the surface of the cave floor.

References: White 1976:26-27

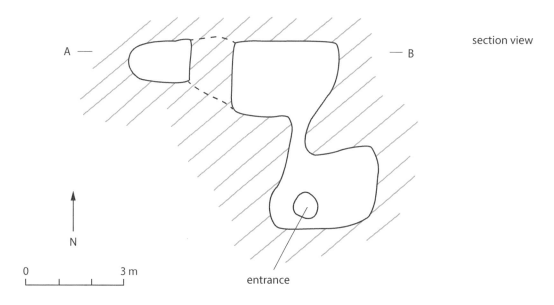

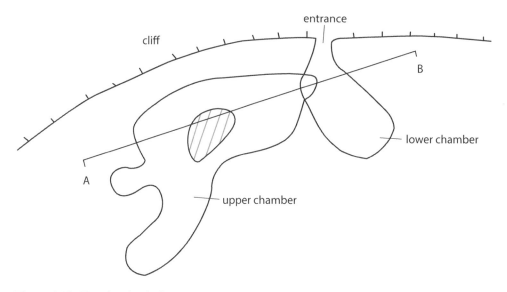

Figure 3.13. Site sketch of Ch-8, Portrero del Cerro (Cave 3).

CH-8 PORTRERO DEL CERRO (CAVE 3)
(Figure 3.13)

Site Type: Ceremonial cave

Occupation: Protoclassic, Early Classic, Late Postclassic

Location and Setting: (see Ch-6 and Ch-7) This site is located approximately 50 m west of Ch-7 at the base of a cliff, 2 km south of Río Yayahuita.

Environmental Stratum: Evergreen Seasonal Forest

Description: The cave consists of two chambers. The first lower chamber is entered by way of a small round mouth less than a meter in diameter. It is approximately 3.5 m by 2 m in area and 2 m high. Near its top is another narrow opening that gives way to a slightly larger chamber that measures 7 m by 3 m and is approximately 2 m in height. Inside were found several bags of sherds and a human cranium fragment.

References: White 1976:26-27

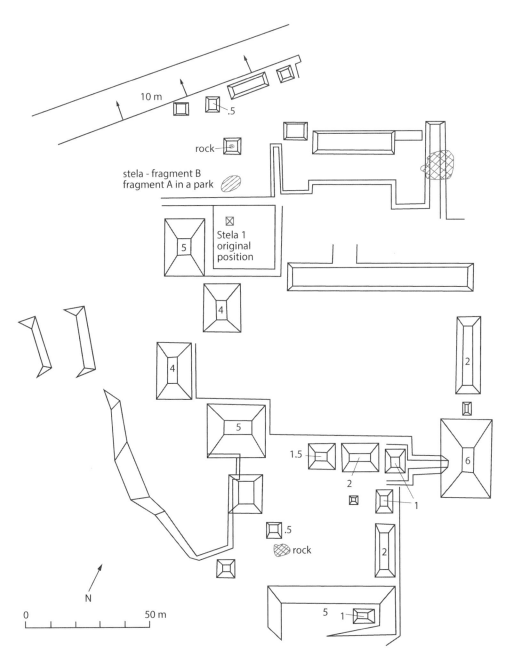

Figure 3.14. Site sketch of Ch-9, Piedra Labrada.

CH-9 PIEDRA LABRADA
(Figures 3.14-3.15)

Site Type: Ceremonial and habitation

Occupation: possible Early Classic, possible Middle Classic, Late Classic, Early Postclassic

Location and Setting: Piedra Labrada is located on the southern outskirts of Colonia Piedra Labrada, 150 m east of Río Tachinula. The site sits approximately 20 m above the river level at the base of a mountain slope which has been terraced in the site area. It now lies within the town site and is covered with grass and trees. Townsfolk use the main plaza as a ballcourt.

Environmental Stratum: Evergreen Seasonal Forest

Figure 3.15. Ch-9, Piedra Labrada:
a-b. two views of same stela fragment; c. stela
fragment depicting head of a lord with elaborate
headdress; d. creative refashioning of stelae and
sculpture fragments by townsfolk of Colonia
Piedra Labrada; e. mountain slope behind the site.

Description: The center of the site consists mainly of ceremonial structures arranged around a large open plaza. If any of the structures were occupied as residences, their size and proximity to this elaborate ceremonial center would indicate that they belonged to the elite. The northern part of the site is bounded by an enormous ballcourt (roughly the same size and I-shaped like that found at Co-54) 55 m long and 10 m wide. Between the ballcourt and the plaza is a long narrow mound (75 m by 10 m) that could well have been a Postclassic addition to the site. The southern corners of the plaza are delineated by two large pyramids: one 6 m tall and the other 5 m tall. Between these, on the edge of a terrace overlooking the plaza, are three small temple mounds. They, in fact, form the north edge of a separate smaller plaza, which in turn is formed by smaller temple mounds. In the plaza area are 2-3 small altars. The south edge of this smaller plaza is formed by a huge terrace mound built into the hillside. It is 5 m high and 50 m long.

Returning to the main plaza, the west side is delineated by two large 4 m tall mounds. Just to the north of these is a 5 m tall mound that flanks a large platform with a stela sitting in its original position. To the north of this is another stela fragment, part of which was removed to the main plaza in the Colonia. Five other small platforms are located along the north side of the site, fronting a terrace that drops steeply for 10 m.

The closed nature of the plazas and their formalized layout suggests a Classic date for the bulk of the construction. Only structures such as the 75 m long mound and the small altars are perhaps suggestive of a Late Postclassic reoccupation of the site. But even more important is the location of several stelae fragments at the site and in the Colonia. The discovery of a stela with Maya hieroglyphs, one of which is the outline of an introductory glyph, provides an important anchor for the interpretation of Chicomuselo ceramics and culture history (White 1976:27). Specifically, the style of the stela is similar to others found to the north at Tenam Rosario (Tr-9), Chinkultic

(Navarrete 1984, 1999), and Tonina (Becquelin and Baudez 1982).

References: White 1976:27-29; Lee 1984:119

CH-10 PUEBLO VIEJO (YAYAHUITA)
(Figure 3.16)

Site Type: Ceremonial and habitation

Occupation: Late Classic, Late Postclassic, Colonial, post-Colonial

Location and Setting: Pueblo Viejo is on the south side of Río Yayahuita approximately 4 km west of Chicomuselo. The main part of the site (Ch-10a) sits at the edge of a 15-20 m high terrace overlooking the river. The area is used as a combination of milpa and pasture.

Environmental Stratum: Fields or Pasture

Description: The main part of this site consists of several colonial structures: a church, house mounds, and altars. The church has standing walls 2 and 3 m high. Behind it (towards the river) is a large walled-in area that may have been a cemetery. South of the Church is a small plaza area with a long rectangular house mound that is surrounded by four, low square altars. An irregularly shaped mound sits on the west side of the house platform and forms the border of the plaza. These structures may have been Pre-conquest buildings re-used during the Colonial period.

To the east of the church is a large field that contains an unknown number of house mounds (vegetation was too thick to map them at the time of the survey). These may have been part of the pre-Conquest community in the area. The field is full of cobbles, as are the fence lines, attesting to the number of house platforms that must have been present at one time. The habitation area is roughly 600 m by 100 m. Further east still is another colonial building (Ch-10b) that may also have been a church. It is smaller than the church near the river but still has wall remnants standing 1.5 m high.

This site may have been the location of a hacienda named Yayahuita, a Colonial Period occupation of a former Pre-Hispanic site.

References: White 1976:29-30

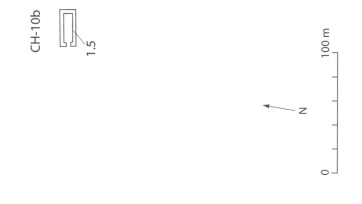

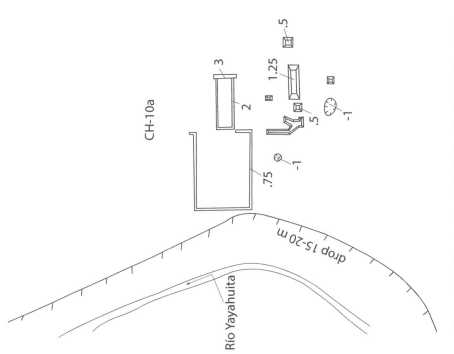

Figure 3.16. Site sketch of Ch-10, Pueblo Viejo (Yayahuita).

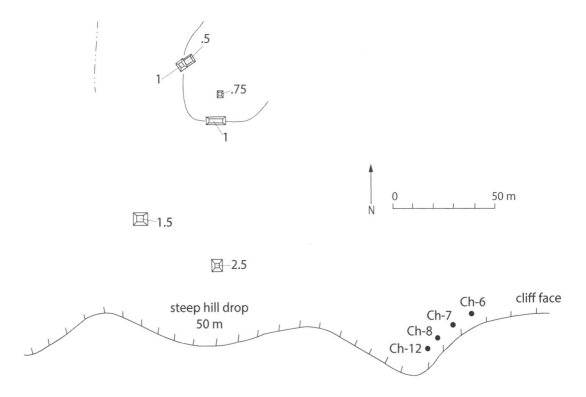

Figure 3.17. Site sketch of Ch-11, Potrero del Cerro.

CH-11 POTRERO DEL CERRO
(Figure 3.17)

Site Type: Ceremonial and habitation

Occupation: Late Classic

Location and Setting: Potrero del Cerro is located 8 km west of Chicomuselo and 2 km south of Río Yayahuita. It is situated on a large mesa-like formation with a commanding view of the surrounding region. To the south is a large steep cliff in which are located four caves that served some sort of ceremonial function (probably burial caves see Ch-6, Ch-7, Ch-8, and C-12). The area is now covered with thick tall grass and is used as pasture.

Environmental Stratum: Evergreen Seasonal Forest

Description: There are only a few mounds at Potrero del Cerro. One group of two mounds near the base of the cliff is comprised of one 1.5 m and one 2.5 m tall platform. These were probably ceremonial pyramids or temple substructures. Just north of these was located a group of three mounds that may have been a residential group. One of the mounds appears to have been an altar and is in a small depression midway between the other two platforms. One of these is a small structure with an extension on the northeast side. The overall layout of these structures suggests a Late Classic date.

References: White 1976:30

CH-12 PORTRERO DEL CERRO (CAVE 4)
(no map)

Site Type: Ceremonial cave

Location and Setting: This is the easternmost of the four caves located in the face of a large cliff to the south of Ch-11. The other sites are Ch-6, Ch-7, and Ch-8.

Environmental Stratum: Evergreen Seasonal Forest

Description: Ch-12 is the largest cave in the series of caves along the cliff face. A small opening gives way to a large chamber which had little cultural material visible. On the floor of the chamber was an opening that led to a lower, smaller chamber. It was in this second chamber that a number of large sherds and almost complete vessels were found. Many of them were embedded in lime deposits.

References: White 1976:30

CH-13 (Figure 3.18)

Site Type: Ceremonial (?) and habitation

Ceramic Phase: Ix

Occupation: Protoclassic, Late Classic

Location and Setting: This site is located 4 km north of Chicomuselo on the east side of Río Chicomuselo. It sits on the grassy river margin 100 m south of it in an area that is used as milpa.

Environmental Stratum: Riparian Forest

Description: There are only two mounds at this site. One is 15 m by 8 m and 1 m high, and was probably a large house platform. The other mound sits 25 m to the south. It is 7 m by 7 m and also 1 m high. This second mound may have been a small ceremonial structure, perhaps an altar. Both were faced with river cobbles.

References: White 1976:30-31

CH 14 (Figure 3.19)

Site Type: Ceremonial and habitation

Occupation: Late Classic, Late Postclassic

Location and Setting: Ch-14 is located 2 km north of Chicomuselo and the confluence of the Yayahuita and Tachinula rivers. It sits on a low hill 1 km east of Río Chicomuselo. The site area is forested and partially cleared for milpa.

Environmental Stratum: Tropical Deciduous Forest

Description: There are two groups of mounds at Ch-14 and only one of these may have had ceremonial functions. It is about 12 m on a side and 1.5 m high. Directly opposite, across a small patio, is a long low house platform. Another small platform sits on the north side of the plaza.

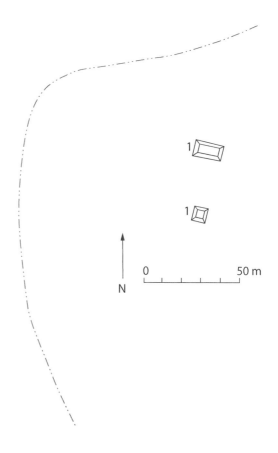

Figure 3.18. Site sketch of Ch-13.

To the south is the other group of four mounds. They include three very low platforms arranged in linear fashion, one of which is 1 m high. Another of these is 20 m long and only 0.25 m high. All of these were probably house platforms, perhaps belonging to the same patio group. Several of the structures were being destroyed at the time of the survey in order to use their river cobble facings for the construction of modern houses.

References: White 1976:31

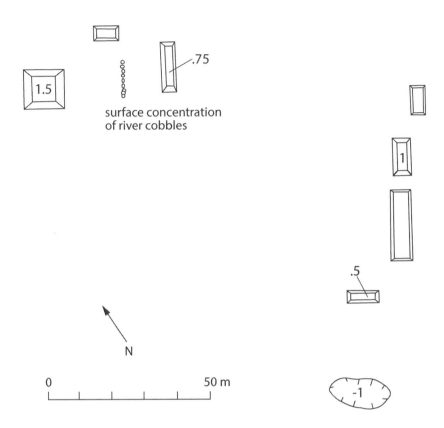

Figure 3.19. Site sketch of Ch-14.

CH-15 LA CEIBA (no map)

Site Type: Habitation

Ceramic Phase: Lato, Jocote

Occupation: Early Preclassic, possible Late Preclassic, Late Classic, Late Postclassic

Location and Setting: La Ceiba is on the top of a low hill in a bend of the Río Chicomuselo 4 km north of Chicomuselo and 300 m east of the river. The land is partially forested but is now used as pasturage.

Environmental Stratum: Tropical Deciduous Forest

Description: There are two possible platforms visible at the site. Each is very low and only about 4 m on a side. They appear to have been constructed of river cobbles. Sherds collected from near them suggest a Late Classic period date. One hundred meters to the northeast of these is an eroded zone at the hilltop which had a number of Early Preclassic sherds washing out of it. It would thus appear that there was an early settlement at the site that did not have any associated structures preserved.

References: White 1976:31

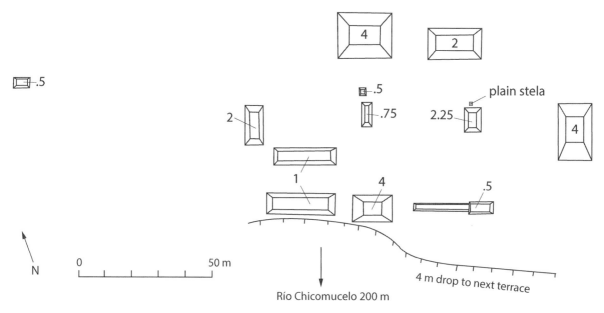

Figure 3.20. Site sketch of Ch-16, Tiju.

CH-16 TIJU (Figure 3.20)

Site Type: Ceremonial

Occupation: Late Classic

Location and Setting: Tiju is located on the west side of Río Chicomuselo 4 km north of that town. The ruins are on a low hill 20 m from the river. At the time of the survey the area was covered with a dense scrub forest, some of which had been cleared for milpa.

Environmental Stratum: Tropical Deciduous Forest

Description: Tiju is one of the larger sites in the Chicomuselo study area. There are three, 4 m high mounds surrounding a fairly compact plaza. On the west side there is a smaller mound but just south of it are two long low mounds that appear to have formed a ballcourt. One long narrow mound blocks off an open section on the south side of the plaza. In the center of the plaza are two small altar platforms and a 2 m high mound. In front of this mound was found a plain stela.

Most of the structures in the main plaza area were faced with river cobbles and many of these have now been removed for modern construction projects.

Very few residential structures were found in the region surrounding the site, perhaps because of the dense vegetation at the time of survey. Two smaller mounds to the west of the main center could have been residential platforms. Approximately 250 m northwest of the main structures in a tilled field were found high quantities of sherds. This distribution suggested a large-scale residential occupation in the zone around the ceremonial center.

References: Lowe 1959:64; White 1976:31-32

CH-17 CHACAJAL 1 (no map)

Site Type: Habitation

Location and Setting: The site is located 4 km south of Chicomuselo on the north side of Río Yayahuita. It is in the river valley, only 100 m away from the river. The area is used as milpa.

Environmental Stratum: Fields or Pastures

Description: There was only one low house mound observed at this site. It was approximately 10 m by 8 m and outlined by a concentration of river cobbles. Although no sherds were recovered, the site layout suggests a possible Late Classic date.

References: White 1976:32

0   5 cm

Figure 3.21. Sherd with textile impression from Ch-19, Cerecillo.

CH-18 CHACAJAL 2 (no map)

Site Type: Habitation

Location and Setting: Chacajal 2 is found 4.5 km west of Chicomuselo on the north side of Río Yayahuita. It is located approximately 200 m from the river in the valley bottom. The area is used as pasture.

Environmental Stratum: Fields or Pastures

Description: There was only a single mound 7 by 7 m and roughly 0.5 m high. The structure is probably a house platform. No sherds were found; however, like Ch-17, the site possibly dates to the Late Classic. The house mound was made of river cobbles.

References: White 1976:32

CH-19 CERECILLO (Figures 3.21-3.22)

Site Type: Ceremonial and habitation

Ceramic Phase: Ix

Occupation: Protoclassic, Late Classic, Postclassic

Location and Setting: Cerecillo is located on a low hill in Río Tachinula Valley. It is 3 km south of Chicomuselo and 90 m west of the river. The area is presently a grass-covered pasture.

Environmental Stratum: Tropical Deciduous Forest

Description: This site is spread out over roughly 250 m by 100 m and consists of five separate house groups and a ceremonial structure. On the northern extremity is a 2.5 m high pyramidal platform that was probably the ceremonial focus of the site. South of it are two isolated mounds that might have been residential mounds. Possibly though, since they are each 1 m high and isolated, they could have been civic-ceremonial buildings flanking a plaza zone in front of the mound. Two additional mounds directly south of the main mound appear to form a house group. West of them by 50 m is an additional house group of two house mounds. There may have been additional platforms but the surface area was very eroded. In this eroded zone the largest sherd sample was found. One hundred meters to the south of these main mound groups was the largest house group. It contained four low platforms around a small patio area. More house mounds may have been located in the zone surrounding the site but erosion might have destroyed a few.

References: White 1976:32

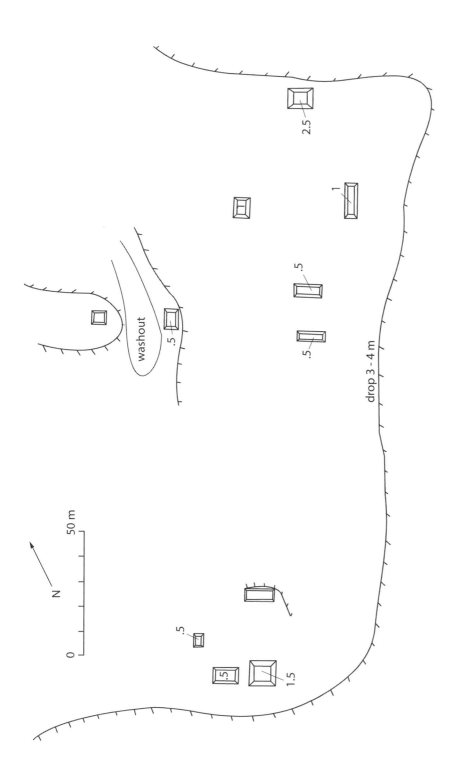

Figure 3.22. Site sketch of Ch-19, Cerecillo.

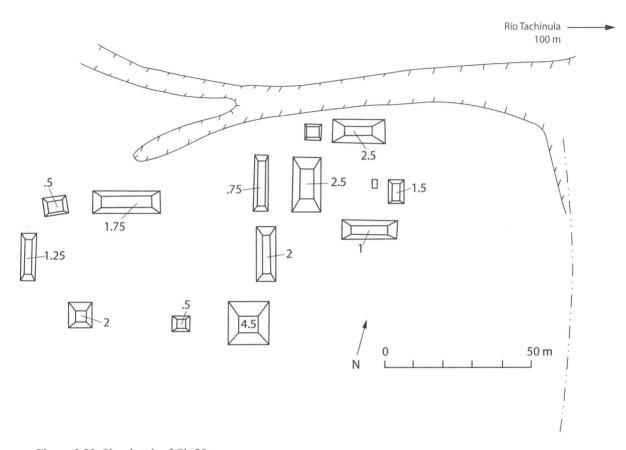

Figure 3.23. Site sketch of Ch-20.

CH-20 (Figure 3.23)

Site Type: Ceremonial

Occupation: Late Classic, Postclassic

Location and Setting: This site is located 5 km south of Chicomuselo on the west side of Río Tachinula, 100 m from the river. It is located on the valley bottom in a zone that is used for milpa.

Environmental Stratum: Tropical Deciduous Forest

Description: The mounds at this site form two plaza groups. The northeast group appears to have mainly ceremonial structures arranged tightly around a small plaza. Two of the mounds in this group are 2.5 m high and approximately 15 m long. Southeast of them are two smaller mounds that close off the plaza. A small altar platform is located directly opposite the smallest mound in the group.

The southwest mound group was approximately twice as large as the first group. The plaza is larger and it also contains the largest mound at the site, which rises to a height of 4.5 m. Opposite to the west is a small altar-like platform and further west a 2 m tall mound. These form the south side of the plaza. The west side is formed by a long low mound that may have been a residence platform. The north and east sides of the plaza are bound by a 0.5 m tall platform and three long narrow mounds. One of these is 23 m long and almost 2 m high. Several of the mounds in the center of the site have been quarried for construction fill. Most of the mounds were faced with river cobbles.

References: White 1976:32-33

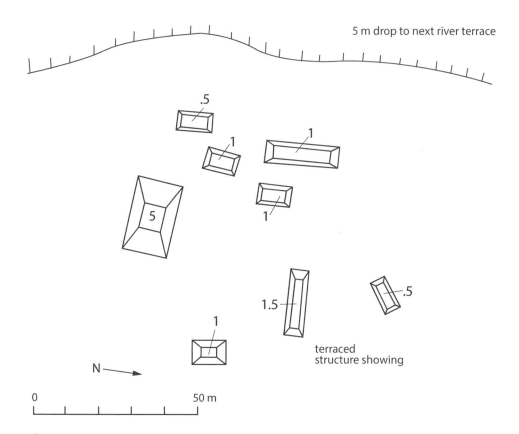

Figure 3.24. Site sketch of Ch-21, La Esperanza.

CH-21 LA ESPERANZA
(Figure 3.24)

Site Type: Ceremonial and habitation

Ceramic Phase: Ix

Occupation: Protoclassic, Early Classic, Late Classic

Location and Setting: La Esperanza is located on the east side of Río Tachinula, 4.5 km south of the Chicomuselo. It sits on the second terrace above the river in an area that is used for pasturage and milpa.

Environmental Setting: Tropical Deciduous Forest

Description: The several mounds at this site are scattered in an irregular pattern around a small plaza facing the largest mound at the site. This mound is 5 m high and sits on the south side of the plaza. Four mounds on the west side of the plaza are quite small and could be residential platforms. One of them is 22 m long and may have been a Postclassic structure since it is generally longer than most Classic period structures of that height (1 m). Another long narrow structure on the north side of the plaza is faced in river cobbles and appears to have been stepped.

References: White 1976:33

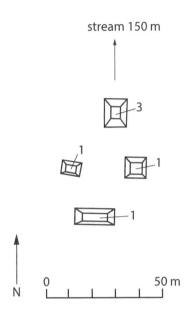

stream 150 m

0   50 m
N

Figure 3.25. Site sketch of Ch-22, Limonal.

CH-22 LIMONAL (Figure 3.25)

Site Type: Ceremonial and habitation

Occupation: Late Preclassic, Late Classic

Location and Setting: This site on the north side of a small stream 5.5 km upstream from its confluence with Río Yayahuita. The site is 30 km west of Chicomuselo. Terrain is rather rugged in the region of the site, which sits on a terrace overlooking the stream 5 m below. The site area is used for milpa.

Environmental Stratum: Evergreen Seasonal Forest

Description: The four mounds at this site appear to include both ceremonial and residential functions. The largest mound is 3 m high and was probably a temple platform. The other three are arranged around a plaza area delineated on the north side by the 3 m mound. These smaller structures are only 1 m high and although many may have had ceremonial functions, they could just as well have been elite residences in this small community. The easternmost mound had been trenched. Thick vegetation prevented recording the additional residential structures surrounding the center.

References: White 1976:33

CH-23 LA PINTA 1 (Figure 3.26)

Site Type: Ceremonial

Occupation: Late Preclassic

Location and Setting: La Pinta is situated on the east side of the Yayahuita, approximately 16 km southwest of Chicomuselo. The river is 130 m northwest of the site zone. Vegetation in the site area consists mainly of scrub-forest, which has been cleared in spots for milpa.

Environmental Stratum: Evergreen Seasonal Forest

Description: Seven mounds were noted at La Pinta 1. The largest is 3 m tall and 15 m by 20 m. It forms the northeast side of a small plaza area that is also bordered by a huge square platform 1.25 m high and 20 m on a side. Two mounds on the west side of the plaza may have been a ballcourt, although they are not the same height nor are they the same length. There are also two small platforms that might have been altars. A large square platform 1 m high and 15 m on a side may form the south side of a secondary plaza. These large square platforms might have been elite residential mounds. There were no definite house mounds surrounding the ceremonial center; perhaps because of the dense vegetation they could not be seen.

References: White 1976:33

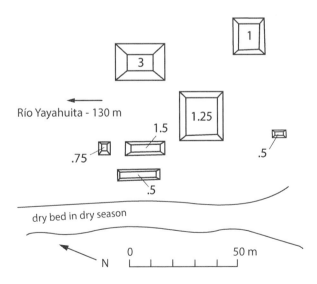

Río Yayahuita - 130 m

dry bed in dry season

0   50 m
N

Figure 3.26. Site sketch of Ch-23, La Pinta 1.

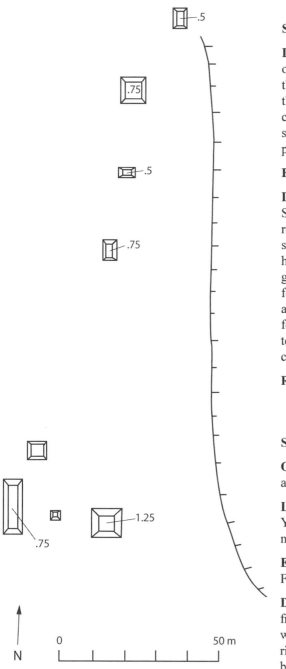

Figure 3.27. Site sketch of Ch-24, San Antonio.

CH-24 SAN ANTONIO (Figure 3.27)

Site Type: Ceremonial and habitation

Location and Setting: San Antonio is located on the north side of Río Yayahuita just south of the point where a small tributary stream enters the river. It sits on a low hill overlooking the confluence of the rivers 200 m to the E. The site zone is covered with grass and used for pasturage.

Environmental Stratum: Riparian Forest

Description: There are eight mounds at San Antonio and most of these appear to be residential mounds. However, there are also several small altar-like mounds which no doubt had ceremonial functions. The largest mound group at the site is to the south and consists of four mounds, the central one of which is a small altar. Sixty meters to the north begin a series of four more mounds spread out along the edge of a terrace drop. Several of these are quite small and could also be altars.

References: White 1976:34

CH-25 LAS MINAS (no map)

Site Type: Historic mine site

Occupation: Postclassic, post-Colonial, abandoned in 1960

Location and Setting: East bank of Río Yayahuita, 17 km west of Chicomuselo. The mines are located on the talus slope.

Environmental Stratum: Evergreen Seasonal Forest

Description: Apparently lead ore was mined from a series of veins approximately 1 hour's walk upslope from this processing site near the river. There were several processing buildings, but no smelter was noted.

References: White 1976:34

0   5 cm

Figure 3.28. Carved stone figure from Ch-26, Zapotec Ventana.

CH-26 ZAPOTEC VENTANA
(Figures 3.28-3.29)

Site Type: Ceremonial and habitation

Occupation: Late Classic

Location and Setting: Zapotec Ventana is located 17 km west of Chicomuselo on the north side of Río Yayahuita. It sits in the river's uppermost area of habitable valley bottom land. The area is used for milpa and pasture.

Environmental Stratum: Evergreen Seasonal Forest-Riparian Forest

Description: The site is a nucleated settlement with roughly 26 platforms irregularly arranged around a long mound. This mound is 30 m long and 7 m wide, yet only 1 m high. It has a low platform extension projecting from its east side. Adjacent to it are the three other largest structures at the site. They are all 1 m to 1.5 m high platforms. All the other structures are less than 1 m high and quite small for house platforms. A few are so small that they might have been altars. None seem to be arranged in clear patio groups.

References: White 1976:34

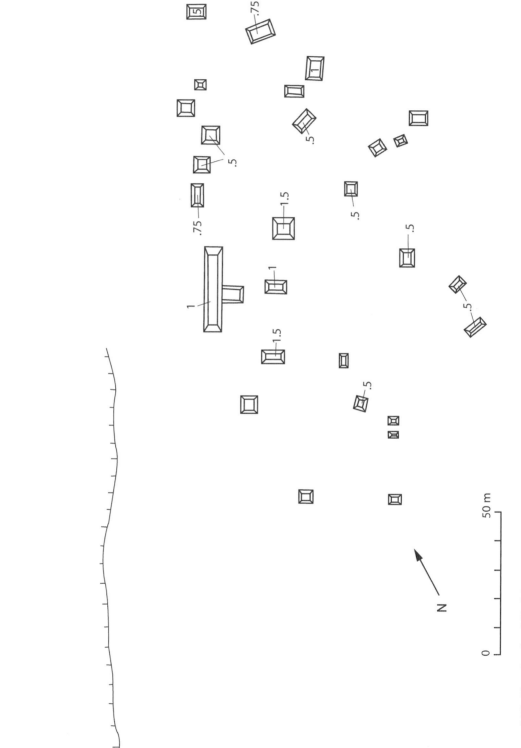

Figure 3.29. Site sketch of Ch-26, Zapotec Ventana.

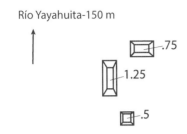

Río Yayahuita-150 m

.75

1.25

.5

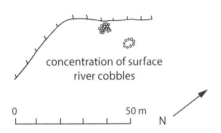

concentration of surface
river cobbles

0   50 m

N

Figure 3.30. Site sketch of Ch-27, La Pinta 2.

CH-27 LA PINTA 2 (Figure 3.30)

Site Type: Habitation

Occupation: Middle Classic, Late Classic

Location and Setting: La Pinta 2 is situated on the south side of Río Yayahuita, approximately 16 km west of Chicomuselo. It is in an area used for milpa agriculture and sits about 150 m back from the river.

Environmental Stratum: Evergreen Seasonal Forest

Description: There are three house mounds arranged around a small patio. The largest mound is 1.25 m high. The others are both shorter and lower than the first. Upslope from these are two concentrations of river cobbles. Since the house mounds were surfaced with cobbles it is possible that these concentrations are the remains of more houses.

References: White 1976:34

CH-28 ZACUALPA (Figure 3.31)

Site Type: Habitation

Occupation: possible Early Preclassic, Late Classic

Location and Setting: Zacualpa is a small habitation site located 2.5 km northwest of Colonia Piedra Labrada. It is located in the wide valley bottom of a stream that flows into Río Tachinula. The land is used as milpa.

Environmental Stratum: Tropical Deciduous Forest

Description: Only three small residential mounds remain at this site. Some may have been destroyed by cultivation and ground leveling. Two of the smaller mounds appear to form a patio group. A third mound is isolated and sits 60 m southwest of the group.

References: White 1976:34-35

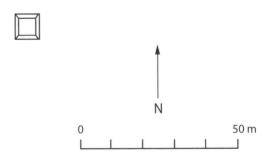

0   50 m

N

Figure 3.31. Site sketch of Ch-28, Zacualpa.

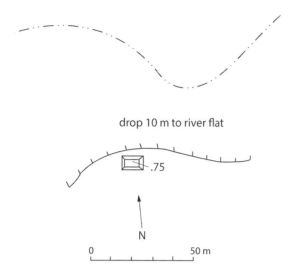

drop 10 m to river flat

N

0   50 m

Figure 3.32. Site sketch of Ch-29, Rancho Guapinol.

CH-29 RANCHO GUAPINOL (Figure 3.32)

Site Type: Habitation

Occupation: possible Protoclassic, Late Classic

Location and Setting: This site is located 5.5 km south of Chicomuselo and 2 km west of Río Tachinula near Colonia Piedra Labrada. It is in the valley of a small stream that flows east towards the Tachinula and sits on a low hill.

Environmental Stratum: Tropical Deciduous Forest

Description: There is only one mound at the site, and it is being quarried for construction fill by a modern household nearby. The mound is a house platform in the Classic period style. It measures 10 m by 7 m and is .75 m high. In addition to Classic sherds, there were also some Late Preclassic-Protoclassic sherds in and around the mound. More house mounds may exist in the surrounding region but vegetation was too dense to detect them.

References: White 1976:35

CH-30 (no map)

Site Type: Habitation

Occupation: Late Classic

Location and Setting: Located on the west side of the Río Tachinula and some 2 km north of Piedra Labrada.

Environmental Stratum: Riparian Forest

Description: Consists of two partially destroyed stone outlines.

References: White 1976:35

CH-31 (Figure 3.33)

Site Type: Habitation

Ceramic Phase: Enub, Ix

Occupation: Middle Preclassic, Protoclassic, Late Classic

Location and Setting: Ch-31 is directly across Río Tachinula from Colonia Piedra Labrada. It is located on a terrace 200 m from the river. The site area is covered in grass and a modern house is built on one of the mounds.

Environmental Stratum: Fields or Pastures

Description: The five mounds at this site form two house groups. The northern group consists of three houses arranged around a small plaza and facing towards the terrace. The southern group has only two mounds but both are higher and somewhat larger than the other group. One is 1 m high and has been more than half destroyed by modern construction. The two houses in this group form an L-shaped configuration around a small patio.

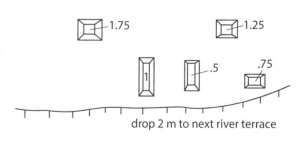

drop 2 m to next river terrace

N   0   50 m

Figure 3.33. Site sketch of Ch-31.

One of the mounds (the 1 m high mound) was partially destroyed and showed earlier interior structure. All of them were surfaced with river cobbles.

References: White 1976:35.

CH-32 EL PARAÍSO 1
(Figure 3.34)

Site Type: Ceremonial and habitation

Occupation: Late Classic, Postclassic

Location and Setting: El Paraíso 1 is directly across Río Tachinula from Colonia Piedra Labrada. It is approximately 150 m east of the river in the valley bottom. The site area is now grassed over and used as pasturage.

Environmental Stratum: Fields or Pasture

Description: The site consists of three house mounds and a small (2 m high) temple mound surrounding a small patio in the middle of which is an altar. One of the structures is elevated on a small natural terrace riser that overlooks that patio and the other structures. All the structures are made from or at least surfaced with river cobbles. This site is probably part of the same large dispersed community opposite the site of Piedra Labrada that includes Ch-31, 33, and 34.

References: White 1976:35

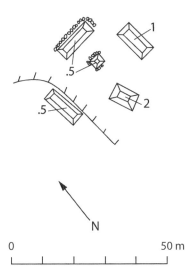

Figure 3.34. Site sketch of Ch-32, El Paraíso 1.

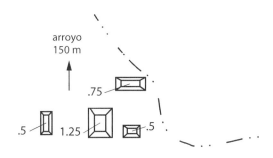

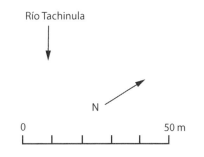

Figure 3.35. Site sketch of Ch-33, El Paraíso 2.

CH-33 EL PARAÍSO 2
(Figure 3.35)

Site Type: Habitation

Occupation: Protoclassic, Late Classic

Location and Setting: El Paraíso 2 is directly across Río Tachinula and slightly south of Colonia Piedra Labrada. It sits in the river valley in a grassy area that is mostly used as pasturage.

Environmental Stratum: Fields or Pastures

Description: The four mounds at this site are arranged in a patio group. They are all probably house mounds and could be a residential outlier of the large Classic site (Piedra Labrada Ch-9) just across Río Tachinula. Like the mounds at Ch-9, these too were surfaced with river cobbles. Three of the house mounds form a U-shaped patio group facing a small arroyo or stream. A fourth structure sits just to the southwest of the largest mound.

References: White 1976:35-36

CH-34 EL PARAÍSO 3 (Figure 3.36)

Site Type: Habitation

Location and Setting: Ch-34 sits just to the north of Ch-33 on the west bank of Río Tachinula and directly across from Colonia Piedra Labrada. The site is in the river valley bottom in an area now used for pasture.

Environmental Stratum: Fields or Pasture

Description: Only two small mounds were recorded at this site. The largest one is only about 5 m by 4 m and 0.75 m high. It could have been a small house mound. The other is even smaller and may have been a house group altar. There may have been other houses in the group that were built directly on the ground surface, and therefore, evaded detection. These mounds are within 300 m of three other house groups that may all be part of the same dispersed community (Ch-31 to Ch-33).

References: White 1976:36

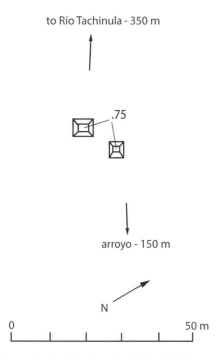

Figure 3.36. Site sketch of Ch-34, El Paraíso 3.

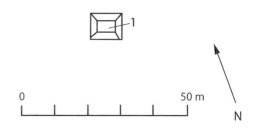

Figure 3.37. Site sketch of Ch-35.

CH-35 (Figure 3.37)

Site Type: Habitation

Occupation: possible Middle Preclassic, Postclassic

Location and Setting: Ch-35 is located 7 km northwest of Colonia Nueva Independencia on the west side of the Río San Miguel. It is in a rocky area covered with small scrub forest and sits alone atop a high hill. The area is used as pasturage.

Environmental Stratum: Tropical Deciduous Forest

Description: This single mound sits on a hilltop and no other mounds or cultural material was noted in the vicinity. The mound is 10 m by 7 m and 1 m high. It could be either a house mound or an isolated ceremonial structure. The structure was surfaced with flat angular sandstone slabs.

References: White 1976:36

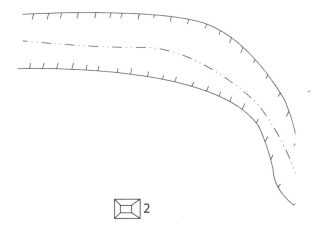

Figure 3.38. Site sketch of Ch-36.

CH-36 (Figure 3.38)

Site Type: Ceremonial and habitation

Occupation: Late Classic

Location and Setting: Ch-36 is 5 km northwest of Colonia Nueva Independencia on the west side of the Río San Miguel. It is in an area of rolling rocky plain and roughly 50 m from the nearest seasonal stream. The region is covered with trees and scrub forest and is used as pasturage.

Environmental Stratum: Tropical Deciduous Forest

Description: There were only three mounds noted at this site, all about 20 to 90 m from each other. The largest mound is 2 m high and approximately 10 m by 7 m. It was probably a small ceremonial structure, perhaps a temple platform. The other two structures are 5-6 m on a side and could have been small residential platforms. The largest mound was surfaced by angular sandstone slabs found in the arroyos nearby.

References: White 1976:36

CH-37 (Figure 3.39)

Site Type: Ceremonial and habitation

Occupation: Postclassic

Location and Setting: This site is 9 km northeast of Chicomuselo in Río San Miguel canyon. It is on the west side of the river in an area of terraces sitting at the base of a cliff. The site is about 40 m above the river level and 200 m from the water. Dense grass and small trees cover the site used as pasturage.

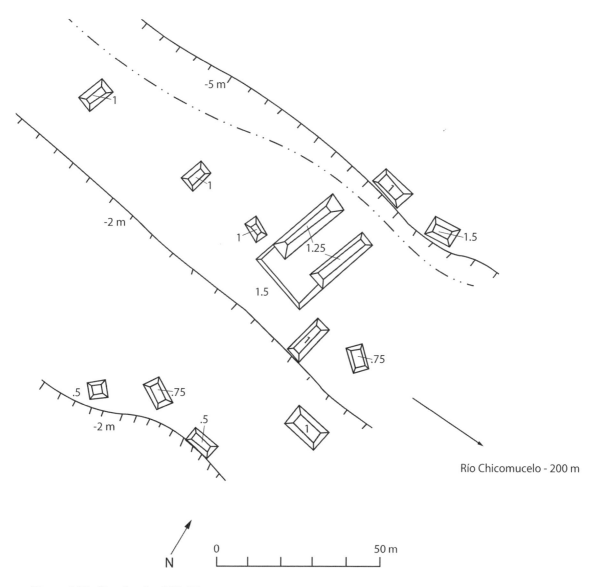

Figure 3.39. Site sketch of Ch-37.

Environmental Stratum: Tropical Deciduous
Forest

Description: Ch-37 sits on a series of three
terraces overlooking the river. The main part of
the site includes an I-shaped ballcourt formed
by two long 1.25 m high mounds, parts of which
are faced with stone slabs. On the same terrace,
which itself is faced with river cobbles and stone
blocks, are five other mounds that appear to be
house mounds, although they are not arranged
in distinct patio groups. Upslope on the next
terrace were two additional platforms; one is 1.5

m high—the tallest at the site. These two could
have been the bases for small temples. On the
terrace below the ballcourt were an additional
four low platform mounds. These were all about
the size of house mounds, although they too
were irregularly arranged. Most of the mounds
were faced with or partially constructed of river
cobbles.

There may be more mounds in the zone
surrounding the site but because of extremely
dense vegetation it was not possible to find more.

References: White 1976:37

CH-38 CALZADA DE LA CRUZ
(Figures 3.40-3.41)

Site Type: Ceremonial and habitation

Ceramic Phase: Enub, Mix

Occupation: Middle Preclassic, Late Classic, Postclassic

Location and Setting: Calzada de la Cruz is situated on a hilltop in an area of rolling terrain. It is 5 km north of Colonia Pablo Sidar. Vegetation in the site area consists mainly of scrub forest and grassy clearings. It is used as pasturage and milpa. There is a spring near the site.

Environmental Stratum: Tropical Deciduous Forest

Description: The site consists primarily of a single large ceremonial center with some residential structures nucleated around the main center. The main plaza is almost completely rectangular and measures 65 m by 100 m. It is bounded on all but the northwest side by 14 large rectangular mounds. These mounds range from 1 m to 4 m in height. Four of them are 20 m or longer. Inside the plaza area is the largest mound at the site, which may in fact form the northwest end of the plaza. It is 25 m by 15 m and 4.5 m high. Three small altars are located to the southeast of this pyramid. Most of the mounds have been surfaced with limestone blocks, as has part of the plaza.

Just outside of this band of main plaza structures are 40 or so residential platforms. The closed nature of the main plaza means that they were relatively shut off from access to the ceremonial center. Many of the house platforms are arranged in patio groups and some have small altars associated. One group to the southeast of the center had five structures arranged around a patio. Two of the platforms were 2 m tall and could have been either elite houses or ceremonial structures within the house group. Dense vegetation prevented mapping of many more house mounds at the site. Houses covered the surrounding valley bottom to an estimated extent of 60 ha. This community size and layout is much like other Terminal Classic sites on the north side of Río Grijalva and Río Santa Inéz Valley.

Conspicuous by its absence is a ballcourt. At this time period such large sites usually had at least one. This may mean that an even larger or more politically important ceremonial center is located within the zone neighboring this site.

References: White 1976:37-39

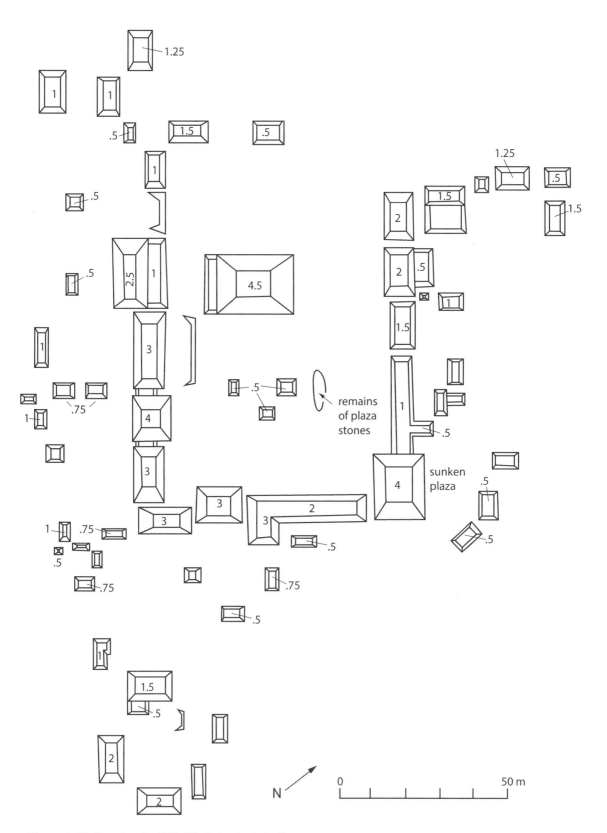

Figure 3.40. Site sketch of Ch-38, Calzada de la Cruz.

Figure 3.41. Views of two figurine heads from Ch-38, Calzada de la Cruz.

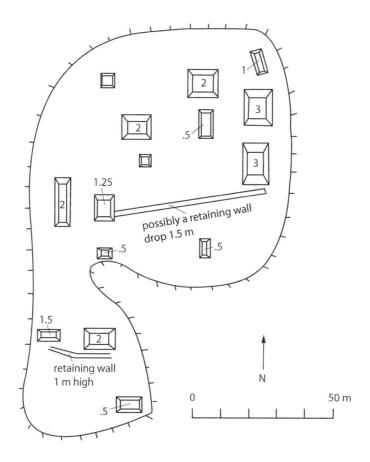

Figure 3.42. Site sketch of Ch-39, Jobo 1.

CH-39 JOBO 1 (Figure 3.42)

Site Type: Ceremonial and habitation

Location and Setting: This site is located on a high hilltop 13.5 km northwest of Chicomuselo. The hill projects above the surrounding terrain, which is mainly rolling hills and flats with occasional small stream valleys. One small stream is about 300 m northwest of the site. The site is densely covered with thorny bushes and tall grass. It is used for pasturage.

Environmental Stratum: Pine-Oak Forest

Description: There are 15 mounds on this site which covers the top of the hill. Several of the largest mounds surround a small plaza area

roughly 45 m by 20 m on each side. The south side is defined by a low terrace retaining wall about 1.5 m high. There are twin, 3 m high mounds on the east side of the plaza and three, 2 m high mounds on the north and west sides. Within the plaza area are several smaller and lower mounds, one of which is probably an altar. Several other small mounds are located in the zone surrounding the plaza, but none of them form distinct house groups. A larger residential population may have been located in the zone around the base of the hill but because of dense vegetation none were recorded.

References: White 1976:39

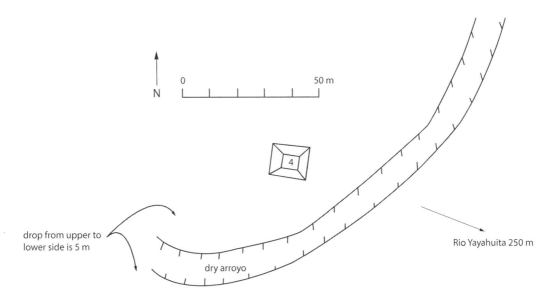

Figure 3.43. Site sketch of Ch-42.

CH-40 MISHOLAR (no map)

Site Type: Habitation

Occupation: possible Middle Preclassic, Late Classic

Location and Setting: Misholar is in a small stream valley 14 km northwest of Chicomuselo. It is in a modern house yard.

Environmental Stratum: Pine-Oak Forest

Description: There is only one small mound at this site and a scatter of poorly preserved sherds. It is a platform only 2 m by 3 m and so was probably a simple house group altar mound.

References: White 1976:39

CH-41 (no map)

Site Type: Habitation

Occupation: possible Middle Preclassic, Late Classic

Location and Setting: Just south and almost directly above the ranch house of Finca Jobo on the road to the settlement of Misholar. A small stream is located 300 m northwest; the land is in pasture. To the west some 500 m is Ch-39.

Environmental Stratum: Pine-Oak Forest

Description: A single housemound with a few eroded sherds.

References: White 1976:39

CH-42 (Figure 3.43)

Site Type: Ceremonial

Occupation: Late Classic

Location and Setting: Located near the road to the settlement of Misholar. Mound is located near a deep dry arroyo and some 250 m east of the Río Yayahuita.

Environmental Stratum: Evergreen Seasonal Forest

Description: Dense vegetation covers the area of the single recognizable mound, obscuring other possible platforms or occupation. The observable mound is roughly 10 by 15 m and is some 4 m in height, representing too much labor to be a common residence. Only a few sherds recovered.

References: White 1976:40

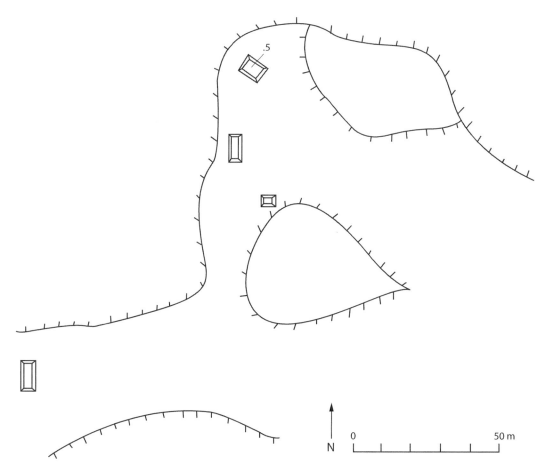

Figure 3.44. Site sketch of Ch-44, Cruz Ocote.

CH-43 LA PIEDAD
(no map)

Site Type: Historical

Occupation: post-Colonial

Location and Setting: located southwest of the primary finca buildings of La Piedad. The land is in pasture.

Environmental Stratum: Tropical Deciduous Forest

Description: Lower portion of an end wall with a window area, segments of the side walls, and a building corner; it may have been a church or hacienda building.

References: White 1976:40

CH-44 CRUZ OCOTE
(Figure 3.44)

Site Type: Habitation

Location and Setting: Forested land located approximate 1 km southwest of the rural settlement of Santa Monica.

Environmental Stratum: Tropical Deciduous Forest

Description: Each of the 0.5 m platforms was outlined with a stone retaining wall. No sherds recovered.

References: White 1976:40

CH-45 NUEVA ESPAÑA
(no map)

Site Type: Habitation

Location and Setting: Located in a milpa with corn and squash. Site location is not clear from documentation.

Environmental Stratum: Tropical Deciduous Forest

Description: Sherds recovered from a dry well in a milpa near Nueva España; vegetation too dense to see more.

References: White 1976:40

CH-46 NUEVA AMERICA
(no map)

Site Type: Habitation

Occupation: possible Late Classic

Location and Setting: in the town of Nueva América.

Environmental Stratum: Tropical Deciduous Forest

Description: A few sherds located in the central plaza of this community. This area is probably within the settlement area of Ch-47.

References: White 1976:40

CH-47 ALFONSO CORONA DEL ROSAL
(Figure 3.45)

Site Type: Ceremonial and habitation

Occupation: Late Classic

Location and Setting: Located on the northern edge of a hilly plateau region at the point of descent to the Río Grijalva approximately 3 km to the northeast. Land is in milpa. Drinking water provided to the local ejido of the same name courtesy of wells with fresh water 2 m below surface.

Environmental Stratum: Tropical Deciduous Forest

Description: Survey documented more than 140 structures, platforms and mounds, over a wide area. The main plaza and related mounds cover an area of some 80 by 130 m or in excess of 1 ha. This plaza is dominated by a 10 m high mound at its southeast end. Directly across the plaza is a blank stela was located between an altar and a smaller mound; perhaps the stela had initially been placed atop the altar. A second altar is located in the plaza in front of two "twin" mounds of similar shape. The mounds in the plaza appear to have originally been faced with roughly squared limestone, which is locally available.

A second smaller plaza is located to the south of the main plain and large 10 m high mound. Two mounds, 3 and 4 m respectively, define the southern corner. Just south of this secondary plaza is a *plazuela* (Willey et al. 1965:572), a courtyard arrangement of low secondary platforms on a basal platform.

Surrounding the primary and secondary plazas are numerous courtyard arrangements of mounds, ranging in height from 0.5 to 2.5 m, and extending out from all sides, although only the most prominent structures were included in the sketch map. Habitation is estimated to extend at least 900 m to the southwest and northeast and may encompass an area of 80 ha.

References: White 1976:40-42

Figure 3.45. Site sketch of Ch-47, Alfonso Corona del Rosal.

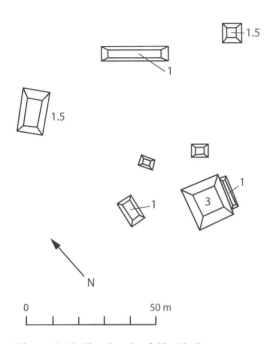

Figure 3.46. Site sketch of Ch-48, Santa Monica 1.

CH-48 SANTA MONICA 1 (Figure 3.46)

Site Type: Ceremonial and habitation

Occupation: possible Late Preclassic, Protoclassic, Late Classic

Location and Setting: The site is found just outside of ejido Santa Monica and is currently in pasture. The site is elevated with an excellent view of the surrounding plains.

Environmental Stratum: Tropical Deciduous Forest

Description: The site of consists of 7 mounds, probably ceremonial in function although the six smaller mounds are not neatly arranged around the 3 m high mound. The large cut has been mad through the center of the primary mound.

References: White 1976:42

CH-49 SANTA MONICA 2 (Figure 3.47)

Site Type: Habitational

Occupation: Late Classic

Location and Setting: The site is northeast of ejido Santa Monica and 300 m northwest of Ch-49. Located in pasture.

Environmental Stratum: Tropical Deciduous Forest

Description: Site consists of a single 1.5 m high mound and is probably related to Ch-49. Few sherds recovered.

References: White 1976:42

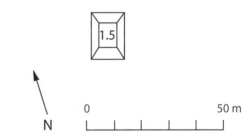

Figure 3.47. Site sketch of Ch-49, Santa Monica 2.

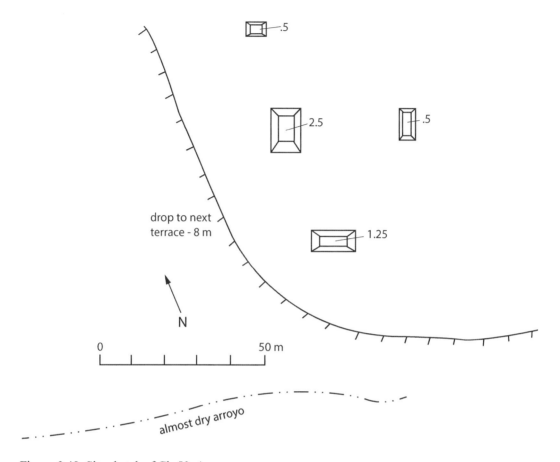

Figure 3.48. Site sketch of Ch-50, Aurora.

CH-50 AURORA (Figure 3.48)

Site Type: Ceremonial and habitation

Occupation: possible Early Classic, Late Classic

Location and Setting: This site lies on a terrace above a seasonal arroyo. Located in milpa.

Environmental Stratum: Tropical Deciduous Forest

Description: This site consists of three mounds arranged around a courtyard, with one low house mound to the north.

References: White 1976:42

CH-51 LA PALMA 1 (Figure 3.49)

Site Type: Habitation

Location and Setting: Site lies 20 m from the Río Yayahuita and is in pasture.

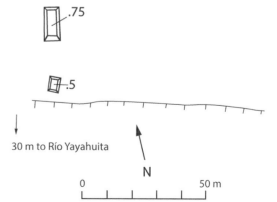

Figure 3.49. Site sketch of Ch-51, La Palma 1.

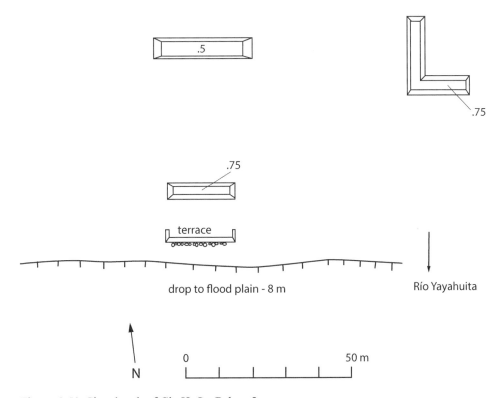

Figure 3.50. Site sketch of Ch-52, La Palma 2.

Environmental Stratum: Riparian Forest

Description: Two low mounds are surfaced in river cobbles. No sherds recovered.

References: White 1976:42

CH-52 LA PALMA 2 (Figure 3.50)

Site Type: Habitation

Location and Setting: Located some 80 m east of Ch-51 and on a higher ground 8 m above the floodplain; the Río Yayahuita is 90 m to the southwest. Land is in pasture.

Environmental Stratum: Riparian Forest

Description: Site consists of 3 mounds. Two are oriented east-west, elongated and low-lying; while a third is L-shaped. There is a short terrace in the riverbank of the site. All of the mounds are faced with river cobbles. No sherds were recovered.

References: White 1976:43

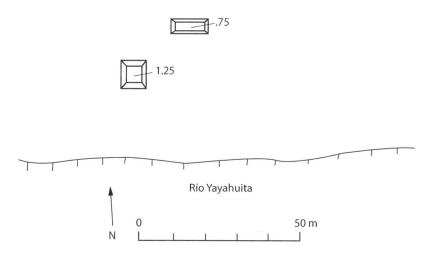

Figure 3.51. Site sketch of Ch-53, La Palma 3.

CH-53 LA PALMA 3 (Figure 3.51)

Site Type: Habitation

Location and Setting: Site is located 20 m from the Río Yayahuita and 300 m west of Ch-51. Land is in pasture.

Environmental Stratum: Riparian Forest

Description: Site consists of two mounds both faced with river cobbles. No sherds were recovered.

References: White 1976:43

CH-54 LA PALMA 4 (Figure 3.52)

Site Type: Ceremonial and habitation

Occupation: possible Middle Preclassic, possible Protoclassic, Late Classic, Postclassic

Location and Setting: Located in a bend of the Río Yayahuita, some 100 m from the water at the closest point. Site is in grass and coyol palm and used for pasture.

Environmental Stratum: Riparian Forest

Description: Site consists of five mounds faced with river cobbles. The primary mound is 3 m high and the five mounds appeared to be grouped around a courtyard or small plaza. An additional small house mound is located northeast of the courtyard group.

References: White 1976:43

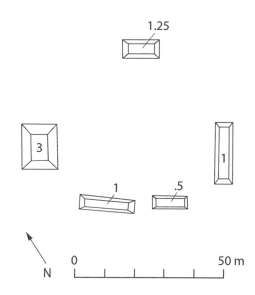

Figure 3.52. Site sketch of Ch-54, La Palma 4.

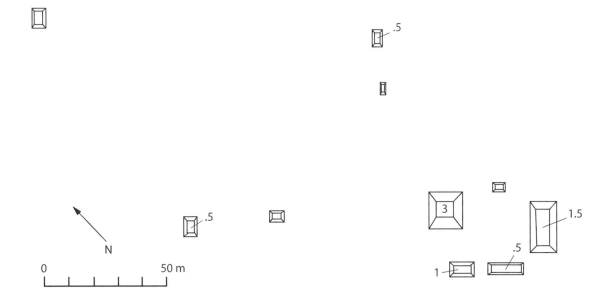

Figure 3.53. Site sketch of Ch-57, Rancho Santa Teresa 1.

CH-55 LA PALMA 5 (no map)

Site Type: Habitation

Occupation: possible late Middle Preclassic, Postclassic

Location and Setting: Site is in grass and coyol palm and used for pasture. Located some 200 m from the Río Yayahuita.

Environmental Stratum: Riparian Forest

Description: Sherd scatter

References: White 1976:43

CH-56 (no map)

Site Type: Habitation

Occupation: Late Postclassic

Location and Setting: Location not well-defined; land use in milpa.

Environmental Stratum: Fields or pastures

Description: Sherd scatter over 0.5 ha.

References: White 1976:43

CH-57 RANCHO SANTA TERESA 1 (Figure 3.53)

Site Type: Ceremonial and habitation

Occupation: Protoclassic, possible Early Classic, Late Classic

Location and Setting: Junction of the Ríos Tachinula and San Rafael. Site is in milpa and pasture. Mounds are being systematically destroyed by aggressive tractor use and by pothunting.

Environmental Stratum: Riparian Forest

Description: This site was the likely the focus point for the other settlements nearby (Ch-58, Ch-59, and Ch-60). The four sites are located with the junction of the Ríos Tachinula and the San Rafael which flows down from town of Lázaro Cárdenas. Although recorded as distinct sites, the artefactual remains and locations indicate contemporaneity of occupation. Sherd scatters are seen all over the banks of the Tachinula and inland.

The largest mound currently still stands at 3 m in height and faces a long platform mound across a small plaza, which is enclosed by three other smaller mounds. The largest mound is faced with river cobbles and has numerous looters' pits. Smaller mounds are dispersed further to the north; more mounds may have been present but have been worn down from ploughing.

References: White 1976:43-44

CH-58 RANCHO SANTA TERESA 2 (no map)

Site Type: Habitation

Occupation: Middle Preclassic, Early Classic, Late Classic, Postclassic

Location and Setting: Located 100 m from the Río Tachinula on a low terrace. Area is in milpa.

Environmental Stratum: Riparian Forest

Description: Sherd scatter over approximately 2 ha. See Ch-57.

References: White 1976:44

CH-59 SANTA TERESA 3 (no map)

Site Type: Habitation

Occupation: Postclassic

Location and Setting: Located close to the junction of the Ríos Tachinula and San Rafael. Approximately 50 m southeast from the Río Tachinula. Area is in milpa and also likely floods in the rainy season.

Environmental Stratum: Riparian Forest

Description: Sherd scatter over approximately 2 ha. See Ch-57.

References: White 1976:44

CH-60 SANTA TERESA 4 (FIGURES 3.54-3.55)

Site Type: Habitation

Occupation: Postclassic

Location and Setting: Located 50 m east of the Río Tachinula in the area south of the junction

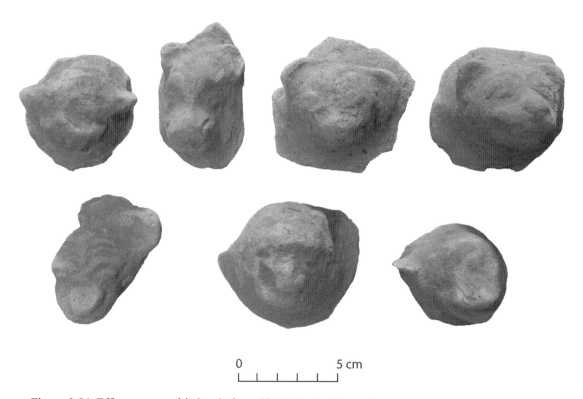

0   5 cm

Figure 3.54. Effigy zoomorphic heads from Ch-60, Santa Teresa 4.

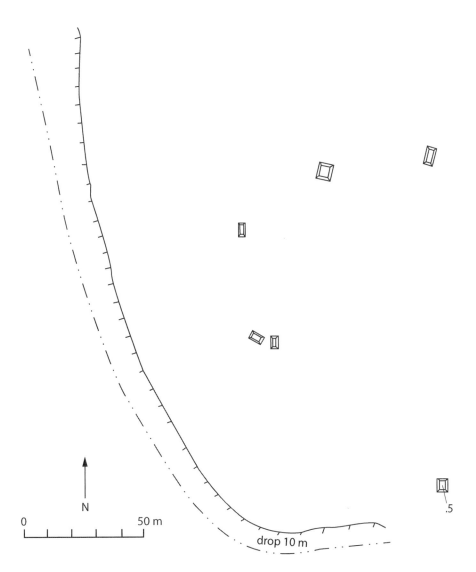

Figure 3.55. Site sketch of Ch-60, Santa Teresa 4.

of the Ríos Tachinula and San Rafael. Area is in milpa.

Environmental Stratum: Riparian Forest

Description: Site consists of 6 house mounds, faced with river cobbles, dispersed throughout the milpa area. Dense sherd scatters are also present in the area of the mounds. See Ch-57.

References: White 1976:44

CH-61 CHICOMUSELO 1 (no map)

Site Type: Habitation

Occupation: Late Classic, Late Postclassic

Location and Setting: Road cut along the banks of the Río Yayahuita; road cut is located in the northern tip of town of Chicomuselo.

Environmental Stratum: Riparian Forest

Description: Dense deposit of sherds in a road cut.

References: White 1976:44

CH-62 CHICOMUSELO 2 (no map)

Site Type: Habitation

Occupation: Early Classic, Postclassic

Location and Setting: Brickyard lies 20 m from the Río Yayahuita; brickyard is located in the northern tip of town of Chicomuselo.

Environmental Stratum: Riparian Forest

Description: Abundant sherds recovered from a clay quarry in a brickyard. There appears to have been a (now destroyed) house mound.

References: White 1976:45

CH-63 CHICOMUSELO 3 (no map)

Site Type: Habitation

Occupation: Postclassic, possible Colonial

Location and Setting: Located in the northern tip of Chicomuselo on municipal land also used as a dumping site; located near the margins of the Río Tachinula.

Environmental Stratum: Riparian Forest

Description: Sherds eroding out of area of run-off down to the river.

References: White 1976:45

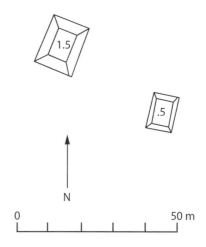

Figure 3.56. Site sketch of Ch-64, El Chachagual.

CH-64 EL CHACHAGUAL (Figure 3.56)

Site Type: Habitation

Occupation: Late Classic

Location and Setting: Located some 200-300 m from the Río Yayahuitla, north of the town of Chicomuselo. Land is not in use; currently covered in scrub grass and coyol palms.

Environmental Stratum: Riparian Forest

Description: Consists of two small house mounds.

References: White 1976:45

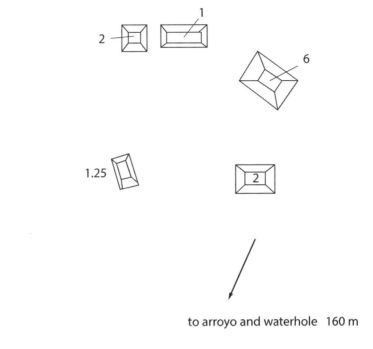

to arroyo and waterhole 160 m

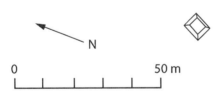

N

0 50 m

Figure 3.57. Site sketch of Ch-65.

CH-65 (Figure 3.57)

Site Type: Ceremonial and habitation

Occupation: Late Preclassic, Protoclassic, Postclassic

Location and Setting: West of the town of Pablo Sidar, this site is located on a prominent hill commanding an excellent view to the south and east. An arroyo is located 160 m to the southeast.

Environmental Stratum: Tropical Deciduous Forest

Description: Site consists of seven mounds, with five of them loosely arranged in a courtyard group. The mounds were faced with slightly water-worn, flat, locally available stone. The largest mound has looters' pits.

References: White 1976:45

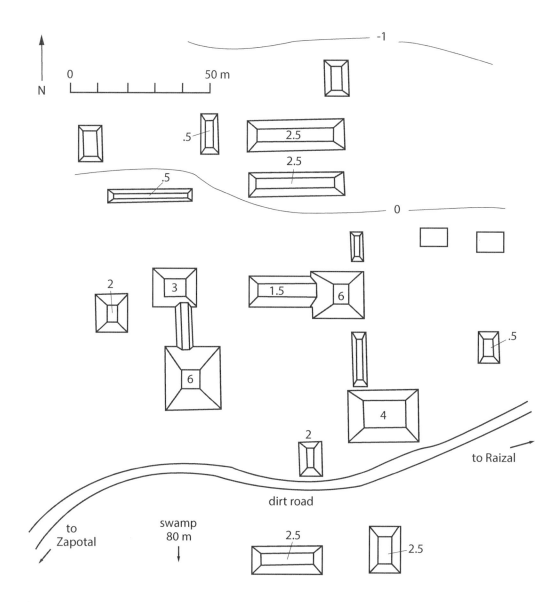

Figure 3.58. Site sketch of Ch-66, Zapotalcito.

CH-66 ZAPOTALCITO
(Figure 3.58-3.59)

Site Type: Ceremonial

Location and Setting: Site is in milpa with a few large guanacaste and zapote trees. Site is divided by a road to Zapotal (west) and El Raizal (east). A swamp is located some 80 m to the south

Environmental Stratum: Tropical Deciduous Forest

Description: This site has a number of large mounds around a plaza area. The largest at 6, 4 and 3 m in height, also have lower rectangular platforms attached to them. A ballcourt is found north of the primary plaza.

Figure 3.59. Views of stone pestle from Ch-66, Zapotalcito.

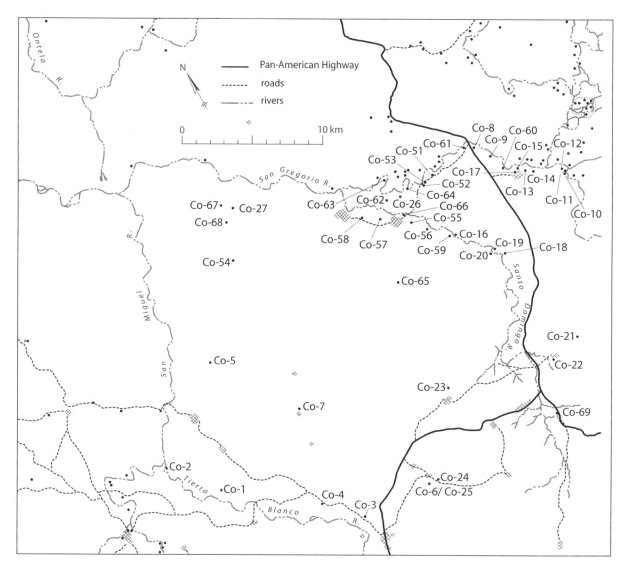

Figure 4.1. Map of site locations in the municipality of Frontera Comalapa (close up of map in Figure 1.7).

CHAPTER 4

SITE DESCRIPTIONS: MUNICIPIO FRONTERA COMALAPA

Michael Blake, Thomas A. Lee Jr., James M. White, John E. Clark, and Mary E. Pye

CO-1 (Figure 4.2)

Site Type: Ceremonial and habitation

Occupation: Late Classic, Postclassic, Colonial

Location and Setting: Between Comalapa and Colonia Nueva Libertad on the north side of Río Blanco on the dirt road to Finca San Miguel.

Environmental Stratum: Tropical Deciduous Forest

Description: Co-1 may be the site of Utatlán, an early colonial settlement and church mentioned in 16th century documents. The accompanying sketch map shows the layout of the remnants of the community. The church is almost 20 m long with the front wall still standing to a height of 10 m. The rear and side walls are only 5 to 6 m high and the rest, of course, has long since collapsed. On the north side of the church are a series of steps near the entrance—possibly from an old well a few meters to the north. In front of the church are two small altars (B and C), as well as another small platform (D). These may be contemporary with the church, but some of the sherds associated with them indicate a Postclassic date. Another small group of mounds (E and F) are located 60 m to the south of the church. They appear to be a small house group, perhaps the priest's residence or a Postclassic elite household. There are undoubtedly many more houses around the church perhaps too ephemeral to have been visible on the surface.

References: Markman 1984

CO-2 GUAPINOLE (Figure 4.3)

Site Type: Ceremonial

Occupation: Late Classic, Late Postclassic

Location and Setting: Co-2 is located approximately 5 km northeast of Chicomuselo.

The site is situated in a canyon on the east bank of the Río Blanco, at its confluence with the Río San Miguel. The terrain in the vicinity of the site is characterized by gently rolling plain. Vegetation in the site area consists primarily of grassland and low, deciduous trees and is used for pasture.

Environmental Stratum: Tropical Deciduous Forest

Description: Guapinole is a small site with only a few structures remaining. Two long low mounds (A and B) appear to form an open-ended ballcourt. To the northwest of them is Structure C, another fairly long rectangular mound. Fifty meters to the west is Mound D, which is a 3 m high pyramid.

The long rectangular nature of the mounds in the A-C group, plus the ceramics collected, indicate a Postclassic date. Mound D on the other hand, is more in the style of Late Classic ceremonial structures at small sites. The landowners reported that all the mounds had been faced with river cobbles, most of which had been removed. In fact, all of the mounds have suffered from removal of fill as well, and so were probably higher.

CO-3 CUXU (Figure 4.4)

Site Type: Ceremonial and habitation

Occupation: possible Late Classic, Postclassic, Colonial

Location and Setting: Co-3 is located 1.5 km north of the center of Frontera Comalapa, 100 m east of the road leading to Guadalupe Grijalva. The Río Blanco passes approximately 750 m west of the site. The terrain in the site area is gently rolling plain. Vegetation consists of grasses and scrub trees.

Environmental Stratum: Fields or Pastures

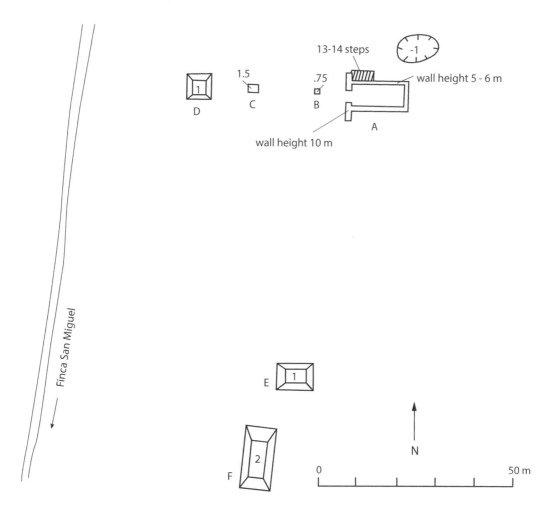

Figure 4.2. Site sketch of Co-1.

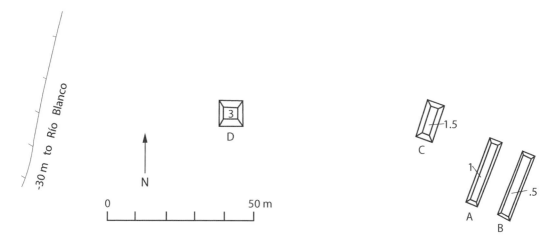

Figure 4.3. Site sketch of Co-2, Guapinole.

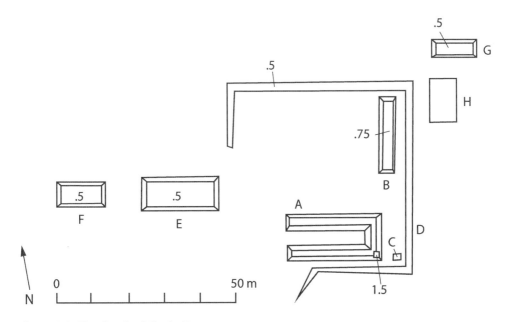

Figure 4.4. Site sketch of Co-3, Cuxu.

Description: Cuxu is an Early Colonial period church with some residences nearby. The collapsed church (A) has some masonry remaining in one corner. The front wall is completely missing. One long structure (B) flanks a plaza area supported and surrounded by a square terrace (D). Facing the church structure are two more low platforms half a meter high (F and E). These may have been elite residences within the center of the community. The only other group of structures noted is a house platform group (G and H).

Some of the ceramics indicated a Postclassic occupation, but this may simply be a stylistic continuation into the Early Colonial period. At any rate, the long rectangular shape of the mounds is similar to the Postclassic construction style throughout the study area.

References: Lee and Markman 1977; Markman 1984

CO-4 GUADALUPE GRIJALVA (Figure 4.5)

Site Type: Ceremonial

Ceramic Phase: Chacaj

Occupation: Early Preclassic, Late Preclassic

Location and Setting: Co-4 is located at the northwest edge of the community of Guadalupe

Grijalva. The site is situated in an area of gently rolling plain. Approximately 200 m west of the site is a small stream draining into the Río Blanco, just 750 m southwest of the site. The vegetation in the site area consists mainly of grasses and low deciduous scrub trees.

Environmental Stratum: Tropical Deciduous Forest

Description: The site at Colonia Guadalupe Grijalva consists of only one large mound 12-15 m on a side and 4 m high. There may have been

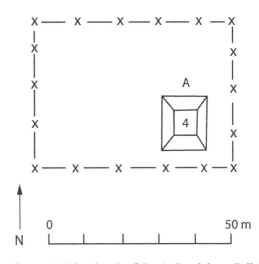

Figure 4.5. Site sketch of Co-4, Guadalupe Grijalva.

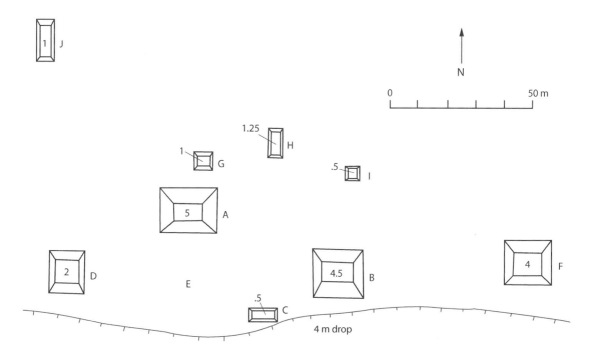

Figure 4.6. Site sketch of Co-5, Los Borditos.

residential structures surrounding the mound but they could have been destroyed by modern-day construction in and around the colonia.

CO-5 LOS BORDITOS (Figure 4.6)

Site Type: Ceremonial and habitation

Occupation: Late Classic

Location and Setting: Co-5 is located 3.5 km northeast of Colonia Nueva Independencia. The site is situated in an area of rolling plain with low deciduous forest and grasses the predominant vegetation. The Río San Miguel passes approximately 2.5 km to the west of the site.

Environmental Stratum: Tropical Deciduous Forest

Description: Los Borditos is a large ceremonial center with several pyramidal mounds and a few smaller residential mounds. The largest mound (A) is approximately 5 m high and fronts a large plaza (E) which is about 75 m by 35 m. The south side of the plaza may have eroded away. Two other large mounds (B and D) and a third mound (C) bounded the plaza. To the east of this

main mound group was another large mound (F) which was 4 m high. Surrounding these large ceremonial mounds are four other small platforms that may have been house platforms (as in the case of H and J) or altars (as in the case of G and I).

The overall layout of the site (if parts have not been eroded away) is much like Late Preclassic centers found throughout the region, although no ceramics were recovered from that era.

CO-6/CO-25 EL SABINO (Figure 4.7)

Site Type: Ceremonial and habitation

Occupation: Middle Preclassic, possible Late Preclassic, possible Protoclassic, Late Classic

Ceramic Phase: Enub

Location and Setting: This site is located approximately 400 m south and slightly west of Colonial El Portal. The site is situated on a hillside in an area of rolling-to-broken hilly terrain. Vegetation in the site area consists mainly of grasses with stands of low deciduous forest nearby. A stream, the Sabinal, passes approximately 200 m to the north of the site.

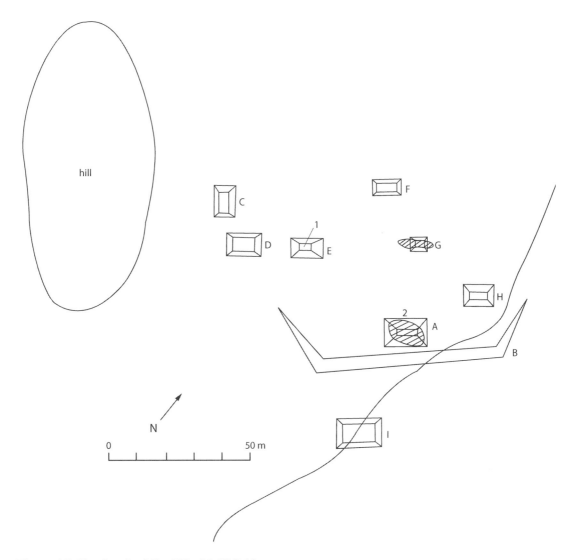

Figure 4.7. Site sketch of Co-6/Co-25, El Sabino.

Environmental Stratum: Evergreen Seasonal Forest

Description: El Sabino consists of a nucleated group of mounds on a hillslope. Some of the mounds (such as A and G) were badly destroyed. Apparently, Mound A had been dynamited in the 1940s by a military party who tried to lift the floor of the mound. Some of the mounds (such as C, D, and E) may form a house group upslope from Mounds A and H. These last two mounds are supported by a large terrace (B). Downslope from these is another platform (I), which also may have been a house mound.

CO-7 (Figure 4.8)

Site Type: Ceremonial and habitation

Occupation: possible Protoclassic, Colonial

Location and Setting: Co-7 is located near Colonia Costa Rica. It is in an area of trees and bush with some grassy areas. The land is used as pasturage.

Environmental Stratum: Tropical Deciduous Forest

Description: Two main groups of structures were noted at the site. The main group consisted

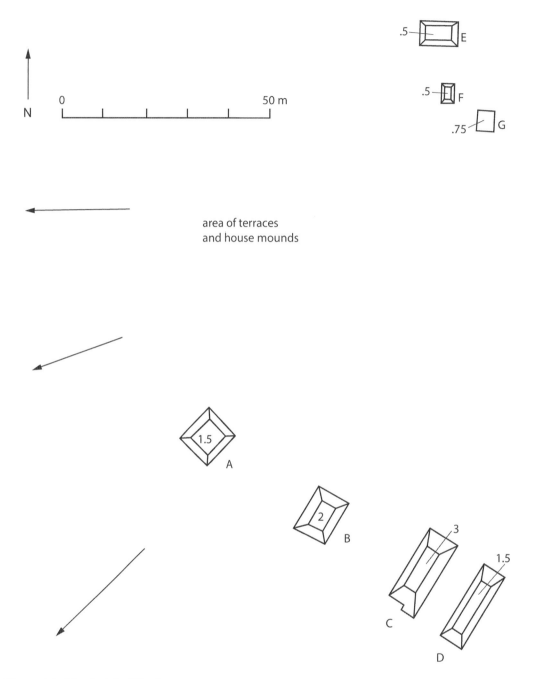

Figure 4.8. Site sketch of Co-7.

of an alignment of four structures: two low platforms (A and B) and a ballcourt (C and D). The ceremonial structures were faced with squared limestone slabs common in the region. Mound C in the ballcourt was 3 m high. Ninety meters north of this group was a second smaller group of structures. The largest (Mound E) was probably a house platform. Two others (F and G) may have been altars or peripheral structures.

Many additional house structures and terraces were located in the area upslope. Unfortunately, the site area was too densely covered with vegetation to map.

Río San Gregorio

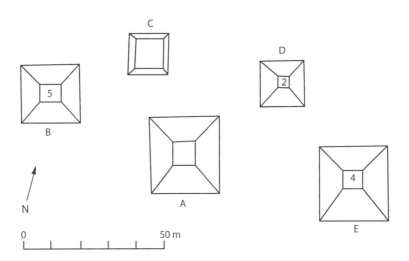

Figure 4.9. Site sketch of Co-8, Chamic.

CO-8 CHAMIC (Figure 4.9)

Site Type: Ceremonial

Occupation: Late Preclassic, Protoclassic, Late Classic

Location and Setting: Co-8 is located 2 km northwest of Colonia Joaquín Miguel Gutiérrez. The site is situated on the south bank of Río San Gregorio, 250 m east of where the river passes under the Pan-American Highway. The site, in the valley of Río San Gregorio, is in an area of gently rolling plain. Vegetation in the site area consists of grasses with riparian trees along the river channel and is used as pasture.

Environmental Stratum: Riparian Forest

Description: This large Late Preclassic ceremonial center is similar to many other such sites in the study area. The largest mound (A) is in the central part of the site and is surrounded on three sides by many other large mounds. Two of these (D and E) form a small plaza area on the east side of the center. Mounds B and C form a slightly smaller plaza area on the west side of the site. There may well have been additional small mounds of simple houses on the surface that were too low to be visible in the vegetation. Furthermore, river flooding may have covered them over with sediments during the past two thousand years.

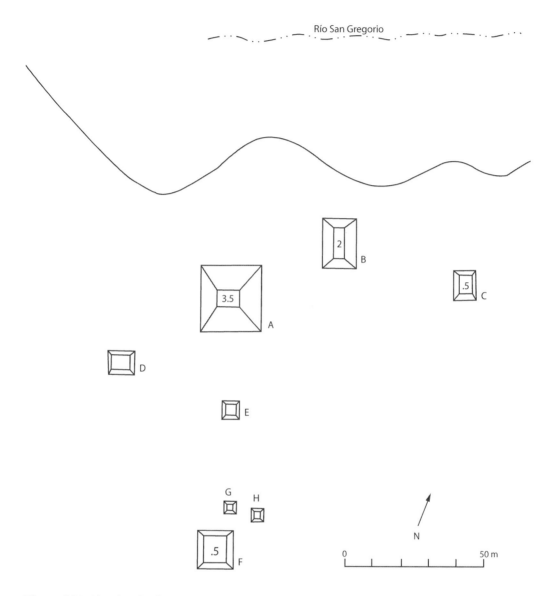

Figure 4.10. Site sketch of Co-9.

CO-9 (Figure 4.10)

Site Type: Ceremonial and habitation

Occupation: Late Classic

Location and Setting: Co-9 is located 2 km northwest of Colonia Joaquín Miguel Gutiérrez on the south bank of Río San Gregorio. The Pan-American Highway passes approximately 500 m west of the site. The site area is used as a milpa.

Environmental Stratum: Riparian Forest

Description: Co-9 consists of two large pyramidal mounds and several smaller platforms and altars clustered near Río San Gregorio. Although there may have been a Late Preclassic nucleus, the bulk of the construction appears to be Late Classic. The main mound (A) is 3.5 m high and faces southeast towards Mounds E, G, H, and F with which it is aligned. The area between these mounds probably formed the main plaza. One small mound (D) flanks this plaza area on the west side. Just to the north of Mound A was located the next largest mound (B)

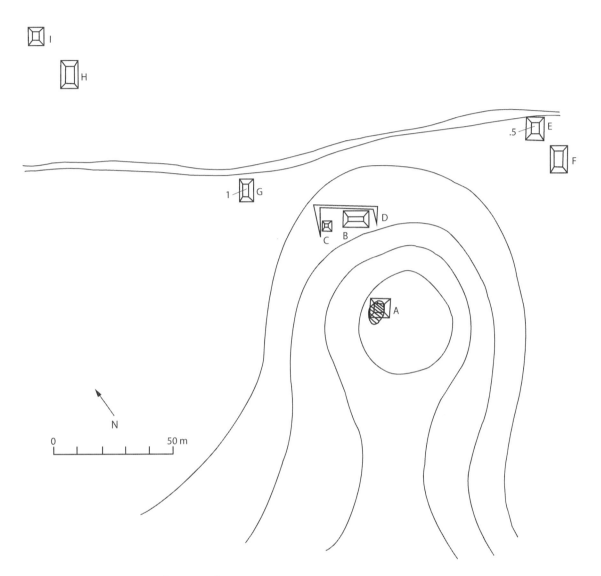

Figure 4.11. Site sketch of Co-10, Platanar.

which was 2 m high. A possible house platform (C) is located a further 35 m to the E. All of these structures form a settlement pattern most reminiscent of the Late Classic period; however, most Late Classic sites with a ceremonial center as large as this have many more residential structures around the main mound group. It is possible that (at least at this site) houses were built directly on the ground. Certainly the valley area along this stretch of the San Gregorio has fewer cobbles and boulders that could be used to construct permanent house platforms.

CO-10 PLATANAR (Figure 4.11)

Site Type: Habitation

Occupation: Middle Preclassic, Late Classic

Location and Setting: Co-10 is located approximately 3 km east and slightly south of Colonia Joaquín Miguel Gutiérrez. The site is situated on a hillside on the west bank of Río Rincón Tigre. Approximately 500 m downstream of the site, the river converges with Río Dolores. Co-10, Co-11, and Co-12 are clustered closely together along Río Rincón Tigre in this area.

Vegetation at the site consists of grasses and low deciduous trees.

Environmental Stratum: Riparian Forest

Description: Platanar is a small habitation site with the remains of eight structures. One of the mounds (A) is located at the top of a small hill overlooking the valley bottom. It has been partially destroyed and dug away. Downslope from Mound A is a small house group supported on a terrace (D). The house structure (B) is flanked by a smaller structure (C) that may have been an altar. To the west 75 m is a small house group with two house platforms (E and F). To the northwest of the B-D House Group are the single structure (G) and another more isolated house group (H and I). This site is typical of small Late Classic settlements throughout the region.

CO-11 CAMINO A LA BOMBA
(Figure 4.12)

Site Type: Habitation

Occupation: Late Preclassic

Location and Setting: Co-11 is located approximately 3 km east and slightly south of Colonia Joaquín Miguel Gutiérrez. The site is situated on a hillside on both sides of a dry arroyo on the west bank of Río Rincón Tigre. Vegetation in the site area consists of grassland and low deciduous trees. Approximately 500 m downstream from Co-11, Río Rincón Tigre converges with Río Dolores. Several other sites are also clustered in this area.

Environmental Stratum: Riparian Forest

Description: The site has a number of house groups scattered over an area of about 500 m by 300 m. Among these are also several individual structures. Some (such as Mounds C, D, and E) are arranged around a small patio area (F). The group comprised of Mounds U and V has a small structure (W), which might have been an altar. Altogether, there are approximately eight house groups and five isolated structures. The distance between the groups ranges from 40 m to 150 m.

CO-12 (Figure 4.13)

Site Type: Ceremonial and habitation

Occupation: possible Early Classic, Late Classic

Location and Setting: Co-12 is located approximately 2.5 km east and slightly south of Colonia Joaquín Miguel Gutiérrez. The site is situated on a hillside on the west bank of Río Rincón Tigre. Three hundred meters downstream of the site, Río Rincón Tigre converges with Río Dolores. Several other sites are clustered in this area. Vegetation in the site area consists of grasses and some low deciduous trees, and sections of it were cleared for milpa.

Environmental Stratum: Tropical Deciduous Forest

Description: This site is a habitation area consisting of at least 17 mounds. There may be others hidden by the vegetation that were not mapped. The main part of the site is located atop a low hill in the center of which were located the largest mounds. Mound A may have been a small temple mound, although it is possible that it was a large elite residence platform. Surrounding it were several rather ill-defined house groups. Two structures (M and N) are isolated from the main group and could have been single residences. The only other structures mapped were about 100 m north and downslope from the main group. They may have comprised one or two separate house groups.

CO-13 (Figure 4.14)

Site Type: Ceremonial and habitation

Occupation: possible early Middle Preclassic, Late Classic

Location and Setting: Co-13 is located 750 m east of Colonia Joaquín Miguel Gutiérrez. The site is situated on the second terrace above the south bank of Río San Gregorio. Vegetation in the site area consists mainly of grass which is used as pasturage. It is also used as milpa.

Environmental Stratum: Fields or Pastures

Description: This large site includes a large ceremonial center, as well as two distinct

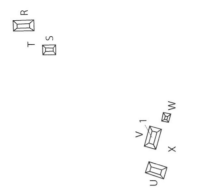

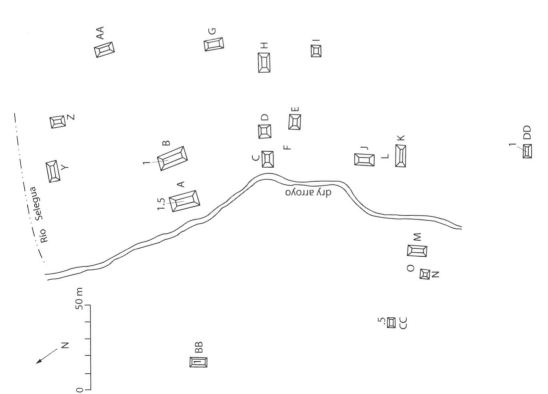

Figure 4.12. Site sketch of Co-11, Camino a la Bomba.

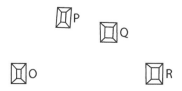

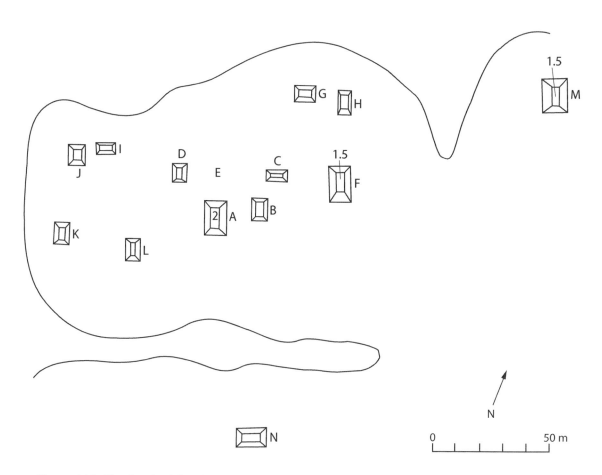

Figure 4.13. Site sketch of Co-12.

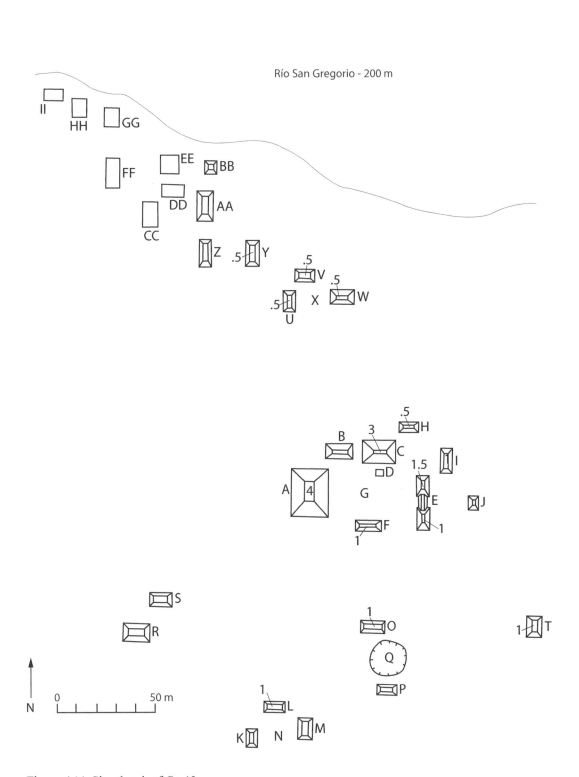

Figure 4.14. Site sketch of Co-13.

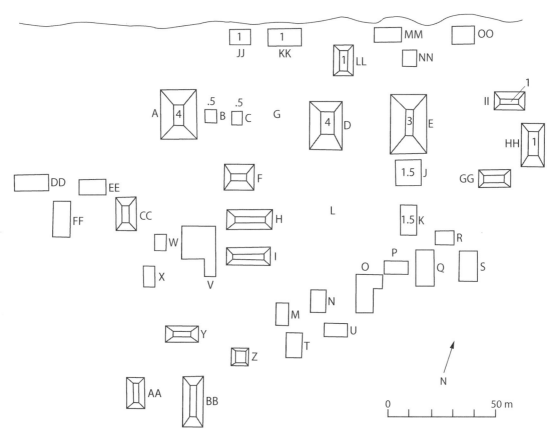

Figure 4.15. Site sketch of Co-14.

residential areas. The ceremonial precinct has nine separate mounds surrounding a well-defined plaza (G). The largest mound (A) is 4 m high and 20-25 m on a side. Directly opposite is Mound E, a two pyramid mound joined to a small connecting platform. The other mounds surrounding the main plaza include a large pyramid mound (C) and several smaller platforms that could have been elite residences. Mound C bears a small platform that may have been an altar.

The largest residential group begins 65 m north of the ceremonial precinct and extends in linear fashion another 200 m to the northwest. Most of the platforms appear to form distinct house groups, such as Mounds U, V, and W, which are arranged around the house group patio (X).

Another more scattered residential area lies to the south of the Main Plaza. There appear to be three separate house groups and one isolated structure (T). One group (O and P) sit on either side of a small depression (Q) which may have been a well. A larger house group consists of Mounds K, L, and M that surround a small house patio. The house groups in this part of the site are separated by between 35 and 60 m.

More intensive survey might recover evidence of additional house structures and perhaps concentrations of artifacts in the ploughed fields.

CO-14 (Figure 4.15)

Site Type: Ceremonial and habitation

Occupation: Middle Preclassic, Late Classic

Location and Setting: Co-14 is located approximately 100 m east of the northeast edge of Colonia Joaquín Miguel Gutiérrez. The site is situated on the second river bench, 150 m south of Río San Gregorio. Vegetation in the site area consists primarily of grasses used as pasturage.

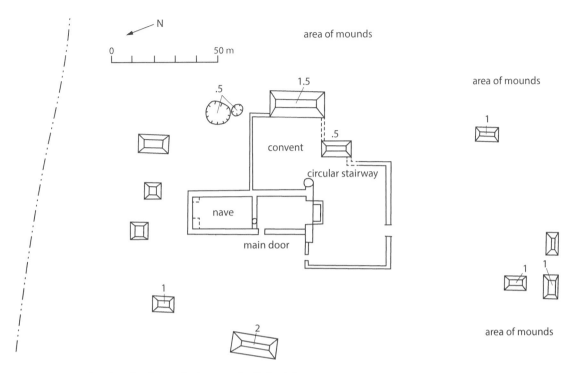

Figure 4.16. Site sketch of Co-15, Aquespala Colonial.

Environmental Stratum: Fields or Pastures

Description: This large nucleated community consists of a central ceremonial precinct, tightly surrounded by many residential structures. The main ceremonial structures include two large mounds (D and E) on the north side of the plaza (L). The west side of the plaza is formed by one mound (F) and a large open-ended ballcourt made up of Mounds H and I. Outside of this main plaza area is another plaza (G) to the west of Mound D. This latter mound faces Mound A, which is one of the largest mounds at the site. Between the two are the small platforms (B and C) that might be altars.

A group of large low platforms to the east of the main mound group is possibly an elite residential group. These structures (GG, HH, and II) form a small patio group facing Mound E. Most of the other smaller platform mounds that were probably house mounds also front the main mound group. There were no isolated mounds mapped so all the house mounds probably belong to smaller house groups. One large structure (V) near the ballcourt is an irregularly shaped low platform of unknown function.

A more detailed and intensive survey at the zone surrounding this site would probably reveal many more house mounds, although some might have been built at ground level without supporting platforms. The general layout of the community appears to be most similar to the Classic pattern throughout the area.

CO-15 AQUESPALA COLONIAL
(Figure 4.16)

Site Type: Ceremonial and habitation

Occupation: Late Preclassic, Late Postclassic, Colonial

Location and Setting: Aquespala is located approximately 250 m north of Colonia Joaquín Miguel Gutiérrez. The site is situated on the first bench above the south bank of Río San Gregorio. Several other sites are clustered immediately across the river from this site. Vegetation in the site area consists primarily of grasses.

Environmental Stratum: Fields or Pastures

Description: Aquespala is the site of one of the many early Colonial Churches in the

Figure 4.17. Views of an axe from Co-16, Niagara.

upper tributaries region. This community was visited by Fray Alonso Ponce in 1586 (Ciudad Real 1993). The indigenous people who were congregated into the town spoke Coxoh, a variant of Tzeltal Maya (Campbell and Gardner 1988).

The site, when mapped in 1974, consisted of the remains of the church and convent as well as a walled-in forecourt. Our sketch map only shows the main mounds surrounding the church structure. These were probably Early Colonial residences, but some may be part of a pre-Hispanic occupation as well. To the north, east, and south of the ceremonial center were located a number of low house mounds. These were not mapped at the time because of the dense weeds.

References: Lee and Markman 1977; Markman 1984

CO-16 NIAGARA
(Figures 4.17-4.18)

Site Type: Ceremonial and habitation

Occupation: Late Preclassic, Middle Classic, Postclassic

Location and Setting: Co-16 is located 4 km southeast of Colonial San Caralampio. The site is situated on the east bank of Río Santo Domingo in an area of gently rolling plain. The site of Guajilar (Co-59) is located across the river. Vegetation in the site area consists of grasses and dense riparian growth along the river channel.

Environmental Stratum: Riparian Forest

Description: More than 30 mounds lie along the Río Santo Doming with an orientation just west of north. The primary group, consisting of the largest mounds, is roughly center (A through F). Mounds A-E are located on a pentagon-shaped platform some 120 m at its widest and 160 m at its longest. Mound A is roughly 35 m in diameter and over 5 m in height; Mound B is 40 m in diameter and 5 m in height; Mound C measures 20 m in diameter and 1.2 m in height; and Mound E is 50 m in diameter and 5 m in height. Mound F lies to the west and is L-shaped; it is at least 6 m high. These mounds are arranged in a pentagon shaped layout around a plaza. A group of smaller mounds lies just north of Mounds A and B. Large depressions to the northeast, north, and west may have been the source of the matrix for the large mounds and platforms.

Further north lies another group of smaller mounds (L through P) along a slight rise adjacent to the river. To the south of the primary ceremonial complex, numerous small mounds cluster near Mound K on a rise above the river; Mound K is 2 m in height and 15 by 20 m.

Notably, there appears to be no ballcourt at the site.

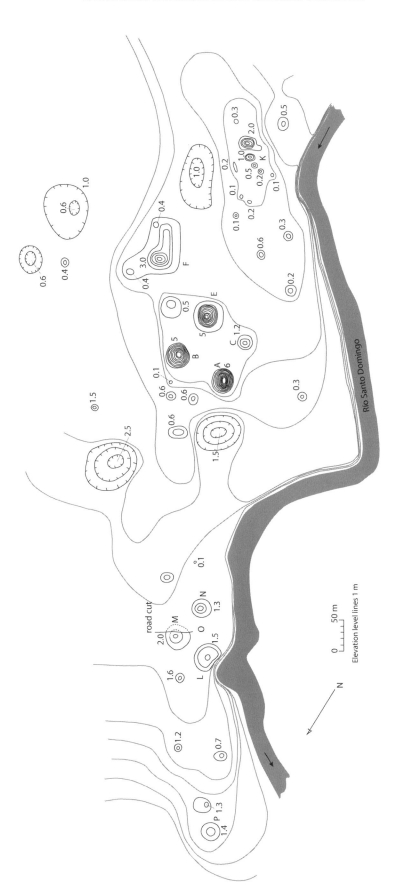

Figure 4.18. Site sketch of Co-16, Niagara; mapped by Eduardo Martínez.

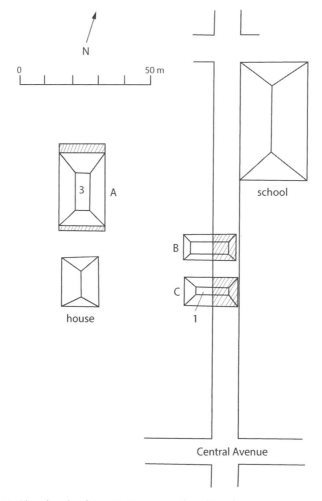

Figure 4.19. Site sketch of Co-17, Joaquín Miguel Gutiérrez.

CO-17 JOAQUÍN MIGUEL GUTIÉRREZ
(Figure 4.19)

Site Type: Ceremonial and habitation

Occupation: Late Classic, Postclassic

Location and Setting: Co-17 is located at the north edge within the community limits of Colonia Joaquín Miguel Gutiérrez. The site is situated in an area of gently rolling plain within approximately 500 m of Río San Gregorio.

Environmental Stratum: Plains or Fields

Description: Only three mounds remain of this site, which has been badly destroyed by recent construction within the community. The largest mound (A) is still 3 m high, but the ends have been somewhat dug into. Portions of Mounds B and C have been completely cleared away in order to create the street in front of the community's school. These two mounds may have been part of an elite residence near the ceremonial center. No other mounds were noted.

References: Lee 1985:table 1

CO-18 TRES LAGUNAS
(Figure 4.20)

Site Type: Ceremonial and habitation

Occupation: Protoclassic, Late Classic

Location and Setting: Co-18 is located near the small village of Tres Lagunas, 7 km southeast of Colonia San Caralampio and approximately 1.75 km west of the Pan-American Highway. The site

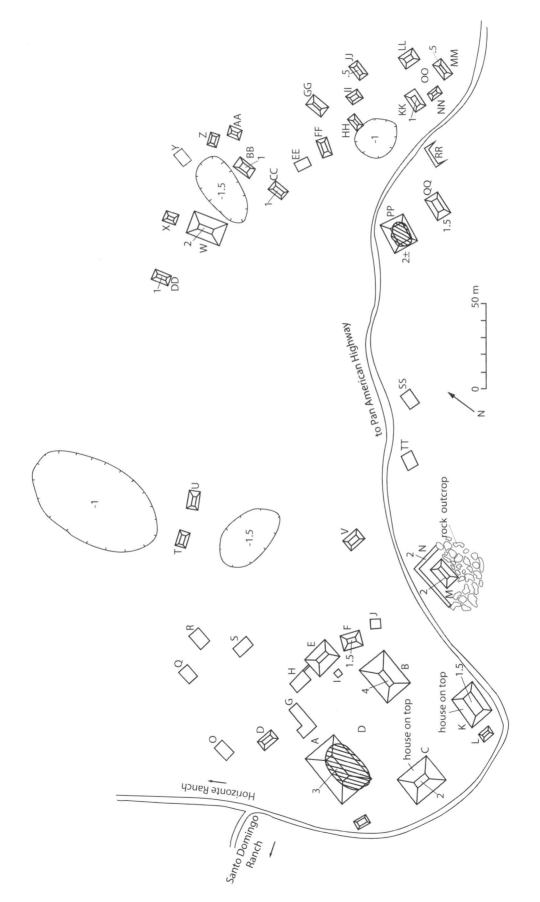

Figure 4.20. Site sketch of Co-18, Tres Lagunas.

is situated on the river margin on the east bank of Río Santo Domingo. It is in an area of rolling plain; vegetation consists of grasses and low deciduous tress, with riparian vegetation along the river.

Environmental Stratum: Riparian Forest

Description: Tres Lagunas consists of two main sections, both of which appear to have been contemporaneous, based on the similarity of construction and layout. The largest section is on the south part of the site and consists of three large mounds (A, B, and C), several smaller mounds around the main plaza, and some small house groups. The main plaza (D) is closed off on the north side by Mounds G, H, E, F, and J. These mounds are tightly arrayed around the one side that is opposed to the other residential parts of the community. The largest mound at the site (A) is badly destroyed—a good deal of the fill has been removed. Two of the mounds (C and K) have modern houses built on top of them.

A large structure (M and N) is built into a rock outcrop on the east side of the plaza. It probably formed the far eastern side of the ceremonial center.

The other section of the site begins approximately 230 m to the northeast. It has only one of two large mounds that may have been ceremonial structures. One of them (PP) is badly destroyed. Near it are several house groups, one of which has four house mounds arranged around the patio (OO). The other house groups are not as well defined. There are four large depressions around the site between 1 m and 1.5 m deep. These may have been barrow pits or perhaps seasonal lagoons from which the site takes its name.

The layout of the ceremonial structures and the houses are all very similar to the basic Late Classic pattern. It is likely that there are more house mounds scattered throughout the zone.

CO-19 TRES LAGUNAS 2
(Figure 4.21)

Site Type: Habitation

Ceramic Phase: Enub

Occupation: Middle Preclassic, Late Classic

Location and Setting: Co-19 is located 6.5 km southeast of Colonia San Caralampio and 2.5 km west of the Pan-American Highway. The site is situated on the river margin of the east bank of Río Santo Domingo in an area of gently rolling plain. Vegetation in the site area consists mainly of grasses, with riparian growth along the river.

Environmental Stratum: Fields or Pastures

Description: This small habitation site had only four mounds. Mounds A, B, and C form a clear house group around a small patio. Other structures may be present in the surrounding zone but none were noted during survey.

CO-20 SANTO DOMINGO
(Figure 4.22)

Site Type: Ceremonial and habitation

Occupation: Late Classic

Location and Setting: Santo Domingo is located 6 km southeast of Colonia San Caralampio. The site is situated on the river margin on the west bank of Río Santo Domingo in an area of gently rolling plain. Vegetation in the site area consists mainly of grasses, with riparian growth along the river.

Environmental Stratum: Riparian Forest

Description: Santo Domingo is a nucleated settlement with nine structures mapped. The main mound (A) faces southwest onto a small plaza area. Several of the mounds, such as D, E, and G, are quite small and may have been altars. The other structures were probably house platforms. Two of these (F and I) form a fairly distinct house group. Although it is likely that additional structures are present in the surrounding environs, none were noted during the survey.

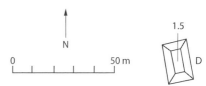

Figure 4.21. Site sketch of Co-19, Tres Lagunas 2.

CO-21 (Figure 4.23)

Site Type: Ceremonial

Occupation: possible Late Preclassic, Late Classic

Location and Setting: Co-21 is located 1.75 km east and slightly north of Colonia Sabinalito. The site is situated in a small valley in an area of rolling hilly terrain. A stream passes 200 m to the south of the site. Vegetation in the site area consists of grasses and low deciduous trees.

Environmental Stratum: Tropical Deciduous Forest

Description: The only mound at this site is partially eroded away. It was 2.5 m high and probably was a ceremonial pyramid for a small community, although no other mounds were noted in the immediate vicinity.

CO-22 SABINALITO (Figure 4.24)

Site Type: Ceremonial and habitation

Ceramic Phase: Foko

Occupation: late Middle Preclassic, possible Late Preclassic, Late Classic

Location and Setting: Co-22 is located at the south edge of Colonia Sabinalito. The site is situated in a small valley in an area of rolling hilly terrain. Vegetation in the site area consists of grasses and low deciduous trees. A small stream that drains into Río Santo Domingo passes approximately 300 m west of the site.

Environmental Stratum: Pine-Oak Forest

Description: Only four mounds remain at Sabinalito. One large mound (A) is 3 m high, but the north end of it had been removed for construction fill. Two other mounds (C and D)

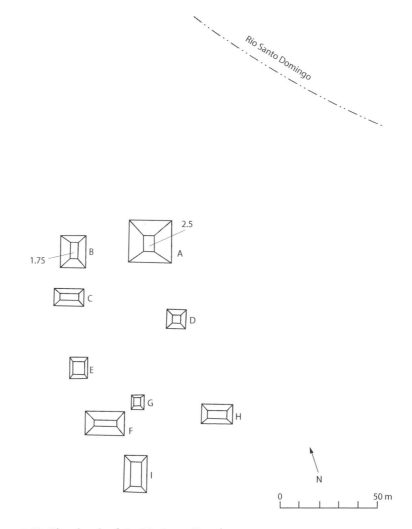

Figure 4.22. Site sketch of Co-20, Santo Domingo.

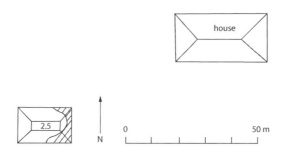

Figure 4.23. Site sketch of Co-21.

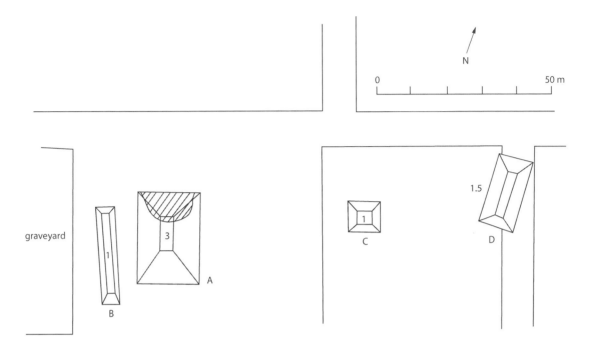

Figure 4.24. Site sketch of Co-22, Sabinalito.

are 40 and 30 m east of Mound A, respectively. Mound D has also been partly destroyed by construction. An additional mound (B) is located just to the west of Mound A. It is in the long narrow style characteristic of the Late Postclassic, and in fact, may have been built after the other principal mounds in the group. These other mounds are laid out much like other small Late Classic ceremonial centers. It is highly likely that the colonia has destroyed many of the smaller residential mounds surrounding the site.

References: Lee 1985

CO-23 EL GUANACASTE
(Figure 4.25)

Site Type: Ceremonial and habitation

Occupation: Late Classic

Location and Setting: Co-23 is located approximately 500 m to the northeast of Colonia Verapaz. The site is situated in a small valley in an area of gently rolling hills. Vegetation in the site area consists of grasses with stands of deciduous forest nearby and is used as milpa. A stream passes approximately 200 m east of the site.

Environmental Stratum: Tropical Deciduous Forest

Description: El Guanacaste consists of a small ceremonial complex surrounded on the north side by several residential structures. Main Plaza structures include Mounds A to E. Mounds A and B form the northern edge of the plaza and Mounds C and D, which appear to be two ballcourt mounds, are on the south side of the plaza. Another large mound (E) may have been either a ceremonial platform or an elite residence.

One cluster of residential structures is located to the west of the main plaza and these mounds (G to J) could have formed one house group. To the north about 60 m is another group of five structures that may have formed another large house group. Ninety meters to the east is an isolated residential mound (P). Other mounds are likely distributed around the site's immediate zone and would be revealed by more intensive survey. The presence of the ballcourt indicates that this site was probably larger or at least its ceremonial center served a larger area than the number of structures mapped would suggest.

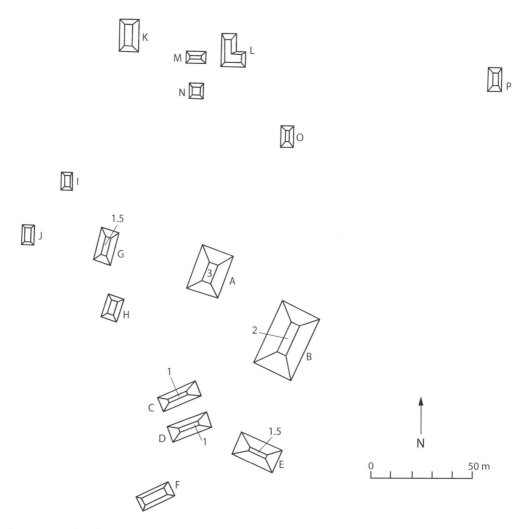

Figure 4.25. Site sketch of Co-23, El Guanacaste.

CO-24 EL MARITO
(Figure 4.26)

Site Type: Habitation

Occupation: Late Preclassic?

Location and Setting: El Marito is located approximately 500 m southeast of Colonia El Portal, on the east side of the road to Colonia Monte Redondo. The site is situated in a valley in an area of rolling-to-broken hilly terrain. Vegetation in the site area consists of grasses, with stands of low deciduous forest nearby. No water source was recorded for this site.

Environmental Stratum: Evergreen Seasonal Forest

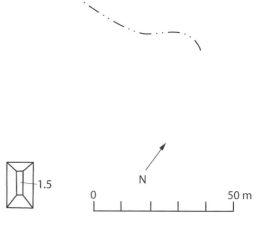

Figure 4.26. Site sketch of Co-24, El Marito.

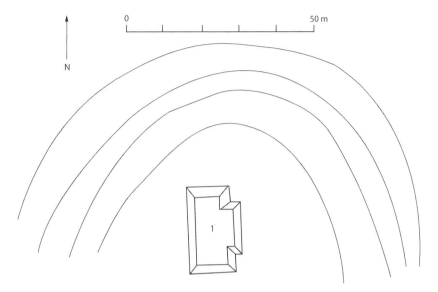

Figure 4.27. Site sketch of Co-26.

Description: Only one small mound was noted at the site. There may have been other less substantial structures nearby that were not visible in the vegetation.

CO-25 (see CO-6)

CO-26 (Figure 4.27)

Site Type: Habitation

Occupation: Late Classic

Location and Setting: Co-26 is located 1.25 km northeast of Colonia San Caralampio. The site is situated on top of a low hill, overlooking Río San Gregorio to the north. Vegetation in the site area consists mainly of grasses, with riparian growth along the river.

Environmental Stratum: Riparian Forest

Description: This single mound was 10 m by 20 m and 1 m high. The east side had a short extension that was probably a staircase. This isolated structure could have been a residence, but more likely it is some form of ceremonial structure since it is larger and more elaborate than most isolated houses in the region.

CO-27 (Figure 4.28)

Site Type: Habitation

Location and Setting: Co-27 is located 1 km east and slightly south of Colonia Sinaloa. The site is situated on a low hill, approximately 250 m east of a river that flows into Río San Gregorio. Vegetation in the site area consists of low deciduous trees and grasses. The land is used for pasturage.

Environmental Stratum: Tropical Deciduous Forest

Description: The two sections of this site are separated by 150 m. The section with the ceremonial structure (Mound A) is located on the edge of a 1 m high limestone outcrop. The mound itself is 3 m high and about 60 m from the nearest mounds to the west of it. These structures are mainly house groups comprising two to three residential platforms. The northeast group of residential structures has about 25 mounds and small platforms. These are quite nucleated on a small hill with the mounds arranged in formal groupings. One mound (S) has an attached lower platform perpendicular to it. In front of it are three very low small platforms (T, U, and V),

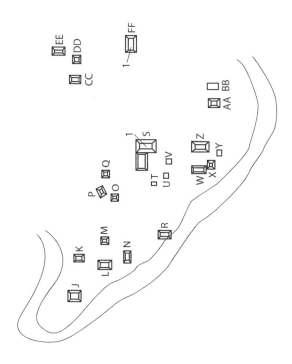

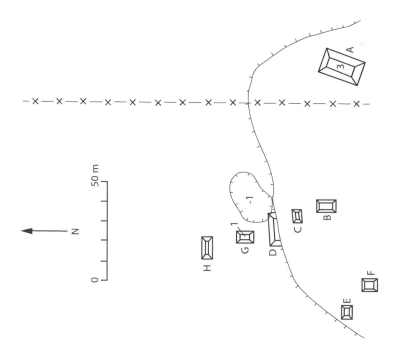

Figure 4.28. Site sketch of Co-27.

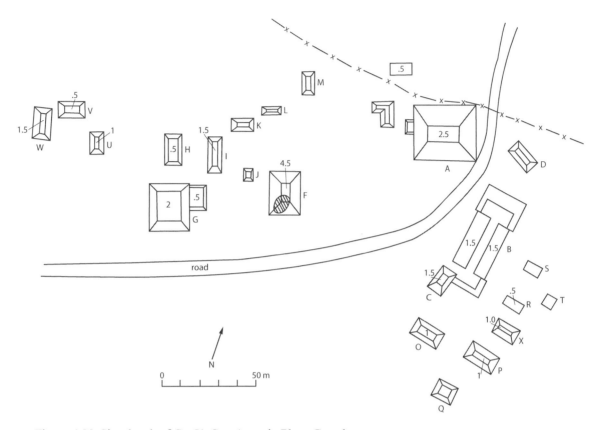

Figure 4.29. Site sketch of Co-51, San Antonio Playa Grande.

which may be altars. This configuration is much like the Late Postclassic style. Another group (W to Z) also has some platforms that are tightly clustered (ex. west and X), as well as a small altar (Y). An isolated structure (I) is located 70 m to the east of this group.

Both sections are probably Late Classic but the possibility remains that at least part of the main residential area in the east portion of the site was occupied during the Postclassic.

[Note: There is a break in the site sequence numeration. There are no sites from Co-28 to Co-50.]

CO-51 SAN ANTONIO PLAYA GRANDE (Figure 4.29)

Site Type: Ceremonial and habitation

Occupation: late Middle Preclassic, Late Preclassic, Late Classic

Location and Setting: Co-51 is located 3.5 km northeast of Colonia San Caralampio. The site is situated on the river margin or the south bank of Río San Gregorio. Vegetation in the site area consists mainly of grasses, with riparian growth along the river, and is used as pasturage.

Environmental Stratum: Riparian Forest

Description: San Antonio is a large ceremonial center with several temple mounds arranged around a plaza area. The east side is formed by an I-shaped ballcourt, formed by two long rectangular mounds, each 1.5 m high (B). The largest mound at the site is A, which while only 2.5 m high, is approximately 30 m on a side.

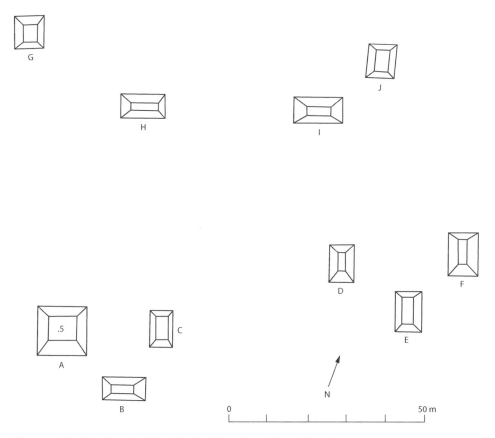

Figure 4.30. Site sketch of Co-52, San Francisco Playa Grande.

Two other large mounds (G and F) are situated on the west side of the plaza area. Mound F has been partly looted. South of the ballcourt and northwest of murals G and F are several clusters of what appear to be rectangular residential mounds. Some (like mounds U, V, and W) are clearly arranged around a small patio. Others (such as Mound M) are more isolated. It is probable that more residences are located in the fields nearby but were covered with vegetation during the survey.

CO-52 SAN FRANCISCO PLAYA GRANDE
(Figure 4.30)

Site Type: Habitation

Occupation: Late Classic

Location and Setting: Co-52 is located approximately 2.5 km northeast of Colonia San Caralampio. The site is located in the valley on the south bank of Río San Gregorio. Vegetation in the site area consists of grasses and low deciduous trees and bush.

Environmental Stratum: Riparian Forest

Description: The structures mapped at this site include four nucleated house groups. Two of them have three house platforms each, arranged around small patios. The other two house groups have two house platforms each. No ceremonial structures were noted in the immediate vicinity of the site, although a larger center with a ceremonial structure is located 200-300 m to the north (Co-53).

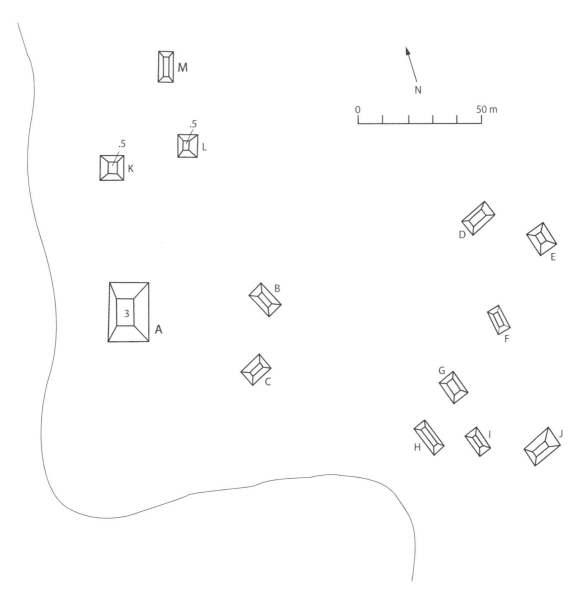

Figure 4.31. Site sketch of Co-53, San Francisco Playa Grande 2.

CO-53 SAN FRANCISCO PLAYA GRANDE 2
(Figure 4.31)

Site Type: Ceremonial and habitation

Occupation: Late Classic

Location and Setting: Co-53 is located 3 km northeast of Colonia San Caralampio. The site is situated in the valley on the south bank of Río San Gregorio. Vegetation in the area consists of grasses and low deciduous trees and bush.

Environmental Stratum: Riparian Forest

Description: San Francisco Playa Grande 2 is much like Co-52 to the south, except that it has a few additional house platforms as well as a pyramidal mound (A). Since there are differing orientations among the various structures, it is possible that they are not all contemporaneous. Some of the house platforms (like the B and C group and the G, H, and I group) are in well-defined clusters around small patios. The house groups are separated from each other and from the main mound by about 30 to 60 m.

CO-54 (Figure 4.32)

Site Type: Ceremonial and habitation

Occupation: Late Preclassic, Early Postclassic, Late Postclassic

Location and Setting: Co-54 is located 3.5 km south of Colonia Sinaloa. The site is situated on the east bank of an arroyo that may have been an old stream channel that drained into Río San Gregorio. The site is on a high hilltop. Vegetation in the site area consists of thick deciduous trees and bush.

Environmental Stratum: Tropical Deciduous Forest

Description: The site covers the slopes and summits of several small hills. The largest structure is Mound AA, which is about 14 m high and has a staircase on one side. It faces a small mound (BB), and another slightly larger mound (CC) flanks the two. Together, these mounds form a ceremonial focus for the western zone of the site. Surrounding them are a numerous house platforms most of which are on terraces. Some terraces had no house platforms on them and may have supported simple houses built on the ground surface.

The eastern zone of the site has a very nucleated center with seven large pyramidal mounds. The tallest is Mound A at 8 m. Beside it are two other large mounds (B and O) that surround a small plaza area in the middle of which is a possible altar platform (N). Adjacent to all these large pyramids are several small platforms that could have been part of the elite residential complex. Some are at the same level as the main plaza (such as Mound P), while others form small house groups on terraces below the main plaza level (e.g., Mound T, supported by Terrace U). Even one of the large pyramids (K) sits below the level of the main plaza.

The two distinct ceremonial foci at the site suggest either that each may be a different temporal component or that they represent two distinct social groupings within the site. If the latter was the case, then the different layouts and arrangements of the structures in each group may indicate separate origins or political affiliations.

CO-55 SAN CARALAMPIO (TEMPISQUE) (Figure 4.33)

Site Type: Ceremonial and habitation

Occupation: Late Classic

Location and Setting: Co-55 is located approximately 1.25 km southeast of Colonia San Caralampio. The site is situated on a low hill 200 m east of Río Santo Domingo. Topography in this area is gently rolling hills. Vegetation in the area consists mainly of grasses, with sparse low deciduous trees and is used as milpa land.

Environmental Stratum: Fields or Pastures

Description: The site, as recorded, is mainly a ceremonial center, although there are most likely many more residential structures nearby. The main mounds at the site are supported on the hilltop by a 140 m long terrace system (C). The largest mound (A) is 6 m high and forms the northeast edge of the plaza. To the south is an I-shaped ballcourt (F), which is comprised of two long rectangular mounds (D and E). On the other side of the plaza is a 4 m high mound (B). Several other mounds are found nearby, but they do not form distinct groupings. G and H are, in fact, oriented in a slightly different direction from the other main mounds and so could be of a different date. The small group (M, N, and O) just south of Mound L is probably a residential group.

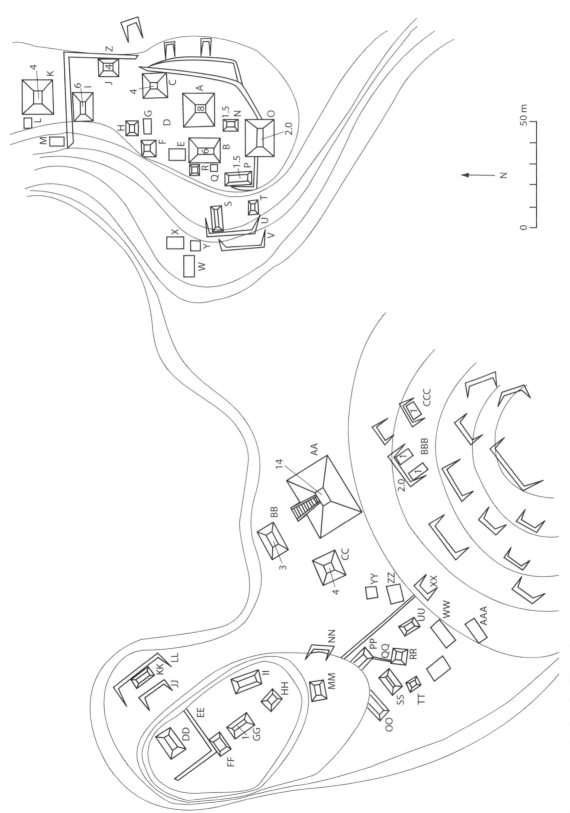

Figure 4.32. Site sketch of Co-54.

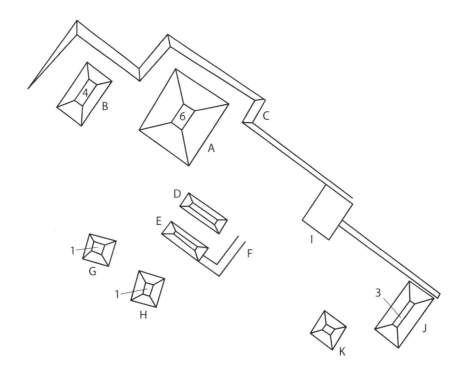

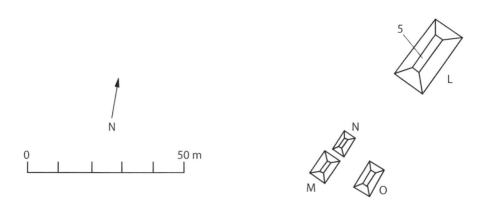

Figure 4.33. Site sketch of Co-55, San Caralampio (Tempisque).

CO-56 CARALAMPIO
(Figure 4.34)

Site Type: Ceremonial and habitation

Occupation: Late Classic

Location and Setting: Co-56 is located 1.75 km southeast of Colonia San Caralampio. The site is situated in the valley on the west bank of Río Santo Domingo. Topography is generally a rolling plain, bisected by the river valley in which the site sits. Vegetation in the site area consists mainly of grasses and is used for pasture.

Environmental Stratum: Riparian Forest

Description: This site is a dispersed linear arrangement of residential structures and two ceremonial mounds. These two mounds (A and B) are located near the north end of the site. Mound A, the largest, is 5 m high. To the north are five smaller platforms that probably supported house structures. Mounds D, E, and F form a small patio group. Thirty meters south of the ceremonial mounds is another house group with Mounds H, I, and J arranged around a small patio. To the south an additional 80 m is a large house group with five platforms. They surround a larger patio area. No other house platforms were recorded, although it is quite possible that a more intensive search would produce a number of low mounds along the river margin near the site.

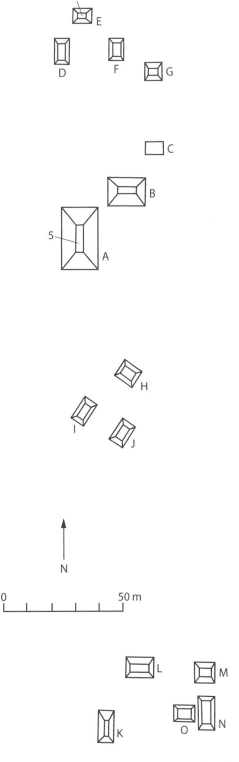

Figure 4.34. Site sketch of Co-56, Caralampio.

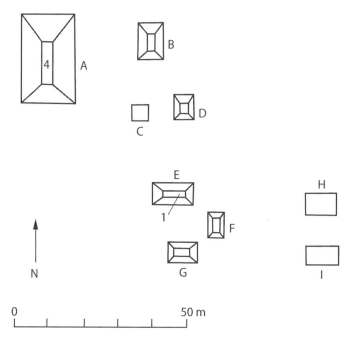

Figure 4.35. Site sketch of Co-57, San Caralampio El Vado.

CO-57 SAN CARALAMPIO EL VADO (Figure 4.35)

Site Type: Ceremonial and habitation

Location and Setting: Co-57 is located 1.25 km northwest of Colonia San Caralampio. The site is situated on a low hill, 500 m west of Río Santo Domingo in an area of gently rolling hills. Vegetation in the area consists mainly of grasses, and the land is used as milpa and pasture.

Environmental Stratum: Fields or Pastures

Description: The few structures at the site include a large pyramid mound (A) 4 m high on an altar platform (C) and several other platforms that were probably house mounds. One group includes Mounds E, F, and G, arranged about a small patio. Mound H and I were lower mounds that formed a small house group. These mounds all appear to be contemporaneous since they have the same orientation.

CO-58 ENCIERRA DE ESTORAQUE (Figure 4.36)

Site Type: Ceremonial and habitation

Occupation: Early Classic, Late Classic

Location and Setting: Co-58 is located 2 km northwest of Colonia San Caralampio on the road to Colonia Tierra Blanca. The site is situated in an area of gently rolling hills approximately 600 m west of Río Santo Domingo. Vegetation in the site area consists mainly of grasses.

Environmental Stratum: Riparian Forest

Description: Encierra de Estoraque is a large site with three distinct zones of construction. The western one is situated on a ridge several meters above the surrounding level terrain. Mound A is the largest mound on the ridge and was probably a temple platform. It is flanked on either end by two smaller platforms. South of it is a small house group (Mounds F, G, and H), which may have formed an elite house group located on the ridge. Two additional small platforms sit on the north end of the ridge. To the east and overlooked by Mound A is a large ballcourt (I).

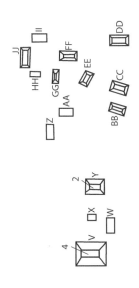

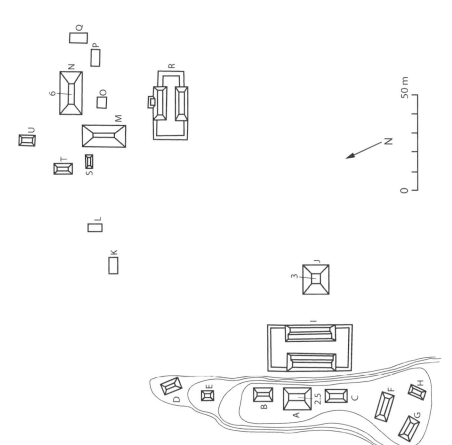

Figure 4.36. Site sketch of Co-58, Encierra de Estoraque.

Directly opposite it is another small pyramid (J) which is 3 m high.

Approximately 150 m east of this group is another mound group that consists primarily of a ceremonial plaza and associated mounds. The largest (N) is 6 m high. Mound M is also a large temple mound and adjacent to it and Mound N is a small square platform (O) that was probably an altar. An I-shaped ballcourt (R) forms the south side of the plaza. Several smaller platforms (e.g., P and Q) surround this mound group and were probably house platforms.

The eastern group of mounds begins another 100 m to the east. It has a small ceremonial precinct with Mounds V and Y that flank a small plaza with a central altar platform (X). Further east are a number of small platforms forming a series of tightly nucleated house groups.

All three groups have quite different layouts and could therefore be from different time periods. Alternately, they may represent individual social groups within one contemporaneous site.

CO-59 GUAJILAR
(Figures 4.37-4.40)

Site Type: Ceremonial and habitation

Ceramic Phase: Guajilar, Ix, Mix

Occupation: Late Preclassic, Protoclassic, Late Classic, Early Postclassic, Late Postclassic

Location and Setting: The site is located 3.6 km southeast of Colonial San Caralampio. The site is situated on the west bank of Río Santo Domingo in an area of gently rolling plain. The site of Niagara (Co-16) lies across the river. Vegetation in the area consists of dense riparian growth along the river channel.

Environmental Stratum: Riparian Forest

Description: The ceremonial center and surrounding residences cover approximately 16 ha. The site is laid out in a linear fashion with the six large mounds parallel to the Río Santo Domingo at approximately 70 degrees west of north. The largest mound is 17 m in height (42). A large 14 m high mound (54) is located off-line

Figure 4.37. Ceiba tree at Co-59, Guajilar.

40 m west of the axis along which the six largest mounds are aligned. The main plaza is bordered by two of the axial mounds while flanked to the northeast by a large 3 m high platform and to the southwest by a 4 m high mound. The plaza is completely enclosed by terraces and appears to be sunken below the level of the surrounding surface. Two ballcourts are present. One defines a secondary plaza along with Mounds 29 and 42; the other, a T-shaped ballcourt, is found on the backside of Mound 50 and faces Mound 42. Forty house mounds were recorded during the mapping at the site; more were noted beyond the perimeter of the area mapped.

Two field seasons were undertaken by the NWAF in 1976 and 1978. Excavations in Mound 51 uncovered a cache with 39 jade celts and a

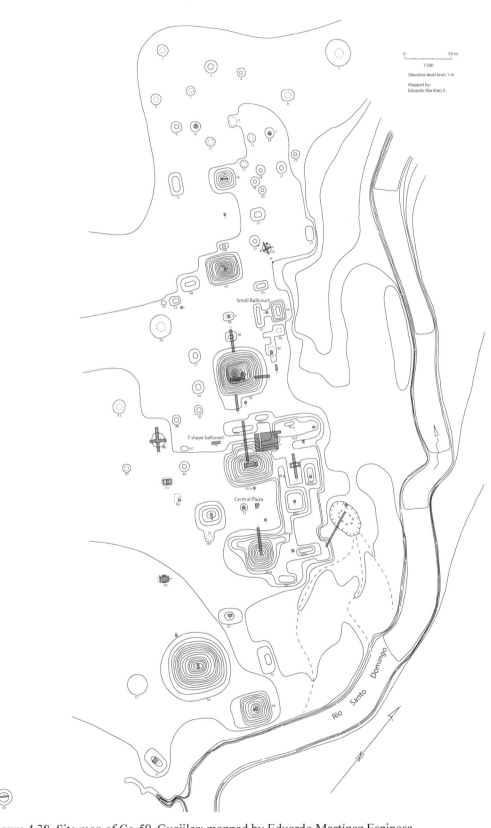

Figure 4.38. Site map of Co-59, Guajilar; mapped by Eduardo Martínez Espinosa.

Figure 4.39. Co-59, Guajilar. Environment near Río Santo Domingo.

Figure 4.40. Río Santo Domingo at the edge of site Co-59, Guajilar.

large mollusk shell full of jade and shell beads, which dates to the Late Preclassic period.

References: Blake 2010:270-271; Lee 1985; Lee and Bryant 1996:63; Wells 2015

CO-60 (Figure 4.41)

Site Type: Ceremonial

Occupation: Middle Preclassic, Late Classic

Location and Setting: Co-60 is located 1.75 km north and slightly west of Colonia Joaquín Miguel Gutiérrez. The site is situated in the valley on the west bank of Río San Gregorio. Vegetation in the site area consists mainly of grasses, with riparian growth near the river.

Environmental Stratum: Riparian Forest

Description: Only three mounds were recorded at this site. The largest (A) is 7 m high. Together with two additional mounds measuring 3 and 5 m in height, respectively (C and B), the group forms an open plaza.

References: Lee 1985

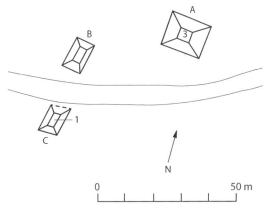

Figure 4.42. Site sketch of Co-61, San Gregorio.

CO-61 SAN GREGORIO (Figure 4.42)

Site Type: Ceremonial and habitation

Occupation: possible Late Preclassic, Late Classic

Location and Setting: On the margins of the Río San Gregorio, approximately 400 m east from the main road to Comitan-Ciudad Cuauhtemoc.

Environmental Stratum: Riparian Forest

Description: Three mounds present, the largest was 3 m in height. Five smaller mounds were noted west of the main mound but were not mapped.

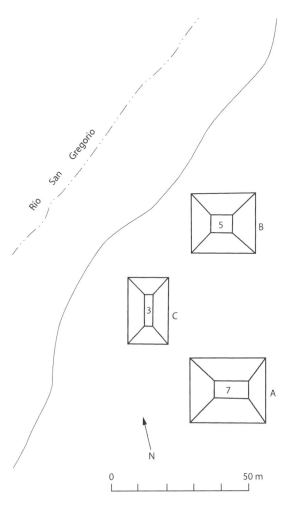

Figure 4.41. Site sketch of Co-60.

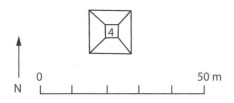

Figure 4.43. Site sketch of Co-62, Santa María Esquintenango (Bebedero El Reparo).

CO-62 SANTA MARÍA ESQUINTENANGO (BEBEDERO EL REPARO) (Figure 4.43)

Site Type: Ceremonial?

Occupation: Late Classic, Late Postclassic, Colonial

Location and Setting: Located 300 m west or south from the Río Santo Domingo, approximately 1 km north of San Caralampio.

Environmental Stratum: Fields or Pastures

Description: Site consists of a single mound 4 m in height.

CO-63 SANTA MARÍA ESQUINTENANGO (Figure 4.44-4.45)

Site Type: Ceremonial

Ceramic Phase: Guajil, Mix

Occupation: Late Preclassic, Late Classic

Location and Setting: Located in a long narrow bend or oxbow of the Río San Gregorio, approximately 3.5 km east of Tierra Blanca.

Environmental Stratum: Riparian Forest

Description: The site consists of 13 primary mounds with 3 smaller platforms on the eastern edge (N-P). The layout likely reflects the different occupations at the site. There is a central plaza, although not sharply defined, given the placement of Platform F and Mound C. The largest mound (H), located in the northern quadrant, appears to have had projections or perhaps stairways on four sides. A well-defined ballcourt (D) lies on the east side of the site.

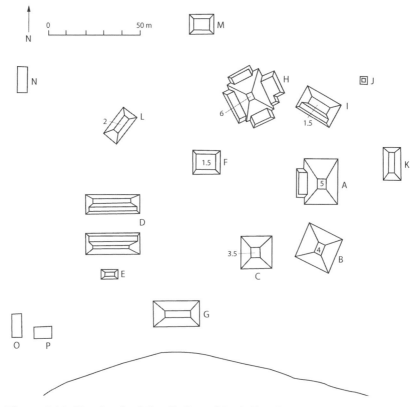

Figure 4.44. Site sketch of Co-63, Santa María Esquintenango.

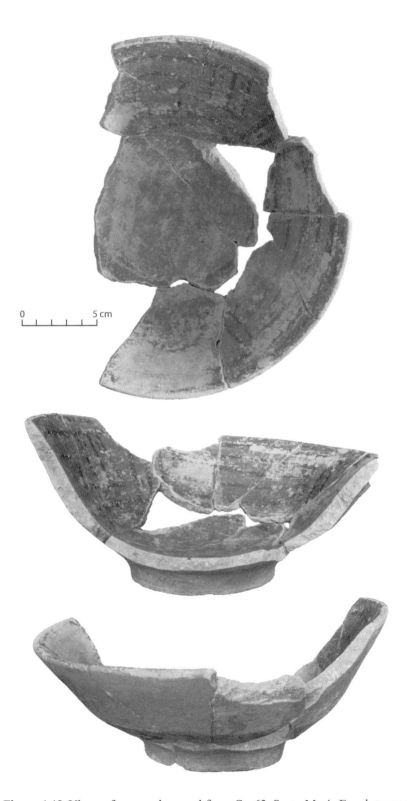

Figure 4.45. Views of a ceramic vessel from Co-63, Santa María Esquintenango.

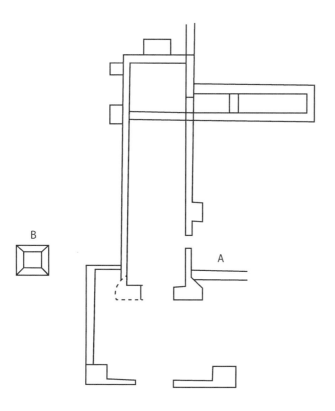

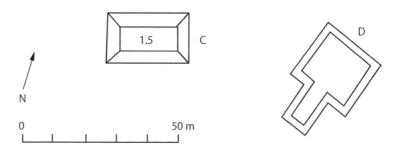

Figure 4.46. Site sketch of Co-64, Santa María Esquintenango (Colonial).

CO-64 Santa María Esquintenango (Colonial)
(Figure 4.46)

Site Type: Ceremonial

Occupation: Colonial

Location and Setting: Site is located some 50 m from the Río San Gregorio near a series of sharp bends in the river. It lies approximately 2 km northeast from San Caralampio.

Environmental Stratum: Riparian Forest

Description: Site consists of the remains of a Colonial church and three additional mounds.

References: Markman 1984

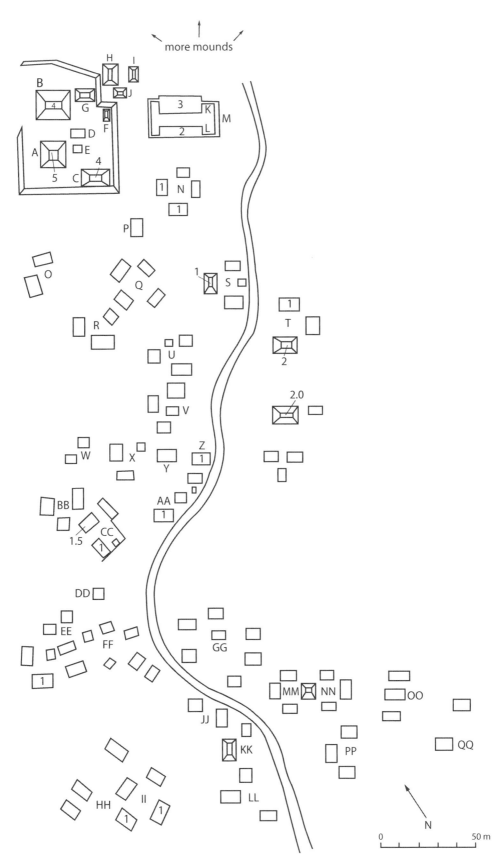

Figure 4.47. Site sketch of Co-65.

CO-65 (Figure 4.47)

Site Type: Ceremonial and habitation

Occupation: Late Classic

Location and Setting: Located 2.5 km south of San Caralampio and 3.6 km west of the Río Santo Domingo. Site area is densely vegetated gently rolling valley lands

Environmental Stratum: Tropical Deciduous Forest

Description: This large ceremonial center and habitation site is spread over a wide area, at least 500 m by 200 m, with more housemounds apparent to the north, east, and south, which were not included in the sketch map. Still, over 100 housemounds were drawn, comprising at least a dozen or more identifiable house groups.

The ceremonial center of the site is located in the northern section of the map, with an area of some 120 by 75 m. Seven mounds are located atop a square platform, the largest three measuring 5 (A) and 4 (B, C) m in height, respectively. To the east of this compound is a well-defined I-shaped ballcourt. A group of three smaller mounds (H, I, J) are located just below the platform mound group to the northeast.

Two crossed-arms sculptures were also reported to have come from this site and were purportedly taken to the municipal building of San Caralampio.

CO-66 (Figure 4.48)

Site Type: Habitation

Occupation: Protoclassic, Late Classic

Location and Setting: Located 0.5 km east of San Caralampio and approximately 100 m south of the Río Santo Domingo.

Environmental Stratum: Riparian Forest

Description: Site consists of two house platforms.

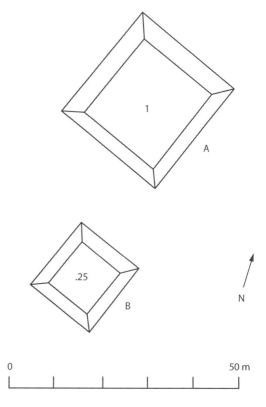

Figure 4.48. Site sketch of Co-66.

CO-67 SINALOA (Figure 4.49)

Site Type: Ceremonial and habitation

Occupation: Protoclassic, Late Classic

Location and Setting: Located approximately 1 km southeast of Colonia Sinaloa, along the bank of the Arroyo El Zapotal.

Environmental Stratum: Riparian Forest

Description: The site is oriented northeast-southwest over an area of at least 290 by 60 m. Currently, the site is divided among three ranchos: the northern section lies in Rancho el Zapote; the middle in La Chaperna, and the southern in Encierro de la Mora. Over 30 mounds were drawn with three possible ceremonial precincts apparent in the northern, middle, and southern sections. The middle section has an I-shaped ballcourt.

Cremated remains in a large olla were located between two altars near Mound F.

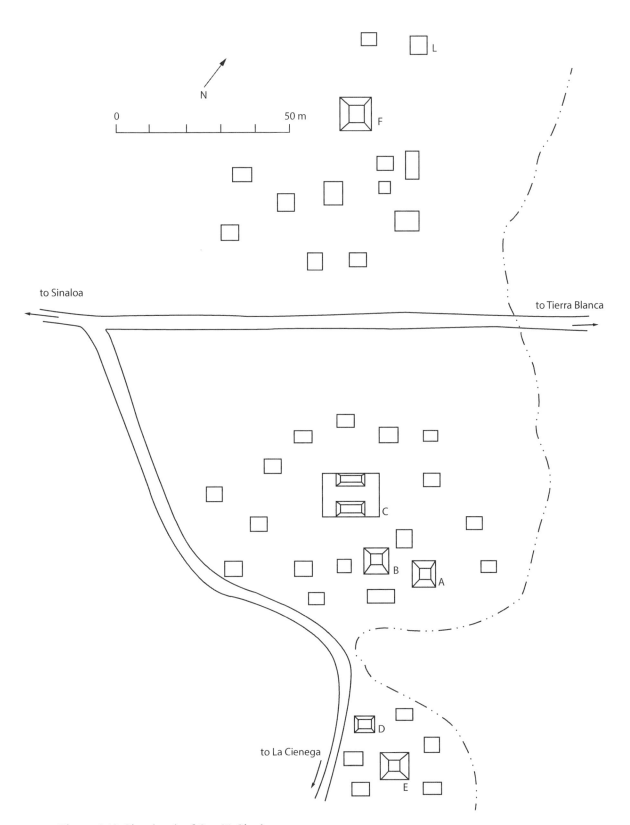

Figure 4.49. Site sketch of Co-67, Sinaloa.

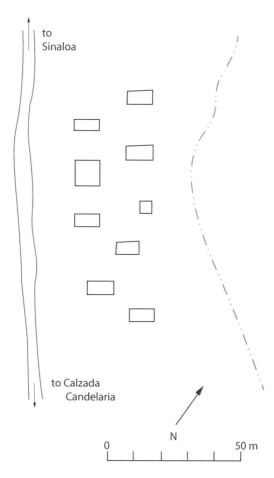

Figure 4.50. Site sketch of Co-68, Buena Vista el Zapote.

CO-68 BUENA VISTA EL ZAPOTE (Figure 4.50)

Site Type: Habitation

Location and Setting: Located on the eastern outskirts of Colonia Sinaloa, along the banks of a dry arroyo.

Environmental Stratum: Tropical Deciduous Forest

Description: Nine housemounds were noted, although the vegetation was dense and would have covered the remains of other low-lying occupations. The bases of the nine mounds had 2-3 rows of stone foundations.

CO-69 JOCOTE (Figure 4.51)

Site Type: Ceremonial and habitation

Occupation: Late Preclassic, Late Classic

Location and Setting: Located on the edge of the Pan-American Highway, approximately 0.5 km north of El Ocotal (Ciudad Cuauhtemoc) on the left side of the road. The ruins are near the intersection of the highway going east (and ultimately south) to the coast. The area is valley floor near the bank of the Río Ocote.

Environmental Stratum: Tropical Deciduous Forest

Description: Site consists of three mounds, one of which was partially destroyed by the construction of the Pan-American Highway. The exposed section of the mound revealed several building phases, each constructed of stone and fill, and with walls faced with river cobbles and adobe plaster.

The two undisturbed parallel mounds, 1.5 to 2.0 m in height, comprise a ballcourt with open ends. The long axis is north-south and playing alley measures 7 m wide and 24 m long.

References: Shook 1956:23, 37

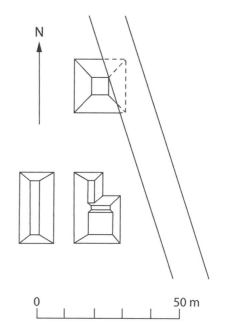

Figure 4.51. Site sketch of Co-69, Jocote.

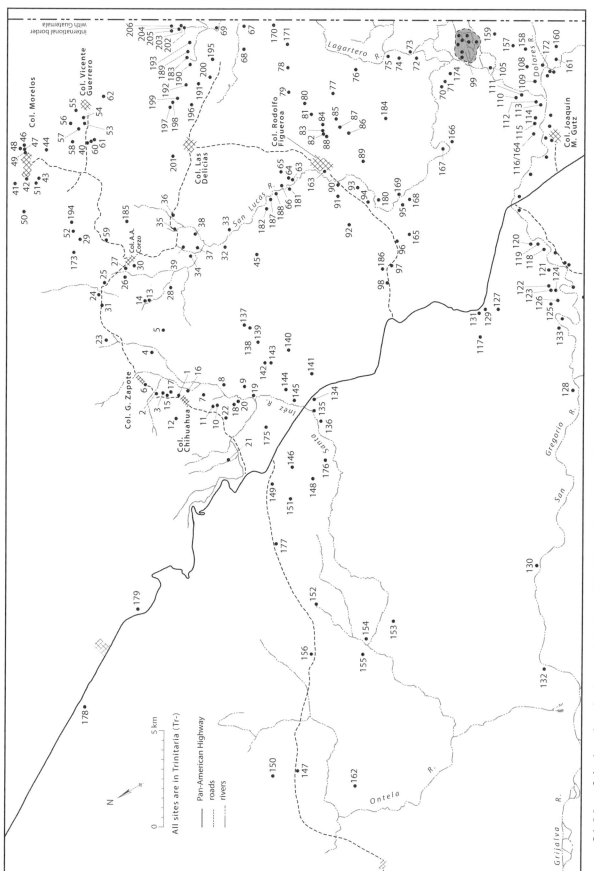

Figure 5.1. Map of site locations in the municipality of La Trinitaria (1 to 107) discussed in Chapter 5 (close-up of map in Figure 1.7).

CHAPTER 5

SITE DESCRIPTIONS: MUNICIPIO LA TRINITARIA TR-1 TO TR-107

Michael Blake, Thomas A. Lee Jr., James M. White, John E. Clark, and Mary E. Pye

TR-1 CHALIB (Figure 5.2)

Site Type: Ceremonial and habitation

Ceramic Phase: Mix

Occupation: Late Classic, Early Postclassic

Location and Setting: The site is located approximately 200 m northeast of the center of Colonia Chihuahua and 400 m west of a branch of Río Santa Inés. It is in an area of low rolling hills covered by low trees, shrubs, and grassland. There is a good spring approximately 100 m north of the site.

Environmental Stratum: Short Tree Savannah/ Thorn Woodland, Riparian Forest

Description: This site consists of four separate groups of archaeological features. The largest group (Inset 1) contains nine mounds and a system of terraces. Most of these mounds, except perhaps the tallest one (Mound I) are residence platforms. They are arranged in clusters that may have been house groups: A and B to the west form a loose group; C, D, and E may have outlined a central patio; F is relatively isolated on the edge of Terrace K; and G, H, and I outline a large patio facing Terrace J. Most of Terrace K and all of Terrace L had no evidence of habitation structures. Many of the structures in this group appear to have similar orientations on north-south, east-west axes. They are also linked together by the terrace network (J, K, and L), with the exception of Mounds A and B. The other three groups are much less complex. Two residential mounds (Inset 3) are located 240 m east of the main group. These mounds probably form the northern and western boundaries of a patio. Another cluster of three house mounds (Inset 2) is located 420 m northeast of the main group. These three mounds also form a house group. They are on the edge of a deep sinkhole 10 m in diameter. The last group (Inset 4) is

located only 150 m northwest of Mound A in the main group. It contains the largest mound on the site (M), which is 4 m tall and 20 m by 20 m at the base. A double-tiered mound (N) was located 20 m to the northwest and a possible house platform (O) was associated with it. All of the mounds are upslope from a 50 m long terrace.

None of the groups of mounds at the site appear to be obviously related to the others, and it is difficult to tell if they were even contemporaneous. Alignments vary from group to group and even within the main group.

References: de Montmollin 1989c:133-134, 174-175

TR-2 CASTELLANO (Figure 5.3)

Site Type: Ceremonial and habitation

Ceramic Phase: Mix

Occupation: possible Early Classic, Late Classic

Location and Setting: This site is situated 1 km west of Colonia Guadalupe Zapote on the west side of Arroyo Castellanos which has permanent water flow. The site straddles both sides of the road that runs between Guadalupe Zapote and Colonia Chihuahua. It lies on a ridge that runs north-south along the arroyo and overlooks an area of rolling hills. There is riparian forest in the arroyo but the surrounding land is used as milpa.

Environmental Stratum: Short Tree Savannah/ Thorn Woodland, Riparian Forest

Description: The ridge that runs along the west side of Arroyo Castellano is covered for a length of 530 m by temple mounds, platforms and terraces. There are at least nine terrace structures, eight house platforms, four temple mounds, one ballcourt, and one altar. The main ceremonial complex sits on the highest part of the ridge (Structures A through G) and is situated in the central part of the site. The tallest mound (D) is

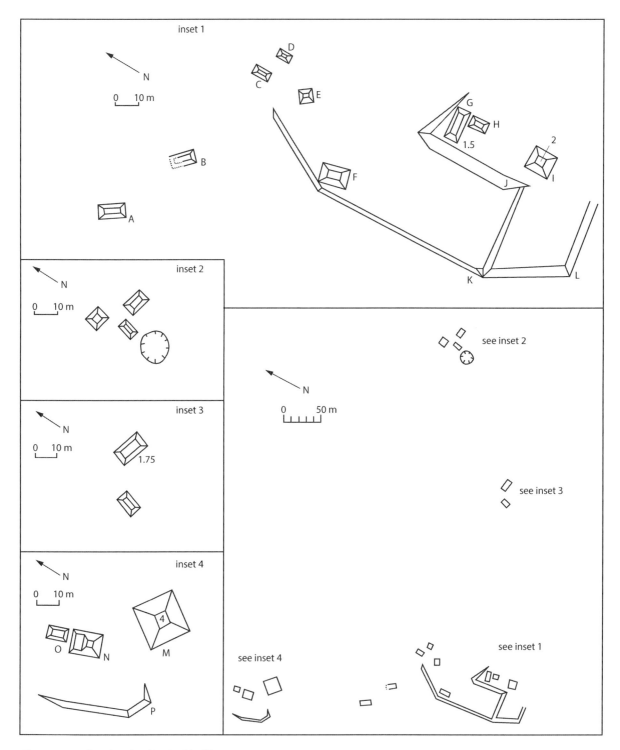

Figure 5.2. Site sketch of Tr-1, Chalib.

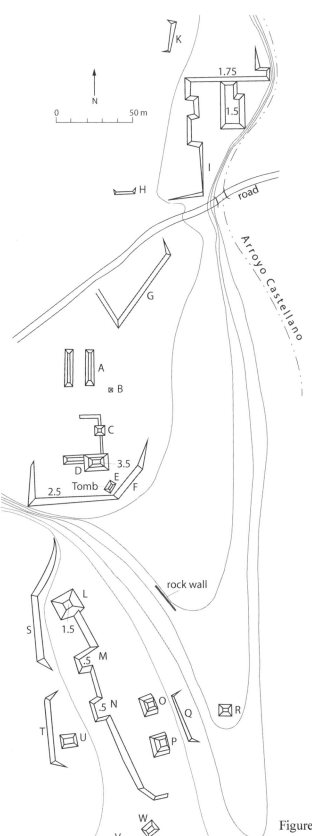

Figure 5.3. Site sketch of Tr-2, Castellano.

3.5 m high and is linked to two other mounds; one is a low platform extension and the other (Mound C) is connected by a low rock wall. These outline the central plaza area. An open-ended ballcourt (A) sits at the northern edge of the plaza area and is flanked on the southeastern side by a small altar (B). This whole complex is bounded on the south by a long 2.5 m high terrace (Terrace F). A small platform mound (E) had been looted and showed evidence of having held a tomb.

Extending north from the ballcourt are a series of long terraces that probably provided level ground for residences overlooking the arroyo to the east. Terrace G is 60 m long and Terrace I provides two protruding platform terraces that face onto a plaza area overlooking the arroyo. Structure J is an L-shaped mound in the center of the plaza and is one of the largest mounds at the site.

The portion of the site to the south of the central complex includes structures L to V and is located on a natural terrace downslope from the ballcourt group. This portion has three levels of terracing: S-T, N-M, and Q. The S-T terraces extend north-south for 150 m and only have one mound on the surface they provide (Mound U). The M-N terrace is about 130 m long, runs parallel to S-T and terminates at the north in a large mound (L). The points on the terrace indicated by the letters M and N are possibly house platforms protruding downslope. Two larger temple mounds (O and P) are located 25 m upslope from this terrace and are partially built into the hill on their eastern sides.

The extensive use of terraces over the entire site, its linear arrangement, and the consistent orientation of the mounds in the central group all suggest that most of the structures were contemporaneous.

References: de Montmollin 1989c:111-112

TR-3 TRAPICHE VIEJO (Figure 5.4)

Site Type: Ceremonial and habitation

Ceramic Phase: Chacaj, Mix

Occupation: Early Preclassic, Late Classic

Location and Setting: This site is located 1.1 km northeast of the eastern edge of Colonia

Chihuahua on the south side of the dirt road between that community and Colonia Guadalupe Zapote. The site is in an area of open undulating terrain with some minor arroyos nearby. Most of the short tree forest in the area has been cleared for cornfields and pasture. It is midway between Tr-1 (Chalib) and Tr-2 (Castellano), each a kilometer away.

Environmental Stratum: Short Tree Savannah/ Thorn Woodland, Riparian Forest

Description: The site is a scattered collection of small mounds ranging from 0.5 m to 2.0 m in height. There are small clusters of mounds which may be domestic groups, as well as many mounds that appear to be relatively isolated from their neighbors. Two mounds (A and B) may form a patio group. Four mounds (C through F) and two associated terraces (G and H) are also arranged in a cluster around an open level area. The mounds in this group have a similar orientation to each other but offset 45 degrees from the A-B group 60 m to the north. The mounds I, J and K also form a cluster oriented the same direction as the C-F group but separated by about 35 to 40 m. This group contains the largest mound (J) which is both the tallest and has the largest basal dimensions (23 by 15 m). Several other mounds (M through Q) form the southern edge of the site but are not grouped and all have different orientations from each other and the other groups. This suggests that the structures at the site may not be contemporaneous or, if they are, that the site layout was unplanned.

References: de Montmollin 1989c:78-80, 109-111

TR-4 CHULTÚN (Figure 5.5)

Site Type: Ceremonial and habitation

Ceramic Phase: Mix

Occupation: Middle Classic, Late Classic

Location and Setting: The site is located 1 km southeast of Colonia Guadalupe Zapote. It is in a hilly area with thick small tree and brush cover. Within 200 m on either side of the site are several intermittent stream channels that flow south eventually linking up with Río Santa Inés.

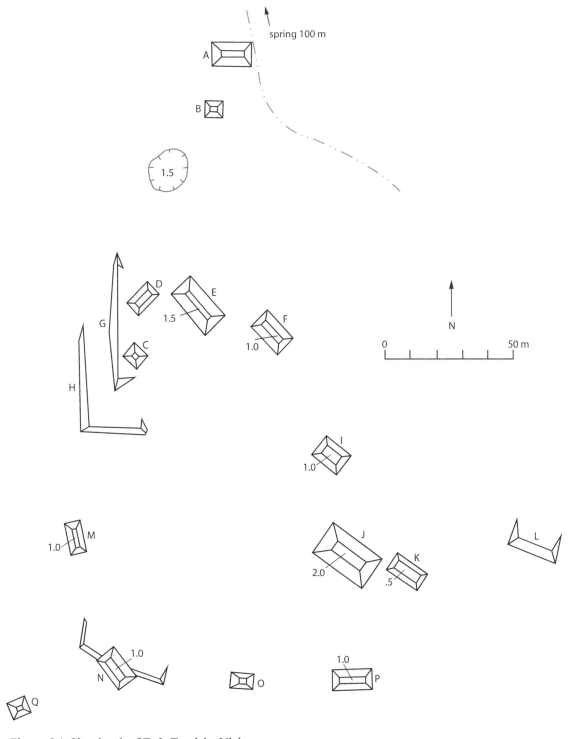

Figure 5.4. Site sketch of Tr-3, Trapiche Viejo.

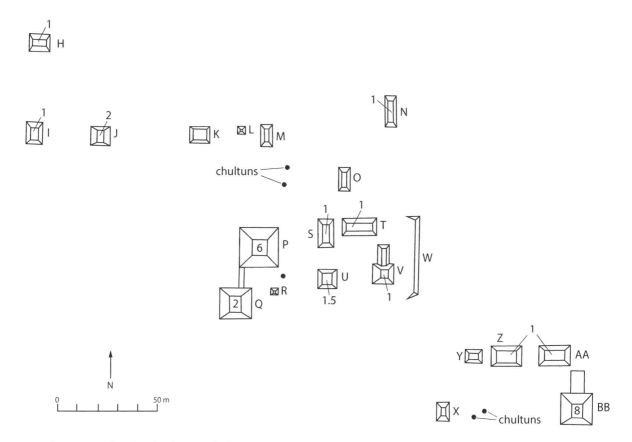

Figure 5.5. Site sketch of Tr-4, Chultún.

Environmental Stratum: Short Tree Savannah/ Thorn Woodland

Description: The site consists of three main groups of temple mounds, house platforms, terraces and *chultunes*. The northern group is 120 m north of the central group and consists of six mounds and a terrace (A through G). The terrace (G) probably supported a residential structure on the hill slope. The largest mound in this group (B) is only 2 m high. Another mound (C) is low but has an additional low mound extending from its eastern side. Together with D it may form a domestic group. Mounds E and F may also be an associated domestic group.

The central group of mounds is the largest (H through W). There are several tight clusters of mounds surrounding plaza areas, as well as some more isolated mounds (e.g., H, I, J, and N). Mounds K, M, and O seem to face onto a plaza area which contains two chultunes and a possible altar (L) between K and M. Just 20 m to the south of this group is a well-arranged cluster of platforms with a large temple mound (P). Mound P is linked by a terrace to another large mound (Q) and, along with Mound U, they form a plaza area with a central altar (R) and a chultún. Another plaza area to the east is formed by Mounds S, T, U, V, and Terrace W.

Another group of mounds (X to BB) is located 50 m southeast of the central group. This group forms a well-defined plaza area that contains two chultunes and has the south side open. The largest pyramid at the site (BB) is located in this group. It has a low platform extending northwards.

All three groups, although separated from each other seem to be systematically arranged with the main axes of each mound oriented to the same directions. It is likely that the whole site represents a contemporaneous unit.

References: de Montmollin 1989c: 67-69, 125-126

TR-5 LA TRINIDAD (Figure 5.6)

Site Type: Ceremonial and habitation

Ceramic Phase: Mix

Occupation: Late Classic

Location and Setting: This site is located 2.5 km southeast of Colonia Guadalupe Zapote. It is situated at the southern edge of a high, flat mesa. The surrounding terrain is under milpa cultivation. Pine-covered ridges are located within 0.5 km to the northeast and southwest of the site.

Environmental Stratum: Short Tree Savannah/ Thorn Woodland

Description: This site consists of one stepped pyramid, five low platforms, and two terrace features. The whole complex is located close to the southern edge of the mesa, hence the terracing. The complex is arranged in a linear manner along the central axis of the mesa.

The mounds appear to be divided into three groups, each consisting of two mounds arranged around possible plaza or patio areas. Each group is separated by ca. 20-30 m. The central group includes a large two-level temple mound that measures 2 m on the lower level and 4 m on the upper level; this mound faces across a plaza to a low rectangular mound (B). This mound pair is partially enclosed by a long zigzagging terrace (H). The terrace appears to provide level ground for mounds A and B, and possibly for other structures not visible on the surface.

A second pair of mounds (C and D) is located 30 m northwest of the central group. These two low rectangular mounds, which have the appearance of being arranged around a patio, were probably a residential compound.

A third pair of mounds (F and E) is located at the southern end of the site near the mesa edge. Associated with this pair is another terrace, which extends out of the southern corner of Mound F. The terrace appears to follow the southern contour of the mesa, providing level ground for the E/F pair. Although the pair is not as tightly clustered as the C/D pair, it is probably another residential compound.

The linear arrangement of the three mound groups, along the central axis of the ridge, and the regular spacing between mound groups, suggests that they were built according to a plan. Judging by the contour of the ridge and the location of the terraces, it is probable that the structure of the site is dictated more by the natural contour of the mesa than by formal considerations.

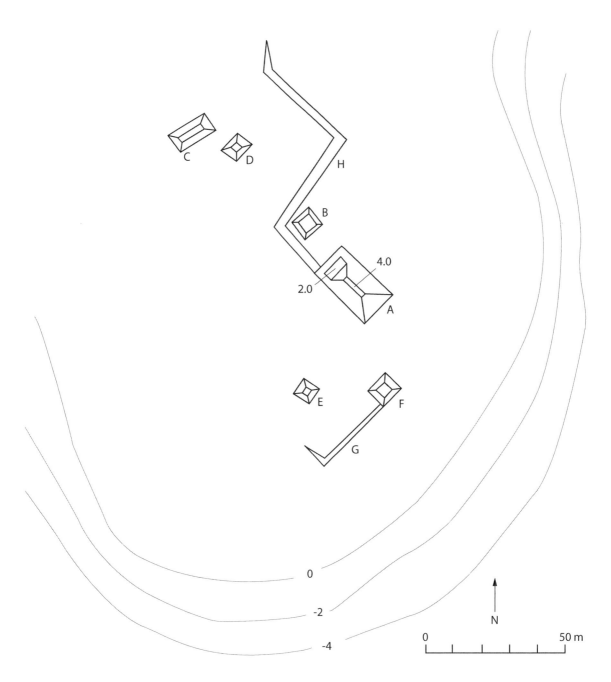

Figure 5.6. Site sketch of Tr-5, La Trinidad.

TR-6 GUADALUPE ZAPOTE (Figure 5.7)

Site Type: Ceremonial and habitation

Ceramic Phase: Mix

Occupation: Late Classic

Location and Setting: The site is located on the western edge of Colonia Guadalupe Zapote, straddling the road leading west to Colonia Chihuahua. Archaeological features were observed at the southern base of a small hill, and there may be some terracing on the southern slope of the hill. The local topography is hilly country. An arroyo is the main water source for Colonia Guadalupe Zapote. The local vegetation consists of low tree cover with some milpa.

Environmental Stratum: Short Tree Savannah/Thorn Woodland, Riparian Forest

Description: The site consists of four mounds, and three small terraces. The visible extent of the site is approximately 150 m by 80 m. In addition, there may be more terraces up the slope.

The largest structure (A) is a rectangular mound measuring 2 m high. It is located at the base of the hill, in a slightly prominent position relative to the other mounds. Just 25 m south of A on a flat spot at the base of the hill is another large low mound (B), measuring 14 m by 17 m and 1 m high. Two small mounds (C and D), situated side-by-side, are located 70 m west of B. These may have been house platforms or perhaps altars.

In addition to the group of mounds, three terraces are visible at the base of the slope. Although there are no architectural remains visible on the terraces, the fact that there are structures directly downslope of them suggests they were not agricultural terraces but were used to support house platforms.

Both the layout and the orientation of structures and terraces appear to be governed by the contour of the hillslope, rather than to formal considerations. The site was probably a residential hamlet with a small ceremonial precinct.

References: de Montmollin 1989c:107-108

TR-7 PROVIDENCIA (Figure 5.8)

Site Type: Habitation

Ceramic Phase: Mix

Occupation: Late Classic

Location and Setting: The site is located 1 km directly south of Colonia Chihuahua, in an area of flat plain dotted with isolated knolls. Providencia sits atop a large knoll surrounded by flat plain. Approximately 400 m to the east flows Río Santa Inés. The local vegetation is characterized by grass, low bushes, and an occasional mulato tree (*Bursera* sp.).

Environmental Stratum: Short Tree Savannah/Thorn Woodland, Riparian Forest

Description: The site consists of a tight cluster of 13 low mounds and one terrace, concentrated on the wide southern portion of the knoll. The maximum extent of visible features measures 50 m northeast-southwest by 55 m northwest-southeast.

There appear to be two types of mounds on the site: long, low, rectangular mounds and small square mounds. There is little variation in the size or height within these two classes. The long, rectangular mounds, which probably represent residential structures for the most part, range in size from 8 to 10 m by 4 to 6 m. Most are approximately 0.5 m in height. Two exceptions to this pattern are Mounds A and J. Mound A, located in the center of the site, is 1.5 m high. Its central location and slightly prominent height suggest that it may be a communal structure of civic or ceremonial significance. Mound J, at the western edge of the site is 1 m high, slightly higher than the others. This structure was built on uneven ground, and an attempt has been made to keep the building level by constructing walls of different heights. This probably accounts for the greater height of the mound relative to the others.

The square mounds are mostly very small. Three of these (L, M, and N) are circa 2 m by 2 m and only 0.25 m high. Its greater dimensions, as well as its proximity to Mound A suggest that it may be part of a civic/ceremonial complex.

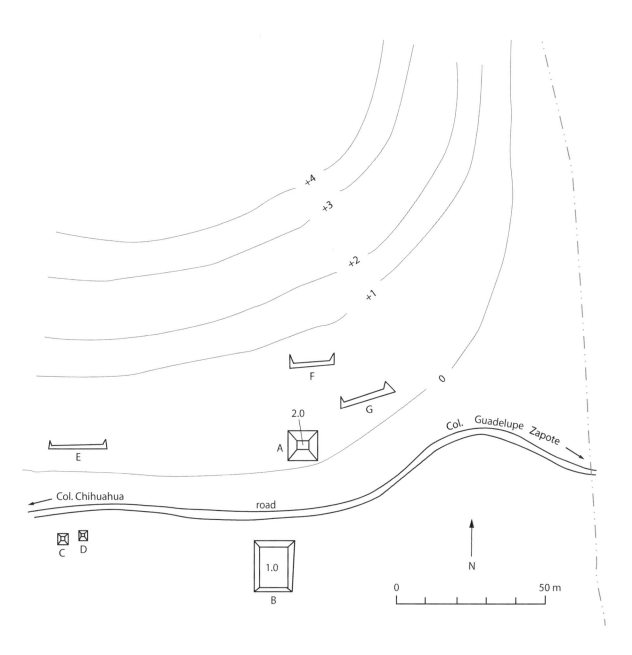

Figure 5.7. Site sketch of Tr-6, Guadalupe Zapote.

Structure H is a terrace near the edge of the hill and may have held a house.

There appear to be at least two groups of mounds arranged around patios or plazas. In the central area, mounds A, B, C, D, E, (and possibly even F) appear to be arranged around a large open area (O), suggesting that the structures may have functioned together as a group. A second group (J, K, and L) appears

to be organized around a patio area (P). This probably represents a domestic compound. Structures M and N are probably small outbuildings or features associated with either of these plaza/patio groupings.

The overall uniformity of structure orientation suggests that the site could have been constructed as a single planned unit. All structures are oriented either parallel or at

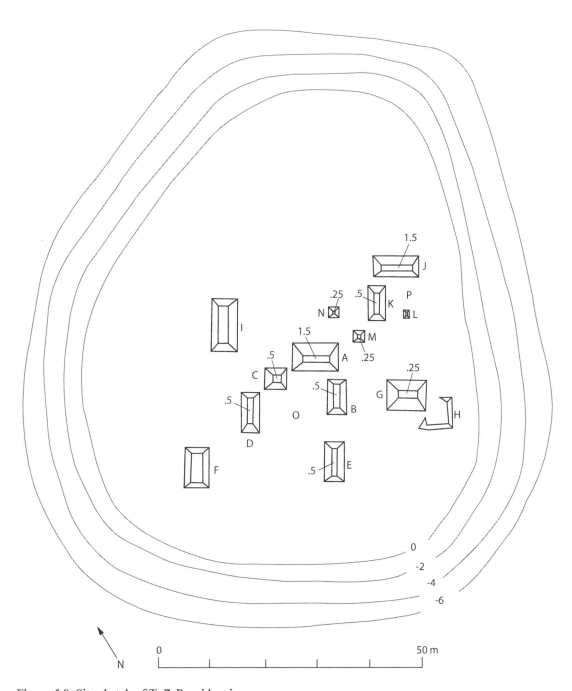

Figure 5.8. Site sketch of Tr-7, Providencia.

right angles to each other, along the northeast-southwest central axis of the hilltop.

The site appears to be a small residential hamlet, with some possible ceremonial activity centered around Mound A. Some minor artificial modification of the landscape is indicated by the terrace (H) and Mound J.

References: de Montmollin 1989c:175-176

TR-8 (Figure 5.9)

Site Type: Habitation

Ceramic Phase: Mix

Occupation: Early Classic, Late Classic

Location and Setting: This site is located some 2 km southwest of Colonia Chihuahua, and 1 km south of Tr-7. The local topography around the site consists of a flat plain dotted with isolated knolls. Tr-8 is situated atop of one such low knoll. Río Santa Inés flows 100 m west of Tr-8. The local vegetation is predominantly grasses, bushes and isolated trees.

Environmental Stratum: Short Tree Savannah/ Thorn Woodland, Riparian Forest

Description: The site consists of a series of low rectangular mounds. Six mounds were recorded and more, of similar size and shape, were observed on the southern portion of the site. The latter were not recorded because heavy brush cover obscured their visibility.

Of those recorded, there appear to be three pairs of mounds. Each of these consists of a larger mound and a smaller mound. The large mounds range in size from 7 by 4 m (A), 5 by 5 m (C), and 7 by 6 m (E). The small mounds range from 2.5 by 2.5 m (B, D) to 6 by 4 m (F). No mound exceeds 2.5 m in height. The house groups are arranged around patios. This is especially true of the C/D and the E/F pair. The site appears to be a small residential hamlet, with no ceremonial precinct.

References: de Montmollin 1989c:178-179

TR-9 TENAM ROSARIO (Figures 5.10-5.11)

Site Type: Ceremonial and habitation

Ceramic Phase: Kau, Mix

Occupation: Early Classic, Middle Classic, Late Classic, Postclassic

Location and Setting: This large center is located 3.2 km south of Colonia Chihuahua on the west side of Río Santa Inés (sometimes known as Rosario). It is located on a hilltop approximately 100 m above the river valley and surrounding terrain. The hilltop is accessible on all sides only by a steep climb from the valley bottom. There is an extremely rocky and shallow soil cover on the site, which has led to its protection from agricultural use. Agrinier (n.d.:12) has written of the vegetation: ". . .the site is now covered by thick underbrush and fairly large trees which are the main source of the thin layer of humus covering the rock formation. The vegetation has been very much undisturbed due to the shallowness of the soil which makes the place unfit for agriculture. It probably offers a good example of the original flora of the surrounding area and it is now being set aside as wood reserve by the inhabitants of the Colonia Chihuahua. The surrounding valley bottom has been almost completely used for modern agricultural purposes since there are deep fertile alluvial soils..."

Environmental Stratum: Short Tree Savannah/ Thorn Forest

Description: Archaeological work at the site from 1976 to 1979 by Pierre Agrinier (1979a, 1979b, 1983, 1984) of the NWAF has contributed greatly to our understanding of this important center. Subsequent work undertaken by Olivier de Montmollin (1989a, 1989b, 1989c, 1992, 1995) has focused on the settlement patterns of the wider Rosario Valley in which the site is located.

This description will present a brief summary of the intra-site settlement pattern. The main part of the site covers the hilltop plateau with divisions of approximately 300 m north-south by 500 m east-west. The entire southern and eastern edge of the plateau is surrounded by a large terrace wall, 950 m long, which may have been constructed for defense. The largest structure at the site is located near the northern edge of the plateau. It is a platform 60 m wide by 70 m long and approximately 4 m high with two long rectangular mounds at each end. On the south side of the platform is a smaller mound and opposite it on the north side are two smaller mounds that sit on a raised bench. This complex faces south onto a plaza which is flanked by two 3 m high temple mounds. To the west of this plaza and the platform temple complex is another major arrangement of structures. On both the northern and eastern sides of this plaza are double temple mounds. The southern side is bounded by a

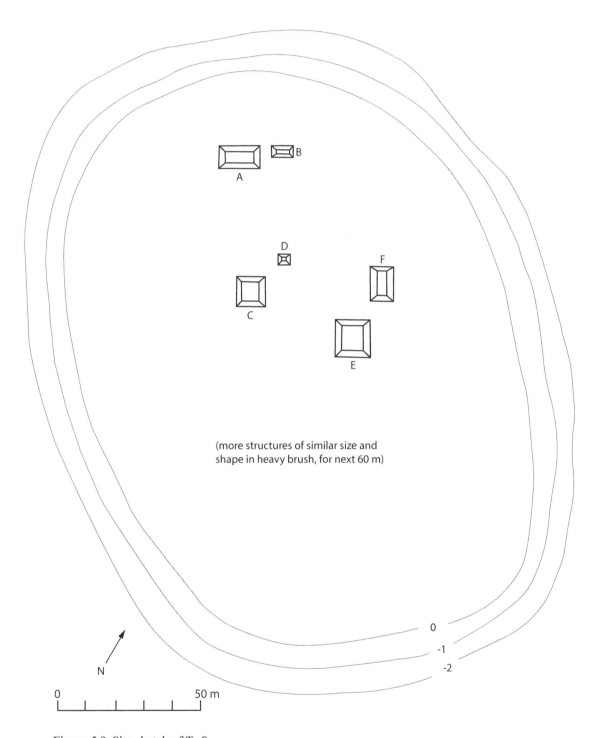

(more structures of similar size and
shape in heavy brush, for next 60 m)

N

0   50 m

Figure 5.9. Site sketch of Tr-8.

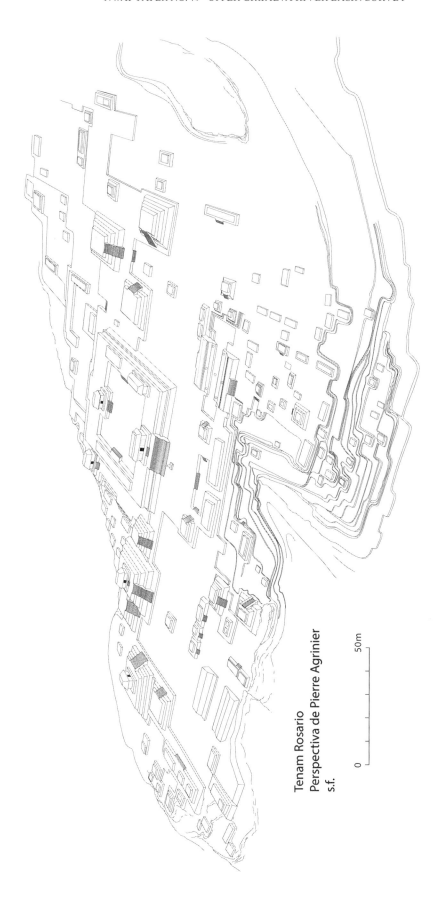

Tenam Rosario
Perspectiva de Pierre Agrinier
s.f.

50m

0

Figure 5.10. Perspective sketch of Tr-9, Tenam Rosario.

ballcourt, and a series of smaller mounds. On the eastern side of the large platform complex are another three large temple mounds ranging from 5 m to 10 m high. These partially surround a plaza that faces south onto another ballcourt. This I-shaped ballcourt has flanking mounds 25 m long and end-zones defined by smaller mounds. The end-zone to end-zone length is about 60 m. To the south of this ballcourt are at least three additional small temple mounds and at least 25 low house mounds. The major residential portion of this hilltop area within the walled zone is to the east of the temple complexes and plazas. There are at least 80 house mounds and some small temples. The house mounds range from 50 cm high to no more than 2 m high. Many of these seem to be arranged in domestic units around patios.

To the southwest of the main ceremonial complexes and outside of the main wall are located nearly 50 house mounds, many of which are built on terrace platforms. These extend for a distance of at least 200 m over a vertical drop of 60 m.

Numerous *chultunes* were found on the hilltop within the walled zone. Twenty-six of these were found within the eastern residential area, and another five or so were found in the ceremonial precinct.

The orientation of all of the mounds at the site is consistently 40 degrees east of magnetic north. This, combined with the cohesiveness of the ceremonial center, would suggest that almost the entire visible site may have been occupied simultaneously.

References: Agrinier n.d., 1979a, 1979b, 1983, 1984, 1991, 1993; Blom and Duby 1957 II:41, 42, fig. 6; de Montmollin 1989a, 1989b, 1989c:62-67, 209-210, 1992, 1995, 1997; Lee 1975:39, 1985; Lee and Bryant 1996:55; Shook 1956:23

TR-10 (Figure 5.12)

Site Type: Ceremonial

Occupation: Protoclassic

Location and Setting: Tr-10 is situated atop a knoll, approximately 1 km directly south of

Colonia Chihuahua. The knoll lies in an area of flat plain, dotted with isolated knolls. The local vegetation is characterized by grasses, low bush, and isolated trees. A small tributary of Río Santa Inés flows immediately to the east of the site.

Environmental Stratum: Short Tree Savannah/ Thorn Woodland

Description: The site consists of a single pyramid (A) and one low rectangular mound (B). The pyramid measures 12 m by 12 m and is 30 m high. The low mound is circa 5 by 8 m and 0.25 m in height. The two mounds are arranged in a straight east-west line along the central axis of the knoll, suggesting they conform to a consistent overall plan; however, the distance between the two structures suggests that they were not a single functional complex. The absence of other structures indicates that it was not a residential site but rather used primarily for ceremonial purposes.

References: de Montmollin 1989c:180

TR-11 (no map)

Site Type: Habitation

Ceramic Phase: Mix

Occupation: Late Classic

Location and Setting: This site is located 1.8 km south of the west entrance to Colonia Chihuahua and 300 m north of Tr-10. It is in an area of rolling hills on fairly level land 200 m west of a small seasonal tributary stream of Río Santa Inés. The site area is almost completely cleared of trees for both milpa and pasture purposes.

Environmental Stratum: Short Tree Savannah/ Thorn Woodland

Description: There are six low habitation mounds at this site. Unfortunately, they are almost entirely destroyed by plowing and little information concerning layout and position of the mounds was available.

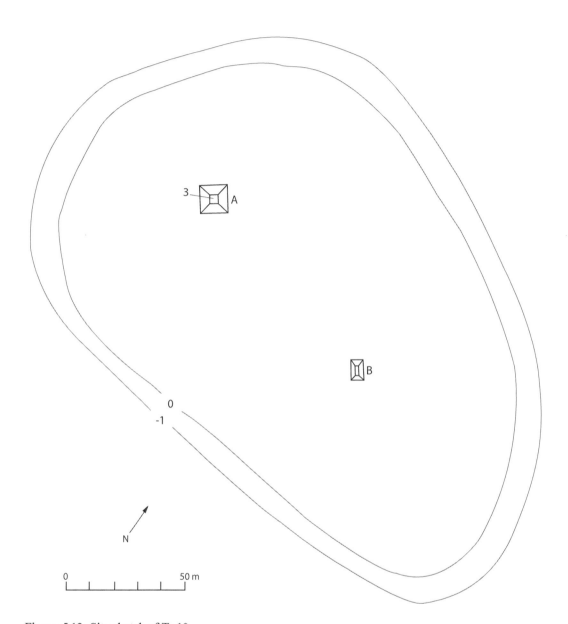

Figure 5.12. Site sketch of Tr-10.

TR-12 CUEVA DE LOS NEGROS (no map)
(Figure 5.13)

Site Type: Cave

Occupation: Postclassic

Location and Setting: This cave is located 2.3 km northwest of the center of Colonia Chihuahua. It is located in the high limestone cliff face. Parts of the cliff face and surroundings are covered in thick forest.

Environmental Stratum: Pine-Oak Forest

Description: A small solution cave formed near the base of a cliff. There are sherds both inside the cave and extending to the foot of the cliff some several meters to the south.

0   5 cm

Figure 5.13. Textile impression on resin on worked ceramic disk lid from site Tr-12, Cueva de los Negros.

TR-13 EL LIMÓN 1 (Figure 5.14)

Site Type: Ceremonial and habitation

Ceramic Phase: Nichim, Tan

Occupation: Protoclassic, Late Classic, Early Postclassic, Late Postclassic

Location and Setting: The site of El Limón 1 is located approximately 5 km northeast of Colonia Chihuahua, and 2.5 km southwest of Colonia Ángel Albino Corzo. It is approximately 2 km south of Tr-14. El Limón 1 is situated atop a steep knoll, overlooking a small stream at the western base of the knoll. The area is used for pasture and milpa land, with paths of dense tree cover.

Environmental Stratum: Short Tree Savannah/ Thorn Woodland, Riparian Forest

Description: This small site consists of three rectangular mounds and two large terrace features. The three mounds, all of different dimensions, are clustered together within an area of 50 by 35 m at the center of the knoll top. Mound A (the largest) is rectangular, measuring 25 by 10 m, with a height of 1 m. Mound B measures 12 by 8 m by 1 m high. Mixed-in with the debris of Mound B were found pieces of well-made stucco plaster. The smallest mound (C) measures 9 by 5 m by 0.25 m high. The three mounds are arranged around an open area (D), which probably served as a common plaza area for the three structures. The orientation of the structures, either parallel or at right angles to each other indicates a degree of planning of the complex, suggesting that they were used (and possibly even built) contemporaneously.

The unusually large size of Structure A suggests that this may have served as a civic-ceremonial building. On the other hand it may represent an elite residence, or even an extended family dwelling. The two smaller mounds probably represent residential structures.

This site is located less than 1/2 km from Tr-14 (see below).

TR-14 EL LIMÓN 2 (Figures 5.15-5.17)

Site Type: Ceremonial and habitation

Occupation: Postclassic

Location and Setting: Tr-14 is situated atop a large spur or ridge. The site is immediately north of Tr-13, 3.5 km east of Colonia Guadalupe

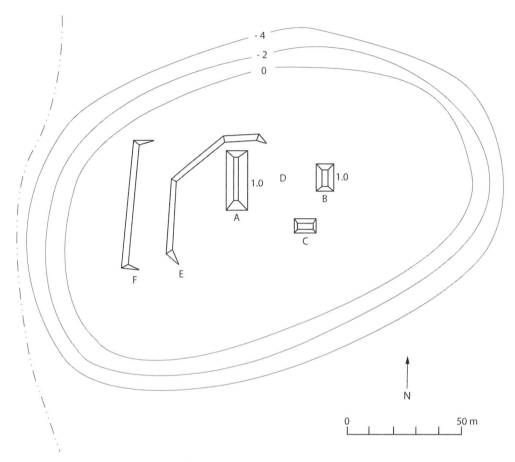

Figure 5.14. Site sketch of Tr-13, El Limón 1.

Zapote, and 2 km southwest of Colonia Àngel Albino Corzo. To the east and west of the site flow small streams which converge south of Tr-13 to form a tributary of the Río San Lucas.

The local topography can be characterized as small alluvial valleys dissected by ridges and knolls. Vegetation is dominated by milpa and grassy pasture with paths of dense tree cover.

Environmental Stratum: Short Tree Savannah/ Thorn Woodland, Riparian Forest

Description: Tr-14 consists of a ceremonial precinct on the northeast portion of the site and a large residential sector dominating the western portion of the hilltop and the southern slope of the hill. The residential area on the top of the hill has been outlined, but the number of features has not been counted or mapped.

The ceremonial complex consists of ten structures arranged around a large plaza area

(K). These structures include two very long, low mounds (A and B), three pyramids (C, D, and F), and five lower rectangular structures. The two long low mounds A and B measure 34 by 8 m by 1 m, and 51 by 8 m by 1 m respectively. These form the northern and eastern edge of the plaza (K). The western border of the plaza group is formed by Mounds C and D, which are 5 m and 6 m in height. Between C and D is a small low structure. This may have functioned as an altar serving the two larger pyramids. A lower structure (Mound E), measuring 2 m in height, is situated immediately to the northeast of D. At the southern end of the plaza area sits Mound F, 5 m high.

Slightly south, but still in view, of the plaza complex are located two low square-shaped mounds (G and H). Mound G, measuring 16 by 16 m by 1 m, has a small stairway built into its northern wall. This pair of structures probably

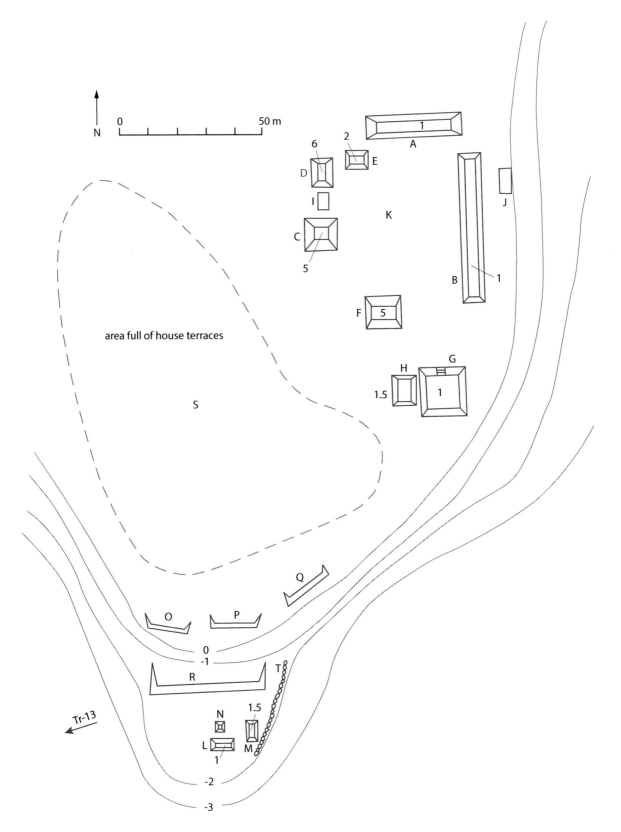

Figure 5.15. Site sketch of Tr-14, El Limón 2.

Figure 5.16. Site Tr-14, El Limón 2, view south, Mounds H and G.

Figure 5.17. Site Tr-14, El Limón 2; cobble alignment in background; Mounds M and L to the left.

represents an elite residence, perhaps occupied by persons involved in the operation of the ceremonial structures.

To the west and southwest of the ceremonial complex, the residential complex is located. This consists of a few residential structures (L, M, and N), a series of house terraces (O, P, Q, R, and S), and a long cobble wall (T). The terraces appear to follow the general contour of the southern slope of the hill. The terraces are relatively small, for the most part measuring 15 m long (with the exception of R, at 35 m long). The size of the terraces and the absence of structures upon the terraced land suggest that these were non-elite residential terraces. Below the terraces on a small flat area of the knoll, three small low rectangular mounds (L, M, and N) were noted. These mounds, arranged around a small patio, appear to form a house group. Immediately east of this mound group is a long cobble alignment (T) that acts as a retaining wall or erosion control feature, reinforcing the natural slope of the hill.

The overall layout of the site, particularly the ceremonial complex, suggests it was occupied over a relatively long period of time. Buildings in the ceremonial complex demonstrate planning in their arrangement (around a plaza) and orientation (either parallel or perpendicular to each other).

References: Blake 2010:263-265 (Blake refers to this site as TR-13); Lee 1985; Lee and Bryant 1996:55

TR-15 (Figure 5.18)

Site-Type: Ceremonial and habitation

Ceramic Phase: Mix

Occupation: Late Preclassic, Late Classic

Location and Setting: Tr-15 is located on a low ridge, approximately 500 m north of Colonia Chihuahua and 1.5 km south and slightly west of Colonia Guadalupe Zapote. The ridge on which the site is located overlooks a small arroyo. The local topography is hilly country. Local vegetation is mainly milpa, with low bush cover and isolated trees.

Environmental Stratum: Short Tree Savannah/ Thorn Woodland

Description: Tr-15 appears to represent a residential hamlet with a possible ceremonial structure. The maximum extent of the site measures approximately 200 m by 140 m. It consists of 11 low mounds and one large mound located in the center of the site. The small mounds are arranged in groups of two, a larger and a smaller mound (B/C and D/E) or isolated larger mounds (H, I, J, K, and L). These groupings probably represent residential structures arranged around a patio. The isolated mounds may represent individual residential structures or the remaining evidence of residential patio groups.

The single larger mound (A) located in the center of the site measures 15 by 11 m, with a height of 2 m. This structure may have served as the ceremonial center of the hamlet. Nearby is Mound F, a probable altar.

Two terrace features (M and N) are located towards the southern end of the site. These were probably constructed to level the uneven surface of the ridge top for houses.

There does not appear to be any formal structure to the layout of the site; rather, it was probably dictated by the natural contours of the ridge on which the site is located.

References: DeMontmollin 1989c:112-113

TR-16 (Figure 5.19)

Site Type: Ceremonial

Ceramic Phase: Mix

Occupation: Middle Preclassic, Late Classic

Location and Setting: Tr-16 is located approximately 200 m southeast of Colonia Chihuahua. The site is situated on a valley floor on the west bank of a small stream. The local topography is a flat plain with occasional rises and knolls. The surrounding vegetation consists primarily of milpa, grasses, and palm.

Environmental Stratum: Short Tree Savannah/ Thorn Woodland

Description: The site consists of a pair of very large primary platforms sitting on the

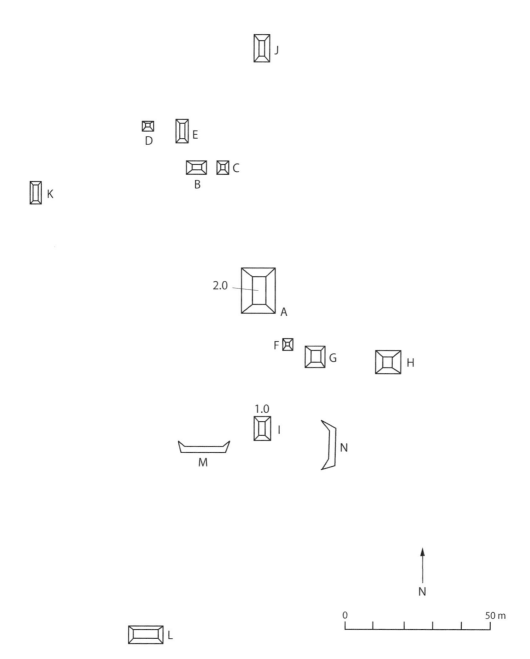

Figure 5.18. Site sketch of Tr-15.

valley floor. The maximum extent of the site is 100 by 40 m. The taller of the two mounds (A) measures 30 m on a side and has a height of 4 m. Immediately north of this mound and offset slightly to the west is Mound B, also measuring 30 by 30 m with a height of 2 m. Structures A and B are separated by a plaza (C) measuring 40 m across. Pyramid A and platform Mound B form a ceremonial unit. The absence of residential structures suggests this ceremonial complex may be a 'vacant center' that served a dispersed surrounding population. It is also possible that low house mounds would be discovered in the vicinity with more intensive survey.

References: de Montmollin 1989c:121-122

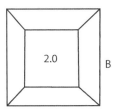

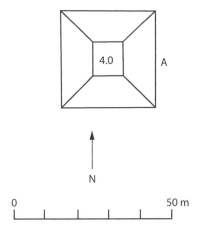

Figure 5.19. Site sketch of Tr-16.

TR-17 (Figure 5.20)

Site Type: Habitation

Ceramic Phase: Mix

Occupation: Late Classic

Location and Setting: Tr-17 is located approximately 500 m north of Colonia Chihuahua, just east of the road to Colonia Guadalupe Zapote. The site is spread over a long low ridge, alongside a small arroyo. It is in area of rolling plain with isolated hills. The local vegetation consists of milpa with low bush and occasional trees.

Environmental Stratum: Short Tree Savannah/ Thorn Woodland

Description: The site consists of eight small low platforms, scattered across the long axis of the ridgetop. The maximum extent of the site is approximately 200 by 70 m. The mounds range in size from 12-15 m long by 5-6 m wide. One very small mound (C) measures approximately 4 m by 4 m and probably served as an altar. Most of the mounds range in height from 0.2 m to 1 m. Only Mound A reaches a height of 1.5 m. This slightly larger mound may be an elite residence or perhaps the locus of local ceremonial activity.

The mounds are clustered in small groups of two to three (D/E/F; H/I; and possibly B/C). Their arrangement around small common areas, especially visible in the D/E/F group and the H/I group, suggests these are residential compounds arranged around a patio (e.g., G, J). The site appears to be a small residential hamlet with no evidence of substantial civic-ceremonial structures.

TR-18 (Figure 5.21)

Site Type: Ceremonial and habitation

Location and Setting: Tr-18 is located approximately 2 km south of Colonia Chihuahua. The Río Santa Inés flows 250 m east of the site. The site is situated on the low eastern hilly base of a hill that forms the eastern boundary of the valley. The local vegetation consists of milpa with low bush and occasional trees.

Environmental Stratum: Short Tree Savannah/ Thorn Woodland-Riparian Forest

Description: The site of Tr-18 consists of a single pyramid, an elite residential compound, and a series of low house mounds and house terraces. The visible extent of the site is approximately 150 m along the contour of the hillside, and stretches 150-200 m up the hillslope. The majority of platform mounds are situated on the basal part of the hill. House terraces are located further upslope where leveling of the natural terrain would be necessary for stable construction.

The largest structure on the site (Mound A) measures 15 by 12 m, with a height of 4 m. This structure is somewhat isolated and does not appear to form part of a complex.

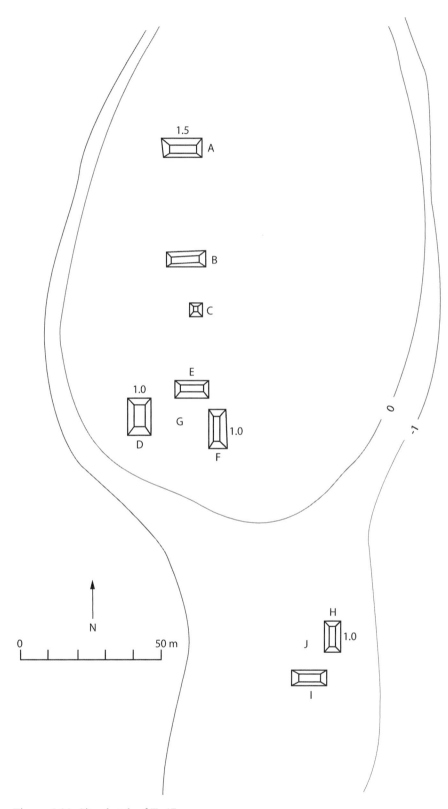

Figure 5.20. Site sketch of Tr-17.

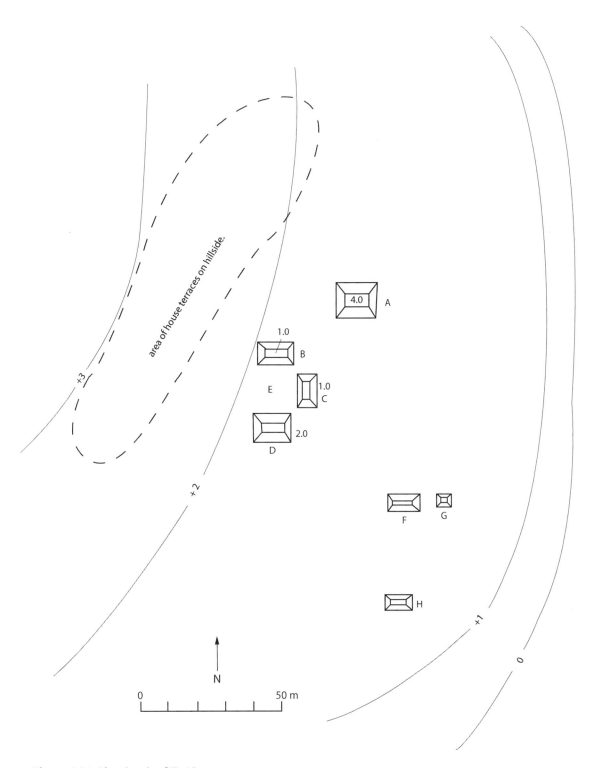

Figure 5.21. Site sketch of Tr-18.

Southwest of the pyramid is a cluster of low mounds (B, C, and D) arranged around a common patio area (E). Two of the structures (B and C) measure 1 m in height and 12-14 m by 7-8 m in basal dimensions. Mound D is slightly larger, measuring 15 by 10 m and 2 m high. The arrangement of this complex, its greater dimensions, and its proximity to the pyramid suggests that it is an elite residential compound. Mound D may even represent a combination of residential and civic or ceremonial functions.

Toward the southern end of the site are located three, small low rectangular mounds. Mounds F and G clustered together appear to be a domestic unit. It is not clear if Mound H was associated with the F/G compound.

This site appears to be a small residential hamlet with a modest ceremonial structure and possible elite residence compound.

References: de Montmollin 1989c:185

TR-19 SANTA MARTA ROSARIO
(Figure 5.22)

Site Type: Ceremonial and habitation

Occupation: Early Preclassic, Middle Preclassic, Late Preclassic, Protoclassic

Location and Setting: This site is located on the eastern floodplain of Río Santa Inés 500 m southwest of Tr-9 (Tenam Rosario). It is at the confluence of a small seasonal river which flows eastward into the Santa Inés. The floodplain at the site has been plowed recently for cotton, but the river margin still preserves a thick riparian growth.

Environmental Stratum: Short Tree Savannah/ Thorn Woodland, Riparian Forest

Description: There were eleven mounds at this Late Preclassic ceremonial center. Unfortunately, many have been leveled for cotton production, and only four mounds remain. The site was excavated from February to May in 1979 by David Bathgate for the New World Archaeological Foundation. His Master's Thesis (1980) discusses in depth the site characteristics and the artifacts and features recovered. This presentation will be restricted to a description of the site layout and some of the relevant features found during excavation.

The largest mound at the site (Mound 1) measured 6.4 m tall. Excavation showed it to be a square, stepped pyramid with an orientation from northwest to southeast. Mound 4 is about 50 m southwest of this mound and reached a height of 3.6 m. It too was square and had the same orientation as Mound 1. Two other mounds that still exist are to the northeast of Mound 1. Seven of the mounds that were leveled sat to the south of Mound 1. The largest of these (Mound 11) was approximately 4.7 m tall, square in shape and oriented the same direction as Mound 1. These two large mounds form the axis of the site with an enormous central plaza between them and flanked on several sides by other smaller mounds. A random sampling program of excavations at the site, revealed evidence of several structures, probably habitation, buried beneath the surface. These consisted of floors, burials, and cobble wall alignments that had been covered by recent alluvial deposits from Río Santa Inés. Some of these structures appeared to be residences that were raised on low platforms above the natural ground surface.

References: Bathgate 1980; de Montmollin 1989c:208-209

TR-20 (Figure 5.23)

Site Type: Ceremonial and habitation

Ceramic Phase: Hun, Ix

Occupation: Protoclassic, Late Classic

Location and Setting: Tr-20 is located 2.5 km south of Colonia Chihuahua and just 200 m south of Tr-18. It is in an area of rolling plain, dotted with hills. Río Santa Inés forms the eastern boundary of the site. The surrounding vegetation consists of milpa.

Environmental Stratum: Short Tree Savannah/ Thorn Woodland

Description: The site consists of a single large mound (A), two smaller mounds (B and C), and two areas of cultural debris (D and E). The maximum extent of the site is 190 by 150 m.

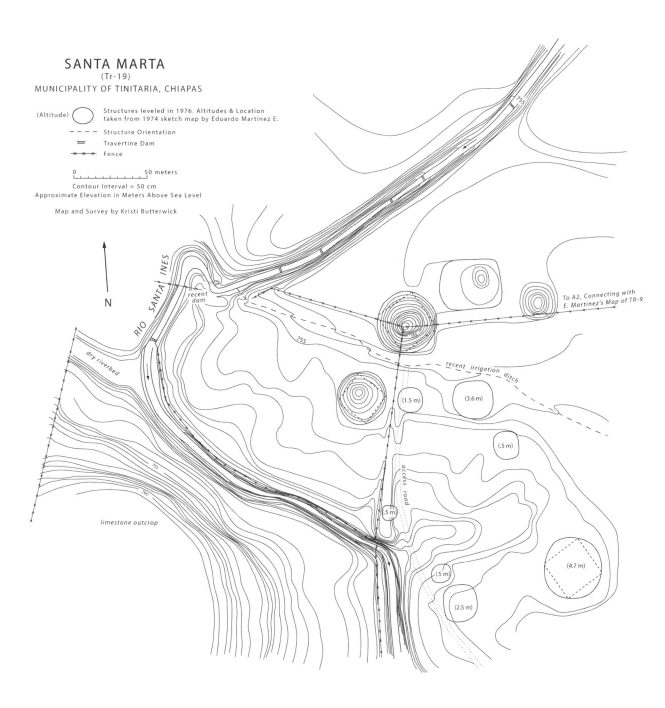

Figure 5.22. Site sketch of Tr-19, Santa Marta Rosario.

The central feature (Mound A) is the largest structure. Measuring 30 by 25 m with a height of 4 m, this pyramid formed the ceremonial center of the site. Thirty meters southeast is Mound B, a low rectangular mound measuring 15 m by 10 m and only 1 m high. Southeast of

Mound B is another low rectangular mound (D). To the southwest of Mound A is a large concentration of surface artifacts (D) with no visible structures.

References: de Montmollin 1989c:180-181

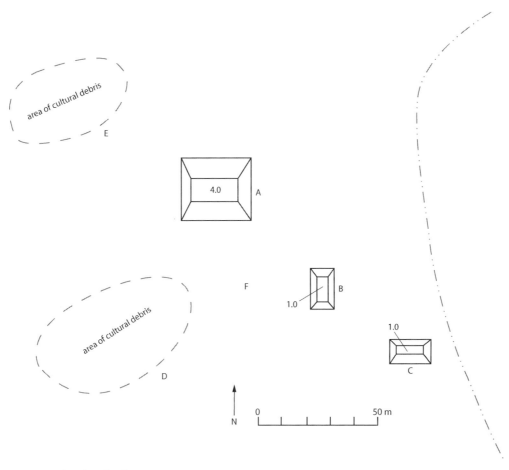

Figure 5.23. Site sketch of Tr-20.

TR-21 (Figures 5.24-5.25)

Site Type: Ceremonial and habitation

Ceramic Phase: Mix

Occupation: Protoclassic, Late Classic

Location and Setting: Tr-21 is located 3.5 km west of Colonia Chihuahua on a small stream tributary to Río Santa Inés. The site is located in an area of rolling hills and ridges. The vegetation consists of dense bush and tree cover.

Environmental Stratum: Short Tree Savannah/ Thorn Woodland, Riparian Forest

Description: Tr-21 consists of several large ceremonial structures and a series of residential clusters. Three very large mounds and eleven low rectangular mounds were observed and there

were two areas where mounds were outlined and counted but not mapped.

The ceremonial precincts are centrally located and arranged in two groups. The largest mounds (A and B) are located side by side, in the center. The larger of the two (Mound A) is a pyramid measuring 25 m on a side with a height of 7 m. Mound B sits 45 m to the east, across a plaza (E). This large, low double-tiered platform, measures 20 m by 30 m and is 0.5 m high on the lower level and 1 m on the upper level. South of A and B, and probably associated with them, are two smaller structures (C and D). Mound C, directly south of A, is a small square structure and measures 10 by 10 m and 1.5 m high. Finally, east of C and south and offset slightly to the west of B, is Mound D, a long rectangular mound measuring 20 by 12 m. The east and west

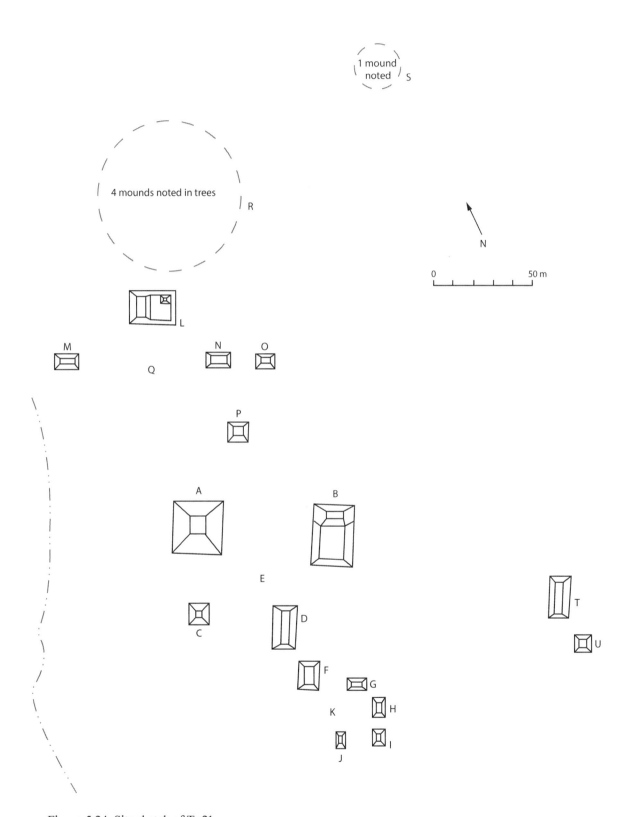

Figure 5.24. Site sketch of Tr-21.

Figure 5.25. Site Tr-21.

walls of Mound D are of uneven heights (1 m and 3 m respectively) probably owing to uneven ground surface. The symmetrical orientation and arrangement of A, B, C, and perhaps D, suggest that this was a planned complex.

In the southeast corner of the site is a cluster of five low rectangular mounds (F, G, H, I and J). This group, arranged around a patio area (K), probably represents an elite residence, possibly associated with the ceremonial core.

North of the large ceremonial complex is another mound group, including a large double-tiered platform and a series of smaller mounds. The center of this group (Mound L) measures 23 by 15 m, with the lower tier at 0.5 m and the higher tier at 1.5 m. Perched on the northeast corner of the lower tier is a small mound. The arrangement of these mounds (M, N, and P) around an open space (Q) suggests this may be a plaza group.

Five mounds of unspecified dimensions are located north of this latter group. We suspect these are also residential mounds.

Finally, another pair of mounds (T and U) is located at the eastern edge of the site. Mound T, measuring 20 m by 10 m and 2 m high, may have been an elite house platform or perhaps another civic-ceremonial structure.

The overall plan of this site suggests the structures were not all constructed as a planned unit. It appears there are two sections to the site, one associated with the large mounds (A and B) and a second associated with the smaller mound (L) to the north. Both sections look like ceremonial centers surrounded by residential mounds.

References: de Montmollin 1989c:73, 186-187

TR-22 (Figure 5.26)

Site Type: Habitation

Ceramic Phase: Mix

Occupation: Late Classic

Location and Setting: Tr-22 is located approximately 2 km south of Colonial

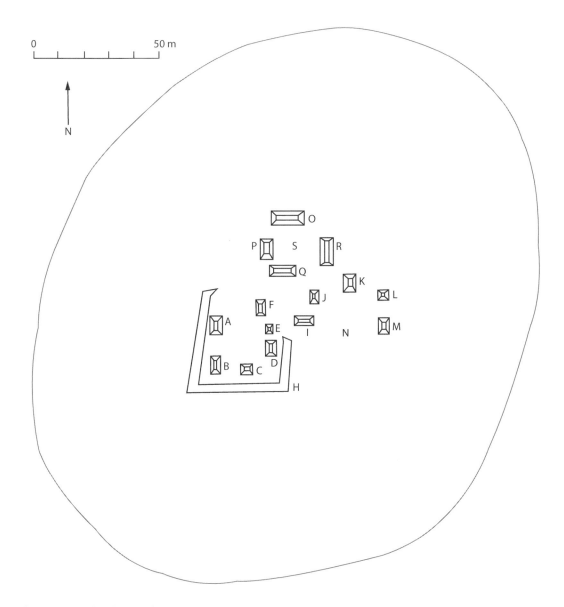

Figure 5.26. Site sketch of Tr-22.

Chihuahua, and just 300 m south of the road leading to Colonia Chihuahua from Colonia Guadalupe Zapote. The site is situated on a low hill in an area of flat plain, dotted with isolated knolls. Local vegetation consists of milpa, grassy plain, low bush, and isolated trees.

Environmental Stratum: Short Tree Savannah/ Thorn Woodland

Description: This site consists of 15 low residential mounds and one large terrace clustered tightly together on top of a low hill.

The maximum extent of the site measures 75 by 80 m. No ceremonial structures were observed.

The house mounds appear to form at least three and perhaps four patio groupings. A large cluster of low mounds (A-F) grouped around Patio G may be a household compound. This cluster is reinforced on three sides by a large terrace (H). None of these mounds exceed 0.5 m in height.

A second group of mounds (I-M) on the east side of the site are situated around an open area (N). This group is more widely dispersed than the A-F group, and may represent more than one compound group.

Finally, a third cluster (O-R) at the northern boundary of the site is arranged around a patio (S). Mounds P, Q, and R, which measure 1 m in height, are slightly higher than the other mounds on the site, suggesting this may be an elite residential compound.

The site represents a small nucleated residential hamlet. The close-packing of sites is probably a function of the hill contour on which the site is located, as is indicated by the form of Terrace H. The regular orientation of the mounds suggests the site was constructed as a planned unit.

References: de Montmollin 1989c:181-182

TR-23 DOLORES ZAPOTE (Figure 5.27)

Site Type: Habitation

Location and Setting: Tr-23 is located 2 km northeast of Colonia Guadalupe Zapote, and roughly 500 m north of the road leading to Colonia Ángel Albino Corzo. It sits on the northern tip of a small ridge that is footed along its western base by a small stream. Local terrain consists of hills and ridges, located at the base of the more rugged dissected terrain that climbs up to the highlands. Vegetation in the vicinity of the site consists mainly of low bush and grasses, and sparse tree cover running along the ridges.

Environmental Stratum: Short Tree Savannah/ Thorn Woodland

Description: This site consists of a single long, low, rectangular mound located at the northern end of a ridge. Although no ceramics or other artifacts were found in association with this mound, it has the general shape and height of large house platforms common in the Late Classic period.

References: de Montmollin 1989c:118-119

TR-24 EL PARAÍSO (Figures 5.28-5.30)

Site Type: Ceremonial and habitation

Ceramic Phase: Nichim

Occupation: Early Classic, Late Classic, Early Postclassic

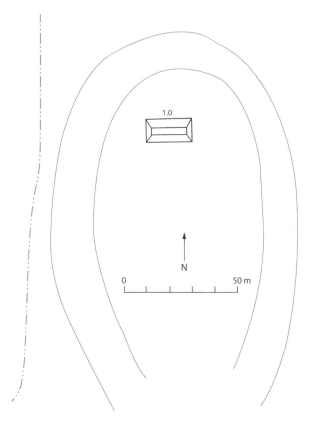

Figure 5.27. Site sketch of Tr-23, Dolores Zapote.

Location and Setting: Tr-24, El Paraíso, is located 2 km northwest of the modern Colonia Ángel Albino Corzo, and roughly 200 m north of the road between Colonia Guadalupe Zapote and Ángel Albino Corzo. It is in an area of rolling hills and ridges, at the base of the more rugged hills which climb into the highlands. The site itself spreads from the base and up the south slope of a steep hillside. The local vegetation consists mainly of grasses, low shrubs, and isolated trees.

Environmental Stratum: Short Tree Savannah/ Thorn Woodland

Description: El Paraíso consists of a small pyramid and several associated low mounds, several elite residential mounds, and a series of substantial terraces. The site is arranged in two groupings, with a ceremonial sector on the northwest side of the site high on the hillslope, and a residential sector covering the southeastern side of the site.

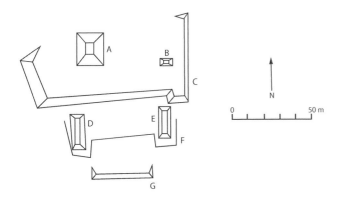

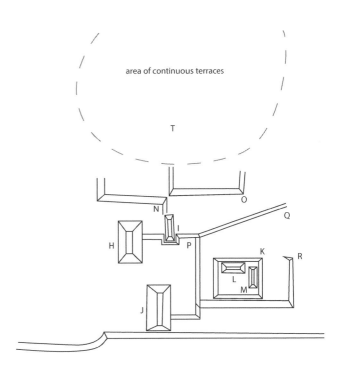

Figure 5.28. Site sketch of Tr-24, El Paraíso.

The northern ceremonial sector consists of a 3 m high pyramid (A) enclosed in a large three-sided terrace (C). East of the pyramid, also within Terrace C, is a small low mound that probably functioned in association with the pyramid. Below this terrace group on the slope are two low rectangular mounds measuring 1 m in height. These are enclosed by Terrace F. Finally, below these mounds is another terrace (G) upon which no structures were observed.

Figure 5.29. Site Tr-24, El Paraíso.

Figure 5.30. Modern cut into terrace at site Tr-24, El Paraíso.

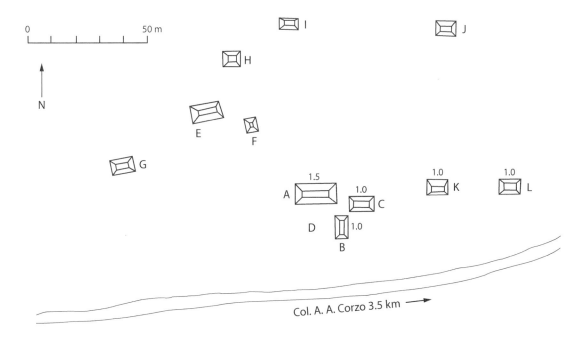

Figure 5.31. Site sketch of Tr-25.

Two hundred and fifty meters southeast of this complex is a series of terraces (T). On the lower slope, Mounds H, I, J, K, L, and M are interconnected by a complex network of terraces (N, P, Q, and R).

The mounds in this area appear to be large elite residential structures. Mounds H and J (15 by 26 m and 15 by 29 m, respectively) possibly have civic-ceremonial functions as well. Mounds L and M form a residential compound situated atop a very large low mound. This entire section appears to have been artificially leveled by terracing.

The site appears to be a nucleated village with a ceremonial complex and elite residential area and a non-elite residential sector.

TR-25 (Figure 5.31)

Site Type: Habitation

Ceramic Phase: Mix

Occupation: Early Classic, Middle Classic, Late Classic

Location and Setting: Tr-25 is located 1.3 km northwest of Colonia Ángel Albino Corzo, just north of the road between Ángel Albino Corzo and Guadalupe Zapote. It sits in a saddle, in an area of hills and ridges. The vegetation in the immediate vicinity of the site is primarily milpa, with dense forest within less than 0.5 km to the east and west.

Environmental Stratum: Short Tree Savannah/ Thorn Woodland

Description: Tr-25 is a small nucleated hamlet with eleven low house mounds. No ceremonial structures were observed. The maximum extent of the site measures 100 by 170 m. The mounds appear for the most part to be scattered about the site in an unstructured manner. Only one group of mounds (A, B, and C) appears to form a cluster, perhaps around a patio (D). This latter group may have been an elite residence, judging by the large size of A, which measures 17 by 9 m by 1.5 m. The other mounds range in size from 5-12 m long, by 4-7 m wide, with heights ranging from 0.25 to 1.5 m.

References: Lee 1985

TR-26 (Figure 5.32)

Site Type: Ceremonial

Location and Setting: Tr-26 is located 0.5 km west of Colonia Ángel Albino Corzo. The site is on the top of a small ridge in a zone of rolling hills and ridges. A branch of Río San Lucas flows 300 m east of the site. Milpa grows on the site. Higher ridges with pine are located 0.5 km to the west.

Environmental Stratum: Short Tree Savannah/ Thorn Woodland

Description: Tr-26 is a small ceremonial center located in a prominent position atop a small ridge. The site includes a single pyramid (A) with a low rectangular platform (B) extending out from the west wall of the pyramid. The southwestern corner of Platform B has an associated small low platform (C). Mounds B and C may be residential structures associated with the pyramid. Unfortunately, no ceramics were found associated with the site during survey.

TR-27 (Figure 5.33)

Site Type: Ceremonial and habitation

Occupation: Late Classic

Location and Setting: Tr-27 is on the northwest outskirts of Colonia Ángel Albino Corzo approximately 100 m east of Río San Lucas. The area is in milpa cultivation.

Environmental Stratum: Short Tree Savannah/ Thorn Woodland

Description: The two main portions at this site are separated by 100 m. The northwestern section consists of several house groups (e.g., B and C, E and F, and G, H, I, and J) surrounding a 3 m high pyramid (D). The southeastern group has a much more dispersed collection of house mounds with no clear ceremonial focus. The largest structure in this group is Mound P, which is 1.5 m high and has a 1 m high extension. This is the only double-tiered mound at the site. Along with its two neighboring mounds (Q and R) it helps enclose a patio area and was probably part of a house group. Other mounds in this sector at

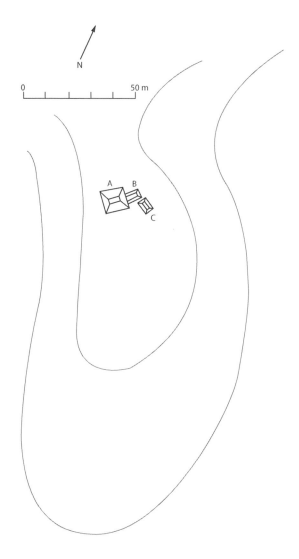

Figure 5.32. Site sketch of Tr-26.

the site also form house groups (e.g., L and M), but most are rather isolated.

The two sectors of the site suggest it was occupied by two separate but related social units, perhaps lineages (providing, of course, that they were occupied contemporaneously).

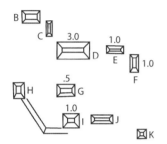

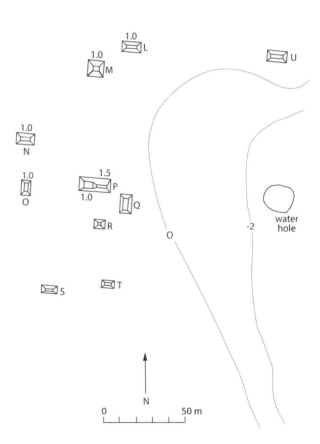

Figure 5.33. Site sketch of Tr-27.

TR-28 LOS HERMANOS
(Figures 5.34-5.35)

Site Type: Ceremonial and habitation

Ceramic Phase: Mix

Occupation: Late Classic

Location and Setting: Tr-28 (Los Hermanos) is located 2.5 km southeast of Colonia Ángel Albino Corzo. The site is situated on slightly rolling land approximately 300 m west of a small headwater tributary of Río San Lucas.

Environmental Stratum: Short Tree Savannah/ Thorn Woodland

Description: The site of Los Hermanos consists of a central civic-ceremonial complex, with groups of residential mounds surrounding the center, and with more residential mounds scattered in a linear manner across the extent of the site. The maximum extent of the site measures 150 by 400 m north-south.

The civic-ceremonial complex, located towards the north end of the site, consists of a large rectangular temple mound (A) and a low double-tiered platform mound (C). In addition, two rectangular platforms (B and E), each measuring 1 m in height, also probably functioned as civic-ceremonial structures. These four structures appear to be arranged around an open plaza (D).

Surrounding the central complex are low residential mounds. Some are arranged in tight clusters suggesting compound groups (e.g., K and L; M, N, and O) while others are less clustered. A burial was found in Mound Q. The burial was in a plain brown jar, with a kill-hole in the bottom. In the southern portion of the site the house mounds are distributed in a more dispersed pattern, with generally greater distance between structures than was observed for the northern area.

The regular orientation of the structures, either parallel or perpendicular to each other, suggests the site was constructed according to an ordered plan and that the structures may have been occupied contemporaneously.

Figure 5.34. Site sketch of Tr-28, Los Hermanos.

Figure 5.35. View from the site Tr-28, Los Hermanos (Alejandro Sánchez).

TR-29 LOS CIMIENTOS
(Figures 5.36-5.39)

Site Type: Ceremonial and habitation

Ceramic Phase: Mix

Occupation: Late Classic

Location and Setting: This site is located 2.75 km north and slightly east of Colonia Ángel Albino Corzo. It is in a zone of short tree forest and fairly dense vegetation. There is some good soil in the area, and small arroyos and tributaries of Río San Lucas seasonally carry water to the south. The site itself is on a low, gently sloping hillside in an area with many limestone outcrops. There are several small sinkholes and caves in the vicinity.

Environmental Stratum: Short Tree Savannah/ Thorn Woodland

Description: This site was visited in the 1920's and is briefly mentioned in Blom and Duby (1957, II: 45) and Basauri (1931: 12). It was

not until 1976, however, that a major study was undertaken at the site by Sonia Rivero in collaboration with the NWAF. A description of the site and its settlement pattern, as well as the results of excavations, can be found in her several publications (1978, 1987, 1990). The description presented here will be restricted to a brief summary of the intra-site settlement pattern so that it may be compared with other sites in the survey. It is primarily based on the work of Rivero (1987), as well as the initial survey in 1973 (Lee 1975).

The site covers a roughly square zone of some 650 m by 650 m. There are two major groups of habitation mounds at the site. The west group consists of 67 square mounds and 62 rectangular mounds grouped together in 55 habitation clusters or terraces. The east group has 60 square mounds and 32 rectangular mounds for a total of 37 habitation clusters. In addition, there are small altar-like structures associated with most of the house clusters. The two groups are separated by an arroyo which ranges from 50 m to 150 m wide and

Figure 5.36. Foundation of house platform from Tr-29, Los Cimientos (Alejandro Sánchez).

is up to 4 m deep. Both the east and the west groups can be further subdivided. In each quadrant of the site there is a temple mound at least 3 m high that may have served as the ceremonial focus for distinct social groups within the community. These are larger and more elaborate than the house mounds. The house mounds consist of well-made cut stone and earth fill platforms ranging from 25 cm to 1 m high. Rivero's excavations of four household or residential units, one from each quadrant of the site, also revealed other structures. She found building foundations at ground level, as well as outbuildings such as small rectangular sweatbaths.

Another feature at the site is the large number (18-20) of stone semi-circles, similar to ones found in other Late Classic sites in the survey area. These circles are interspersed among the household units, and they vary in diameter from 5 to 15 m, some of which have inner stone circles and a large central pit. The ones that Rivero excavated had a large amount of fire-cracked limestone, ash, and refuse. One

hypothesis is that they served as burning ovens, but it is also possible that they were used as roasting pits.

The ceremonial structures are different from most Late Classic sites in the survey in that they are isolated from other large temple mounds and surrounded by house mounds, not much different from the bulk of mounds at the site. However, one similar site is Tr-142 (El Rosario) studied by de Montmollin (1989c:209). The ceremonial structures are oriented to face downhill or southwest as are almost all of the structures at the site. Ceramics excavated from the house mound sample in each quadrant of the site showed that the occupation was Late/Terminal Classic. The majority of households were probably occupied contemporaneously and the community was perhaps primarily a large residential zone with ceremonial facilities to fulfill its own needs.

References: Basuari 1931:12; Blom and Duby 1957, II:45; de Montmollin 1989c:209; Lee 1975: 39; Rivero 1978, 1987

Figure 5.37. Ceremonial structure at Tr-29, Los Cimientos.

Figure 5.38. Ceremonial structure at Tr-29, Los Cimientos.

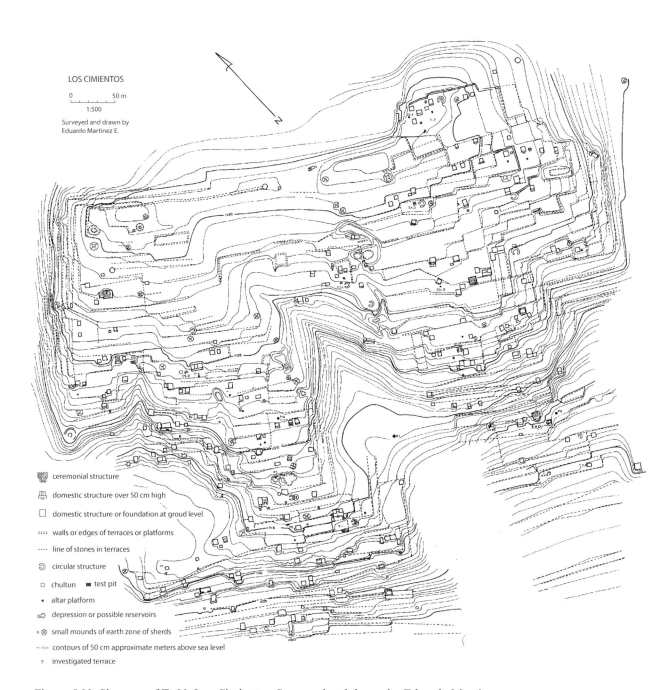

LOS CIMIENTOS

0   50 m

1:500

Surveyed and drawn by
Eduardo Martínez E.

🔲 ceremonial structure

⌂ domestic structure over 50 cm high

☐ domestic structure or foundation at groud level

:::: walls or edges of terraces or platforms

---- line of stones in terraces

ⓢ circular structure

☐ chultun   ■ test pit

• altar platform

🐚 depression or possible reservoirs

∘⊗ small mounds of earth zone of sherds

-·1100-· contours of 50 cm approximate meters above sea level

τ investigated terrace

Figure 5.39. Site map of Tr-29, Los Cimientos. Surveyed and drawn by Eduardo Martínez.

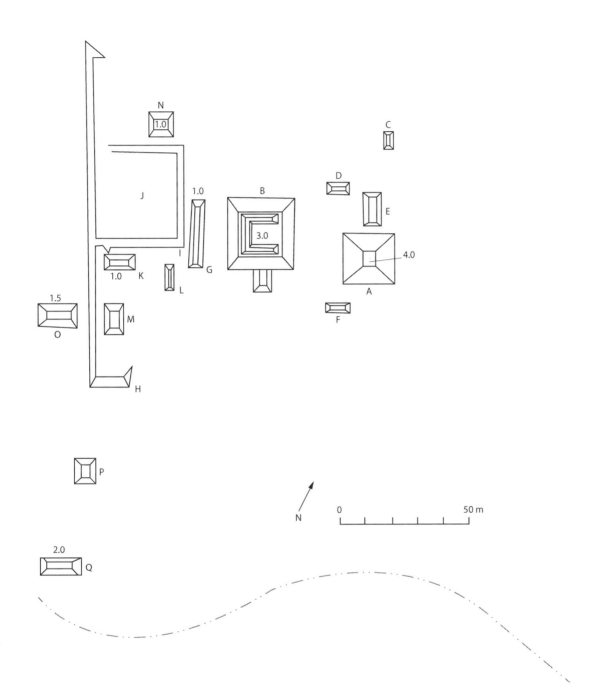

Figure 5.40. Site sketch of Tr-30, El Amate.

TR-30 EL AMATE (Figure 5.40)

Site Type: Ceremonial and habitation

Ceramic Phase: Mix

Occupation: Late Preclassic, possible
Protoclassic, Late Classic

Location and Setting: The site of El Amate,
Tr-30 is located 300 m south of Colonia Ángel
Albino Corzo. It is situated on a low hill,
overlooking an arroyo to the south. The local
topography is characterized by flat plain with
isolated hills. Predominant vegetation in the

vicinity of the site consists of milpa, grasses, low shrubs, and isolated trees.

Environmental Stratum: Short Tree Savannah/ Thorn Woodland

Description: Tr-30 consists of a substantial civic-ceremonial complex, a series of low mounds, and an unusual terrace system. Most structures are clustered closely together atop a hill within an area of 150 by 150 m.

The eastern border of the civic-ceremonial center of the site is formed by a 4 m high temple mound (A). West of A, across a plaza area, is a large basal platform (B). Atop this platform is a three-sided wall foundation with the eastern wall left open on the plaza area, facing Mound A. Protruding out of the southern wall of B is a small platform extension. Behind Platform B, to the west, is a long low platform (G) which, together with the east wall of Platform B, may have been an open-ended ballcourt. Both north and south of the A/B complex are a series of small low platforms (C, D, E, and F) that may have housed an elite population associated with the operation of the ceremonial sector.

The western border of the site is formed by a long terrace (H). This terrace extends 130 m northwest-southeast and appears to have been constructed to provide level ground for the construction of the series of mounds immediately enclosed within the terrace system. Included is a large platform-plaza (J) formed by the construction of Terrace I. Enclosed within the Terrace H area are three low platforms (K, L, and M). These mounds (as well as mounds N and O located outside of the terrace enclosure) may have been elite residential structures.

South of the terrace complex, downslope, are two isolated mounds (P and Q). Mound Q, measuring 2 m in height, is slightly larger than the other mounds.

The compact nature of the site, as well as the regular orientation of structures with respect to each other, suggests it was constructed as a planned unit.

TR-31 SANTA CECILIA (no map)

Site Type: Habitation

Ceramic Phase: Mix

Occupation: Late Classic

Location and Setting: Tr-31 is located approximately 2.2 km northwest of Colonia Ángel Albino Corzo, on the north side of the road leading to Colonia Guadalupe Zapote. It sits on the northern tip of a long ridge. The surrounding topography consists of rolling hills and ridges and the site area itself is now mainly pasture and milpa.

Environmental Stratum: Short Tree Savannah/ Thorn Woodland

Description: This site consists of house terraces, terraces with no evidence of architecture, and chultunes. One chultún, which measures approximately 2 m in diameter, has a round slab covering fill. This site, although not mapped, is a westward residential extension of Tr-24 and may in fact be part of the same site. (See Rivero 1990: 303, fig.34 for a map of the two sites together, Tr-24 and Tr-31.)

TR-32 (no map)

Occupation: Protoclassic, Late Classic

Location and Setting: Tr-32 is located 6 km northwest of Colonia Rodolfo Figueroa and 5 km southwest of Colonia Las Delicias. It is situated on a low ridge overlooking Río San Lucas to the east. Vegetation in the site area consists of dense tree cover.

Environmental Stratum: Short Tree Savannah/ Thorn Woodland

Description: No map of the site was made. The site consists of a primary pyramid and a basal platform.

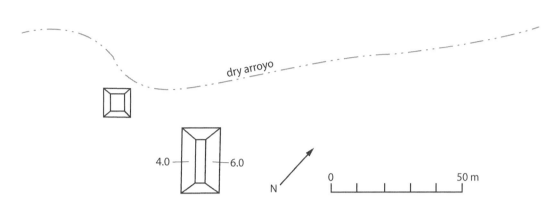

Figure 5.41. Site sketch of Tr-33.

TR-33 (Figure 5.41)

Site Type: Ceremonial

Ceramic Phase: Mix

Occupation: Late Classic

Location and Setting: Tr-33 is located 5.5 km northwest of Colonia Rodolfo Figueroa, and 4 km southwest of Colonia Las Delicias. The site is about 200 m east of Río San Lucas and overlooks a small arroyo which, although dry at present, may have been a water course at the time of the site's occupation. The site is in an area of rolling hills and ridges with some milpa in the area, and tree-covered ridges nearby. Dense riparian vegetation exists along the river.

Environmental Stratum: Riparian Forest

Description: This small site consists of a single large temple platform 4-6 m high and a much smaller platform. The latter may be a residential mound. Very little pottery was found on the site.

TR-34 LA CANDELARIA (Figure 5.42)

Site Type: Ceremonial and habitation

Ceramic Phase: Mix

Occupation: Late Classic

Location and Setting: La Candelaria sits on a narrow ridge 3 km south of Colonia Ángel Albino Corzo, near the confluence of Río Las Tres Marías and Arroyo Tuminte. Site vegetation is primarily milpa with some low bush and occasional trees lining the water courses nearby.

Environmental Stratum: Short Tree Savannah/ Thorn Woodland

Description: Tr-34, La Candelaria, consists of a single temple platform and 15 low mounds. The structures are clustered tightly together on the ridge top in an elongated pattern. The extent of the site is 150 by 80 m, with the majority of structures concentrated in an area of 80 by 60 m.

The largest mound (A), which measures 3 m in height, is located at the southwestern corner of the main concentration. North of this is a very small mound (B) that may have been an altar associated with A. A third mound (C) just west of B may also have been a house platform.

In the center of the concentration is a series of mounds (D, E, F, G, and possibly H), which appear to be clustered around a patio (I). This arrangement around a large patio or plaza in a prominent central position, as well as their greater than average size, suggests they were elite residences or possibly even civic-ceremonial structures. North of this group are another series of four mounds, two large (J and L) and two small (K and M), which were also probably residential structures. Finally, Mound N at the northwest corner, and Mounds O, P, and Q scattered at the southeast end of the site also seem to be residential mounds.

The site appears to be a nucleated hamlet with a modest civic-ceremonial complex.

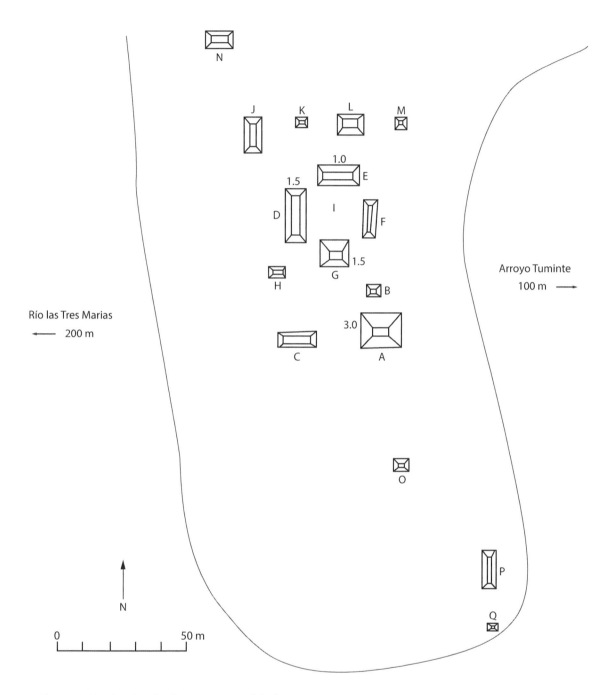

Figure 5.42. Site sketch of Tr-34, La Candelaria.

TR-35 BRASILAR (Figure 5.43)

Site Type: Ceremonial and habitation

Ceramic Phase: Mix

Occupation: Late Classic

Location and Setting: The site is 3.5 km west and north of Colonia Las Delicias beside a small headwater tributary of Río San Lucas. It sits on a small hill. The local vegetation is primarily low bush cover that has been cleared in spots for milpa. The streamside has denser riverine

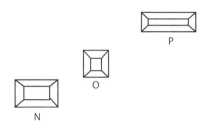

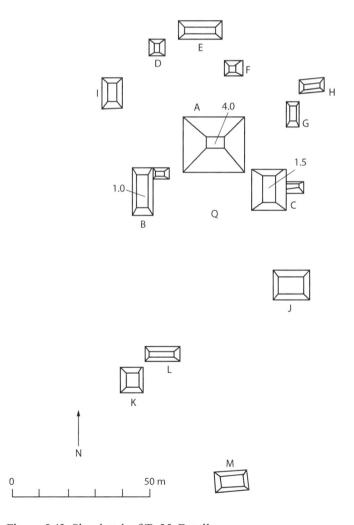

Figure 5.43. Site sketch of Tr-35, Brasilar.

vegetation. Tr-36 is located 0.5 km directly east of this site on a similar headwater tributary of Río San Lucas.

Environmental Stratum: Short Tree Savannah/ Thorn Woodland, Riparian Forest

Description: This site consists of a pyramid, two large platforms, and a series of residential platforms. The maximum extent of the site is approximately 250 by 100 m; however, the majority of structures are concentrated in an area of about 100 by 80 m.

In the center of the concentration is a 4 m high pyramid (A). Flanked on either side, slightly to the south, are two large platforms (B and C). These two structures have an added feature: a small low platform extending out from the eastern wall of the main part of the mound. These structures may have been arranged around an open area (Q).

Scattered around the ceremonial complex area, within the central concentration, is a series of mounds (I; D, E, and F; G and H; and J), which appear to be arranged as residential compounds. The proximity of these structures to the ceremonial group suggests that they may have been elite residences.

Further to the south and separated from the main group by 60 m is another series of mounds (K, L, and M). Finally, at the north end of the site, also separated from the main group by 60 m, is another group of mounds (N, O, and P). They may also have been residential.

This site appears to be a nucleated hamlet with a substantial ceremonial sector.

TR-36 SAN LUCAS (Figure 5.44)

Site Type: Ceremonial and habitation

Ceramic Phase: Mix

Occupation: Late Classic

Location and Setting: Tr-36 is located 3 km west and slightly north of Colonia Las Delicias on a low hill overlooking the east bank of a small headwater tributary of Río San Lucas. The local terrain is hilly with occasional ridges. The area is used primarily for milpa.

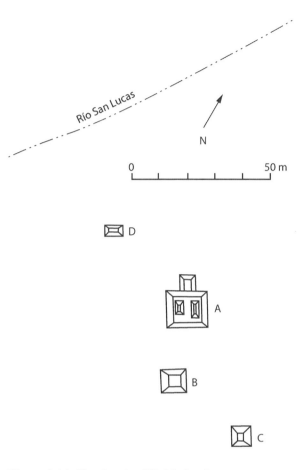

Figure 5.44. Site sketch of Tr-36, San Lucas.

Environmental Stratum: Short Tree Savannah/ Thorn Woodland, Riparian Forest

Description: This site consists of a temple mound (A) and three low platforms. The temple mound, which measures 15 by 13 m, has two low rectangular platforms constructed atop it. In addition, a low rectangular platform protrudes out of the northwest side of the mound. Southeast of the platform are two low platforms (B and C) that may have been residential mounds. West of the temple mound is another low structure (D), which also may have been a residential structure.

The site appears to be an isolated ceremonial center with a few residential structures, probably associated with the maintenance and operation of the civic-ceremonial complex.

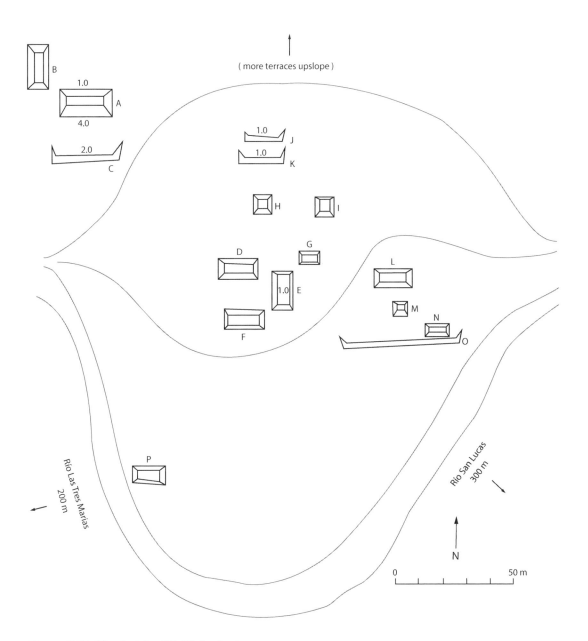

Figure 5.45. Site sketch of Tr-37, La Junta.

TR-37 LA JUNTA (Figure 5.45)

Site Type: Habitation

Ceramic Phase: Mix

Occupation: Late Preclassic, Late Classic

Location and Setting: La Junta is 3 km south of Colonia Ángel Albino Corzo and 4.5 km west of Colonia Las Delicias. It sits on a hill between the Ríos Las Tres Marías and San Lucas, 350 m north of their confluence. The terrain surrounding the site is gentle rolling hills with occasional ridges. Vegetation on the site is primarily milpa with isolated trees, while dense riverine vegetation lines the water courses.

Environmental Stratum: Short Tree Savannah/ Thorn Woodland, Riparian Forest

Description: This site consists of 12 low platform mounds and several terraces. The mounds tend to be clustered in groups, taking advantage of the natural terracing on the hillside.

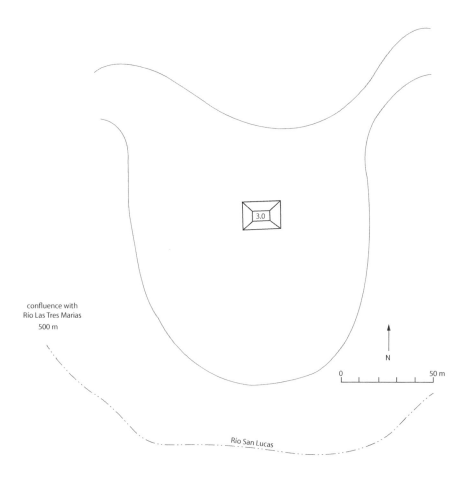

Figure 5.46. Site sketch of Tr-38.

One such group (A C) is located at the northwest edge of the site. This group, reinforced by Terrace C, is isolated from the other mounds. In the case of Mound A, the uneven heights of the north and south walls are is probably an attempt to compensate for the uneven terrain upon which it is built. This may have been an elite residence and perhaps even served some civic-ceremonial function.

In the center of the site, on a large level area, is a cluster of six mounds (D, E, F, G, H, and I) which appear to form at least one residential compound (and probably more). Mounds D, E, and F, grouped around an open patio, comprise one such house group. Mounds G, H, and I, all smaller structures, may represent one or more separate residential compounds. Terraces J and K, upslope from the house mounds, probably held residential structures.

Downslope to the east is another group (L, M, and N) that may have been a single house compound, constructed upon an artificial terrace (O). Finally, in the southwestern corner of the site is another low mound (P) which was also probably a residential structure. Upslope from the main area of occupation, more terraces were observed, but these were not counted or mapped.

This site appears to be a nucleated hamlet with no obvious ceremonial complex.

TR-38 (Figure 5.46)

Site Type: Ceremonial

Ceramic Phase: Foko, Hun

Occupation: late Middle Preclassic, Late Preclassic, Protoclassic

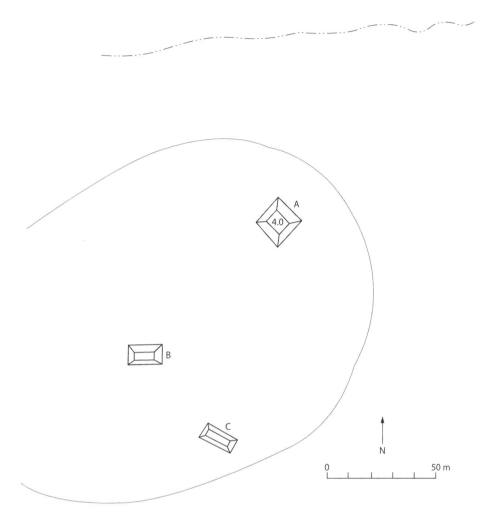

Figure 5.47. Site sketch of Tr-39, Tuminte.

Location and Setting: Tr-38 is located 3 km southwest of Colonia Ángel Albino Corzo on a low terrace overlooking the west bank of Río San Lucas. It is 1 km north of its confluence with Río Las Tres Marias. This site is 900 m northeast of Tr-37. It is in an area of hilly country, primarily used for milpa. The nearby water course is densely covered with riverine vegetation.

Environmental Stratum: Short Tree Savannah/ Thorn Woodland, Riparian Forest

Description: The site consists of a single temple platform measuring 20 by 15 m, by 3 m in height. It is located on a prominent position on a low river terrace which juts out into Río San Lucas. The single structure may have served as a ceremonial center for surrounding hamlets.

TR-39 TUMINTE (Figure 5.47)

Site Type: Ceremonial and habitation

Ceramic Phase: Mix

Occupation: Late Classic

Location and Setting: Tr-39 is 2.5 km south of Colonia Ángel Albino Corzo. It is situated on a river terrace overlooking the east bank of the Arroyo Tuminte, 500 m north of its confluence with Río Las Tres Marias. The local terrain consists of rolling hills, mainly used for milpa. The nearby arroyo is lined with riverine vegetation.

Environmental Stratum: Short Tree Savannah/ Thorn Woodland

Description: Tr-39 consists of a single temple platform (A) and two low rectangular mounds (B and C). The maximum extent of the site is 100 by 70 m. The largest mound (A) measures 15 by 15 m, and 4 m in height. The two remaining low mounds (B and C) are probably residential platforms. This site may have served as a ceremonial center for surrounding hamlets.

TR-40 COPALAR (Figures 5.48-5.52)

Site Type: Ceremonial and habitation

Ceramic Phase: Mix

Occupation: Late Classic

Location and Setting: This site is 1.5 km west of the entrance to Colonia Vicente Guerrero. It is in an area of low rolling limestone hills with a very shallow soil layer. There are some small low trees but it is mostly grassland pasture and scattered milpas.

Environmental Stratum: Grassland

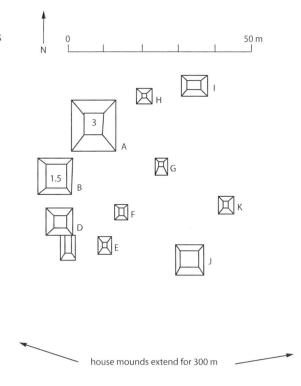

Figure 5.48. Site sketch of Tr-40, Copalar.

Figure 5.49. Area of house mounds at Tr-40, Copalar.

Figure 5.50. Ceremonial center of Tr-40, Copalar.

Figure 5.51. Area of house mounds at Tr-40, Copalar.

Figure 5.52. Close up of wall from circular structure seen from above, Tr-40, Copalar.

Description: The ceremonial center of this site consists of a tight cluster of mounds within a 60 by 50 m area. The largest mound (A) forms the northern part of a plaza with Mounds B, D, E, F, and G forming the west, south, and east sides. Several mounds, such as I, J, D, and B, may have been residential platforms. All of the mounds in the site core have the same north-south orientation and form a cohesive (and probably contemporaneous) complex. Additional house mounds were observed to the east and west of the central core but were not mapped. Near some of these house mounds were circular structures like those found at Los Cimientos (Tr-29) (Rivero 1987).

TR-41 EL CERRO JOCOTE
(Figures 5.53-5.55)

Site Type: Ceremonial and habitation

Ceramic Phase: Mix

Occupation: Late Classic

Location and Setting: This site is situated 500 m northwest of the center of Colonia Morelos on a steep hillside. Most of the hillslope is rocky with a thin layer of soil. At present the land is being used for milpa cultivation.

Environmental Stratum: Fields or Pastures

Description: There is one large mound at this site that is 20 by 20 m at the base and 10 m tall on the downslope side. It is the center of a complex of terraces that cover the hillside surrounding the mound. Only one other mound was noted, and it is a low platform mound that was possibly the base of a residential structure. It sits just to the southwest of the main pyramid and is on one of the terraces. The two mounds partially enclose a plaza terrace that contained a standing stone figure (Lee 1975: 45). It was contained within a low circular dry laid wall (possibly a modern construction).

Some of the terraces at the site are 170 m long and provide level ground that could have been used for habitation and/or agriculture.

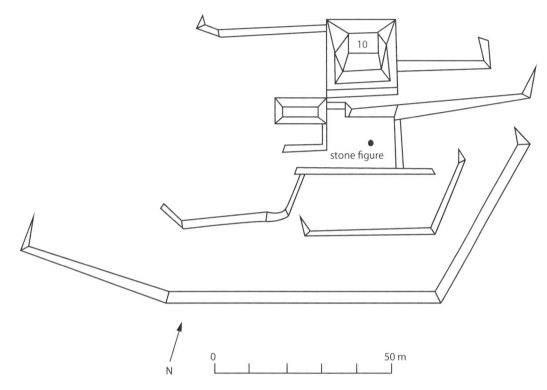

Figure 5.53. Site sketch of Tr-41, El Cerro Jocote.

Figure 5.54. Terraces at Tr-41, El Cerro Jocote.

Figure 5.55. Stone sculpture found at Tr-41, El Cerro Jocote.

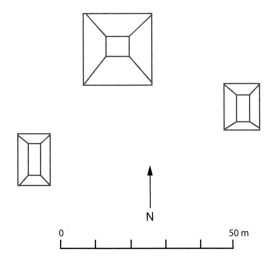

N

0   50 m

Figure 5.56. Site sketch of Tr-42, El Cerrito.

TR-42 EL CERRITO (Figures 5.56-5.59)

Site Type: Ceremonial and habitation

Occupation: possible Early Preclassic, Protoclassic, Early Classic, Middle Classic, Late Classic

Location and Setting: This site is located on a flat hilltop within the western section of the Morelos. The small hill is only about 200 m in diameter and rises to about 60 m above the surrounding valley bottom. There is some tree cover but the soil is very rocky and extremely dry, so little but xerophytic vegetation grows at the site.

Environmental Stratum: Fields or Pastures

Description: The site covers roughly 125 by 150 m of the mesa. Only three mounds were visible on the surface, but many terraces were also present. Excavations have defined in greater detail the cultural sequence at the site, as well as discovering numerous sub-surface features, according to a preliminary report of one season's work by John Clark and Ronald Lowe (1980).

The largest mound at the site, Mound 1, is 5 m tall and commands a view of the entire site, as well as some neighboring sites such as Tr-43 (Santa Rosa). Two more mounds (2 and 3) are located to the southeast and southwest, respectively, of the main mound. The three mounds form the north, west, and east sides of

Figure 5.57. View from Mound 1, Tr-42, El Cerrito.

Figure 5.58. Tr-42, El Cerrito.

Figure 5.59. Looking north upslope towards mound, Tr-42, El Cerrito.

a plaza area. Unfortunately, the large mound has been looted. Clark believes the large mound was a ceremonial structure and that Mounds 2 and 3 were elite residences (1980: 5-7). Test pits revealed the remains of four other habitations buried beneath a shallow layer of fill on the hilltop. Three of these were on the margins of the plaza and an additional one was to the north of Mound 1. In addition, several terraces were located by test pits around the periphery of the central zone on the hillslopes.

Four *chultunes* were found and excavated. One is to the west and the other to the east of the main plaza, while two others were associated with Structure 4 near Mound 2.

There appears to have been a large Protoclassic occupation responsible for the construction of the three large mounds at the site. All had the same orientation (northeast to southwest) and formed a major complex with the habitation structures undoubtedly occupied contemporaneously. There was some Late Classic modification and expansion of

at least Mound 3, but the site layout remained unchanged.

References: Bryant and Clark 1983; Clark and Lowe 1980 (Preliminary ceramic assessment placed this site as primarily Late Preclassic, but this was corrected to Protoclassic after excavating).

TR-43 SANTA ROSA (Figures 5.60-5.63)

Site Type: Ceremonial and habitation

Ceramic Phase: Hun, Kau, Mix

Occupation: Protoclassic, Early Classic, Late Classic

Location and Setting: This site is located on the top of a small hilltop at the southern edge of Colonia Morelos. The site is in a similar setting to Tr-42 (El Cerrito), 400 m to the northwest. The small hill rises approximately 50 m above the valley bottom and has fairly steep sides. Land use is milpa, although it was once sparsely covered with trees.

Figure 5.60. Tr-43, Santa Rosa.

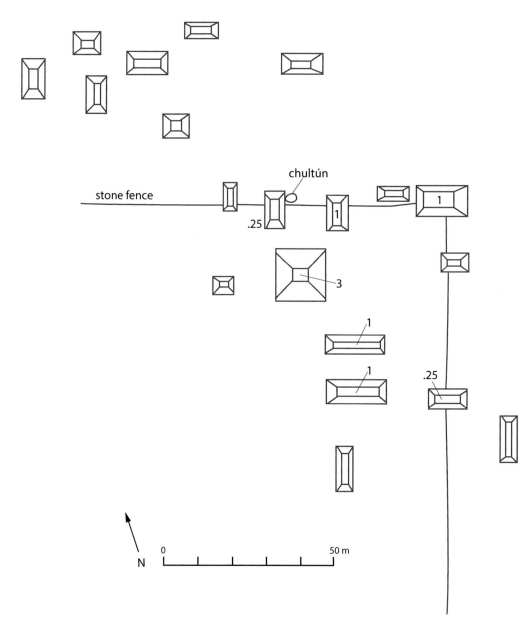

Figure 5.61. Site sketch of Tr-43, Santa Rosa.

Environmental Stratum: Fields or Pastures

Description: There are 19 mounds at this small hilltop site. The largest and most prominent is a 3 m tall, 15 m square mound in the central area of the site. It faces onto a plaza area defined by three smaller mounds (D, G, and H) and a ballcourt (B and C). The ballcourt has two 16 m long mounds that are approximately 1.5 m tall. Other small habitation mounds are located on the

terraces to the southeast of the main plaza (I, J, K, and L). To the north of the main complex is another group of low residential mounds. Many of these appear to be arranged around courtyards or patio, for example Mounds O, P, Q, and N. The whole hilltop is surrounded by a series of rock-faced terraces, typically less than 0.5 m tall. These were probably used to provide level ground for habitations that had either very low or no foundations and are therefore, not visible.

Figure 5.62. Tr-43, Santa Rosa.

Figure 5.63. *Chultún* at Tr-43, Santa Rosa.

They also could have been used for agricultural purposes. All mounds at the site are oriented to just east of the cardinal directions.

TR-44 TENAM SOLEDAD
(Figures 5.64-5.66)

Site Type: Ceremonial and habitation

Ceramic Phase: Kau, Mix

Occupation: Protoclassic, Early Classic, Middle Classic, Late Classic

Location and Setting: This site is located on the top of a very steep hill 600 m east of central Colonia Morelos. The hilltop overlooks a large valley to the east of the colonia. There are many milpas on the slopes of the hill and also patches of sparse forest. The top and sides of the hill are very rocky and soil cover is shallow.

Environmental Stratum: Tropical Deciduous Forest

Description: This large site was a hilltop ceremonial center similar to others in the area like Tr-9 (Tenam Rosario) and Tr-45 (Tenam Concepción). The ceremonial complex is on a flat part of the hilltop, 120 m long and 70 m wide. In total, there are 14 major mounds in this complex. The largest (G) is in the center of the site and measures 17 by 20 m by 6 m tall. Two smaller mounds flank it to the south (H and I) and outline a central plaza with a chultún near the center. The southern edge of this plaza is marked by a ballcourt (J), which is two tiered and has a total height of 1 m. Judging from the end-zone near Mound L, the court was I-shaped and the west end-zone is simply eroded. There is a small platform (K) in the central playing zone of the ballcourt, and it could be a recent altar. North of the big pyramid (C) is a 25 m long low mound (F) forming the southern edge of another plaza group. The other structures surrounding the plaza are small temple mounds (B, C, and E) and larger residential platforms (A and D). The entire hilltop complex has the same orientation to the cardinal directions. The long axis of the site is north-south. Covering the hillslope, surrounding the main part of the site, are numerous terraces with some evidence of habitation debris but not many well-defined house mounds.

Most of the construction at the site is rubble fill with stone facing. Unfortunately, many

Figure 5.64. View from site Tr-44, Tenam Soledad.

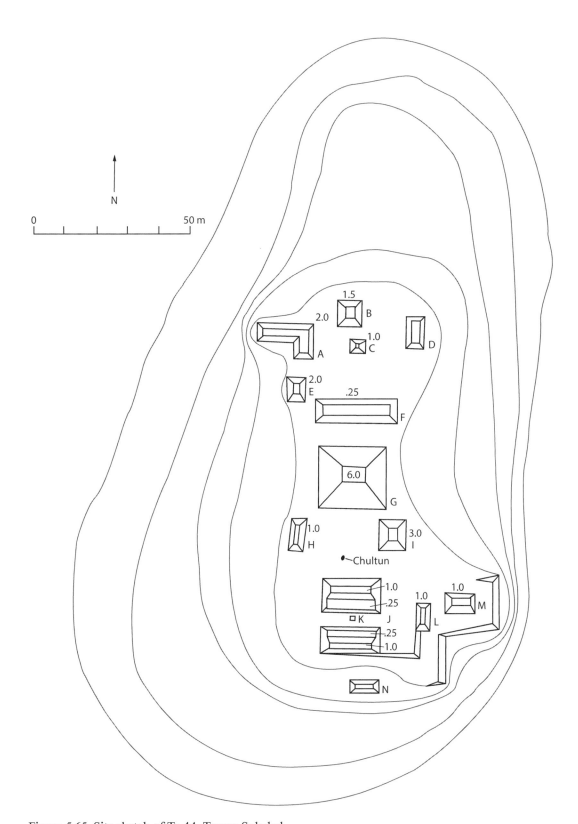

Figure 5.65. Site sketch of Tr-44, Tenam Soledad.

Figure 5.66. Looking northeast toward Mound L, end zone of ballcourt at Tr-44, Tenam Soledad.

of the stones have been robbed for modern constructions, and the large pyramid has also been badly looted.

References: Blom and Duby 1957 II:44 45, fig. 7; Lee 1975.

TR-45 TENAM CONCEPCIÓN (no map)
(Figures 5.67-5.70)

Site Type: Ceremonial and habitation

Ceramic Phase: Mix

Occupation: Protoclassic, Late Classic

Location and Setting: This large site is located 5.5 km northwest of Colonia Rodolfo Figueroa and 1.5 km west of Río San Lucas. It sits on a cliff top that overlooks Río San Lucas Valley to the east and also commands a view of Río Santa Inés Valley 7 km to the west where Tr-9 (Tenam Rosario) is located. The site terrain is fairly flat and rocky with only sparse tree cover. Vegetation is primarily long grass and a few scattered bushes.

Environmental Stratum: Short Tree Savannah/ Thorn Woodland

Description: The ceremonial center of this site has many large pyramids, platforms for residences, and plazas. The largest mound at the site is 10 m high and sits on a huge platform at least 50 m long. There are two enclosed plazas that are surrounded by long mounds on all four sides. One of the large platforms may have been a double stairway on one side, but excavation is needed to confirm this. A fragment of carved stela was located in the center of one plaza, but it was only part of the whole piece, which was broken and since taken from the site. There is an I-shaped ballcourt in very good condition and faced with cut stone. Unfortunately, the grass was too high to permit an accurate sketch map of the site.

Figure 5.67. Tr-45, Tenam Concepción.

Figure 5.68. West end of ballcourt at Tr-45, Tenam Concepción.

Figure 5.69. Tr-45, Tenam Concepción.

Figure 5.70. Tr-45, Tenam Concepción.

Figure 5.71. View southeast of Mound A at Tr-46.

TR-46 (Figures 5.71-5.72)

Site Type: Ceremonial and habitation

Ceramic Phase: Ix, Mix

Occupation: Protoclassic, Late Classic

Location and Setting: This site is 600 m east of the center of Colonia Morelos and 300 m north of Tr-44 (Tenam Soledad). The site is on a flat spot on the hillslope rising out of the valley bottom in which the colonia is located. The terrain is very rocky and vegetation consists of sparse tree cover and grass land.

Environmental Stratum: Grassland

Description: There is one large pyramid and seven other small temple mounds and residence platforms at this site. All are tightly clustered in a 90 by 70 m area on the hillside. The mounds sit on a complex system of terraces which provide for large plazas, like Plaza I, and extend the total area of level ground. The main pyramid (A) is 5 m tall and shows evidence of having contained at least one corbelled vault. This mound was constructed of rubble fill and had cut stone facings. Two other mounds (E and F) on the

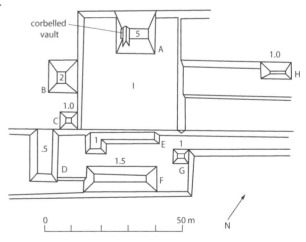

Figure 5.72. Site sketch of Tr-46.

southeast side of Plaza I may have formed an I-shaped ballcourt and then was subsequently remodeled on the west end of Mound E for some other purpose. Other mounds such as D and H probably formed the base of elite residences. There are more terraces on the hillside surrounding this main core, but there is not much evidence of house platforms.

The orientation of all mounds and terraces is from northwest to southeast.

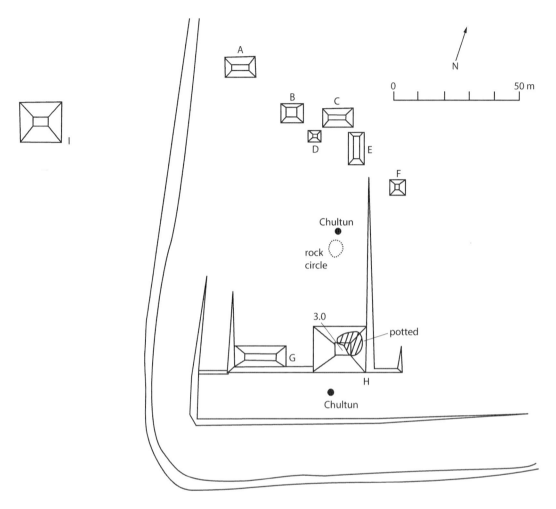

Figure 5.73. Site sketch of Tr-47, Los Cerritos.

TR-47 LOS CERRITOS
(Figures 5.73-5.74)

Site Type: Ceremonial and habitation

Ceramic Phase: Hun, Mix

Occupation: Late Preclassic, Protoclassic, Late Classic

Location and Setting: This site is located on the northeast edge of Colonia Morelos, within 400 m of Tr-46, Tr-48, and Tr-49. It lies on a low hilltop rising above the valley bottom. The land is very rocky and is covered with small bushes, grass, and the occasional large tree.

Environmental Stratum: Grassland

Description: There are nine mounds at this site, arranged atop a terraced hill. Six of the smaller mounds (A to F) are spread in a line along the northern edge with a smaller mound (D), which could be an altar. In the central plaza area is a *chultún* and to the south of it, a circle of upended stone slabs. The southern and eastern sides of the plaza are marked by large mounds and terraces. The largest of these (H) is 3 m tall but badly potted. To the west is a long low mound that could have served as an elite residence platform. An isolated mound (I) was located 80 m to the northwest of the main plaza area. All mounds have the same orientation from northwest to southeast.

Figure 5.74. Circle of upended stones, Tr-47, Los Cerritos.

TR-48 BUENOS AIRES (Figure 5.75)

Site Type: Habitation

Ceramic Phase: Mix

Occupation: Late Classic

Location and Setting: This site is located 800 m northeast of the center of Colonia Morelos on a south-facing hillside. The site is 350 m north of Tr-47 and 200 m northwest of Tr-46. The hillside has fairly shallow soil and is very rocky in spots. The land is used for milpa.

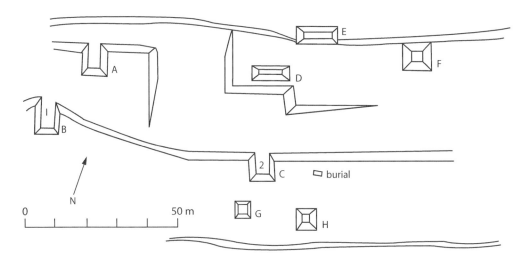

Figure 5.75. Site sketch of Tr-48.

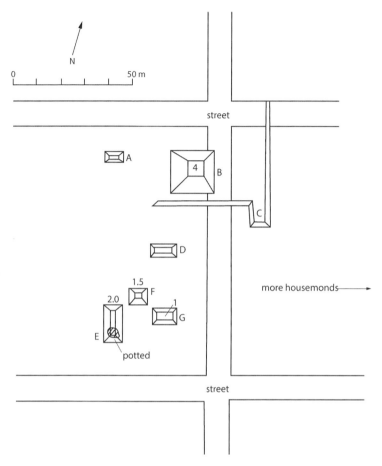

Figure 5.76. Site sketch of Tr-49, Barrio Nuevo.

Environmental Stratum: Grassland

Description: There are several habitation mounds and terraces at this small site. Some of the mounds are free-standing and near the edge of terraces, such as D, E, and F. Others are located in central terrace areas like G and H, which could be a house group around a patio area between them. Three other platforms are simply projections of the terraces (A, B, and C). These house platforms were probably located on leveled terraces to provide flat land for both habitation and agriculture.

An urn burial was reportedly plowed up just to the east of Platform C. No other artifacts were reported. All of the terraces and mounds have the same orientation from northwest to southeast, and so could well have been part of a single contemporaneous community.

TR-49 BARRIO NUEVO (Figure 5.76)

Site Type: Ceremonial and habitation

Ceramic Phase: Kau, Mix, Nichim

Occupation: late Middle Preclassic, Late Preclassic, Early Classic, Late Classic, Early Postclassic

Location and Setting: This site is located on a low ridge within Colonia Morelos, 200 m from the central plaza. The site is in a modern household compound that has several modern buildings and much disturbance.

Environmental Stratum: Grassland

Description: This collection of mounds within the limits of the present-day colonia is essentially confined to the eastern portion of one block (100 by 100 m). The largest mound at the site is B, which is 4 m tall and 17 m square. It is partially

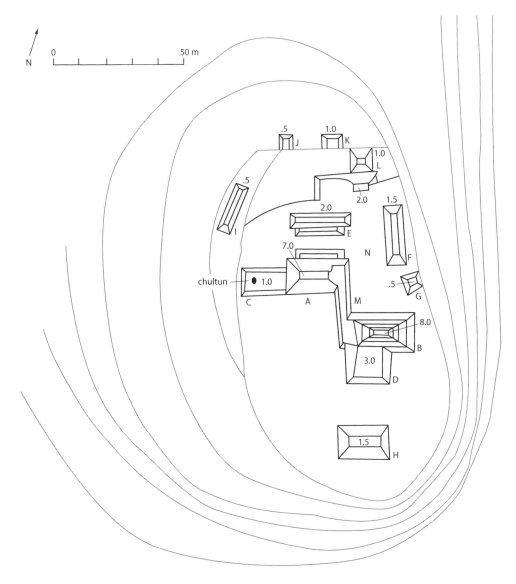

Figure 5.77. Site sketch of Tr-50, Tenam Poco Uinik.

disturbed by a modern street but otherwise is intact. The mound is partly surrounded by a long terrace that also contains a platform extension (C) which may have been the base of a house. To the south of this complex are four other mounds, three of which are arranged in a patio group (E, F, and G). Several other house mounds were recorded 200 m to the southeast, but these were not mapped. The overall configuration may have been larger but modern construction in the colonia has probably destroyed some mounds. All those remaining have the same northwest to southeast orientation and were probably part of a single contemporaneous community.

**TR-50 TENAM POCO UINIK
(Figures 5.77-5.80)**

Site Type: Ceremonial and habitation

Ceramic Phase: Mix

Occupation: Protoclassic, Late Classic

Location and Setting: The site is located 1.7 km west of the center of Colonia Morelos. It is on a hilltop, which has a steep sloping southern periphery and a much more gradual northern slope. The maximum extent of the site is undetermined. The site overlooks a small arroyo

Figure 5.78. Mound B at Tr-50, Tenam Poco Uinik.

Figure 5.79. Terraces at Tr-50, Tenam Poco Uinik.

Figure 5.80. Stucco architectural fragments at Tr-50, Tenam Poco Uinik.

that flows south past Colonia Ángel Albino Corzo and eventually into Río San Lucas. The terrain surrounding the site is primarily milpa.

Environmental Stratum: Tropical Deciduous Forest

Description: The whole complex is a tight cluster of structures that covers an area of 130 by 80 m on the knoll top with never more than 20 m separating any structure from the other. The site appears to be a ceremonial and civic complex that includes two pyramids, one large plaza, two large platforms, one ballcourt, and seven low platform mounds that may have been elite residences. The two large pyramids (A and B) are linked together by a low 10 m long platform (M). Each pyramid has an additional low platform (C, D) extending away from the main plaza. The northernmost pyramid (A) has a ballcourt attached (E). The ballcourt is I-shaped but has no well-defined end zones. This complex, together with the southern pyramid (B) forms the west and south borders of the plaza (N). Most of the possible elite habitation mounds are located on the northern edge of the site, but one large low mound (F), perhaps an elite residence, forms the eastern edge of the plaza. Another (H) is located 16 m south of the largest pyramid (B).

The whole top of the knoll appears to be artificially leveled while the pyramid may take advantage of natural rises in the knoll. A *chultún* was found in a platform that adjoins the northern pyramid and may confirm that the bases of the higher mounds and the pyramids were sculpted from natural formations. The entire site appears to have been a single contemporaneous complex for the following reasons: first, there are several structures joined to each other by architectural features; and second, there is a consistent orientation of the axes of all but one structure (I).

References: Basuari 1931; Blom and Duby 1957 II:44

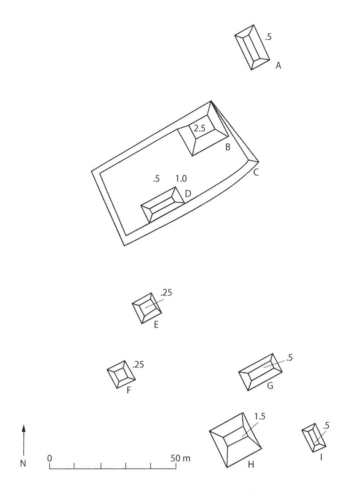

Figure 5.81. Site sketch of Tr-51, La Cieneguilla.

TR-51 LA CIENEGUILLA (Figure 5.81)

Site Type: Ceremonial and habitation

Ceramic Phase: Mix

Occupation: Late Classic, Early Postclassic

Location and Setting: The site is located 700 m southwest of the center of Colonia Morelos and 200 m northeast of the old La Cieneguilla ranch house. It is situated in an area of rolling hills at the base of several steeper slopes to the north. The area of the site overlooks a low-lying swampy area. There is sparse shrub cover in the area and present-day milpas cover the zone.

Environmental Stratum: Tropical Deciduous Forest

Description: The site consists of eight small mounds and a large low platform. Two of the mounds are situated on the platform. The dimensions of the site are about 140 by 90 m and the structures are distributed fairly evenly over this area. The most complex structure at the site is the platform mound (C), which measures 35 by 55 m and is 0.5 m high. The tallest mound at the site (B) sits on the northeast corner of the platform and adjacent to it on the southwest corner is a lower rectangular mound. One mound (A) is to the northeast of the platform complex and all the other mounds which are probably residence platforms are to the south of the platform complex. Three of these mounds (G, H, and I) are arranged in such a way as to suggest they are residences surrounding a plaza. All of the mounds at the site have the same orientation indicating contemporaneity.

References: Marquina 1939:33; Piña Chan 1967:53

TR-52 CUEVA LA CIENEGUILLA OR TONCHUB ROCKSHELTER (no map)

Site Type: Cave

Ceramic Phase: Mix

Occupation: Late Classic, Late Postclassic

Location and Setting: This rockshelter is at the base of a large outcrop 500 m north of Los Cimientos (Tr-29). It overlooks the milpa land of Rancho La Cieneguilla and a low basin. There is sparse shrubby vegetation with a few scattered large trees.

Environmental Stratum: Tropical Deciduous Forest

Description: The large rockshelter is 300 m wide at the mouth and the opening is about 12 m high. The shelter is several meters deep and large enough so that a few cattle can be kept inside. There is evidence of recent human disturbance, and cattle have also contributed to the erosion of the deposits. Sherd, lithic flakes, and bone fragments were observed inside on the floor of the rockshelter. Two smaller shelters were located 15 to 20 m further west along the base of the cliff, but no further information is available for them.

References: Blom and Duby 1957 II:44

TR-53 JOGALY AMATE (Figure 5.82)

Site Type: Ceremonial and habitation

Ceramic Phase: Mix

Occupation: Late Classic

Location and Setting: The site is located approximately 500 m west of Colonia Vicente Guerrero and spans both sides of the road to Colonia Ángel Albino Corzo. It is located in an area of rolling grass-covered hills with very few trees. There is some milpa activity in the vicinity. The terrain is very rocky.

Environmental Stratum: Grassland

Description: There are two groups of low mounds separated by 60 m. In neither group are there any mounds greater than 2 m high. The westernmost group contains 13 mounds

and one platform over an area of 90 by 80 m. All are within 15 m of each other, except for a small group of three mounds to the north (L, M, and N) that is 25-30 m from the nearest mounds. One small mound (I) is built onto a low terrace-platform (H) providing a level spot on the hillside. Several of the mounds form groups of three or so which delineate small plaza areas (i.e., A/B/C; L/M/N; and G/I/J). Another mound (K) is somewhat isolated from the rest. All of the mounds appear to be residence platforms with the exception of A and B, which may be small temple mounds, and E, D, and M which are perhaps small altars. Another group to the east of the group just described contains a total of five mounds. All are tightly clustered in an area of no more than 25 by 30 m, and none of them are more than 5 m apart from each other. They appear to enclose a plaza with an altar (R) in the central area. All of the mounds in both groups have the same orientation. This, combined with their tight clustering, suggests contemporaneity.

TR-54 (Figure 5.83)

Site Type: Habitation

Ceramic Phase: Mix

Occupation: Late Classic

Location and Setting: The site is located on low rolling terrain 100 m northwest of the entrance to Colonia Vicente Guerrero. There is very little vegetation covering the site, primarily grass and some scattered trees. Tr-53, another small site, is located 400 m to the west and may have been closely related to this site.

Environmental Stratum: Grassland

Description: The site consists of 23 small habitation and altar mounds covering an area of about 240 m long and 50 m wide along a low ridge. Most of the mounds are less than 10 m apart from each other, but two groups of three mounds each are about 40 m from the others. One of these groups (A/B/C) forms a possible domestic unit surrounding a plaza. The other (D/E/F) may form a similar configuration, although Mound D and mounds east are both very small and could be altars. Another cluster

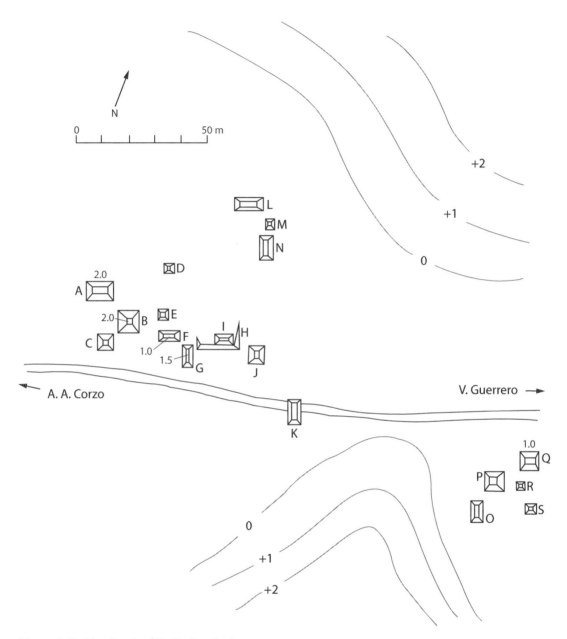

Figure 5.82. Site sketch of Tr-53, Jogaly Amate.

of habitation mounds (G, H, and I) further to the south also appear to cluster around a large plaza, and there is a small mound (K) which may be associated. The large group of mounds (I to U) does not form such a distinct pattern as the previous groups, but they too may be associated with each other around unseen plazas. Small mounds in that group, such as Q, may be altars. There are really no mounds in the site large

enough to be temple structures. The highest mound (N) is only 1.5 m tall. Two mounds (V and W) are more isolated from the others and may represent separate domestic units. Like many of the sites previously described (e.g., Tr-53), all of the mounds appear to have the same orientation, suggesting that they are all part of a contemporaneous community.

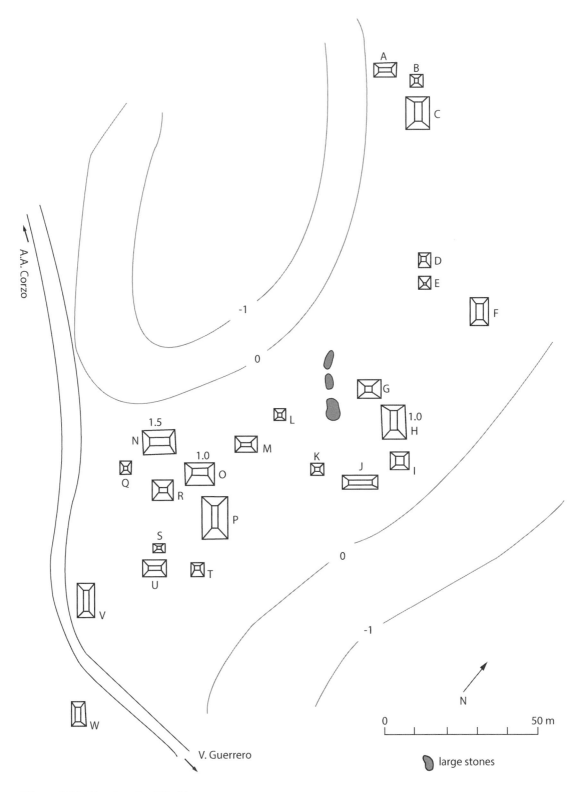

Figure 5.83. Site sketch of Tr-54.

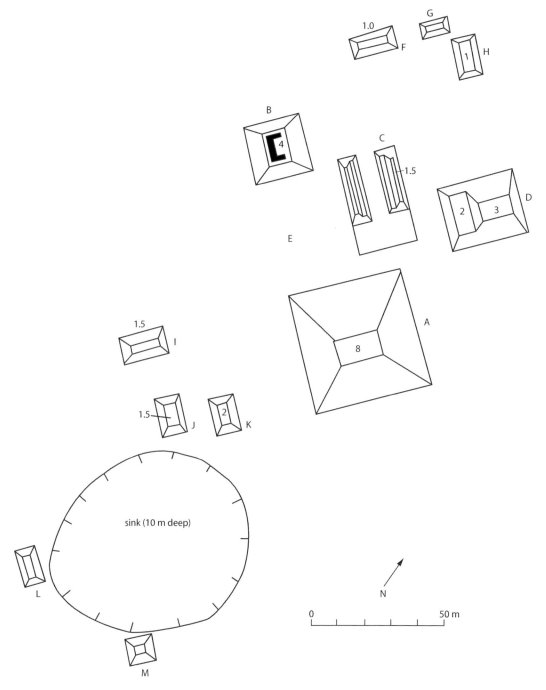

Figure 5.84. Site sketch of Tr-55, San José Las Canoas.

TR-55 SAN JOSÉ LAS CANOAS
(Figures 5.84-5.85)

Site Type: Ceremonial and habitation

Ceramic Phase: Kau, Mix, Ux

Occupation: Protoclassic, Early Classic, Middle Classic, Late Classic, Late Postclassic

Location and Setting: This large site is located about 300 m north of Colonia Vicente Guerrero and approximately 500 m south of San José Las

Figure 5.85. Mound A looking toward Mound B, Tr-55.

Canoas ranch house. It is situated on an area of rolling terrain with very little vertical relief. There are some shrubs growing in the site area itself but few large trees. The zone to the north of the site is under cultivation.

Environmental Stratum: Grassland

Description: The central core of the site covers an area of about 100 by 300 m. In addition to this there is evidence of more low residential mounds and occupational debris stretching several hundred meters to the west. The main part of the site consists of one large temple mound, two smaller ones, a ballcourt, and eight large house mounds. The largest temple mound (A) reaches a height of 8 m. It overlooks the ballcourt (C), which is located on the east side of the main plaza (E). Two smaller temple mounds also face onto the plaza (B and D). The tallest of these (B) is 4 m high and has the remains of a walled building on the top. The wall is approximately 1 m high and the east side is open. It may be colonial. The other temple mound (D) has a 2 m high platform before it finally rises to 3 m high at the top. Three low residential mounds (F, G, and H) were located 30 m north of this large complex

and seem to outline another possible plaza between them and the ballcourt. Another three low mounds seem to fulfill the same function just 30 m to the southwest of the main complex. They probably face onto a plaza, adjacent to the large temple mound (which may have been an extension of E). All structures at the site conform to the same orientation. Two additional mounds (L and M) were located 100 m southwest of Mound A. They overlook a large sink that is 80 m in diameter and 10 m deep.

TR-56 (Figure 5.86)

Site Type: Ceremonial and habitation

Ceramic Phase: Kau

Occupation: Protoclassic, Early Classic, Late Classic

Location and Setting: This site is located 1 km northwest of Colonia Vicente Guerrero and 600 m west of Tr-55 (San José Las Canoas). It is situated on the west side of a low hill and extends for 240 m along the slope. There is little disturbance in the area and the site is covered with forest.

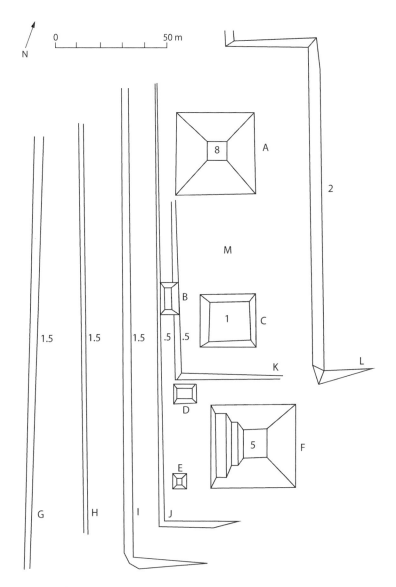

Figure 5.86. Site sketch of Tr-56.

Environmental Stratum: Tropical Deciduous Forest

Description: The site contains two large temple mounds, one large platform, and three smaller mounds as well as a series of six large terraces. The two large mounds at the site (A and F) are separated by a 90 m long plaza (M) that contains a large platform (C). Mound F has three tiers on its western side facing onto a portion of Terrace J, which contains two smaller mounds (D and E). The plaza area (M) is formed on the west by Terrace K and Mound B and on the east by Terrace L which is 2 m high. The western part of the site on the hillslope has three terraces, each 1.5 m high and parallel to each other and extending for a length of 200 m. This whole ceremonial center is oriented on the same axis, including the terraces. More habitation mounds were noted extending upslope towards the east. House mounds were also noted at Tr-55 extending west towards this site, and there may have been a continuous occupation between the two sites.

TR-57 (Figure 5.87)

Site Type: Habitation

Ceramic Phase: Mix

Occupation: Late Classic

Location and Setting: The site is located 1 km west of Colonia Vicente Guerrero and 400 m southwest of Tr-56. It is in an area of rolling fields converted into pastures and milpas. There are some large trees and small bushes in the vicinity.

Environmental Stratum: Grassland

Description: Twelve low habitation mounds were observed at this site. All are less than 10 m on a side and less than 50 cm high except Mound J, which is double-tiered and is 1 m at the highest point. The site has a linear orientation with all structures oriented to the long axis of the site. The most clearly defined patio group is composed of structures F, G, H, I, and J around an open area. The maximum distance between neighboring mounds is 27 m between K and L. A 70 m long terrace extends along the west edge of Mound D and seems to enclose a possible plaza area fronting onto Mounds A, B, C, D and E.

TR-58 CHUMISH (Figure 5.88)

Site Type: Habitation

Ceramic Phase: Mix

Occupation: Protoclassic, Late Classic

Location and Setting: This site is located 2 km northwest of Colonia Vicente Guerrero in a zone of very low hills and sparse trees and shrubs. There is a small seasonal water course on the northeast edge of the site.

Environmental Stratum: Grassland

Description: There are a series of small house mounds in this long linear site. Two larger mounds (F and G) are among the structures at the site, and these were both at least twice as high as the other mounds. Mounds F and G are in the central area and are linked together by an L-shaped wall. These structures together with a small mound (H) enclose a patio area. Two

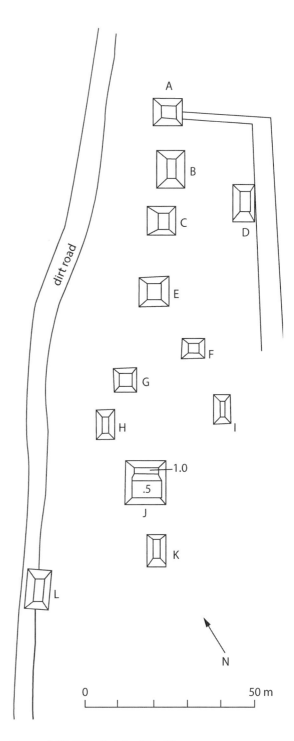

Figure 5.87. Site sketch of Tr-57.

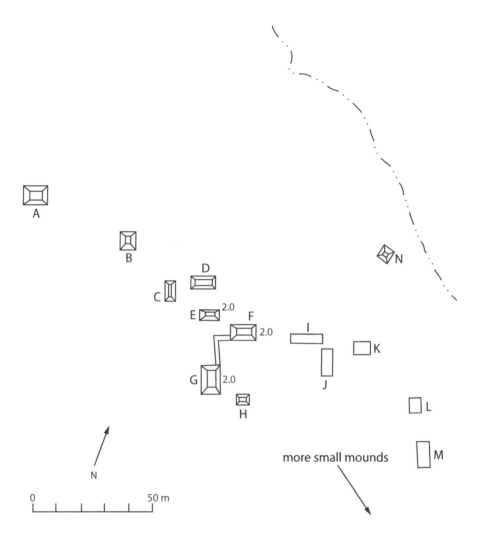

Figure 5.88. Site sketch of Tr-58, Chumish.

smaller structures (I and J), which are outlined by stone foundations, also appear to front onto the same patio. Further to the north, C, D, and E may enclose a small patio and may also have been a domestic group. Other mounds such as A, B, and N were isolated from other mounds. The linear orientation of the site is east-west, but the mounds themselves are oriented west of north. Additional small mounds extend to the east but were not mapped. All of the structures conform to a coherent orientation and apparently planned arrangement. It probably represents one occupation or construction sequence.

TR-59 EL TIMBRAL (no map)

Site Type: Habitation

Ceramic Phase: Mix

Occupation: Late Classic

Location and Setting: This site is located 1.5 km east of Colonia Ángel Albino Corzo on the south side of the road that leads to Colonia Morelos. It is located in a zone of heavy vegetation and tree cover with milpa land interspersed.

Environmental Stratum: Tropical Deciduous Forest

Description: This site consists of house mounds with patios and patio walls and terraces. There is also a circular structure similar to the ones at Tr-60, roughly 5 km to the east.

TR-60 (Figure 5.89)

Site Type: Ceremonial and habitation

Ceramic Phase: Mix

Occupation: Late Classic, Late Postclassic

Location and Setting: This site is located 1.5 km west of Colonia Vicente Guerrero in an area of very low rolling hills with grassland pasturage and sparse tree cover.

Environmental Stratum: Grassland

Description: This large site consists of at least 26 residential mounds, a temple mound, a complex network of terraces, and several semi-circular structures. The entire site is aligned on the same axis, including the terraces. The largest structures are in the central portion of the site, with U, the tallest mound at 3 m, surrounded by plazas and other large mounds such as O and W. One large plaza is defined by terraces and Mounds U, W, X, Y and Z. A semi-circular structure (AAA) sits to the southeast of this unit. Another plaza is defined by Mounds O, N, Q, and U, with Mound P in the central area. To the east is a well-defined domestic unit with Mounds CC and DD as well as a surrounding set of terraces. Other groups of mounds also seem to be systematically aligned in groups of two or three around possible patio areas: A and B; E, F, and G; I and H; J and K; T, EE, and V.

The function of the semi-circular stone structures (C, D, and AA) is not known, but they may have been sweatbaths or lime kilns. AA had a small pile of cobbles in its center, but the others had no such features on the surface. The terrace structures at the site create large level areas and define groups of mounds in plaza or patio arrangements. This gives the impression that the site was built over a relatively short period of time and that most of the structures are contemporaneous. In a disturbed portion of the site between Mound B and the semi-circle C was found a cremation jar with a bowl stopping the opening.

TR-61 CIMA (Figures 5.90-5.91)

Site Type: Habitation

Location and Setting: This site is located 1.5 km west of Colonia Vicente Guerrero and 200 m south of Tr-60. It is located in an area of rolling low hills similar to the terrain near Tr-60. The surrounding vegetation is mostly grassland with scattered low trees. Soil conditions are poor, and the surface of the site zone is covered with large limestone outcrops.

Environmental Stratum: Grassland

Description: The site is a cluster of house mounds and terraces spread over a very low hill. The main center of the site contains a number of mounds that were closely spaced and linked together by long terraces. Two of the largest mounds (H and J) are 2 m high, but most are 1 m high or less. There are few clear patio groups: H, I, and J may face onto a patio, which is also in part formed by a terrace, and the mounds to the east seem to form an isolated cluster 60 m east of the main group. There is a large L-shaped platform (K) in the central area, and it may have been a basal mound for several perishable structures. Just to the south of this platform is a large stone walled semi-circular structure (Q) similar to ones at Tr-60. It stands 50-75 cm high at several points and contains as many as three courses of stones. Most of the stones are irregular cobbles and boulders, heaped on each other and not carefully laid. The outside diameter is 10 m. Rivero (1982) suggest these were used in *cal* or limestone processing. Twenty-five meters west of Mound F is a deep cave, but it was not explored and its cultural significance is not known.

This site, like Tr-60, is interconnected by a complex terrace network. Combined with the standard northeast-southwest orientation of all the mounds and terraces and the compact nature of the site layout, it appears that most of the structures are contemporaneous with each other.

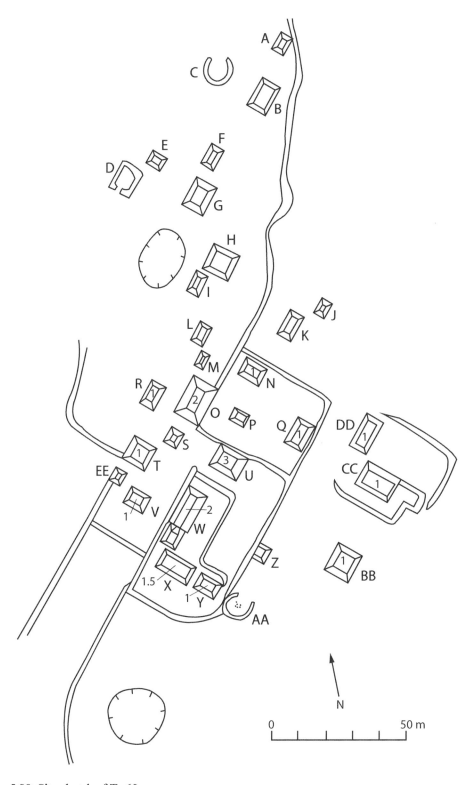

Figure 5.89. Site sketch of Tr-60.

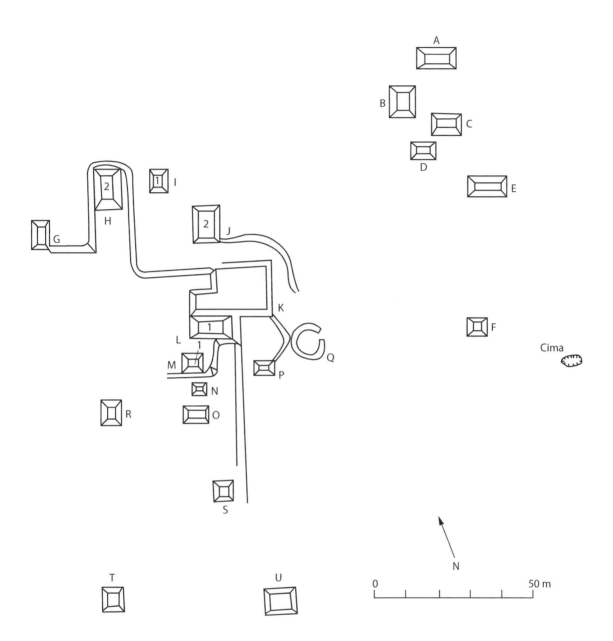

Figure 5.90. Site sketch of Tr-61, Cima.

Figure 5.91. Circular structure with opening (Q) ar Tr-61, Cima.

TR-62 CALVARIO (Figures 5.92-5.95)

Site Type: Ceremonial and habitation

Ceramic Phase: Mix

Occupation: Late Classic

Location and Setting: It is in an area of low hills and rolling terrain, most of which is very rocky. The site itself is on the top of a hill that rises approximately 50 m above the surrounding plain and 1 km south of Colonia Vicente Guerrero. Vegetation cover is very sparse in the rocky soil, but there are small trees scattered over the hillsides.

Environmental Stratum: Grassland

Description: The hilltop setting of the site isolates it from the surrounding locations yet provides a good view of the area. There are 11 mounds at the site, and these are roughly arranged on a north-south axis. The largest mound (F) is 2.5 m high and has a 25 m long terrace extending west from its southwest corner. There is also a long parallel terrace (G) 10 m to the south. Mound F seems to form the southern edge of a plaza area defined on the east by Mounds A, B, and D. A small structure (C), which may have been an altar, is located between D and F, perhaps in the plaza. Another large mound (E) is buttressed by a large terrace enclosing a flat area that the central mound complex sits on. Two platform terraces project on the southeast portion of the hilltop. Mound I sits between them. Two additional mounds (K and L) are located downslope on the northwest slope of the hilltop. The whole complex probably represents a contemporaneous series of small structures with some ceremonial importance. There are also three long rock piles 10 m to the east of Mound B that may have been modern graves. Mound D has located atop it a circular structure 5 m in diameter and built of five courses of cobbles and boulders. It contains two wooden crosses and is now used as a shrine for rain and curing ceremonies by people from Colonia Vicente Guerrero.

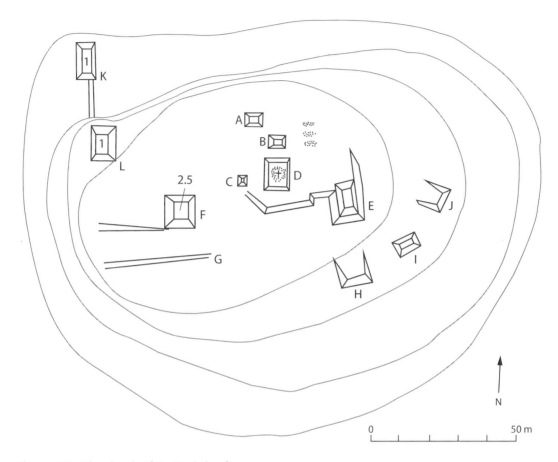

Figure 5.92. Site sketch of Tr-62, Calvario.

Figure 5.93. Pabellon Modeled-carved sherd, Tr-62, Calvario.

Figure 5.94. Modern shrine on Mound 3, Tr-62, Calvario.

Figure 5.95. Close-up of modern shrine on Mound 3, Tr-62, Calvario.

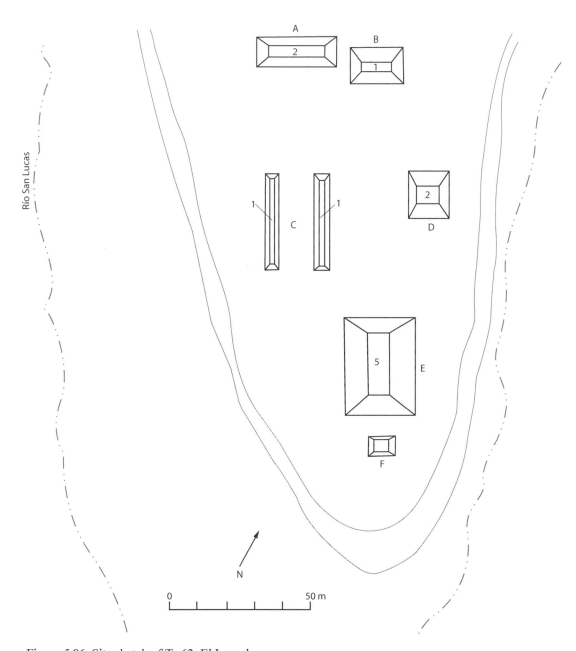

Figure 5.96. Site sketch of Tr-63, El Laurel.

TR-63 EL LAUREL (Figures 5.96-5.98)

Site Type: Ceremonial and habitation

Occupation: Late Classic

Location and Setting: This site is located 1.5 km north of Colonia Rodolfo Figueroa on the east side of Río San Lucas. It is on part of the river bench well above the flood plain, and the terrain is very flat. The land is cleared and plowed for modern milpa activity, but there are isolated large trees and the mounds are covered with small trees and bushes.

Environmental Setting: Short Tree Savannah/ Thorn Woodland, Riparian Forest

Description: The portion of this site that remains consists of five mounds and a ballcourt. The mounds enclose a plaza facing southwest

Figure 5.97. Tr-63, El Laurel.

Figure 5.98. Tr-63, El Laurel.

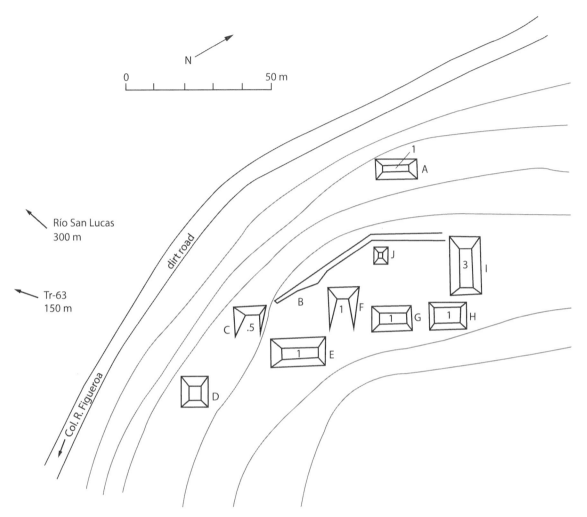

Figure 5.99. Tr-64, Rancho San Antonio.

towards the river. Mounds A and B form the northern part of the plaza; D is on the eastern side; Mound E (the largest mound at 34 by 25 m and 2 m high) marks the southern periphery of the plaza. The smallest mound at the site (F) is just to the south of Mound E. The ballcourt is open-ended and is formed by two long narrow, 1 m high mounds near the central plaza. All of the structures form a tight unit with consistent orientation to the west of north. There may have been smaller habitation mounds surrounding this ceremonial center, but recent agricultural disturbance has probably leveled them.

TR-64 RANCHO SAN ANTONIO
(Figures 5.99-5.100)

Site Type: Ceremonial and habitation

Location and Setting: This site is located 1.75 km north of Colonia Rodolfo Figueroa on the east side of Río San Lucas. Tr-63 is located 200 m to the southwest. Tr-64 is situated on the side of a hill facing Río San Lucas Valley but not more than 20 m above the valley bottom. The site location itself is on the rocky terrain of the hillslope. There is a sparse cover of short trees in the site area but the land is mostly grass covered.

Environmental Stratum: Short Tree Savannah/Thorn Woodland

Figure 5.100. Upslope veiw of Tr-64, Rancho San Antonio.

Description: There are nine mounds on the west-facing hillside that leads up from Río San Lucas, 300 m away. A plaza was formed by the construction of a terrace (B) on top of which are located several mounds (F, G, H, I and J). These mounds are arranged as a group facing downslope with a small mound (J) possibly used as an altar. One mound (A) is isolated from the rest and is situated downslope, while another (D) is also slightly separated to the south. Two mounds (C and F) are really terrace platforms extending out of the hillside and flank Mound E, which is one of the largest at the site. Since this tight cluster of mounds all have the same orientation, they are probably contemporaneous and represent the nucleus of a community.

TR-65 (Figures 5.101-5.102)

Site Type: Habitation

Ceramic Phase: Mix

Occupation: Late Classic

Location and Setting: This site is located 2 km north of the center of Colonia Rodolfo Figueroa on the eastern side of Río San Lucas, 750 m east of the main channel. It is on a small hilltop, which is very rocky and covered with grass and a few small trees.

Environmental Stratum: Short Tree Savannah/Thorn Woodland

Description: The site consists of five small habitation mounds surrounding a much larger mound (F) 1.5 m high. All of the visible mounds cover an area of 55 by 35 m and seem to aggregate as a single domestic compound. They may have been built at roughly the same time since they all have the same orientation.

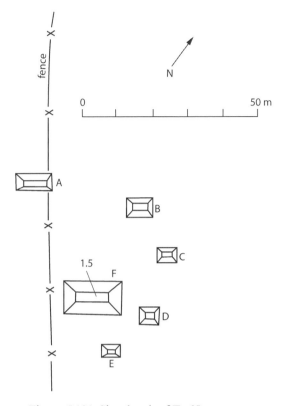

Figure 5.101. Site sketch of Tr-65.

Figure 5.102. Mound A, Tr-65.

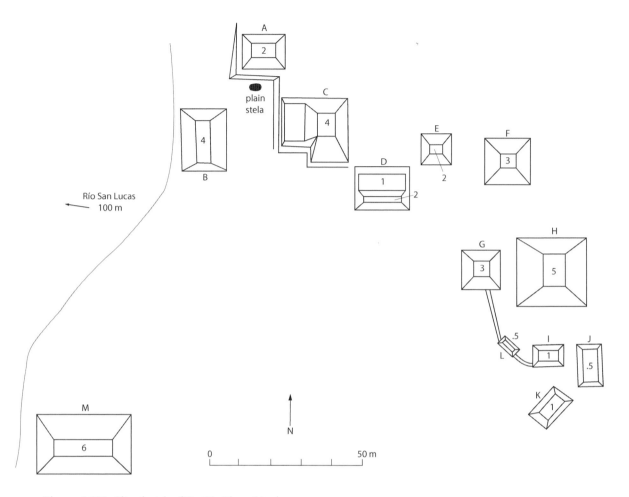

Figure 5.103. Site sketch of Tr-66, Clavo Verde.

TR-66 CLAVO VERDE
(Figures 5.103-5.105)

Site Type: Ceremonial and habitation

Ceramic Phase: Hun, Mix

Occupation: Protoclassic, Late Classic

Location and Setting: The site is located 2.3 km north of Colonia Rodolfo Figueroa on the second bench of Río San Lucas. The site is 100 m east of the river near the edge of the terrace. The terrain is flat except for the steep terrace that drops down to the river. Vegetation consists of small trees on the mounds with the surrounding land under cultivation. The fields nearby have concentrations of stones that may represent prehistoric house foundations.

Environmental Stratum: Short Tree Savannah/ Thorn Woodland, Riparian Forest

Description: There are 12 large mounds in this ceremonial center. The majority lies in a stretch 320 m long and 60 m wide across the river terrace. There is a consistent north-south orientation to all the mounds except for Mounds K and L, two of the smaller ones. The cluster of large mounds is in the northern part of the site and consists of Mounds A, B, C, and D. There is a terrace connecting Mounds A and C. A plain, 5 m tall stela is located between Mounds B and C and in front of Mound A. Mounds C and D, which are side by side, were both double-tiered. Another group of mounds (G through L) is located in the eastern part of the site, but some are offset from the others (K and L), and there is no clear plaza formed. Mounds I, L, and G

Figure 5.104. View toward site Tr-66, Clavo Verde, with Mound H in the background to the left.

Figure 5.105. Plain stela, from two sides, at Tr-66, Clavo Verde (Alejandro Sánchez).

are connected by a long curvilinear terrace. The largest mound at the site is M and it is located 170 m south of the rest. Its dimensions are 60 by 40 m and 6 m high. The zone between Mound M and the rest is plowed and contained evidence of stone fill from destroyed mounds.

The overall orientation of the mounds suggests they were all planned as a single ceremonial center with the exception of Mounds K and L. These two mounds have the same orientation as each other (i.e., northeast to southwest) and may have been built after the main group.

TR-67 (Figure 5.106)

Site Type: Habitation

Ceramic Phase: Mix

Occupation: possible Protoclassic, Late Classic

Location and Setting: This site is 6.4 km southeast of Colonia Las Delicias, only 200 m west of the Guatemala-Mexico border. It is on a hillside sloping down to a small arroyo 100 m to the north. The site is on the edge of a thick forest that faces onto an area of milpa agriculture.

Environmental Stratum: Tropical Deciduous Forest

Description: There are 12 mounds at this site and all of them appear to be habitation mounds. There are two clusters of house mounds, the northern group (A to G) contains seven, and the southern group, separated by 50 m, contains five mounds (H to L). All mounds have the same orientation (i.e., northwest to southeast). Within each group the mounds are tightly clustered, usually no more than 20 m apart from each other.

TR-68 LA SOMBRA (Figure 5.107)

Site Type: Habitation

Ceramic Phase: Mix

Occupation: Protoclassic, Late Classic, Postclassic

Location and Setting: This site is 3.4 km southeast of Colonia Las Delicias. It is situated on the top of an east-west ridge which has

formed between two streams flowing east into Guatemala after converging 300 m east of the site. The ridge that the site is located on has little vegetation other than sparse tree cover that eventually turns to a thicker forest as one moves westward. Milpa lands surround the site.

Environmental Stratum: Tropical Decidous Forest

Description: Eleven habitation mounds extend in a linear fashion for 250 m along the ridgetop. There is a western group consisting of Mounds A to D that seems to be arranged around a patio area. Several more isolated mounds occur to the east at intervals of about 30 to 40 m (E-G) until another possible domestic group is reached (H, I, and J). Mound K is another isolated mound, 30 m farther south. All of the mounds have roughly the same orientation, suggesting that the structures were part of a single community.

TR-69 CANAJASTÉ (Figures 5.108-5.112)

Site Type: Ceremonial and habitation

Ceramic Phase: Tan

Occupation: Early Postclassic, Late Postclassic

Location and Setting: This site is located 5.3 km southeast of Colonia Las Delicias on Río Lagartero. The main part of the site is situated on a horseshoe-shaped bend of the river as it meanders south for 2 km before re-crossing the Mexico-Guatemala border several hundred meters to the east. The site reaches above the river level and sits on several terraces left by the down-cutting of the river. The area was covered by dense forest recently cleared for milpa. The area is fairly dry and the soil is very rocky.

Environmental Stratum: Tropical Deciduous Forest, Riparian Forest

Description: The main part of the site covers a bend in the river that is 250 m long and 175 m wide. It is delineated on the east side by a 2.5 m high stone wall that reaches from the north bend in the river 230 m across the terrace to the southern bend. The river surrounds the north, west, and southern part of the site like a giant moat, while the wall closes off the eastern edge

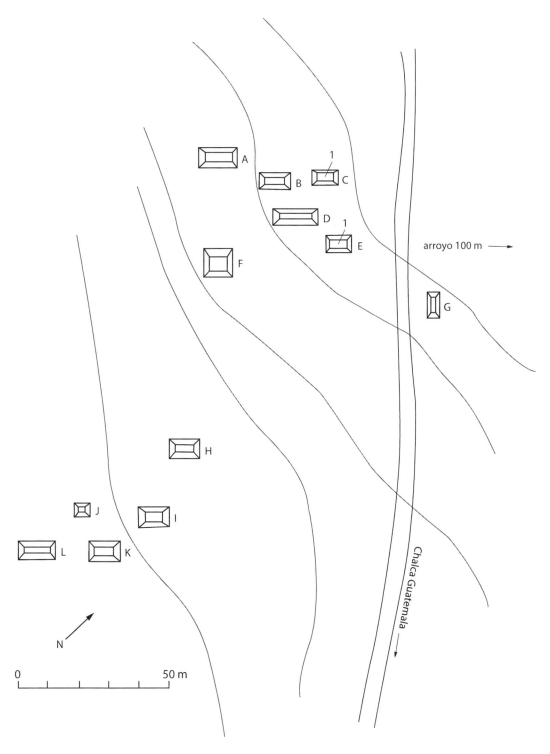

Figure 5.106. Site sketch of Tr-67.

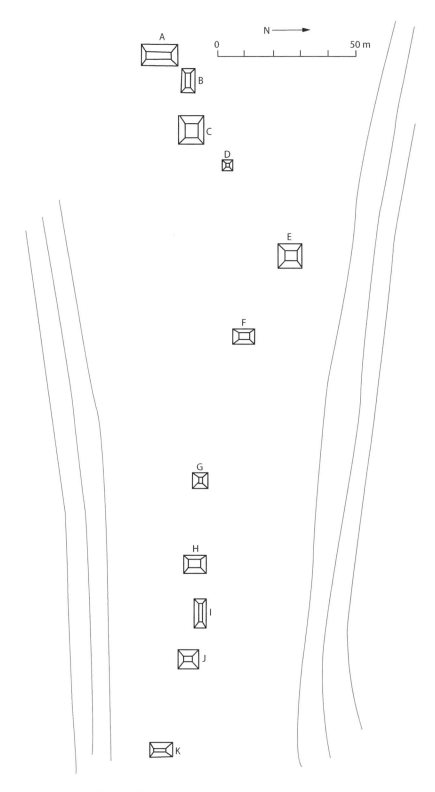

Figure 5.107. Site sketch of Tr-68, La Sombra.

Figure 5.108. House group at Tr-69, Canajasté.

Figure 5.109. Section of wall fortification at Tr-69, Canajasté.

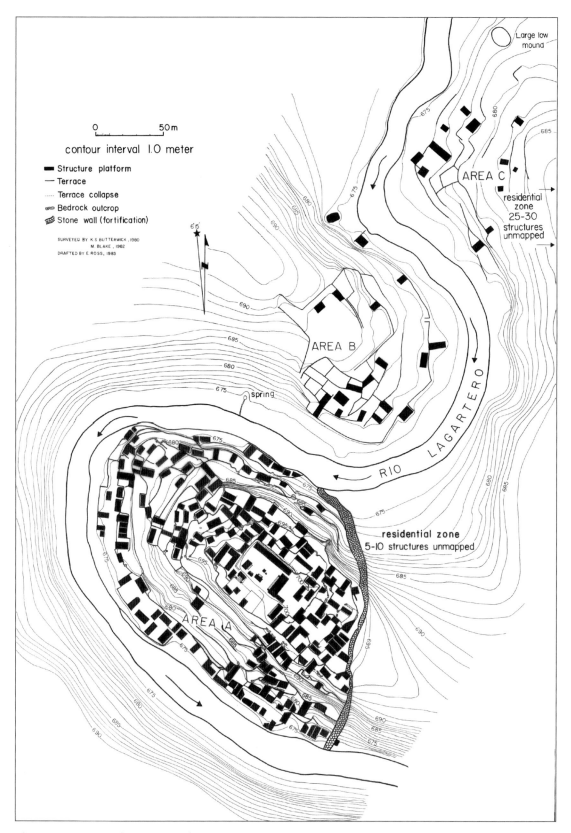

Figure 5.110. Map of Tr-69, Canajasté.

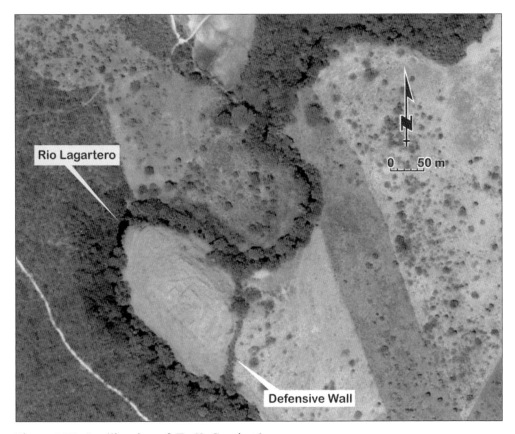

Figure 5.111. Satellite view of Tr-69, Canajasté.

Figure 5.112. Terraces at Tr-69, Canajasté.

of the site. The wall is constructed of local cobbles and boulders and reaches a height of 3 m in spots and ranges from 2 to 4 m wide. The whole enclosed area is approximately 36,000 m², and almost all of it appears to be densely occupied.

Within this zone is a central core separated by yet another wall that is also 3 m high in spots and up to 10 m wide. This central core is enclosed on three sides by stone walls and on the northwest side by a natural rock wall. This area has dimensions of 115 by 70 m, enclosing an area of 8,050 m². Within this core are several large mounds that appear to have been elite residences, some of which enclose patios. There are some walls exposed in a potted zone that have white plaster remaining and evidence of painting in red, green, blue, black, white, and yellow. There are no large temple mounds at the site, but some of the large low mounds in the central core area are very elaborate. Two of these, which face onto the main plaza, have balustraded stairways. Several other low habitation mounds, low platforms, and stone foundation outlines are located in the central core.

Outside of the inner wall, but still within the main part of the site are at least 11 low mounds and stone foundation outlines of an additional 30 house floors or patios. The average dimensions are 5 by 10 m, but there are many larger and smaller outlines. Across the river, on the bend to the north are nine additional low house mounds separated by 50 m or more from each other and scattered among 30 to 40 rectangular outlines of stone house footings. These are the same as the stone alignments on the main part of the site. Some may be house footings, but the larger ones could have been fences, patio boundaries, or low terrace edges. There are still more low house mounds and stone alignments 300 m north of the site core on the same side of the river. Some of these are arranged in groups of two or three and possibly represent domestic units. Reconnaissance of the zone has revealed large numbers of sparsely scattered house mounds on the west side of the river, but none of these was mapped.

The site is located in a very defensible location. The quantity of tightly clustered house mounds in the central zone suggests that a fairly large population lived under the protection of the enormous wall.

References: Blake 2010; Lee 1985; Lee and Bryant 1996

TR-70 JOMANIL 1 (Figures 5.113–5.115)

Site Type: Ceremonial and habitation

Ceramic Phase: Mix

Occupation: Late Classic

Location and Setting: This site is located 6 km north of Colonia Joaquín Miguel Gutiérrez and 1.2 km west of Río Lagartero. It is on a hilltop that faces south to a large agricultural plain, which lies to the west of the Lagartero swamp. The area is covered in trees and milpa lands and at the base of the hilltop is pasturage.

Environmental Stratum: Tropical Deciduous Forest

Description: There are two main groups of mounds on the hilltop. The northwestern group is slightly higher than the southeastern group and roughly separated by a zone 55 m long which contains only three mounds. The northwest group has one large temple mound 3 m tall (J) and six smaller rectangular house mounds that are 50 cm high. Two of these (G and H) are 15 m long parallel mounds that may have formed a small ballcourt whose end-zones are partly formed by Terrace I. There are also two houses outlined by stone footings around very low platforms (A and E). A projection (C) on the large terrace (D) that almost completely surrounds the site may have been a house mound base. Almost all of the structures in this group are within 10 m of each other, except Mounds K and L, which are 23 m to the southeast of Mound J, and may be associated with the southeast group. That group also contains a large, 3 m tall temple mound (P) surrounded by eight smaller house mounds. Most of these are 50 cm or less tall but one (V) is 1 m tall. Three of these mounds (M, O, and S) are long rectangular mounds all with one end near Mound P and extending out radially, almost pointing to all the cardinal directions except for south. Two of them (O and S) combined with

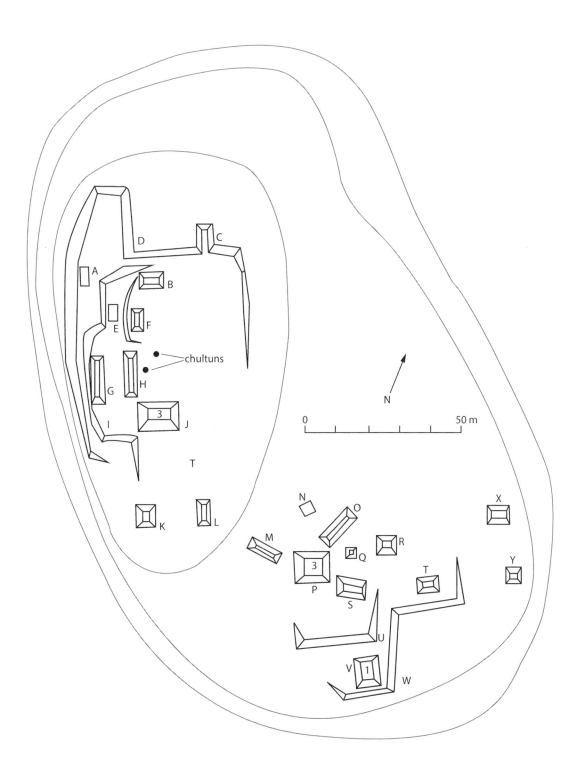

Figure 5.113. Map of Tr-70, Jomanil 1.

Figure 5.114. Tr-70, Jomanil 1.

Figure 5.115. View from site Tr-70, Jomanil 1, to the south.

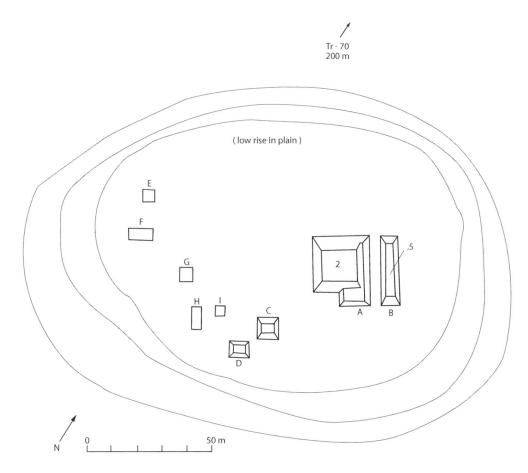

Figure 5.116. Map of Tr-71, Jomanil 2.

P and R enclose a plaza area that contains a small mound (Q), probably an altar. Two fairly large terraces (U and W) provide flat space at the site.

Two *chultunes* were found in the plaza area of the northwest group.

All of the mounds at the site, in both groups, have the same orientation to the west of north, except for the three mounds fronting on Mound P.

TR-71 JOMANIL 2 (Figure 5.116)

Site Type: Ceremonial and habitation

Location and Setting: This site is 200 m south of Tr-70 on a hummock that rises off a fairly flat plain. The plain is near the bottom of the hill on which Tr-70 is located. It is 6 km north of Colonia Joaquín Miguel Gutiérrez and 1.2 km west of Río Lagartero. The land now has little vegetation and is being currently used as pasturage.

Environmental Stratum: Tropical Deciduous Forest

Description: The site is a small cluster of nine mounds in an area 110 m long by 50 m wide. The largest mound (A) is 20 by 25 m by 2 m high and may form the western half of a ballcourt. Mound B is the eastern half and is the same length but only 0.5 m tall. Two other mounds (C and D) seem to form a residential unit around a possible patio. The other mounds at the site are less than 25 cm tall and may also be grouped into residential units. All of the structures have the same orientation; that is, from northwest to southeast, and were probably occupied at the same time.

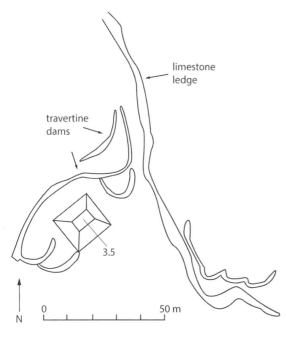

Figure 5.117. Map of Tr-72.

TR-72 (Figures 5.117-5.118)

Site Type: Ceremonial

Location and Setting: This site is 8 km north of Colonia Joaquín Miguel Gutiérrez and 200 m west of Río Lagartero. It is located on a plain to the east of some large hills. There are numerous travertine deposits where the stream used to flow, but now it is dry and only the travertine buildups remain. The area is used as pasturage.

Environmental Stratum: Fields or pastures

Description: The site consists of a single mound, 18 by 18 m along the base and 3.5 m tall. It is very rounded and the site map shows the estimated corner locations. The mound appears to be entirely an earthen construction, and this, combined with its shape, may indicate that it is from the Preclassic period. Unfortunately, no sherds were found, and there was no evidence of other structures.

Figure 5.118. Primary mound of Tr-72 located center-left.

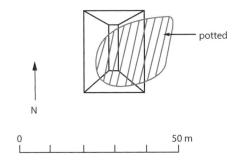

Figure 5.119. Map of Tr-73.

TR-73 (Figure 5.119)

Site Type: Ceremonial

Ceramic Phase: Mix

Occupation: Late Classic, Late Postclassic

Location and Setting: This site is 7 km southeast of Colonia Rodolfo Figueroa, 100 m east of Río Lagartero, and 400 m northeast of Tr-72. It is on a flat plain area that is now being used as pasturage.

Environmental Stratum: Herbaceous Swamp/ Wetland Formations

Description: There are two mounds at this small site. The largest mound is 20 by 25 m and severely potted on the east side. It may have been 3 m tall before its destruction. To the northwest 50 m is another much smaller mound. It is only 1 m tall and may have been an elite residence. Both mounds are stone filled. There may have been more small mounds surrounding these, but they are not now visible. The two mounds are aligned on a north-south axis.

TR-74 BOLSA PLÁTANO
(Figures 5.120-5.122)

Site Type: Ceremonial and habitation

Ceramic Phase: Mix

Occupation: Late Classic, Late Postclassic

Location and Setting: This site is 6.5 km southeast of Colonia Rodolfo Figueroa and 300 m west of Río Lagartero. It is on a hillslope at the base of a range of large hills that separate the Lagartero drainage from that of Río San Lucas to the west. The vegetation is mostly grassland with scattered small trees.

Environmental Stratum: Herbaceous Swamp/ Wetland Formations

Description: This site is large and complex. It is a ceremonial center with three large pyramids, a ballcourt, and 19 lower mounds that could have been used for temples or elite residences. The two largest pyramids (J and S) are square and are 30 m on a side. The larger of the two is S, with a height of 7 m while J is only 4 m tall. To the west of these mounds are a series of smaller mounds that are at most 1 m high. Some of them, such as K through P, are at an orientation to the east of the north-south orientation of the large pyramids. L, M, N, and O are arranged as though they surround a patio area. Mound K is extraordinarily long; at 38 m it is one of the largest for its height and width (1 m and 5 m, respectively). It is not aligned with any other mounds on the site. Farther to the west and to the north are a series of 2 m tall mounds (I, H, G, and F). They range from 10 to 20 m apart. Mounds G and H are probably an open-ended ballcourt. Mound F is a large complex mound 41 m long with an additional 8 m long platform projecting from its east end. It has two components: one is a 3 m tall mound and the other is 2 m tall. This mound sits on a large platform (Y) that also supports Mounds A through E. These five mounds outline an inner plaza and were probably elite residences associated with the ceremonial group.

At the south end of the site is another smaller complex of mounds (U through X) all on a terrace (T) which is 110 m long from east to west. These four mounds appear to surround a

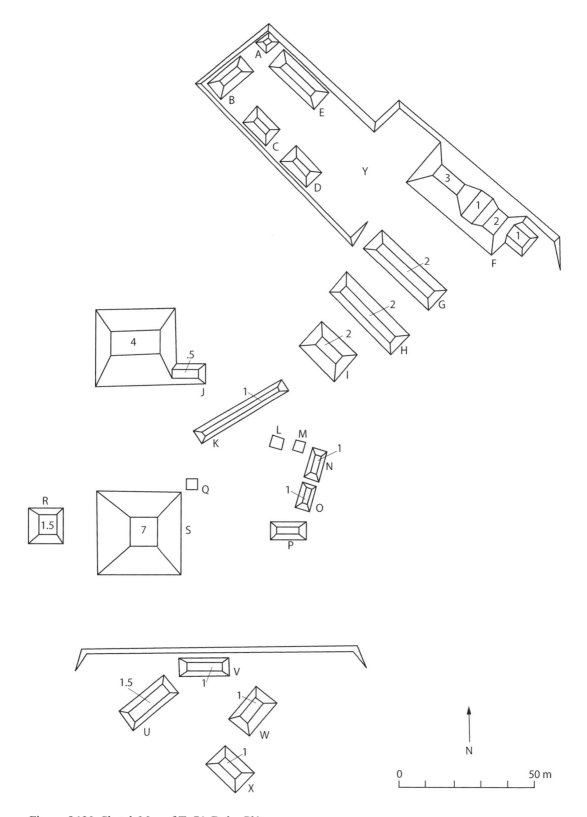

Figure 5.120. Sketch Map of Tr-74, Bolsa Plátano.

Figure 5.121. View from highest point at site of Tr-74, Bolsa Plátano.

Figure 5.122. Tr-74, Bolsa Plátano.

plaza area and are arranged to enclose all but the south side.

The overall orientation of the mounds is very irregular and can be divided into three groups. The northern group, including Mounds A to I and Terrace Y, are all aligned and probably contemporaneous. The large pyramids (J and S) as well as Mound R may be from a different building phase. All of the other mounds at the site are also unaligned with other groups and as such could be from different occupations; however, there is no ceramic evidence to confirm this. This site is unlike other Late Classic period sites, which typically have a uniform orientation for all mounds (e.g., Tr-9, Tr-29).

TR-75 (Figures 5.123-5.125)

Site Type: Ceremonial and habitation

Occupation: Late Classic, Late Postclassic

Location and Setting: This site is 6.2 km southeast of Colonia Rodolfo Figueroa on the west side of Río Lagartero. It is 600 m north of

Tr-74. The site sits on a small hilltop 30 m above the swampy floodplain of the river. There are some scattered small trees and grass covering the hill, as well as the full range of swamp-associated vegetation.

Environmental Stratum: Herbaceous Swamp/ Wetland Formations

Description: There are four sets of archaeological features at this site: two ceremonial areas and two habitation zones. The main ceremonial area at the site is near the center of the hilltop. It is a large platform (D) 65 by 55 m and approximately 50 cm high. On its east side is an additional platform (C), which contains two more mounds (A and B). This complex faces a smaller mound (E) that may have been an elite residence. To the south of this 40 to 60 m are two more mounds. The largest (G) is 4 m tall, but its south side has been badly disturbed. Mound F is smaller and was probably a residence platform.

The northern part of the hill has several outlines of stone foundations, but these were not mapped. The whole slope is covered with house terraces with terrace walls and house outlines.

Figure 5.123. View of Tr-75.

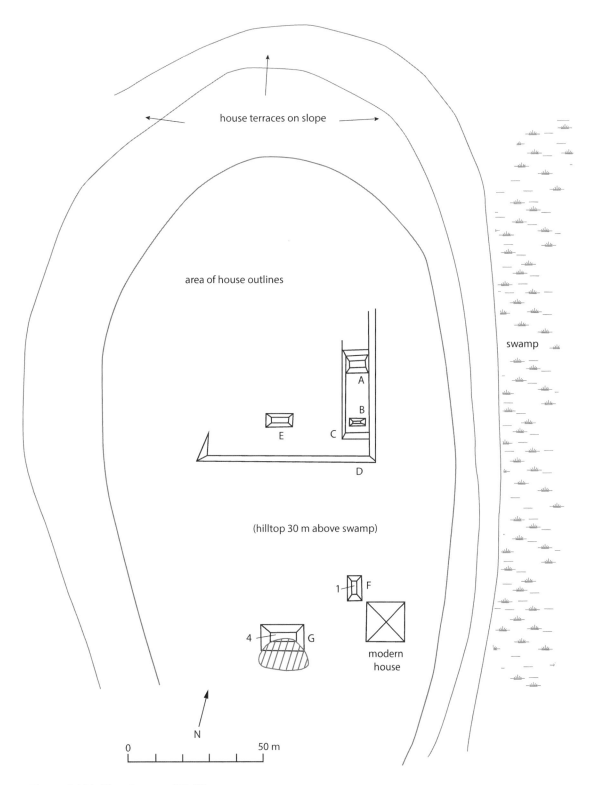

house terraces on slope

area of house outlines

swamp

A

B

C

D

E

(hilltop 30 m above swamp)

1 F

4 G

modern
house

N

0 50 m

Figure 5.124. Sketch map of Tr-75.

Figure 5.125. View of Tr-75.

The habitation area has significant prehistoric refuse.

All of the mounds and the major terraces have the same orientation from northwest to southeast.

References: Blake 2010:265-266

TR-76 (Figures 5.126-5.127)

Site Type: Ceremonial and habitation

Ceramic Phase: Mix

Occupation: Late Classic, Postclassic

Location and Setting: Tr-76 is located approximately 4.5 km east and slightly south of Colonia Rodolfo Figueroa and approximately 0.5 km west of Río Lagartero. It is in an area of rolling hills and ridges and low marshy cienegas. The site itself is situated on a long ridge with three small promontories. The vegetation in the vicinity of the site consists of milpa and isolated thickets of trees. The banks of the river are densely covered with riverine vegetation.

Environmental Stratum: Herbaceous Swamp/ Wetland Formations

Description: This site consists of a large concentration of at least 45 residential mounds, some terracing, and two ceremonial clusters. The structures appear to be grouped in three areas (AA, BB, and CC), each concentrated atop a natural promontory. Areas AA and BB were mapped in detail; however, Area CC is merely outlined as an area with small mounds and no map or mound count was made.

The largest concentration of structures, with at least 32 mounds, is located in Area AA. On a large flat terrace on the northwest slope of AA is a ceremonial complex, including a 4 m temple platform (A) and a ballcourt (B). The ballcourt uses the northwest wall of A as the western boundary of the playing fields. These structures, as well as two smaller mounds, are reinforced on the southwest side by Terrace C.

Surrounding this complex to the east, the south, and up the promontory to the southwest are several low mounds that were probably

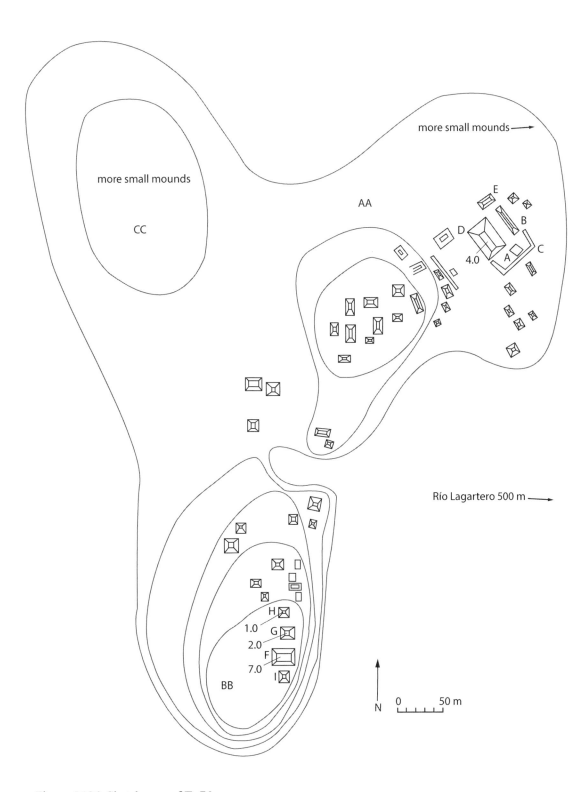

Figure 5.126. Sketch map of Tr-76.

Figure 5.127. Tr-76, Mound A complex.

residential mounds. In the immediate vicinity of the ceremonial complex there are two mounds (D and E) slightly larger than the others, suggesting that these may have been elite residences. Downslope to the west more small mounds were observed, but these were not counted or mapped. The density of mounds tapers off to the south of the AA concentration, although there are at least two house compound groups visible.

A second concentration with 16 mounds is located on top of the southern promontory BB and down the gradual northern slope of this incline. The promontory drops off steeply on the east and south sides, and no structures were observed. A ceremonial group dominates the top of the promontory, including a 7 m temple platform (F) and three lower mounds (G, H, and I). These latter structures, which are slightly taller than the other mounds in the BB concentration, may have been either ceremonial platforms or perhaps elite residences. Down the northern slope of this promontory are several

small mounds that were also probably residential complexes.

This site appears to be a large nucleated village, with at least two civic-ceremonial precincts visible and extensive residential occupation. The concentration of mounds on the natural promontories appears to be an adaptation to the sloping terrain; nevertheless, the presence of a ceremonial complex on each of the two mapped promontories suggests there may have been social correlates of the spatial divisions on the site.

A jade bead and polychrome vessel were found in a small offering in a small mound near the road, off the Tr-76 map.

TR-77 NARANJO (Figure 5.128)

Site Type: Ceremonial and habitation

Ceramic Phase: Hun, Mix

Occupation: Protoclassic, Late Classic

Location and Setting: Tr-77 is 3.5 km east of Colonia Rodolfo Figueroa and 2 km west of

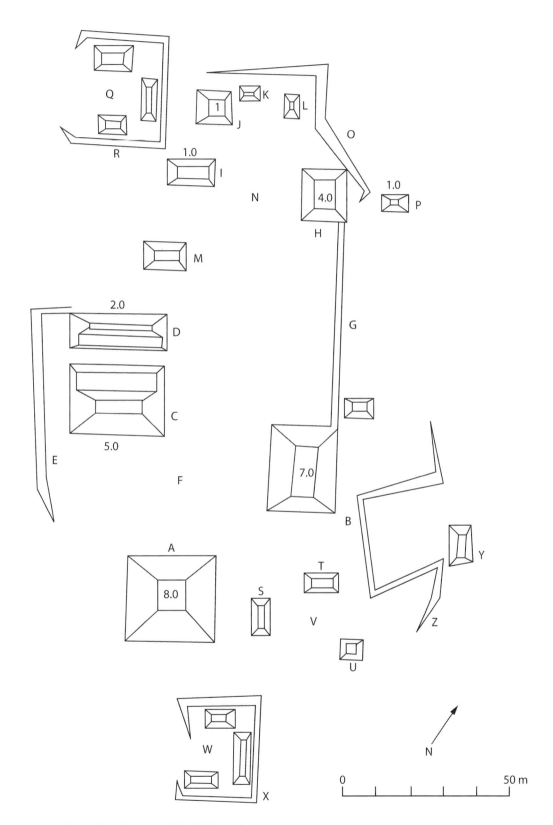

Figure 5.128. Sketch map of Tr-77, Naranjo.

Río Lagartero. The site is located on a low hill overlooking a broad fertile valley to the north. The surrounding topography consists primarily of hills and ridges adjacent to the valley. The vegetation consists of milpa and isolated patches of trees.

Environmental Stratum: Fields or pastures

Description: Tr-77 consists of a series of relatively elaborate ceremonial structures, at least four residential patio groups, and several complex terraces. The maximum extent of the site is approximately 220 by 150 m. The regular elongated orientation of the site appears to conform to the long axis of the hillside, and the terracing is probably an attempt to artificially level ground for construction.

The ceremonial complex, located slightly south of the site center, consists of a large square pyramid (AA) measuring 8 m high. Adjacent to A is a large rectangular temple platform measuring 7 m high. West of A and B, across a plaza (F), is a large almost I-shaped ballcourt (C/D/E). Mound C, which forms the southern bench of the ballcourt, is a double-tiered bench measuring 5 m high at the upper tier. Mound D which forms the northern bench measures only 2 m at the upper tier. The terrace (E) forms the western end zone of the ballcourt; no eastern end-zone is visible. This whole group is arranged around a large open plaza area (F). Finally, northeast of the ceremonial complex connected by Terrace G is another temple platform (H) measuring 4 m high. This may be associated with the ceremonial complex or perhaps with the group of low mounds to the west of H.

East and southeast of the ceremonial group are three residential complexes: S/T/U, arranged around a patio (V); Patio Group W, enclosed by Terrace X; and Mound Y, associated with Terrace Z. The proximity of these to the ceremonial group suggests they may have been elite residential compounds.

Finally, at the northwest end of the site is another group of mounds (I, J, K, L, and possibly M) arranged around an open plaza (N) and partially enclosed by Terrace O. These mounds may have been associated with Temple Platform H, as mentioned above. The height of

Mounds I, J, and even P, suggests these may have been elite residential complexes.

This site appears to be a nucleated community with a substantial ceremonial complex and at least four (or perhaps more) residential complexes. The residential compounds appear for the most part to be large well-made structures. They may have housed an elite population involved in the operation and maintenance of this large ceremonial complex.

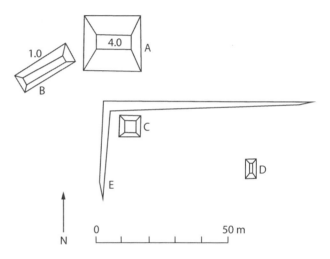

Figure 5.129. Sketch map of Tr-78, San Pablo Miradero.

TR-78 SAN PABLO MIRADERO
(Figures 5.129-5.131)

Site Type: Ceremonial and habitation

Location and Setting: Tr-78 is located 4.5 km northeast of Colonia Rodolfo Figueroa. It is situated on a high natural terrace overlooking the broad fertile valley of Río Lagartero to the south. The surrounding terrain consists of hills and ridges that drop off to the south into the wide Lagartero Valley. The vegetation in the vicinity is mainly grassland and sparse patches of trees.

Environmental Stratum: Short Tree Savannah/ Thorn Woodland

Description: The site Tr-78 consists of a single large temple platform (A), three low mounds (B, C, and D) and a large terrace (E). The temple platform (A) measures 22 by 20 m and 4 m in

Figure 5.130. View from Miradero site of Tr-78, San Pablo Miradero.

Figure 5.131. Modern shrine, Tr-78, San Pablo Miradero.

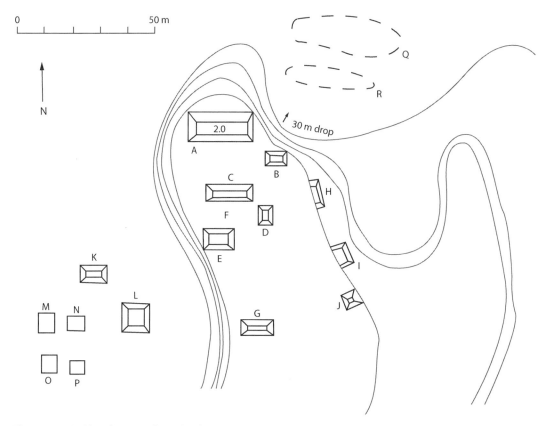

Figure 5.132. Sketch map of Tr-79, El Zapote 1.

height. Immediately west of this site, separated by only 2 m, is a long rectangular mound that measures 22 by 7 m and only 1 m in height. The proximity of these two structures suggests they probably formed a unified complex. South and southeast of this pair are two low mounds (C and D) partially enclosed by Terrace E. These structures may have been residences occupied by people involved in the operation and maintenance of the ceremonial structure.

This site appears to be a modest ceremonial center with a small residential population associated with the ceremonial structures.

TR-79 EL ZAPOTE 1 (Figure 5.132)

Site Type: Ceremonial and habitation

Occupation: Protoclassic

Location and Setting: Tr-79 is located approximately 3.25 km northeast of Colonia Rodolfo Figueroa and approximately 1.1 km west of Tr-78. The site is located atop a ridge overlooking the Lagartero Valley to the south. The local topography has high hills and ridges, that drop off into the broad southern valley. The vegetation consists of grasses and sparse clumps of trees.

Environmental Stratum: Short Tree Savannah/ Thorn Woodland

Description: Tr-79 is a series of low mounds on top of a hill, several wall foundation alignments at the western base of the hill, and a possible ballcourt at the northern base of the hill. The main concentration of mounds is located on the ridgetop (A-E, G-J). The largest mound (A) at the northern end of this group measures 23 by 10 m by 2 m high. This may be a civic-ceremonial structure or perhaps an elite residential structure. Mounds C, D, and E, also slightly larger than most other mounds, form a group arranged around a patio (F). Several other mounds on the ridge top (H, I, and J) appear to be taking advantage of a natural hill terrace.

Another cluster of structures is located at the western base of the slope. Only K and L are actually mounds, whereas M to P are stone wall foundation alignments.

Finally, at the northern base of the slope, two elongated mounds (Q and R) were noted (although these were not mapped in detail). These mounds may have formed an open-ended ballcourt.

This site appears to be a small nucleated settlement with some possible ceremonial structures. The orientation of all of the structures is north to south, except for some of the structures on the eastern hill slope.

TR-80 EL ZAPOTE 2 (Figure 5.133)

Site Type: Ceremonial and habitation

Ceramic Phase: Hun

Occupation: Late Preclassic, Protoclassic

Location and Setting: Tr-80 is located 2.5 km east and slightly north of Colonia Rodolfo Figueroa and approximately 1 km southwest of Tr-79. The site is situated at the southern tip of a long ridge, overlooking the broad valley of Río Lagartero to the south. The local vegetation consists of grasses and sparse tree cover.

Environmental Stratum: Short Tree Savannah/Thorn Woodland

Description: There are six mounds at this site. The maximum extent of the site measures 150 by 70 m. The east-west orientation of the structures seems to follow the contour of the ridges upon which the site is situated.

The three largest mounds (A, B, and C) are clustered together at the western end of the site. These mounds, measuring 1.5 m, 1.5 m and 1 m in height respectively, are arranged around what may be a common patio (D). This group may have been a small ceremonial center or perhaps an elite residential complex.

Scattered across the rest of the site at intervals of 40 to 45 m are three more low mounds (E, F, and G). These structures may have been residences as well.

The site appears to be a very small nucleated community with some possible civic-ceremonial structures.

TR-81 EL RECREO (Figure 5.134)

Site Type: Ceremonial and habitation

Occupation: Protoclassic, Postclassic

Location and Setting: Tr-81 is located approximately 2 km east of Colonia Rodolfo Figueroa and just 0.5 km southwest of Tr-80. It is situated on a hilltop, overlooking the valley that connects the San Lucas Valley with the Lagartero Valley. The surrounding topography consists of

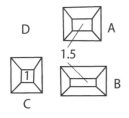

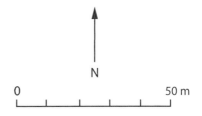

Figure 5.133. Sketch map of Tr-80, El Zapote 2.

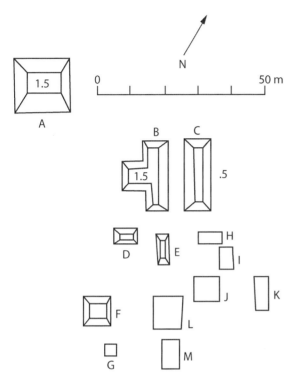

The largest structure on the site (Mound A) is somewhat isolated from the rest of the mounds at the western edge of the site. This mound measures 16 by 16 m with a height of 1.5 m. East of A is an open-ended ballcourt (B/C). The west bench of the ballcourt (B) is slightly taller than the east bench (C): they measure 1.5 and 0.5 m, respectively. In addition to this difference the west bench has a square platform projecting out of the west side of the mound.

South of the ballcourt are a group of structures (D-M) which appear to be arranged in groups, probably residential compounds. Only D, E, and F are mounds, whereas the remaining structures are merely stone wall foundation alignments. This difference may reflect status differences within the community.

This site appears to have been a small nucleated settlement with a moderate ceremonial complex.

TR-82 SAN JUAN VIEJO 1 (Figure 5.135)

Site Type: Habitation

Ceramic Phase: Mix

Occupation: Protoclassic, Late Classic

Location and Setting: Tr-82 is located just 1 km east of Colonia Rodolfo Figueroa and is surrounded on the south and east by Tr-80 and Tr-83 and Tr-84, respectively. The site is situated on the floor of a wide valley connecting the San Lucas and Lagartero Valleys. The surrounding

Figure 5.134. Sketch map of Tr-81, El Recreo.

hills and ridges, descending steeply to the south and into the valley. The surrounding vegetation is primarily grassland with some sparse tree cover.

Environmental Stratum: Short Tree Savannah/ Thorn Woodland

Description: This site consists of a temple mound (A), a ballcourt (B/C), and a series of low mounds.

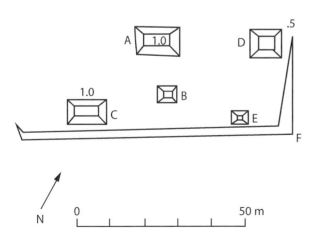
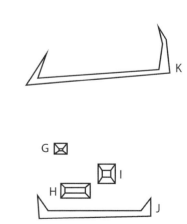

Figure 5.135. Sketch map of Tr-82, San Juan Viejo 1.

area is primarily under milpa cultivation with isolated patches of trees.

Environmental Stratum: Short Tree Savannah/ Thorn Woodland

Description: This site consists of several low rectangular mounds of differing heights and three terraces. The maximum extent of the site measures 150 by 60 m. The mounds are clustered into two groups, enclosed by two of the three terraces. The largest group of mounds (A to E) is located on Terrace F and among these are the three tallest mounds (A, C, and D). This terrace group may have been composed of one or possibly two residential groups. The second group of mounds (G, H, and I) is enclosed by Terrace J. These mounds are all considerably smaller than those on Terrace F. Finally, a third terrace (K) was mapped but no structures were visible.

This was a small settlement with no civic-ceremonial architecture. The size variability of the mounds on the terraces suggests there may have been social differentiation within the settlement.

TR-83 SAN JUAN VIEJO 2
(Figure 5.136)

Site Type: Habitation

Ceramic Phase: Mix

Occupation: Protoclassic, Late Classic

Location and Setting: Tr-83 is located 1.25 km east of Colonia Rodolfo Figueroa. Immediately to the east is Tr-84 and to the west are Tr-82 and Tr-88. The site is situated on the floor of a valley connecting the San Lucas Valley and Lagartero Valley. The surrounding vegetation is sparse and the land is used mainly for milpa.

Environmental Stratum: Short Tree Savannah/ Thorn Woodland

Description: This site consists of three low mounds (A, B, and C) and nine stone foundation alignments. The maximum extent of the site is 150 by 70 m. The main concentration of structures on the site consists of eight wall foundation alignments (D to K) in the center of the site. Scattered around the periphery of the site are three mounds: A in the western corner,

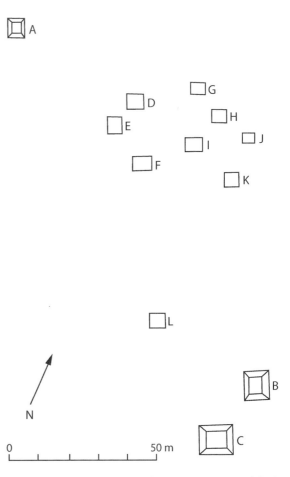

Figure 5.136. Sketch map of Tr-83, San Juan Viejo 2.

and B and C in the eastern corner. Another wall alignment (L) is located nearby the B/C mound pair, and may have been associated with it. These structures appear to be a group of residential compounds.

TR-84 SAN JUAN VIEJO 3
(Figure 5.137)

Site Type: Ceremonial and habitation

Ceramic Phase: Kau, Mix

Occupation: Early Classic, Middle Classic, Late Classic

Location and Setting: Tr-84 is located 1.5 km east of Colonia Rodolfo Figueroa. Immediately to the west are Tr-82, Tr-83, and Tr-88. The site is situated on the floor of a valley connecting the San Lucas Valley and Lagartero Valley. The surrounding vegetation is primarily milpa.

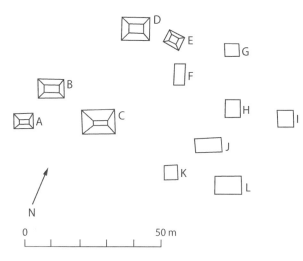

Figure 5.137. Sketch map of Tr-84, San Juan Viejo 3.

Environmental Stratum: Short Tree Savannah/ Thorn Woodland

Description: This site consists of five low mounds and seven stone wall foundation alignments. The structures are concentrated in a 110 by 70 m area. The mounds are all situated on the western side of the site and appear to be arranged in two compound clusters (A, B, C, D, E, and possibly F). The wall foundation alignments are concentrated on the eastern side, but no clear pattern of compound clustering is apparent.

The site appears to be a small residential hamlet with no evidence of ceremonial structures. The difference between house platform preparation types may reflect either social differentiation within the site or adaptation to the topographic situation of the structures on the valley floor.

TR-85 (Figures 5.138-5.139)

Site Type: Habitation

Occupation: Protoclassic, Late Classic

Location and Setting: Tr-85 is located 2.25 km east and slightly south of Colonia Rodolfo Figueroa. It is situated on the south side of the valley floor, in the valley connecting the San Lucas Valley with the Lagartero Valley. The local

Figure 5.138. View of Tr-85.

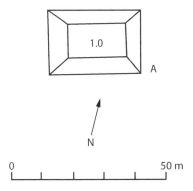

Figure 5.139. Sketch map of Tr-85.

vegetation is sparse and the land is primarily under milpa cultivation.

Environmental Stratum: Short Tree Savannah/ Thorn Woodland

Description: This site consists of a single low mound. There is no evidence of other structures. This was probably a small community with other surrounding structures that were not built on mounds.

TR-86 JICARAL (Figures 5.140-5.142)

Site Type: Ceremonial and habitation

Ceramic Phase: Mix

Occupation: Late Classic

Location and Setting: Tr-86 is located 1.75 km southeast of Colonia Rodolfo Figueroa and Tr-87 is located just 0.5 km to the northeast. The site is situated near the edge of a valley connecting the San Lucas Valley with the Lagartero Valley. The site is at the base of a system of hills and ridges that climb in altitude towards the south. The vegetation surrounding the site is primarily milpa with occasional trees dotting the landscape.

Environmental Stratum: Short Tree Savannah/ Thorn Woodland

Description: This site consists of a platform mound (A), an open-ended ballcourt (B/C), and four low mounds (D, E, F, and G). The mounds are clustered together in an area measuring 110 by 75 m.

The largest mound (A), measuring 23 by 21 m by 3 m high is located at the western edge of the site. The ballcourt (B/C) is oriented at an angle of about 45 to the main platform (A). The remaining mounds (D G) were probably residential structures. Mounds D, E, and F appear to be arranged together around a common patio (H), suggesting this was a single residential compound.

The irregular orientation of the structures suggests that the buildings may not have been constructed as a planned unit. This site appears to be a small settlement with a moderate ceremonial precinct. The proximity of this site to Tr-87 (which has no ceremonial structures) suggests that this site may have served as the ceremonial center for that site.

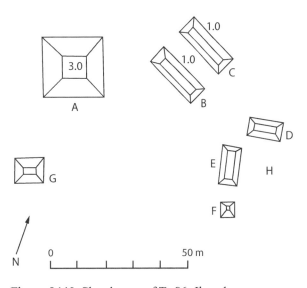

Figure 5.140. Sketch map of Tr-86, Jicaral.

Figure 5.141. Ballcourt at Tr-86, Jicaral.

Figure 5.142. Mound A at Tr-86, Jicaral.

Figure 5.143. Wall foundation alignments at Tr-87.

TR-87 (Figures 5.143-5.144)

Site Type: Habitation

Ceramic Phase: Hun, Mix

Occupation: possible Protoclassic, possible Late Classic

Location and Setting: Tr-87 is located 1.75 km southeast of Colonia Rodolfo Figueroa and just 0.5 km northeast of Tr-86. The site is situated on a small knoll near the edge of the valley bottom connecting the San Lucas with the Lagartero Valley. The area surrounding the site is mainly under milpa cultivation, with occasional trees.

Environmental Stratum: Short Tree Savannah/ Thorn Woodland

Description: Tr-87 has one small low platform mound (A), a *chultún* (B), and several stone wall foundation alignments of differing sizes (C to K). The structures are distributed in an elongated pattern, measuring 150 m north-south by 40 m east-west.

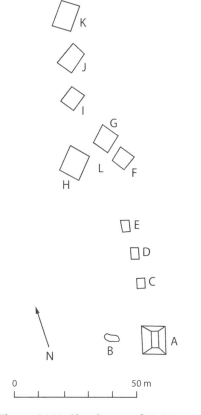

Figure 5.144. Sketch map of Tr-87.

The only mound on the site (A) is located at the southern extreme of the site. The chultún (B) is located approximately 9 m west of A, suggesting the two features were associated. North of A is a string of three small rectangular alignments (C-E), each of which measures approximately 4 by 4 m. North of these are a series of larger wall alignments (F to J). Structures F, G, and H appear to be arranged around a common patio (L), suggesting they form a residential compound.

This site appears to be a small residential hamlet with no evidence of ceremonial structures. The proximity of this site to Tr-86 suggests the latter may have served as a ceremonial center for this site.

TR-88 SAN JUAN VIEJO (Figure 5.145)

Site Type: Habitation

Ceramic Phase: Mix

Occupation: Late Classic, Late Postclassic

Location and Setting: Tr-88 is located approximately 1 km east of Colonia Rodolfo Figueroa. Immediately northeast of the site are Tr-82 and Tr-83. Tr-88 is situated on the edge of the valley bottom connecting the San Lucas Valley with the Lagartero Valley. The land surrounding the site is mainly under milpa cultivation.

Environmental Stratum: Short Tree Savannah/ Thorn Woodland

Description: Tr-88 is a small nucleated settlement with evidence of eight structures. There are two low mounds and six rock wall foundation alignments. The maximum extent of the site measures 120 by 40 m.

The structures appear to be arranged in two or three groups. The only platform mounds (A and B), located at the northern end of the site, are slightly larger than the other structures and may have been elite residential compounds. Finally, Alignment H at the southern end of the site was probably also part of a residential compound.

This site appears to be a residential settlement with no ceremonial precinct.

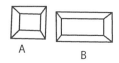

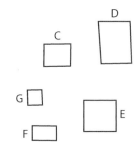

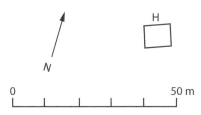

Figure 5.145. Sketch map of Tr-88, San Juan Viejo.

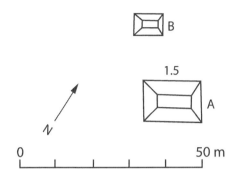

Figure 5.146. Sketch map of Tr-89, Juchuchal.

TR-89 JUCHUCHAL (Figure 5.146)

Site Type: Habitation

Location and Setting: Tr-89 is located 1.5 km south of Colonia Rodolfo Figueroa. It is situated on the north slope of the hilly uplands overlooking Río San Lucas to the north and west. The area around the site is being used for milpa cultivation, with heavily forested uplands to the south.

Environmental Stratum: Fields or pasture

Description: Tr-89 is a small site with evidence of only two structures. Mound A is a small platform measuring 1.5 m in height. Mound B, located just northwest of A, is a much smaller platform. The arrangement of these two structures, as well as the height of Mound A, suggests it may have been a modest ceremonial center. It could, however, have been an isolated residential compound.

TR-90 SAN AGUSTÍN 1
(Figures 5.147-5.148)

Site Type: Ceremonial and habitation

Ceramic Phase: Foko, Guajil, Hun

Occupation: late Middle Preclassic, Late Preclassic, Protoclassic

Location and Setting: Tr-90 is located 0.5 km southwest of Colonia Rodolfo Figueroa, just 100 m west of Río San Lucas. The site is situated on a slight rise above the floodplain. Surrounding the valley bottom the terrain consists of small

hills and ridges. The area surrounding the site is primarily under milpa cultivation.

Environmental Stratum: Fields or pastures

Description: The site of Tr-90 consists of a substantial ceremonial complex as well as some small low mounds. The maximum extent of the site measures approximately 100 by 150 m. The main concentration of ceremonial structures is situated on the western edge of the site, in a straight north-south orientation. The northernmost structure (A) is a pyramid measuring 30 by 33 m, with a height of 6 m. Directly south, across a 16 m plaza, is a lower temple platform (B), which measures 20 m by 20 m and 2 m high. South of this are two low

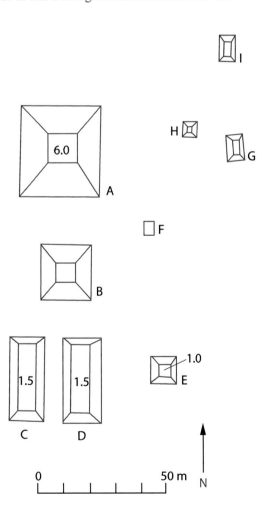

Figure 5.147. Sketch map of Tr-90, San Agustín 1.

Figure 5.148. Tr-90, San Agustín 1.

mounds (C and D) forming a ballcourt. The two
mounds of the ballcourt are of equal heights.
Mound B may form the northern end-zone;
however, no southern end-zone is visible. The
overall symmetry of this complex suggests it was
constructed as planned group.

East of the ceremonial precinct are a series
of low mounds. The proximity of both mounds
E and F to the ceremonial group suggests they
may have had ceremonial functions or perhaps
they form part of residential groups. To the
northeast, Mounds G, H, and I are probably
residential structures.

TR-91 SAN AGUSTÍN 2 (Figure 5.149)

Site Type: Ceremonial and habitation

Ceramic Phase: Mix

Occupation: Protoclassic, Late Classic

Location and Setting: Tr-91 is located
approximately 1 km southwest of Colonia
Rodolfo Figueroa, 0.4 km southwest of Tr-90,
and just 0.5 km west of Río San Lucas. The site

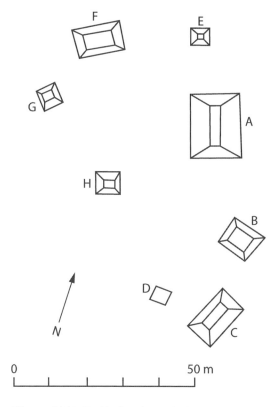

Figure 5.149. Tr-91, San Agustín 2.

is situated on the north side of a valley that opens onto the San Lucas Valley from the west. The vegetation around the site has been cleared and is under milpa cultivation with occasional trees dotting the landscape.

Environmental Stratum: Fields or pasture

Description: Tr-91 is a small cluster of mounds, including one temple platform and seven low mounds. The mounds are concentrated within an area of 90 m by 50 m. The largest mound (A), which measures 17 by 8 m by 2.5 m high, is located in a central position within the group. To the southeast is a group of low mounds (B, C, and D) which may have been a residential group. North and west of Mound A is another series of mounds (E to H) that may have formed parts of residential groups. The irregular orientation of the structures with respect to each other suggests they may not have been constructed as a planned unit. The site appears to be a small nucleated settlement with a modest civic-ceremonial center.

TR-92 SAN JUAN (Figure 5.150)

Site Type: Habitation

Ceramic Phase: Mix

Occupation: Late Classic, possible Postclassic

Location and Setting: Tr-92 is 2.5 km southwest of Colonia Rodolfo Figueroa and 1.5 km south of Tr-91. The site is located in the center of a side valley that opens onto the San Lucas Valley from the west. The vegetation in the vicinity of the site has been cleared and is used primarily for milpa cultivation.

Environmental Stratum: Tropical Deciduous Forest

Description: The site of Tr-92 appears to have been a small streamside camp. The maximum extent of the site measures 60 by 20 m. There are three mounds visible on the site, arranged in a linear pattern, each separated by approximately 10 m. The mounds may represent a single residential compound, with A and B arranged around an open patio (D). The tallest mound (A) measures 10 by 10 m and 1 m high, whereas Mound B, which is only 0.5 m high, has much

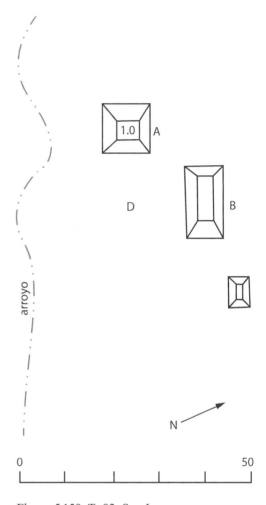

Figure 5.150. Tr-92, San Juan.

larger basal dimensions, measuring 8 by 16 m. The greater height of Mound A could be related to its proximity to the streamside, whereas Mound B is further from the arroyo and out of danger of flooding by the arroyo. Mound C was probably an outlying building associated with the A/B compound.

TR-93 BEBEDERO AMATE (Figure 5.151)

Site Type: Ceremonial and habitation

Ceramic Phase: Mix

Occupation: Late Classic

Location and Setting: Tr-93 is located 1.5 km south and slightly west of Colonia Rodolfo Figueroa. The site is situated on the

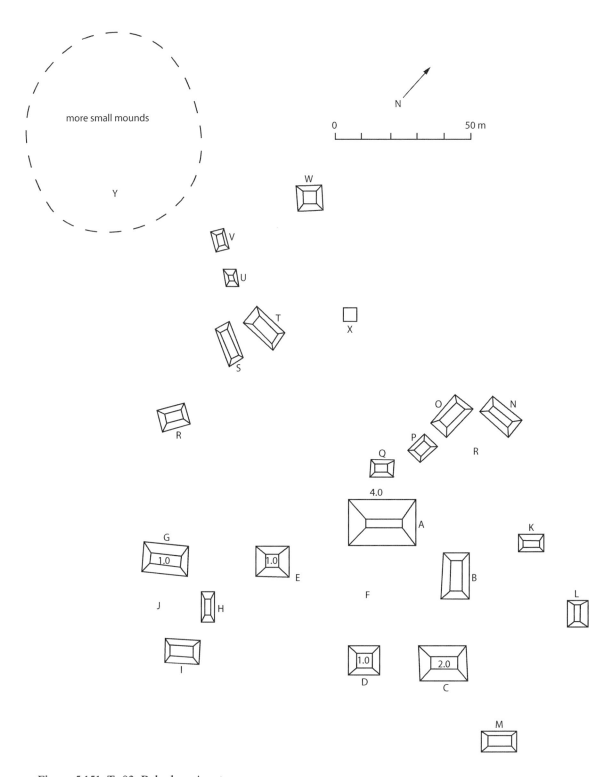

Figure 5.151. Tr-93, Bebedero Amate.

edge of a low bench overlooking the mouth of a wide valley which opens onto the San Lucas Valley from the west. The surrounding vegetation is being utilized primarily for milpa cultivation, with occasional trees dotting the landscape.

Environmental Stratum: Fields or pasture

Description: Tr-93 is a large nucleated hamlet with a central ceremonial complex and several residential structures. The visible extent of the site measures approximately 300 m by 200 m. The ceremonial group in the center of the site is dominated by A, a large 4 m temple platform. Mound A faces onto a large plaza area (F) around the perimeter of which are four smaller mounds (B to E). These latter ones range in height from 0.5 m to 2 m and the basal dimensions, which are generally larger than the others on the site, range from 10-12 m by 11-18 m. These structures probably functioned as civic-ceremonial buildings associated with the main temple platform A.

South of the ceremonial group, separated by approximately 15 m, is a cluster of large platform mounds (G, H, and I) arranged around a common patio (J). Mound G, which measures 11 by 17 m and 1 m high, is the largest residential structure on the site, suggesting that this is an elite compound.

Scattered around the eastern edge of the ceremonial group are three mounds (K, L, and M), each isolated from the others. These were probably residential mounds as well, perhaps associated with structures not visible on the surface. Immediately northwest of the main ceremonial structure (A) is another cluster of mounds (N to Q) that appear to be arranged around a patio (R). The proximity of this group to the ceremonial center suggests this also may be an elite residential compound, although the mean mound area of this group (87.5 m^2) is smaller than the G/H/I group (116 m^2).

In the western portion of the site are a series of low mounds (R to W) and one wall alignment (X) of varying dimensions. The proximity of south to T and of U to V suggests these may have formed part of at least two residential compounds. The remaining structures (R, W, and X) also probably belong to residential compounds.

Finally, several small mounds (Y) were visible at the western edge of the site; however, these were not mapped or counted.

The irregular arrangement of mound clusters with respect to each other suggests that all of the mound groups were not built according to a formal plan. Still, individual clusters (in particular, those around the central ceremonial group) do appear to exhibit a regular pattern of mounds arranged at right angles to each other around a square patio.

TR-94 LOS ENCUENTROS
(Figure 5.152)

Site Type: Ceremonial and habitation

Ceramic Phase: Tan

Occupation: Late Classic, Early Postclassic, Late Postclassic

Location and Setting: Tr-94 is located 2.2 km southwest of Colonia Rodolfo Figueroa. It is situated on the side of a hill in the San Lucas Valley. The hilltop site overlooks the confluence of the Ríos Coneta and Los Encuentros. The site is roughly 200 m from the water course. The local vegetation consists of grasses used mainly for pasture land.

Environmental Stratum: Tropical Deciduous Forest

Description: The site has two mound groups and a residential area. The ceremonial center consists of ten mounds oriented symmetrically around a main plaza. The main plaza, measuring 35 m northwest-southeast and 60 m southwest-northeast, is enclosed by seven mounds (Mounds 1-10). To the northwest a 3 m high pyramid (Mound 3) faces the southwest across the plaza toward a larger 4 m high pyramid, the largest at the site (Mound 8). The west end of the plaza is enclosed by a group of 3 small, 2 m high mounds (Mounds 4-6). The east end of the plaza is open. Just east of the main group is a series of 7 mounds (Mounds 11-17), oriented slightly more to the north than the main group. Mounds 11-12 may define a second plaza area together with Mounds 8-10. The remaining five (Mounds 13-17) to the east define another plaza or perhaps form an elite residential group.

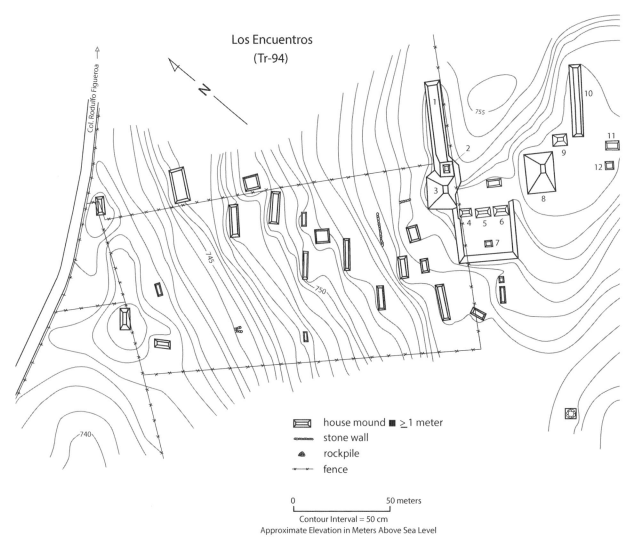

Figure 5.152. Site map of Tr-94.

There is a second mound group located 180 m south of the ceremonial center. There are two 2 m high mounds and a long narrow structure similar to those in the central plaza is located at the southeastern most end of the site. To the northeast of the ceremonial center are a series of likely elite house groups laid out on a slope leading down to the road to Colonia Rodolfo Figueroa.

References: Lee and Bryant 1996; Blake 2010:267-269

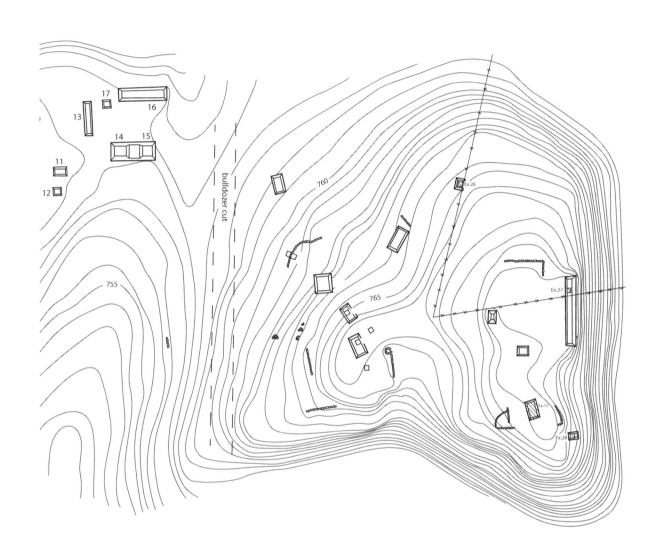

Figure 5.153. Church and attached convent, Tr-95, Coneta.

TR-95 CONETA
(no map, Figures 5.153-5.159)

Site Type: Ceremonial and habitation

Ceramic Phase: Tan, Ux

Occupation: Late Postclassic, Colonial

Location and Setting: The site of Coneta (Tr-95) is located 4 km southwest of Colonia Rodolfo Figueroa. It is situated on the western floor of the San Lucas Valley. To the west, south, and east of the site the terrain rises into hilly, more rugged terrain. The surrounding vegetation is primarily grasses and used mainly as pasture land.

Environmental Stratum: Fields or Pasture

Description: Eighty-six domestic houses, 16 sweatbaths, three churches (one with associated convent), and numerous terraces and other man-made structures were mapped. A grid system of streets was noted in the northwest and southwest sectors of the site (Lee and Markman 1977). The Colonial Coxoh Project, organized by NWAF and Duke University, excavated at the site for one season in 1975. The site map and information on the Precolumbian component

Figure 5.154. Church spire, Tr-95, Coneta.

Figure 5.155. Church, Tr-95, Coneta.

Figure 5.156. Convent, Tr-95, Coneta.

Figure 5.157. Exterior facade, church, Tr-95, Coneta.

Figure 5.158. Brian Hayden, church spire, Tr-95, Coneta.

Figure 5.159. Close-up of window of church, Tr-95, Coneta.

of the site are not available, with the exception of some preliminary data on households (Lee and Bryant 1996; Lee and Markman 1977). The colonial component, however, in particular details and photos of the church and associated convent, can be found in Markman 1984:258-270, 419-427.

References: Lee and Bryant 1996; Lee and Markman 1977, 1979; Markman 1984

TR-96 TRES CRUCES (Figure 5.160)

Site Type: Ceremonial and habitation

Ceramic Phase: Mix

Occupation: Late Classic

Location and Setting: Tr-96 is located approximately 4.8 km southwest of Colonia Rodolfo Figueroa on the road leading from the Pan-American Highway to the Colonia. It is situated on steeply sloping ground in the upland region west of the San Lucas Valley. The surrounding topography is characterized by steep hills and ridges.

Environmental Stratum: Tropical Deciduous Forest

Description: Tr-96 (Tres Cruces) is a large hilltop village with a possible small ceremonial precinct. The site is built on a complex system of terraces. Several compound clusters are visible, as well as individual isolated structures, including both mounds and stone-wall foundation alignments. The terrace system includes both very large complex terrace networks and small individual house terraces. The site appears to represent a substantial amount of labor invested in preparation of land for house construction.

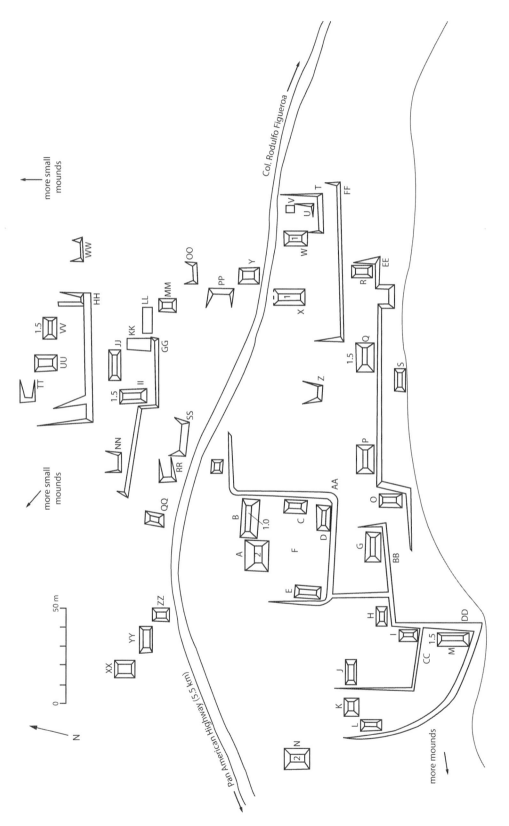

Figure 5.160. Site sketch of Tr-96, Tres Cruces.

The largest structures visible on the site are located on Terrace AA in the west-central portion. This group includes two large mounds (A and B), as well as three other medium-sized mounds (C, D, and E) arranged around a large open plaza (F). This plaza is enclosed on three sides by the large terrace (AA). This terrace is the uppermost part of a large, multi-tiered, interconnected terrace system that covers the southwestern portion of the site. A combination of factors suggests this group is either a civic-ceremonial complex or an elite residential complex: 1) the mounds, especially A and B, are larger than the other mounds on the site; 2) this compound has the greatest concentration of structures on the site; 3) the plaza area is larger and well-defined by both the surrounding structures and Terrace AA. The absence of any other obvious ceremonial structures on the site suggests that this group may have served that function; however, it may have been an elite residential group, perhaps occupied by a large or extended family.

The terrace system continues south and west, providing level ground for several residential mounds. The terraces (including arms BB, CC, and DD) probably enclose at least five residential compounds: G, H/I, J, K/L, and M. At the western edge of the site is a large isolated mound (N), which may also have had ceremonial functions.

In the southeastern corner of the site are two large terraces (EE and FF). These support several more residential mounds and smaller terraces.

North of the road in the northeast section of the site are two more large terraces (GG and HH), which enclose several more house compounds. In addition, scattered over and around the large terraces are a series of small terraces that probably supported individual residential structures. West of these terraces are another series of low residential mounds (QQ, XX, YY, and ZZ) not enclosed by terraces.

Finally, more mounds were visible in areas north, northwest, and west of the main area; however, these were not mapped or counted.

The site appears to be a large, well-planned village. The regular orientation of the structures (arranged at right angles to each other around patios) as well as the overall regularity across compound groups indicates that house groups were built according to an ordered plan.

TR-97 GUAYABITA (Figure 5.161)

Site Type: Habitation

Ceramic Phase: Mix

Occupation: possible Protoclassic, Late Classic

Location and Setting: Tr-97 is located approximately 5.5 km southwest of Colonia Rodolfo Figueroa on the road between the colonia and the Pan-American Highway. The site is situated on a cliff on the south slope of a high hill, in an area of dissected upland topography. The vegetation in the vicinity of the site is mainly sparse tree and brush cover.

Environmental Stratum: Tropical Deciduous Forest

Description: Tr-97 is a large residential community with evidence of several wall foundation alignments, a few mounds, two large complex terrace features, and one small circular structure. The structures appear to follow a linear distribution, arranged in a long narrow band along the contour of the cliff upon which the site is situated.

The site appears to be divided into two concentrations of structures in the northwest and southeast. Each concentration has a terrace structure in a central position with a group of structures upon it. In each area the central terrace group is surrounded by a series of compound clusters. The majority of the structures on the site are visible as stone-wall foundation alignments, with only a few elevated mounds.

The northwestern group is dominated by the central terrace (AAA) upon which is built the largest mound in this area (A). Enclosed within the same terrace are Structures B, C, and D, arranged around Plaza E. The central location of this group, its prominence on the terrace, and the presence of the largest mound suggest that it may have been a civic or ceremonial complex serving this area of the site. The only other mound in this area (J) is an isolated

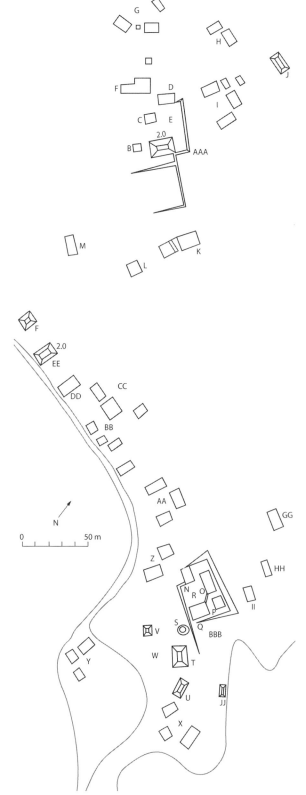

Figure 5.161. Site sketch of Tr-97, Guayabita.

mound at the western edge of the site. At the western edge of this plaza-terrace group are the foundation stones of a large L-shaped structure (F), which may also have formed part of the group. Surrounding the central terrace group are several structures (G to M), most of which were probably residences. On the northwest and north sides, Groups G, H, and I appear to form compounds arranged around patios.

In the southeastern portion of the site, the structures appear to be distributed in a more linear pattern along the cliff edge. In a central position, towards the eastern edge of the site, is another large terrace feature (BBB). This feature encloses four wall foundation alignments (N to Q) arranged around a patio (R). Structures O and Q are connected by a low wall. South of the terrace is a group of low mounds (T, U and V) and a circular structure (S) arranged around an open plaza (W). These two groups may have been civic-ceremonial groups or perhaps elite residences. The round structure (S) may have been a sweat bath associated with either or both of the plaza groups. Surrounding these two central groups and extending along the cliff edge to the west are a series of patio groups (X, Y, Z, AA, and CC), as well as several more isolated structures (DD to JJ) that were probably residential structures.

The orientation of the structures and complexes, particularly in the southeastern area, appears to be an adaptation to the natural contour of the site. The two central complexes, arranged around plazas E and R respectively, do not appear to have any formal arrangement. This would suggest that the site was not built according to a unified plan. The site appears to be a residential community, with possible civic-ceremonial groups in the northwest and southeast sectors.

TR-98 (Figure 5.162)

Site Type: Ceremonial and habitation

Ceramic Phase: Mix

Occupation: possible Protoclassic, Late Classic

Location and Setting: Tr-98 is located approximately 7.25 km southwest of Colonia

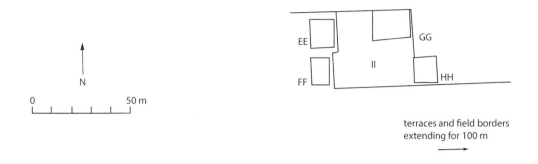

terraces and field borders
extending for 100 m

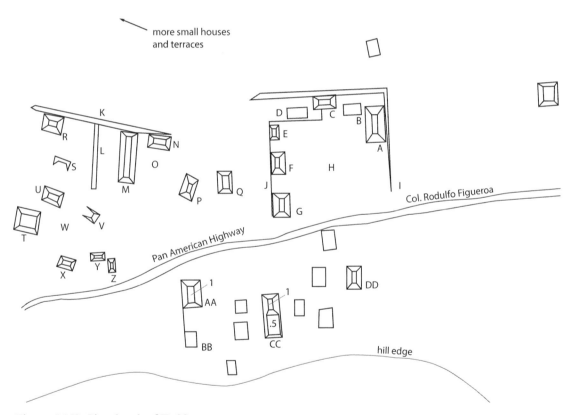

Figure 5.162. Site sketch of Tr-98.

Rodolfo Figueroa on the Pan-American Highway; the road runs through the site.

Environmental Stratum: Tropical Deciduous Forest

Description: Tr-98 is a large community with evidence of civic-ceremonial structures, residential structures, terraces, and field borders.

Both mound structures and stone-wall foundation alignments are visible. The main area of the site is concentrated near the hill edge within an area measuring roughly 150 by 280 m. Other areas with structures were noted northwest and northeast of the main concentration of structures.

The largest cluster of mounds (A to G) is enclosed within Terrace I at the northeast sector of the main area of concentration. This group consists of several small structures arranged around a large open plaza (H). This group is bounded on the west side by a rock alignment (J). At the western edge of the site is another group of low mounds of varying sizes. These mounds are partially enclosed by Terrace K/L, which divides the mounds into at least two groups. The pair of mounds (M and N) on the east side of Terrace L is probably an elite residential compound, judging by the unusually large size of Mound M. Mound P may also have been associated with this group. On the west side of Terrace L, Mound R and the south terrace may have formed part of a residential compound. South of Terrace K/L, Mounds T and U, along with Terrace V and Mounds X, Y, and Z, were probably also residential compounds arranged around patios.

In the southern sector of the site overlooking the hill edge are three mounds (AA, CC, and DD) and several small rectangular wall foundation alignments. Among these structures are the site's tallest structures (Mounds AA and CC), each of which is a maximum of 1 m high. Mound AA is connected by a rock alignment to a rectangular wall foundation (BB). Mound CC in the center of the group, facing the cliff edge, is a double-tiered platform measuring 0.5 m high on the lower tier and 1 m on the upper. This was probably an important ceremonial structure for the site. Surrounding this is a series of wall foundation alignments. These may have been associated with the ceremonial structures or perhaps were part of the households associated with Mounds AA on the west and DD on the east.

At the northeastern corner of the site, a series of rock-wall foundation alignments (EE to HH) appear to represent a household group arranged around Patio II. More terraces and field borders were noted east of this compound but were not mapped or counted. Finally, more small houses and terraces were noted to the northwest, but these were not mapped or counted either.

The site appears to be a large community with one or two civic-ceremonial areas. A wide range of variation in structure size and platform height is visible. The structures are generally oriented in a regular north-south and east-

west manner, suggesting that the site was built according to an orderly plan.

TR-99 LAGARTERO, INCLUDING TR-100, TR-101, TR-102, TR-103, TR-104, TR-106, TR-107
(Figures 5.163-5.178)

Site Type: Ceremonial and habitation

Tr-99: Early Preclassic, early Middle Preclassic, Protoclassic, Late Classic, Early Postclassic, Late Postclassic

Tr-100: Postclassic?

Tr-101, **Tr-102**, **Tr-103:** unknown

Tr-104: Late Classic

Tr-106: Early Classic, Late Classic

Tr-107: Late Classic

Location and Setting: The site of Largartero is located 1 km east of Ejido Cristóbal Colón near the international border with Guatemala. It lies within roughly 8.5 km² of wetlands formed by waters of the Ríos Lagartero and San Lucas and local springs that create shallow lakes called the Lagos de Colón; these waters flow from east to west across the site. The primary area of the site lies on islands and peninsulas projecting into these lakes. The area rests on a limestone formation, which explains the numerous cenotes and sinkholes, and varying depths of the water in the lakes (Rivero 2007b).

Environmental Stratum: Evergreen Seasonal Forest/Gallery Variety-Herbaceous Swamp/Wetland Formations

Description: In 1974, the survey group of Tom Lee, James White, and Nicole Boucher-White divided up the area of Lagartero into distinct sites as the team moved through, hence the assignment of individual site numbers 99-104 and 106-107. Once out of the field, and with the benefit of aerial photos, the assessment shifted to a single site designation (Tr-99) for this unique location, with its connecting ridges and apparently related archaeological features. For the purposes of phase assessment, however, the inital individual site designations will be used.

The first map of the site was a pace and compass version by James White and Nicole Boucher White, and a large format version can

Figure 5.163. View of Largartero.

be found in the backpocket. We also present the map in the following pages along with blow-ups of the former designated sites as field notes and other information are contained in the pace and compass map.

Ekholm and Martínez (1983) present a short history of known visitors to the area since the Spanish Conquest. Some discussion and speculation as to possible Precolumbian hydrology and canal construction are reviewed in Matheny and Gurr (1979) and Ekholm and Martínez (1983). Mapping and initial excavations were undertaken by Ekholm, Martínez, and Gurr of the NWAF; recent activity at the site has been led by Sonia Rivero (see References below).

Archaeological work has focused on Tr-99, which lies in the southeast corner of the site and is located on the largest peninsula, El Limonal/ Limonar. Rivero (2001) reports eleven plazas, 170 mounds, the highest at 18 m, are located in this section, although not all are apparent from the older pace and compass transverse map (see Tenorio et al. 2012:102, fig. 36 for a newer map).

At least two stela fragments were uncovered at Tr-99. Most structures are oriented east of north. One of the largest plazas is outlined by four of the largest mounds; a ballcourt is located behind the southernmost mound of this plaza group. East of this plaza group is the largest plaza, formed by a long platform and three adjacent mounds on a perpendicular creating an L-shaped enclosure. A 2 m wide and 1.5 m high stone wall blocks access to this raised area or peninsula on the southwest side.

Tr-100 is located in the southwest end of the site and lies on the other side of the abovementioned stone wall shared with Tr-99. The topography is an eastward curving ridge of land surrounded by water and marsh. There are relative fewer mounds noted here (16); and there is no obvious plaza organization. The orientations of these mounds are different from Tr-99, with most apparently oriented to the north.

Tr-101 a long sinuous narrow ridge of land oriented southwest-northeast, just northeast of Tr-99. A 1 m high stone wall bisects the ridge in the middle; another wall is located at the northeast end. Most of the mounds lie on the southeast section of the ridge, albeit this is

Figure 5.164. Aerial view of Largartero.

Figure 5.165. Aerial view of Largartero.

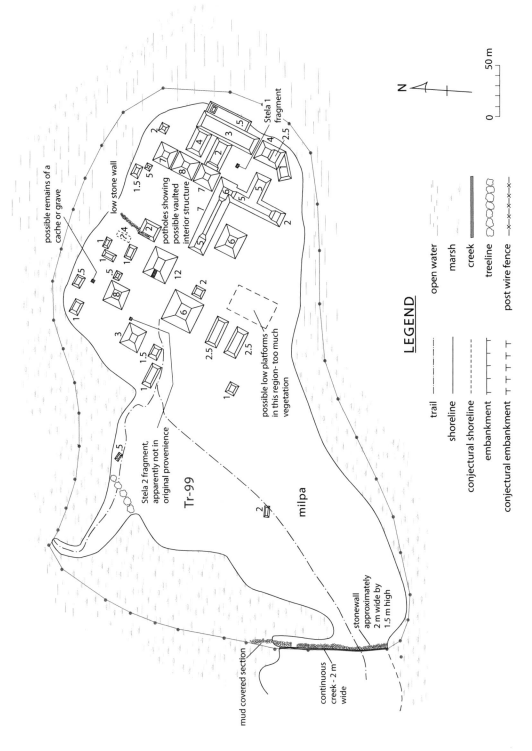

Figure 5.167. Map of Largartero, section Tr-99. Pace and compass traverse map by James M. White and Nicole Boucher White.

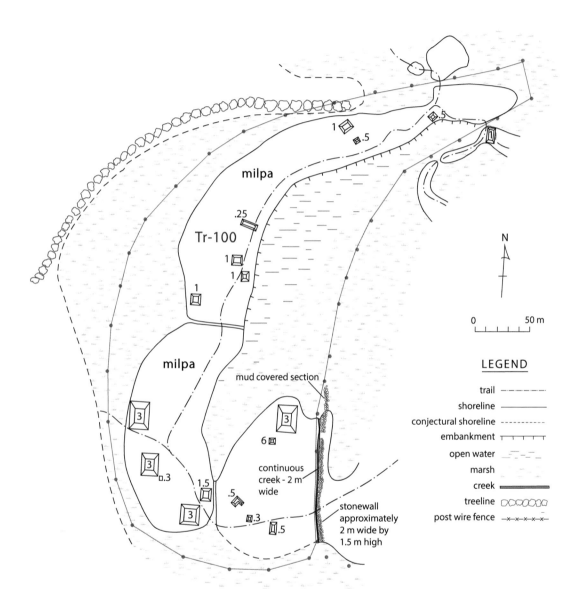

Figure 5.168. Map of Largartero, section Tr-100. Pace and compass traverse map by James M. White and Nicole Boucher White.

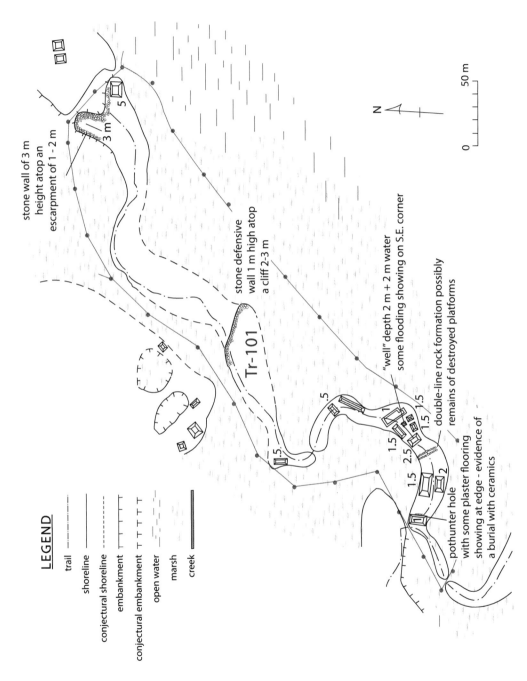

LEGEND

trail

shoreline

conjectural shoreline

embankment

conjectural embankment

open water

marsh

creek

stone wall of 3 m
height atop an
escarpment of 1 - 2 m

stone defensive
wall 1 m high atop
a cliff 2-3 m

Tr-101

"well" depth 2 m + 2 m water
some flooding showing on S.E. corner

double-line rock formation possibly
remains of destroyed platforms

pothunter hole
with some plaster flooring
showing at edge - evidence of
a burial with ceramics

N

0   50 m

Figure 5.169. Map of Largartero, section Tr-101. Pace and compass traverse map by James M. White and Nicole Boucher White.

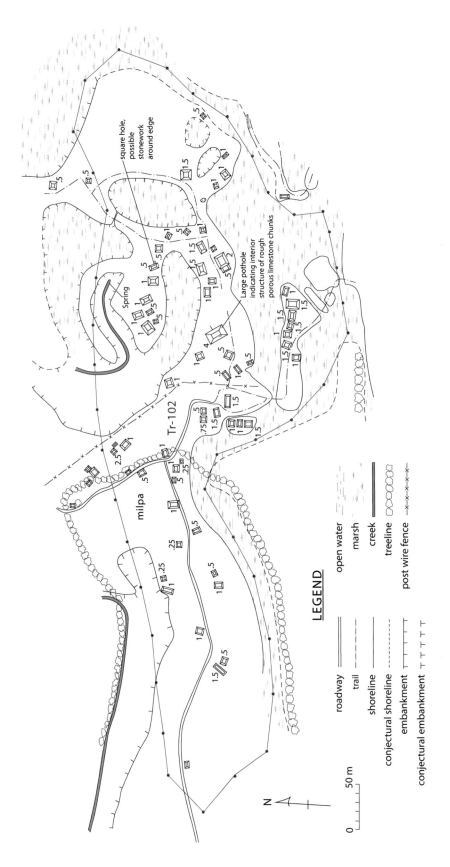

Figure 5.170. Map of Largartero, section Tr-102. Pace and compass traverse map by James M. White and Nicole Boucher White.

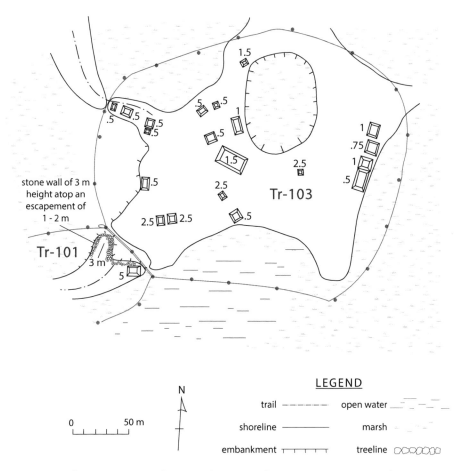

Figure 5.171. Map of Largartero, section Tr-103. Pace and compass traverse map by James M. White and Nicole Boucher White.

the narrowest stretch of the peninsula and the mounds appear to be crowded together blocking easy access across it.

Tr-102 is a large central quadrant of the designated site. It consists of a long peninsula of land jutting into the marsh from the west, while the western half is interspersed with bajos and marsh. Apart from one 4 m high mound in the center, most of the sixty or so mounds are no higher than 1.5 m, and most are grouped together without obvious pattern; mound orientations are varied.

Tr-103 lies northeast of Tr-101 and its stone wall and contains a large bajo. Mounds are generally grouped. The eastern group of four mounds is oriented just east of north. The central group has an orientation west of north with the exception of a rectangular platform in

its midst that is oriented northwest, along with a series of five small mounds blocking access to a ridge of land to the northwest. Two 2.5 m high mounds are located in the center of access to Tr-101.

Tr-104 is located in the northwest section of the site. A series of mostly low-lying mounds are strung along a ridge of land, which is surrounded on both sides by bajos. No discernible plaza patterning is present suggesting that these were probably residential mounds. Two 4 m high mounds are located in the northwest corner, and there were likely other mounds associated with these two, but anything nearby has been destroyed for use as fill in road construction.

Tr-106 lies in the north-central zone of the site. It consists of two areas almost separated

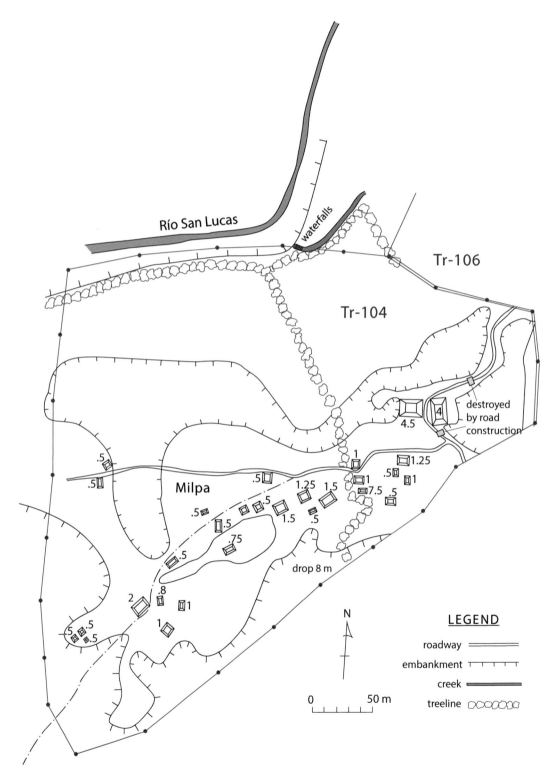

Figure 5.172. Map of Largartero, section Tr-104. Pace and compass traverse map by James M. White and Nicole Boucher White.

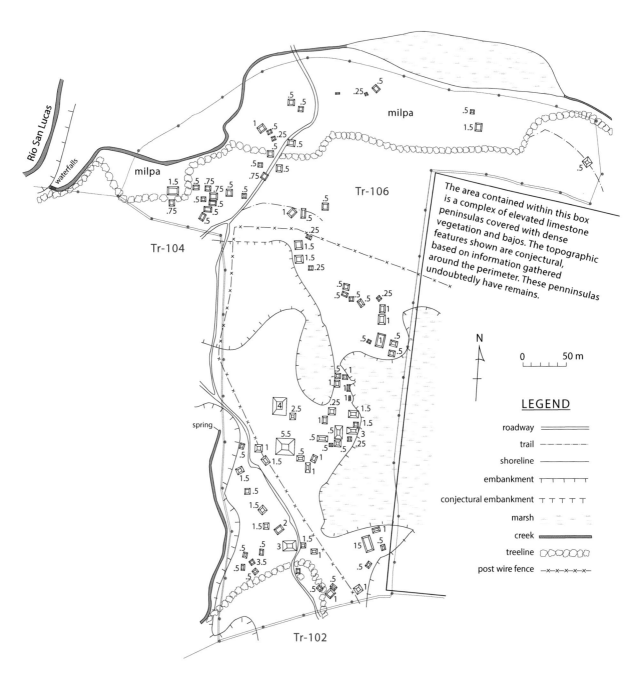

Figure 5.173. Map of Largartero, section Tr-106. Pace and compass traverse map by James M. White and Nicole Boucher White.

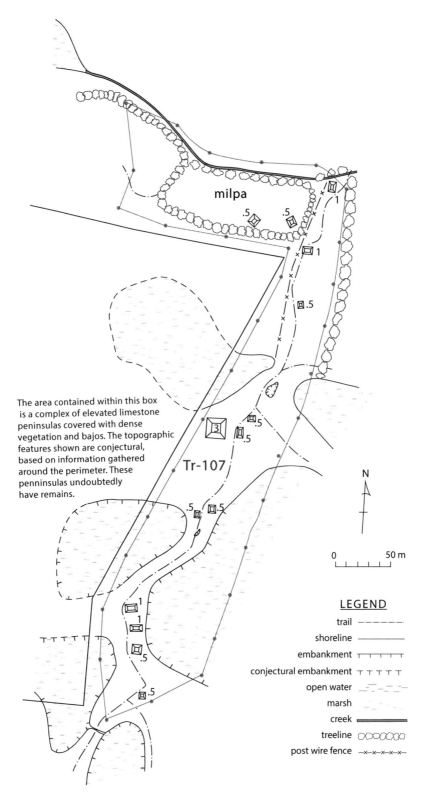

The area contained within this box is a complex of elevated limestone peninsulas covered with dense vegetation and bajos. The topographic features shown are conjectural, based on information gathered around the perimeter. These penninsulas undoubtedly have remains.

milpa

Tr-107

N

0   50 m

LEGEND

trail	— · — · —
shoreline	———
embankment	┬┬┬┬┬
conjectural embankment	⊤ ⊤ ⊤ ⊤ ⊤
open water	— — —
marsh	
creek	▬▬▬▬
treeline	⬭⬭⬭⬭⬭
post wire fence	—×—×—×—

Figure 5.174. Map of Largartero, section Tr-107. Pace and compass traverse map by James M. White and Nicole Boucher White.

Figure 5.175. View of Largartero.

Figure 5.176. View of Largartero.

Figure 5.177. View of Largartero.

Figure 5.178. View of Largartero.

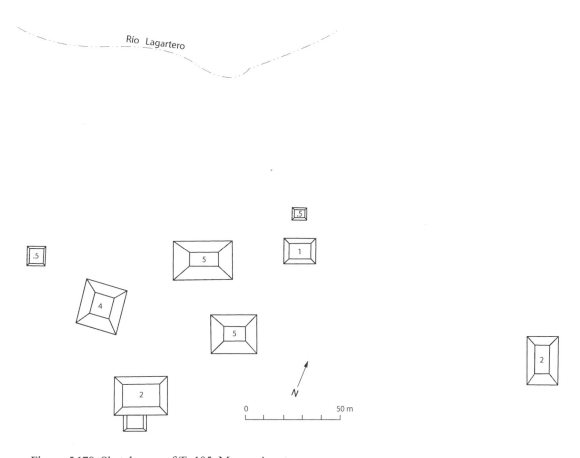

Figure 5.179. Sketch map of Tr-105, Mango Amate.

by penetrating bajos and marshland. A possible plaza lies near the fence line in the southern half of the south. Two mounds of 4 and 5.5 m define it, along with a series of smaller, lower mounds. Clusters of smaller, low-lying mounds are probable residential in nature are located to the north and south of the plaza group. The area between Tr-106 and Tr-107 was not surveyed due to dense vegetation.

Tr-107 lies in the extreme northwest of the site area and consists of a narrow ridge of land with bajos and marsh on either side with a wider area to the north. Some 14 mounds were noted dispersed along its length.

References: Blake 2010:269; Ekholm 1977, 1979a, 1979b, 1984, 1985, 1990; Ekholm and Martínez 1983; Lee 1985; Gurr 1988; Rivero 1996, 1997, 1999, 2001, 2002, 2003, 2006, 2007b; Rivero et al. 2008; Rivero and Tenorio 2005; Tenorio et al. 2012

TR-105 MANGO AMATE
(Figures 5.179-5.180)

Site Type: Ceremonial and habitation

Ceramic Phase: Ix

Occupation: Protoclassic, Late Classic, Early Postclassic

Location and Setting: This site is 45 km northeast of Colonia Joaquín Miguel Gutiérrez on the first bench of the junction of the Ríos Mango Amate and Lagartero. The site is in a fairly arid zone, but the large amount of subsurface water has allowed a heavy vegetation cover. There are now milpas surrounding the site zone.

Environmental Stratum: Evergreen Seasonal Forest/Gallery Variety/Riparian Forest

Figure 5.180. View of Tr-105, Mango Amate.

Description: Eighteen mounds oriented east-west are distributed over two terraces, rising above the river drainages. The ceremonial core of the site lies on one of the terraces and is depicted in the sketch map; the four largest mounds form a plaza.

References: Paillés and Ávila López 1987

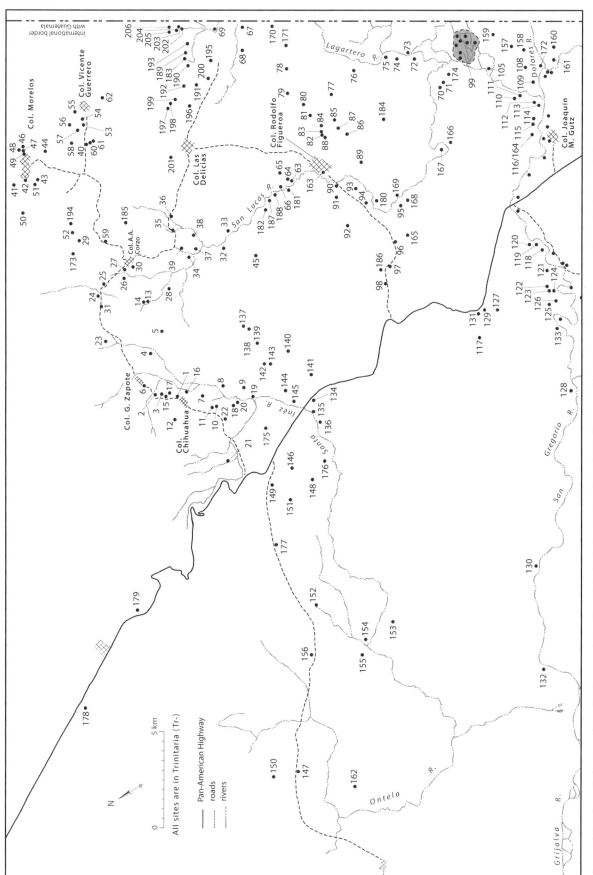

Figure 6.1. Map of site locations in the municipality of La Trinitaria (Tr-108 - 206) discussed in Chapter 6 (close-up of map in Figure 1.7).

SITE DESCRIPTIONS: MUNICIPIO LA TRINITARIA TR-108 TO TR-206

Michael Blake, Thomas A. Lee Jr., John E. Clark, and Mary E. Pye

MUNICIPIO LA TRINITARIA

TR-108 LA LIBERTAD MILPA (ENTRE RÍOS SIN SOMBRA)
(Figure 6.2)

Site Type: Ceremonial and habitation

Ceramic Phase: Enub through Hun and Mix

Occupation: Middle Preclassic, Late Preclassic, Protoclassic, Late Classic

Location and Setting: This site is 3.4 km east of Colonia Joaquín Miguel Gutiérrez, approximately 600 m north of Río Dolores. It is in a zone of almost flat valley bottom that has been cleared for milpa. There are some patches of forest nearby, but for the most part forest in this zone is restricted to riparian setting.

Environmental Stratum: Riparian Forest

Description: There are 20 mounds in the central zone of the site and at least several more in the surrounding fields that were not mapped. There are two main zones The largest includes Mounds A through N and stretches in a linear fashion from north to south with all of the mounds having the same orientation. Within this group several mounds are clustered into plaza groups. Mounds A to D with flanking Mound E completely enclose a plaza area at the north end of the site. To the south of this are several other mounds aligned with each other (F, G, J, and I), some which may partly enclose plazas. Some are isolated (M and N).

The eastern group of mounds at the site (O through T) contains the largest mounds (R and T), which face each other. Together with Mounds Q and S, these enclose a formal plaza, much the same as the north group (A to D). The mounds in both groups are all oriented north-south and arranged so that there is never more than 30 m between neighboring mounds. It is obviously a well-planned ceremonial complex with the bulk of the occupation probably contemporaneous. The site was test excavated in 1977 by members of the NWAF to determine its date and relationship to the large Preclassic center of La Libertad (Tr-157) (see Miller and Lowe 2014), although the site was covered in milpa and inaccurately described by the excavators; limited excavations uncovered Protoclassic material.

References: Miller and Lowe 2014

TR-109 ENTRE RÍOS (Figure 6.3)

Site Type: Ceremonial and habitation

Ceramic Phase: Lato through Dyosan, Hun, Mix

Occupation: Early Preclassic, early Middle Preclassic, Protoclassic, Late Classic

Location and Setting: This site is located on a bench 200 m north of Río Dolores 1 km east of Colonia Joaquín Miguel Gutiérrez. The terrain is flat except for some minor arroyos and old river benches. It has been cleared for agricultural purposes, and there is only minor forest near the stream shores.

Environmental Stratum: Riparian Forest

Description: There are 12 mounds at this site and all have a similar northwest-southeast orientation. The largest (I) is 4 m high and potted on its north side. The others are lower platform mounds that may have been the bases for elite residences. To the north of Mound I is a cluster of three mounds in a compound group possibly surrounding a patio (F, G, and H), or perhaps a ballcourt (F and G). Still farther north is another small group that includes Mound A and two smaller mounds that may have been altars. Mounds D and E are the two largest mounds after Mound I and may have formed the western boundary of a large plaza (M). To the

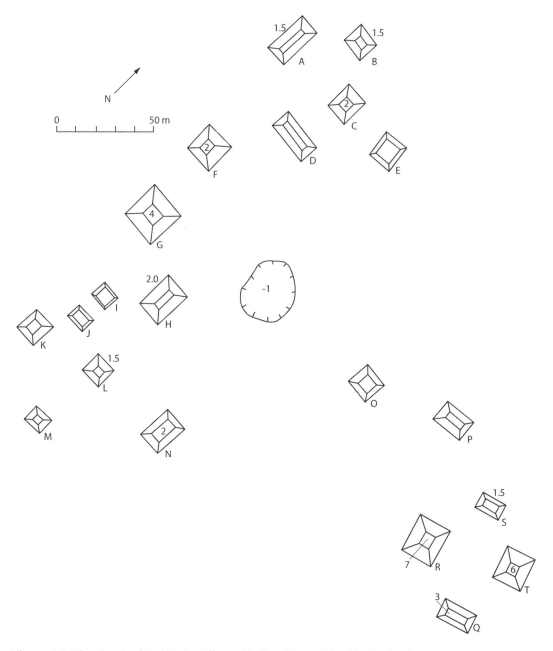

Figure 6.2. Site sketch of Tr-108, La Libertad Milpa (Entre Ríos Sin Sombra).

south of Mound I is a smaller cluster of residence platforms (J, K, and L) that may have formed a domestic group. This site is like many others in the survey area consisting of tight clusters of mounds with some probably being used for ceremonial purposes. The maximum distance between mounds is 40 m, implying they were all used by the same community. The site was tested in 1977 by Miller and Lowe (2014) to determine its relationship with La Libertad (Tr-157). The six test pits showed the site to be primarily Late Classic with a short occupation. Mound construction consisted of rounded river cobbles and evidence of walls also made of river cobbles.

References: Miller and Lowe 2014

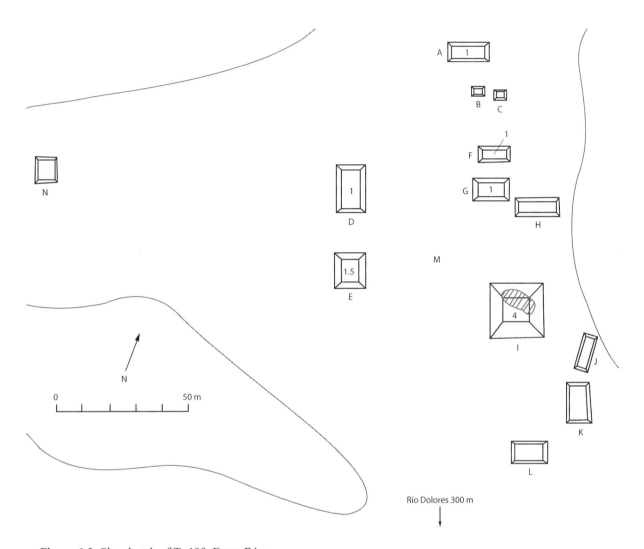

Figure 6.3. Site sketch of Tr-109, Entre Ríos.

TR-110 LA RINCONADA
(No Map)

Site Type: Ceremonial and habitation

Ceramic Phase: Hun

Occupation: Late Preclassic, Protoclassic, Late Classic

Location and Setting: This site is located 2.5 km east of Colonia Joaquín Miguel Gutiérrez and 300 m west of Río Lagartero. It is on a bench above the river and the terrain is flat. The site has been cleared for pasture and now trees are restricted to the riverbanks.

Environmental Stratum: Evergreen Seasonal Forest: Gallery Variety/Riparian Forest

Description: The location of the site map is unknown. From Miller and Lowe's description (2014), the site was composed of at least five large mounds with numerous house foundation outlines; "…two rather large pyramids (approximately 5.5 m tall) [are] arranged on a plaza with a third, low mound to the west side. An elongated mound adjacent to one side of a pyramid forms a ballcourt" (Miller and Lowe 2014:213). The residential area lies to the south of the plaza.

References: Miller and Lowe 2014

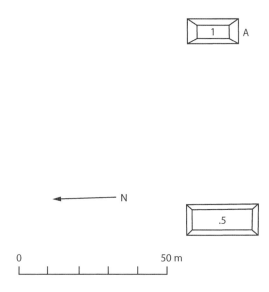

Figure 6.4. Site sketch of Tr-111.

TR-111 (Figure 6.4)

Site Type: Habitation

Location and Setting: This site is located on the west first bench of Río Lagartero approximately 1.2 km north of its confluence with Río San Gregorio. The site is also 2.5 km east of Colonia Joaquín Miguel Gutiérrez and just 300 m south of Tr-110. The site is on a flat bench that is heavily forested with riverine trees.

Environmental Stratum: Evergreen Seasonal Forest: Gallery Variety/Riparian Forest

Description: Unfortunately, only two mounds were visible at this site but since the vegetation cover was so dense there were probably many more which were not discovered. Mound A is the tallest at 1 m, but Mound B is both longer and wider. Both were probably residence platforms. Both have the same alignment.

TR-112 SAN GERÓNIMO (Figure 6.5)

Site Type: Ceremonial and habitation

Ceramic Phase: Mix

Occupation: Protoclassic, Late Classic

Location and Setting: This site is on the first bench of an old stream channel of Río Lagartero, just 250 m west of the present channel and 500 m upstream from its confluence with Río San Gregorio. The site area appears to have been previously forested but has been cleared for pasture.

Environmental Stratum: Evergreen Seasonal Forest:Gallery Variety/Riparian Forest

Description: There are 17 mounds at this site, and all are clustered together on a small protruding section of river terrace. The largest mound (M) is 8 m tall and sits near the east side of the site. The west side is marked by two large mounds (G and H) forming a ballcourt that is enclosed on the east end by Mound J. Another large mound (I) flanks the ballcourt. In the plaza area between the ballcourt and the main temple mound are two small mounds (K and L), which are offset from the ceremonial architecture and may not be contemporaneous with it. Mounds N, O, and P to the east of the main mound and overlooking the terrace edge are probably grouped in an elite residence compound. The northern part of the site has another cluster of mounds with a 6 m tall mound (D) dominating. The other mounds (A, B, C and E) in the group are smaller. Mound E is a double-tiered mound with a large 1 m tall platform and a smaller 1.5 m tall mound. Mound N at the east end of the site is similar.

The community settlement pattern is very different from other sites described. First, there are several mounds that are not oriented with the main mounds or each other. Second, the ballcourt is similar in architecture to Early Classic or Protoclassic construction. Third, small house mounds like K and L are found in the main plaza. Given that the surface ceramics date from Protoclassic and Late Classic, combined with the lack of consistent orientation, strongly suggests that many of the mounds were not contemporary with each other.

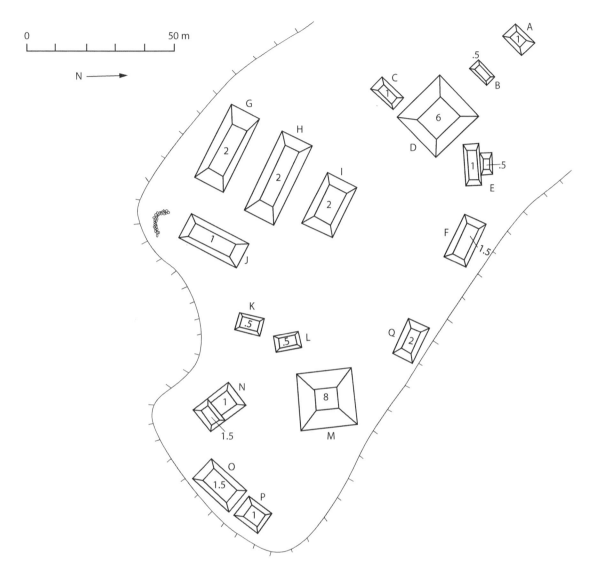

Figure 6.5. Site sketch of Tr-112, Gerónimo.

Test pitting was carried out at the site during 1977 by Miller and Lowe (2014) to determine how the site related to the large Preclassic site of La Libertad (Tr-157). They excavated four test pits in the plaza, the ballcourt, and a small pyramid. A detailed examination of the architecture at the site indicated that it is very similar to that at Lagartero (Tr-99), with cut travertine blocks and earth and rubble fill.

References: Miller and Lowe 2014.

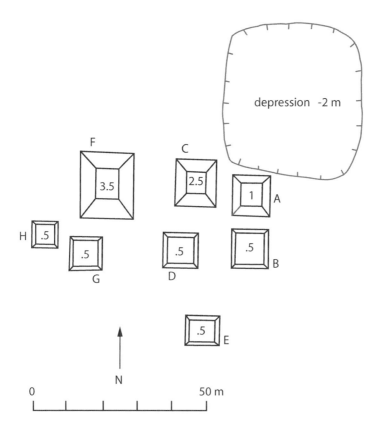

Figure 6.6. Site sketch of Tr-113.

TR-113 (Figure 6.6)

Site Type: Ceremonial and habitation

Ceramic Phase: Guajilar, Mix

Occupation: Late Preclassic, Late Classic

Location and Setting: This site is located 1.5 km east of Colonia Joaquín Miguel Gutiérrez, 250 m north of Río San Gregorio, and 300 m west of Río Lagartero. It appears to be on the bench of an old river channel. It is in a zone of forested vegetation that probably makes use of a high subsurface water table and is surrounded by pasturage.

Environmental Stratum: Evergreen Seasonal Forest: Gallery Variety/Riparian Forest

Description: There are eight visible mounds at this site. The largest (F) is 3.5 m tall and surrounded on two sides by a tight cluster of mounds. The other large mound (C) is aligned directly to the east of Mound F. River cobbles were used as facing on both the pyramids. The maximum distance between the mounds is 12 m but most are within 10 m of each other. To the north of these mounds is a large depression 2 m deep that may have been a barrow pit used in mound construction. More house mounds may be located near the junction of the two rivers.

TR-114 (Figure 6.7)

Site Type: Ceremonial and habitation

Ceramic Phase: Hun

Occupation: Middle Preclassic, Late Preclassic, Protoclassic, Late Classic

Location and Setting: This site is 1.2 km east of Colonia Joaquín Miguel Gutiérrez on the north side of Río San Gregorio. The site is on a bench 250 m northeast of the main channel and has been cleared for pasturage.

Environmental Stratum: Tropical Deciduous Forest

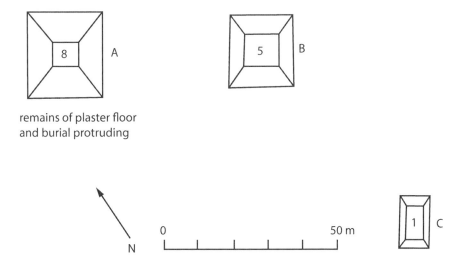

remains of plaster floor
and burial protruding

N   0   50 m

Figure 6.7. Site sketch of Tr-114.

Description: There are only three mounds remaining at this site. The two largest ones (A and B) are aligned from northwest to southeast and are 35 m apart. Mound A is 8 m high and 22 to 24 m on a side. Mound B is slightly smaller at 19 m on a side and 5 m tall. Both are faced with river cobbles. Mound A is slightly disturbed on the northwest side and has a plaster floor and burial protruding from its side. The only other mound is C, just 40 m south of the main complex. All structures have the same alignment and could possibly be contemporaneous. More small mounds may have existed in the fields nearby and have been destroyed by cultivation.

TR-115 (Figure 6.8)

Site Type: Habitation

Occupation: Late Classic

Location and Setting: This site is located 1.1 km northeast of Colonia Joaquín Miguel Gutiérrez on the north side of Río San Gregorio. The site is on a bench 150 m from the river and is in an area of land cleared for pasturage.

Environmental Stratum: Riparian Forest

Description: There are four mounds remaining, and all are arranged around a plaza. They form two groups, each with a major mound and an

adjacent smaller mound. The A/B group is on the north and east sides of the plaza and the C/D group is on the south and west sides of the plaza. Mound D is 1.5 m tall and has a lower northern extension which is 6 m long and 1 m tall. The two larger mounds (A and D) are faced with river cobbles.

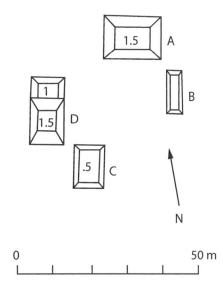

0   50 m

Figure 6.8. Site sketch of Tr-115.

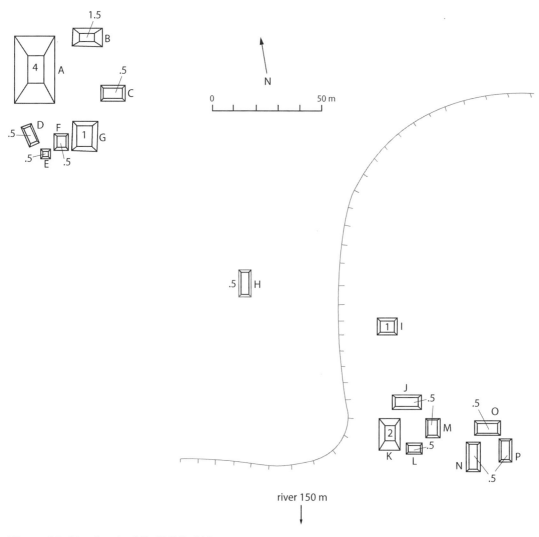

Figure 6.9. Site sketch of Tr-116/ Tr-164.

TR-116/ TR-164 (Figure 6.9)

Site Type: Ceremonial and habitation

Occupation: Late Preclassic, Protoclassic, Late Classic

Location and Setting: This site is 1 km northeast of Colonia Joaquín Miguel Gutiérrez on the other side of Río San Gregorio. It is 150 to 250 m north of the river. It is in an area of land that has been plowed but is used for pasturage.

Environmental Stratum: Fields or pasture

Description: The northwest mound group contains seven mounds. The largest (A) is 4 m

high and forms the west side of a plaza marked on the other three sides by Mounds B, C, and G. There are three additional smaller mounds (D, E and F) to the south of the large mound. The smallest of these (E) may have been an altar. Mound D is oriented a few degrees west of north, while all the rest at the site are oriented a few degrees east of north. The larger mounds were faced with river cobbles.

The southeast section of the site is on a lower terrace approximately 150 m from the previously described mound group. An isolated platform (H) is roughly divided into three separate groups. They include an isolated platform (I) and two residential groups (J to

M and N to P). The J to M group surrounds a courtyard 10 by 15 m with the largest mound (K) on the west side. This replicated on a smaller scale the arrangement of Mounds A to C and G in the northwest mound group. The P group has a similar arrangement around a small courtyard except that it has no large mound like A or K and the south side is open.

TR-117 (Figure 6.10)

Site Type: Habitation

Location and Setting: This site is located 10 km northwest of Colonia Joaquín Miguel Gutiérrez. The site is in a small valley in a hilly zone 4.5 km north of Río San Gregorio and well above its fertile flood plains. The area is forested and some parcels in the zone are used for milpa.

Environmental Stratum: Tropical Deciduous Forest

Description: This small site includes three mounds on a terraced slope. The largest structure (A) is 1.5 m high and forms the east side of a courtyard approximately 20 by 15 m. The north and south sides are formed by the two smaller mounds (B and C), and the west side of the courtyard is formed by the 30 m long terrace. No other mounds or features were noted in the immediate vicinity.

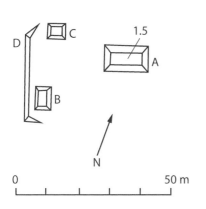

Figure 6.10. Site sketch of Tr-117.

TR-118 TRES CERRITOS
(Figure 6.11)

Site Type: Ceremonial and habitation

Ceramic Phase: Mix

Occupation: Protoclassic, Late Classic, Late Postclassic

Location and Setting: This site is 4.5 km northeast of Colonia San Caralampio on the northern bench of Río San Gregorio and 1.25 km east of the small community of Flor de Mayo. It lies 200 m north of the Río San Gregorio. It is on flat terrain that has been cultivated intensively, but it is presently being used as pasturage.

Environmental Stratum: Riparian Forest

Description: The structure of this site is one of a large ceremonial plaza surrounded by tall mounds and a ballcourt, which are in turn surrounded by smaller residential platforms. The structures surrounding the plaza area include two 6.5 m tall mounds (E and F), a 6 m mound (B), a 5 m mound (C), and a smaller 2 m tall mound (D). The ballcourt (A) is I-shaped with two 1.5 m tall flanking mounds and the end zones enclosed with a continuous low peripheral mound. Adjoining the east corner of the ballcourt is a 1 m tall mound (I). There are two small altars in the main plaza (G and H). Altar H is centrally located and Altar G faces onto Mound B.

On the northwest side of the center are four low platform mounds (L to O). Mounds L and M may be associated with Mound B, while N and O together form a residential unit. These are the only two mounds oriented north-south. The rest are oriented west of north. To the northeast of the main plaza are four mounds (P to S), all arranged around a courtyard with one side open. Mound S is the largest and partly flanks and adjoins a low mound (R). On the south and southeast sides of the main complex are numerous low platforms, the tallest of which were probably residential. Examples are the T to V group and the NN to PP group. In addition, there is a fairly complex group on Terrace LL. This includes FF to KK, all surrounding a central courtyard. There is also an isolated mound (MM). Three additional mounds are located on the east side of the main plaza.

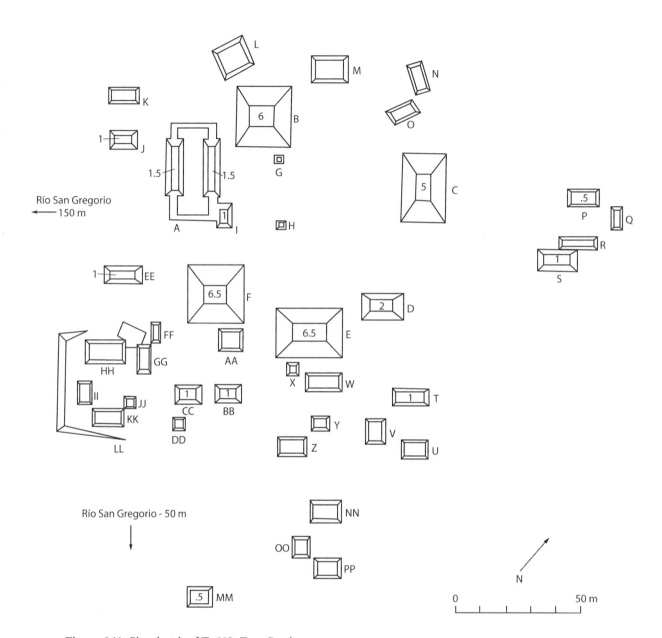

Figure 6.11. Site sketch of Tr-118, Tres Cerritos.

Mound EE may be associated with the terrace group, and K and J could have been associated with the ballcourt.

The similar orientation of all the mounds and their proximity of less than 15 m to a neighboring mound suggest that the site is a compact and well-organized unit.

TR-119 (Figure 6.12)

Site Type: Habitation

Location and Setting: This site is located 5 km northeast of Colonia San Caralampio on the north side of Río San Gregorio and 1.7 km east of the small community of Flor de Mayo. It is on an old second bench well above the modern river level

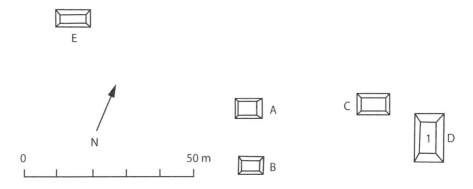

Figure 6.12. Site sketch of Tr-119.

but only 200 m west of the channel. The area has been completely cleared for pasturage and farming, and the only thick vegetation exists along the river margin.

Environmental Stratum: Riparian Forest

Description: This small site consists of five mounds that seem to have been arranged into three groups. One group consists of two low mounds (A and B) facing each other across a 10 m wide courtyard. Mounds C and D may have flanked two adjacent sides of another courtyard about 30 m east of A and B. Mound E is isolated 50 m west of A and B and may have been a lone residential structure. The complex is a few hundred meters east of Tr-118 and may have been a small outlet of that ceremonial center.

TR-120 (Figure 6.13)

Site Type: Ceremonial(?) and habitation

Occupation: Late Classic

Location and Setting: This site is located 5.2 km northeast of Colonia San Caralampio and almost 2 km east of the small community of Flor de Mayo. It is on the first bench of the river, within 100 m of it, and on the north side. The area is under cultivation and pasturage, but previously there may have been a riparian forest.

Environmental Stratum: Riparian Forest

Description: This small site has three mounds, one of which is a compound structure. Mound A

is a large 1 m tall platform, 25 by 20 m, which supports two smaller mounds (B and C). These may have been residential platforms. Mound E is a large platform which is 1.5 m tall and oriented to the northwest, unlike the A mound complex and Mound D which are oriented just a few degrees west of north. Mound D is relatively isolated, about 50 m to the southwest of the other mounds.

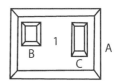

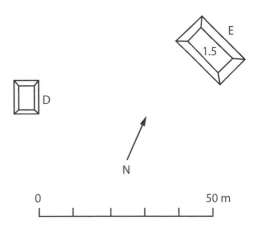

Figure 6.13. Site sketch of Tr-120.

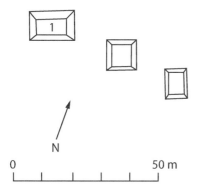

Figure 6.14. Site sketch of Tr-121, Playa Grande.

TR-121 PLAYA GRANDE (Figure 6.14)

Site Type: Habitation

Occupation: Protoclassic, Late Classic, possible Late Postclassic

Location and Setting: This site is 3.7 km northeast of Colonia San Caralampio on the north side of Río San Gregorio and on the eastern edge of the small community of Flor de Mayo It is 250 m north of the river on a higher bench and beside a small arroyo that seasonally drains south into the river. Like most of the good bottomlands of the river, the site zone is cultivated and used for pasturage.

Environmental Stratum: Fields or pasture

Description: There are only three small mounds at the site. They are 10 m from each other and may represent a single residential complex. Mound A is the largest, both in length, width, and height (1 m tall). It is approximately midway between two larger ceremonial centers, Tr-121 and 123 and so could be related to either.

TR-122 (Figure 6.15)

Site Type: Ceremonial and habitation

Ceramic Phase: Mix

Occupation: Protoclasssic, Late Classic, Early Postclassic

Location and Setting: This site is 3.5 km north of Colonia San Caralampio and on the northern edge of the small community of Flor de Mayo. It is situated on a low hill on the north side of Río San Gregorio in rolling terrain 400 m north of the river. The area has been cultivated and is used as pasturage.

Environmental Stratum: Fields or pasture

Description: The linear arrangement of structures is divided into three main groups at this site. The northwestern group is comprised of Mounds A to G. These may have been residential platforms and are arranged in several compound groups such as D and E, B and C, and F and G. The central group (H to M) is a more formalized cluster with all mounds having the same orientation. Mound H is the largest and may have been of ceremonial importance. It faces onto a courtyard bounded by Platform Mounds I, J, and K. To the south are located Mounds L and M, which may have been residential platforms. The southeastern group consists of only two mounds (N and O) forming a courtyard cluster. The three mound groups are separated by 45 to 60 m and (except for the northwestern one) all have the same orientation, west of north.

TR-123 (Figure 6.16)

Site Type: Ceremonial and habitation

Location and Setting: This site is located 3.3 km north of Colonia San Caralampio. It is on the north side of Río San Gregorio and sits on a low hill on the west side of the small community of Flor de Mayo. The site is 300 m from the river, but the fertile lands are often used as milpa or left fallow as pasture.

Environmental Stratum: Fields or pasture

Description: Tr-123 is very similar to Tr-118, which is located 2 km east along the river. The site is a compact ceremonial center with habitation structures. The main plaza is surrounded by several large mounds, and there are large low platforms to the south of the plaza. The west, north, and east sides of the plaza are delineated by a 5 m tall mound (A), two 4 m tall mounds (B and D), and a 3 m tall mound (E). In addition, there are three low mounds around the edge of the plaza (Mounds C, F, and

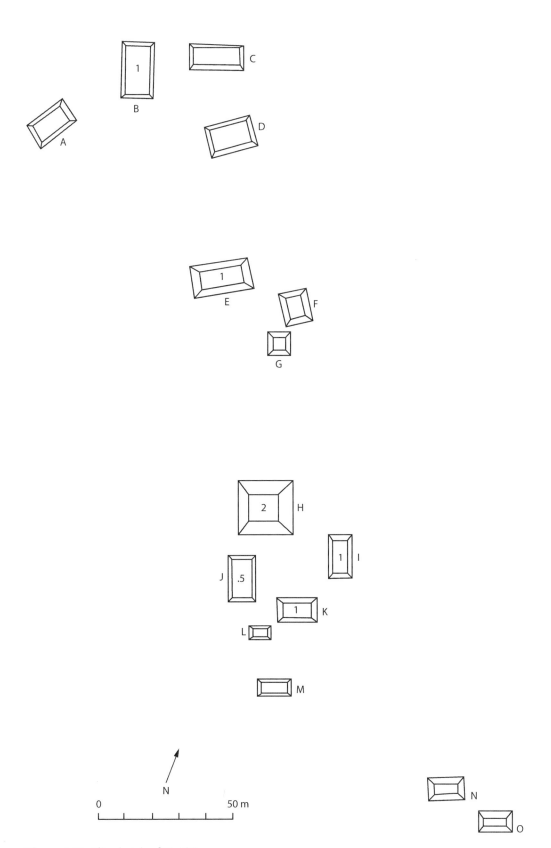

Figure 6.15. Site sketch of Tr-122.

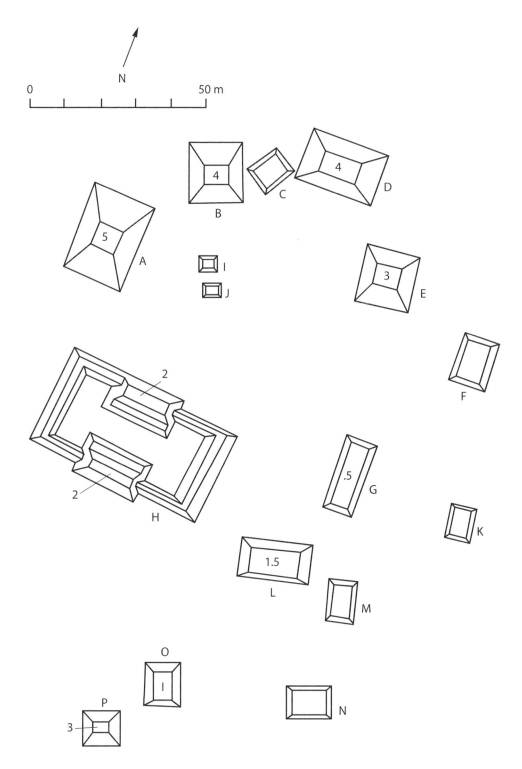

Figure 6.16. Site sketch of Tr-123.

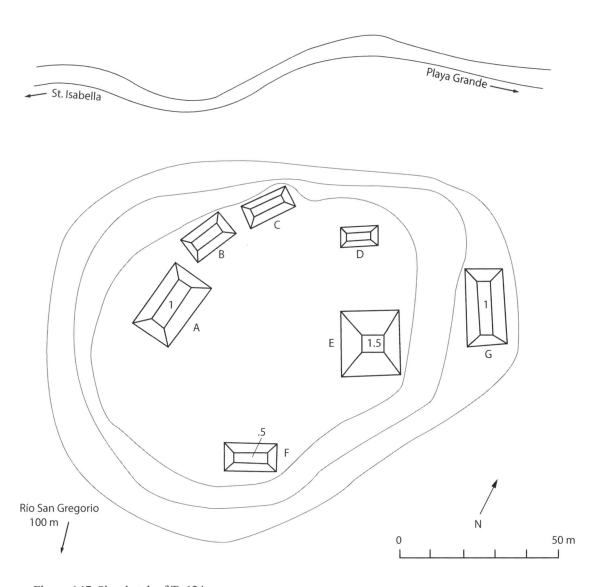

Figure 6.17. Site sketch of Tr-124.

G). Examples of residential platforms arranged around courtyards to the south of the main plaza are Mounds L/M and O/P. The overall alignment of the structures is north-south with some exceptions, like Mounds B and C. The largest structure at the site is the ballcourt (H) which is located on the south side of the plaza. It is I-shaped with two 2 m tall side mounds, each stepped, and a continuous 1 m tall mound surrounding the end-zones. The layout design is similar to Tr-118. Two small mounds (I and J) are probably altars and face onto the largest mound (A).

TR-124 (Figure 6.17)

Site Type: Habitation

Location and Setting: This site is located 3.2 km north of Colonia San Caralampio, on the western side of the small community of Flor de Mayo. It is 100 m north of Río San Gregorio near the edge of a small arroyo. The site is on the fertile first bench and is cultivated as well as left for pasture. Tr-123 is 50 to 75 m north and may be part of the same site.

Environmental Stratum: Riparian Forest

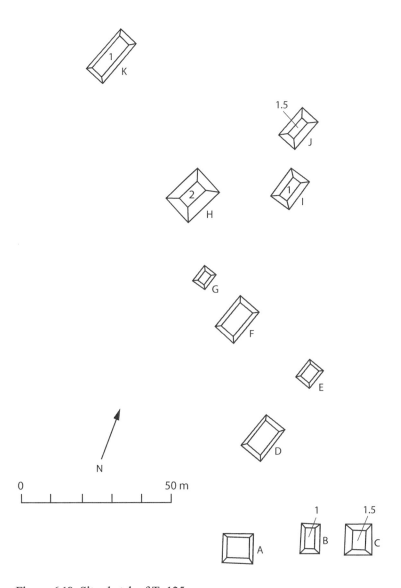

Figure 6.18. Site sketch of Tr-125.

Description: There are seven mounds on this small site situated on a knoll 100 m from the river. All but one of the mounds (G) are laid out so as to surround a plaza. Mounds A to C are arranged end-to-end and face east to the largest mound (E). Mounds D and F flank Mound E on the edge of the plaza. Mound G is a long mound like A and sits downslope from E to just east of it. All of the mounds are continued by the small knoll and so are not oriented in the same direction. Mounds A to C are oriented from north-south to just east of north, while the rest are oriented west of north.

TR-125 (Figure 6.18)

Site Type: Habitation

Occupation: Late Classic

Location and Setting: This site is 3.3 km north of Colonia San Caralampio, 1 km northwest of the small community of Flor de Mayo, and 300 m east of a bend in Río San Gregorio. It is on a low hill well above the river level. The site zone is used as pasturage for a nearby ranch but vegetation may once have been forested.

Environmental Stratum: Tropical Deciduous Forest-Riparian Forest

Description: There are 11 low mounds at this site, most of which probably served as residential platforms. They are spaced from 10 to 30 m apart and for the most part do not seem to form discreet compound clusters. Mound H is the largest at 2 m tall and may have been a ceremonial structure, perhaps the focal point of the community. There are two separate orientation patterns. Mounds A to C are oriented west of north and are located at the south end of the site. Mounds D to K are oriented east of north. These two separate groups may not be contemporaneous.

TR-126 (Figure 6.19)

Site Type: Habitation

Location and Setting: Tr-126 is located roughly 3 km northeast of Colonia San Caralampio and 0.75 km to the west of the small community of Flor de Mayo. The site is situated on a low hill overlooking Río San Gregorio, 200 m to the south. The vegetation surrounding the site is mainly grassy pastureland, cleared of trees.

Environmental Stratum: Tropical Deciduous Forest

Description: This site consists of one isolated mound bisected by the road to Santa Isabel. It may have been an outlier of one of the larger sites nearby, and in fact there may have been more habitations in the vicinity not built on mounds.

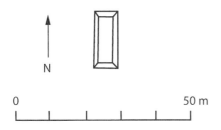

Figure 6.19. Site sketch of Tr-126.

TR-127 (Figure 6.20)

Site Type: Ceremonial and habitation

Ceramic Phase: Mix

Occupation: Late Classic

Location and Setting: Tr-127 is located approximately 6 km northeast of Colonia San Caralampio and almost 3 km north of the small community of Flor de Mayo. The site is located on a low hill at the northern edge of Río San Gregorio basin. In this area the landscape begins to give way to the hilly terrain which is the edge of the plateau. Grassland predominates in the immediate vicinity of the site with forest starting approximately 2 km to the north and northwest in the hilly terrain. A small stream flows by approximately 50 m east of the site, emptying into Río San Gregorio.

Environmental Stratum: Tropical Deciduous Forest

Description: This site consists of a linear arrangement of mounds along a narrow ridge 250 m long. It is divided into three distinct groups. The southern group is comprised of Mounds I to L, the last three of which are located on a rectangular terrace (M). Mounds J to L form a courtyard group with the west side of the patio open. Mound I is probably an associated residential platform although it is just upslope from the terrace. Four mounds (E to H) form a ceremonial complex surrounding the plaza area. The largest mound (G) is 5 m high on the west side and as much as 8 m above the natural ground surface on the eastern downslope side. Mound H is also a large mound: 4 m tall and enclosed the south side of the plaza. Two mounds (E and F) are smaller platforms that may have supported residences. The northern group of mounds includes the ballcourt (C) and a small platform (D). The ballcourt is I-shaped with sunken end-zones. The two flanking mounds (A and B) are symmetrical, except that A is 1 m taller.

The majority of the mounds are oriented north-south.

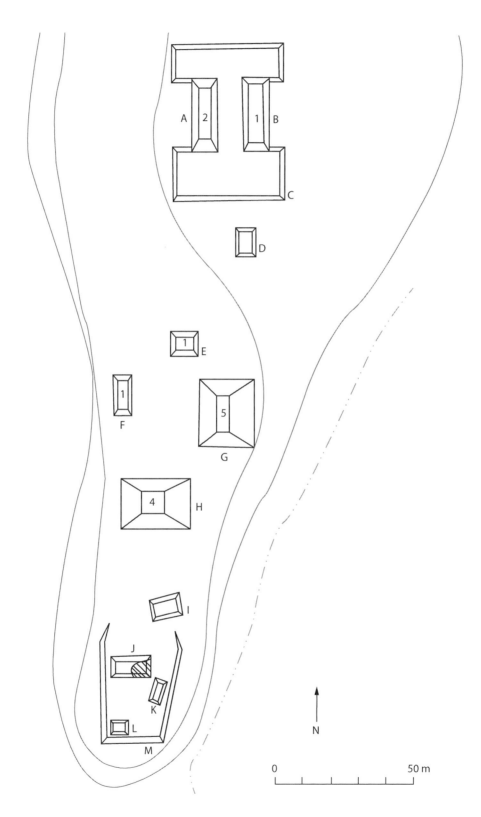

Figure 6.20. Site sketch of Tr-127.

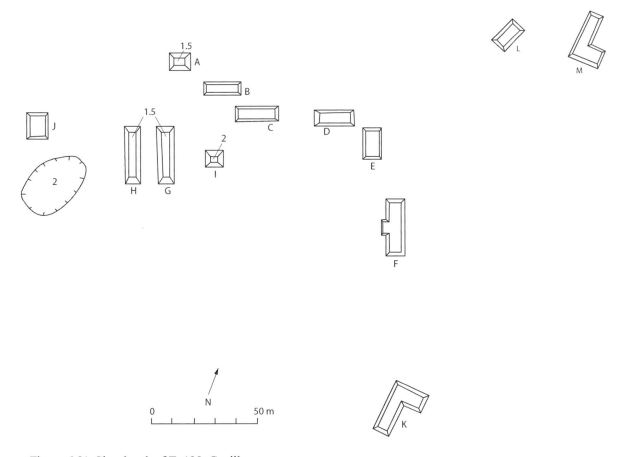

Figure 6.21. Site sketch of Tr-128, Cuajilote.

TR-128 CUAJILOTE (Figure 6.21)

Site Type: Ceremonial and habitation

Occupation: Late Classic, Late Postclassic

Location and Setting: Tr-128 is located approximately 2 km north and slightly east of Colonia Tierra Blanca. The site is situated on a low hill overlooking Río San Gregorio, 200 m to the south. Approximately 0.5 km upstream of Tr-128 is the confluence of Río San Gregorio and Río Santo Domingo. Grassy vegetation surrounds the site, with riparian vegetation along the waterway. Approximately 1 km north of Tr-128 the terrain changes to hilly forested country.

Environmental Stratum: Riparian Forest

Description: There are 13 mounds at this site, most of which form a plaza complex. Mounds C through H enclose the northern half of a plaza

whose south side is open. Mounds H and G are long parallel mounds reaching a height of 1.5 m, and likely define a ballcourt with unmarked end-zones. Mound I is the tallest mound at the site (2 m) and may be a small temple mound or altar within the plaza. The other mounds surrounding the plaza space are notable because they are long, narrow low mounds that were probably platforms for perishable superstructures. Mound F is the only long platform with a central projection facing the plaza. Two other mounds (K and M) are L-shaped and flank the southeast and northeast corners of the site, respectively. Two additional low mounds (L and J) are relatively isolated from the other mounds at the site.

All the mounds have a northwest to southeast orientation, except for the two L-shaped mounds oriented north-south and Mound L which is east of north.

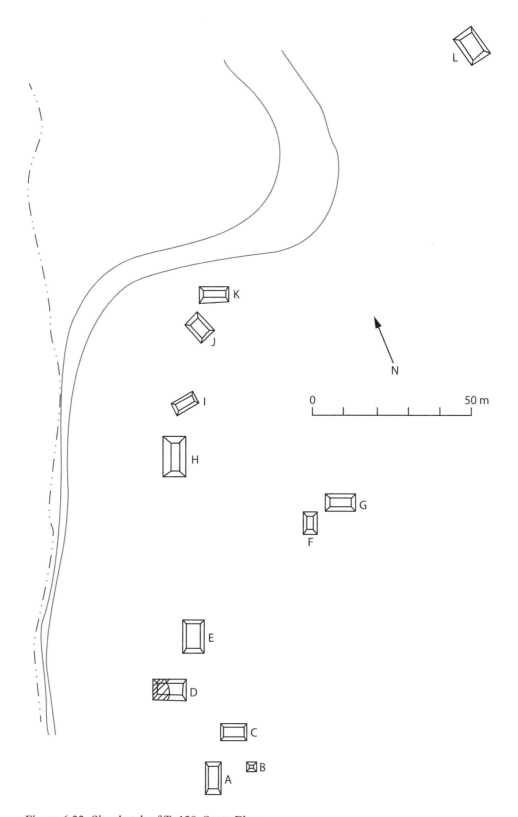

Figure 6.22. Site sketch of Tr-129, Santa Elena.

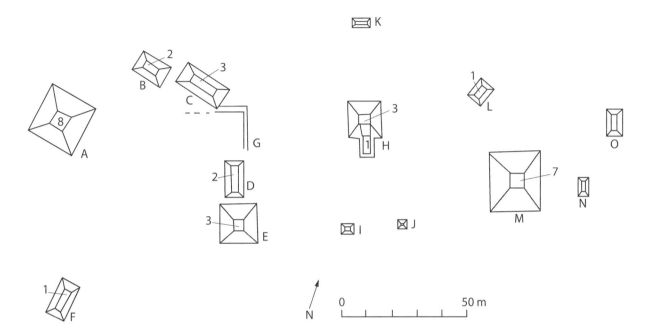

Figure 6.23. Site sketch of Tr-130, El Salvador.

TR-129 SANTA ELENA (Figure 6.22)

Site Type: Habitation

Occupation: Late Classic

Location and Setting: Tr-129 is located approximately 6.75 km northeast of Colonia San Caralampio, 3.2 km north of the small community of Flor de Mayo, and just 100 m west of the Pan-American Highway. The site is situated in a small valley, 50 m south of a stream which flows into Río San Gregorio. The vegetation surrounding the site is mainly grassy with riparian vegetation along the streamside.

Environmental Stratum: Tropical Deciduous Forest

Description: This site seems to be a cluster of residential platforms consisting of two-mound residential units. The mounds within each unit are less than 10 m apart and arranged into courtyard groups; that is, they partially surround a common patio. The distances between courtyard groups vary from 20 to 100 m. Mounds A and C face onto a patio with a smaller mound (B) that may have been an altar. The other courtyard groups each contain two platforms (D and E, F and G, H and I, and J and K). Only Mound L is an isolated residential platform. The largest mound at the site is H at 2 m tall; it may have also served some ceremonial purpose. The orientation of the mounds is predominantly east of north, suggesting that the mounds comprised a contemporaneous hamlet.

TR-130 EL SALVADOR (Figure 6.23)

Site Type: Ceremonial and habitation

Ceramic Phase: Foko, Hun, Mix

Occupation: late Middle Preclassic, Protoclassic, Late Classic

Location and Setting: Tr-130 is located 3 km north and slightly east of Colonia Sinaloa. The site is situated on the eastern plain of Río San Gregorio. Immediately north of the site a small stream converges with Río San Gregorio. Grassy vegetation surrounds the site, with riparian vegetation along the waterways.

Environmental Stratum: Tropical Deciduous Forest-Riparian Forest

Description: There are two main plaza groups at this site, each with a different orientation. The west group consists of four mounds (A to C and F). Mound A is the tallest at the site and forms the western edge of the ceremonial center. The north end of the plaza is formed by two lower mounds (B and C) and the south edge by Mound F. All the mounds in this group have a north-south orientation. The east group is comprised of 10 mounds, all with an orientation of northwest to southeast. The plaza is bounded on the west by Mounds D and E, on the north by Mound H and on the east by Mound M, a 7 m tall mound. Located midway between E and M are two possible altar mounds (I and J). Four other low, probably habitation mounds (K, L, N, and O), are located northeast of the plaza. On the west side of the plaza, perhaps separating the east and west groups, is a low L-shaped terrace (G) that appears to connect Mounds C and D.

The different orientation of each plaza group indicates they may be from different periods in the site's history.

TR-131 (Figure 6.24)

Site Type: Habitation

Ceramic Phase: Mix

Occupation: possible Late Preclassic, Late Classic

Location and Setting: Tr-131 is located approximately 7 km northeast of Colonia San Caralampio, 3.5 km north of the small community of Flor de Mayo, and 100 m west of the Pan-American Highway. The site sits on the west bench of a stream emptying into Río San Gregorio. Grassy vegetation surrounds the site, with riparian vegetation along the streamside. Tr-131 sits approximately 250 m northeast of Tr-129.

Environmental Stratum: Tropical Deciduous Forest

Description: In total, 17 house mounds were mapped at this site; all were clearly visible on the surface and were fairly well-preserved. The site consists of several house groups (e.g., C and D; and N, O, and P) and isolated structures (e.g., K and L) scattered in a linear band 350 m long.

TR-132 SAN FELIPE (Figure 6.25)

Site Type: Ceremonial and habitation

Ceramic Phase: Hun

Occupation: Late Preclassic, Protoclassic

Location and Setting: Tr-132 sits on the north bank of Río San Gregorio, approximately 6 km north by northwest of Colonia Sinaloa. Roughly 2 km downstream of Tr-132, Río San Gregorio converges with the San Miguel. The site sits on flat terrain, while just one kilometer to the north the terrain becomes hilly and forested. Vegetation surrounding the site is primarily grassland, with riparian vegetation along the riverside.

Environmental Stratum: Tropical Deciduous Forest-Riparian Forest

Description: San Felipe has six habitation mounds (B to G) and one pyramid (A). There were probably additional small house platforms surrounding the pyramid, but they were not detected during the reconnaissance. The house platforms form one or two patio groups with only one (B) somewhat distant from the others. The pyramid mound is quite distant from the main group of houses (160-190 m) and so may not in fact be contemporaneous. If it is, then it is likely there are more houses surrounding it.

TR-133 SANTA ISABEL (Figures 6.26-6.27)

Site Type: Ceremonial and habitation

Ceramic Phase: Guajil, Hun

Occupation: early Middle Preclassic, Late Preclassic, Protoclassic

Location and Setting: Tr-133 is located approximately 3.5 km west and slightly north of Colonia Tierra Blanca. The site is situated on the valley bottom 100 m north of Río San Gregorio. Approximately 2.5 km downstream from this site, the Río San Gregorio converges with Río Santo Domingo. The vegetation surrounding the site is primarily tall grass and pasturage.

Environmental Stratum: Riparian Forest

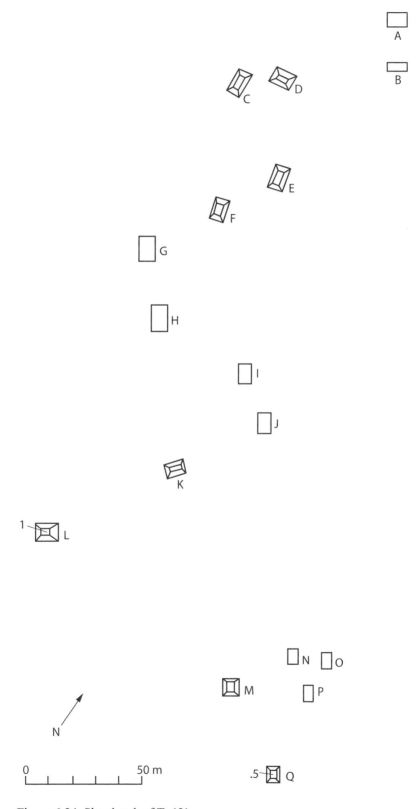

Figure 6.24. Site sketch of Tr-131.

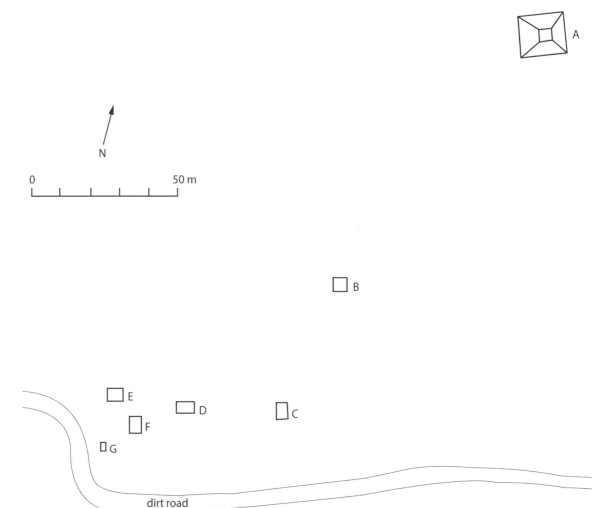

Figure 6.25. Site sketch of Tr-132, San Felipe.

Description: Only the ceremonial center was mapped although there were undoubtedly many more house mounds scattered along the river. The largest mound at the site is Mound F rising to about 7 m and with a low extension attached on the west side. It faces onto a plaza 70 m long by 50 m wide, flanked by Mounds C, D, and E. Further to the west and aligned with this plaza is another large mound (B) approximately 6.5 m high. In addition, a smaller platform (Mound A) was mapped just to the south of this main plaza.

On a small bench rising 6 m above the main valley bottom and 130 m northwest of Mound F is another large related mound (G) with a height of 3 m. Another 80 m beyond it, a low platform mound (H) was mapped. It may have been a residential mound and quite likely there were many more such low house platforms in the vicinity.

References: Lowe 1959:59, 61, fig. 31b, 62

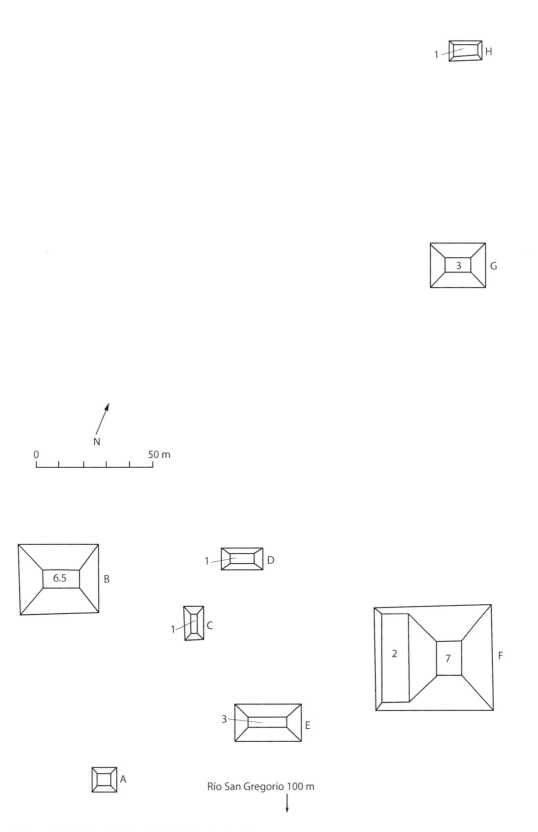

Figure 6.26. Site sketch of Tr-133, Santa Isabel.

Figure 6.27. Sherd found at Tr-133, Santa Isabel.

TR-134 SANTA INÉZ 1 (Figure 6.28)

Site Type: Ceremonial and habitation

Occupation: Late Classic

Location and Setting: Tr-134 is located just 200 m west of the Pan-American Highway, approximately 35 km south of the dirt road turnoff to Colonia Francisco Javier Mujica and Colonia Los Limones (to the west). The site is situated atop a hill. Río Santa Inés flows west approximately 500 m to the north of the site. Vegetation surrounding the site is primarily grassy.

Environmental Stratum: Short Tree Savannah/ Thorn Woodland

Description: Santa Inéz 1 is a compact habitation site located atop a small rise above the surrounding plain. Most of the structures recorded are small house mounds arranged in patio groups. The only ceremonial structure appears to be the small pyramid (II) located towards the east side of the site. Most of the house groups (such as FF, GG, and HH) sit on small terraces (NN) that provide enough level land for habitation. Others are slightly larger and appear to have had higher platforms (such as I, J,

L, and M). This large house group has two small rectangular platforms that may have been altars (K and N).

The regular layout as well as the consistent orientation of the buildings suggests the site was built all at one time, and all the structures were occupied contemporaneously.

References: de Montmollin 1989c:229-230

TR-135 SANTA INÉZ 2 (Figure 6.29)

Site Type: Ceremonial and habitation

Occupation: Late Classic, Late Postclassic

Location and Setting: Tr-135 is located approximately 500 west of the Pan-American Highway, just west of the point at which it crosses Río Santa Inés. The site is flanked on the southeast by Tr-134 (approximately 500 m away) and on the west by Tr-136 (also approximately 500 m away). The site is situated on a low hill, 15 m above and overlooking the Río Santa Inés to the immediate north. Vegetation surrounding the site is primarily grassy with riparian vegetation along the stream channel.

Environmental Stratum: Short Tree Savannah/ Thorn Woodland

Description: Santa Inéz 2 has a small ceremonial center with two pyramidal mounds and a small plaza area. The largest mound (I) is in the center of the site at its highest point. Mound I is about 20 m on a side and rises to approximately 6.5 m. Two other pyramidal mounds (E, which has a small extension, and J) flank the small plaza. Just to the northwest of these buildings is a group of larger low platforms (B, C, D, and F) that may form an elite residential group. These structures are like Mound E, partially supported by a terrace (Z). Nearby the mounds at the site are several other smaller platforms, perhaps house mounds (i.e., Mounds G, H, K, and L). One long platform (N), 1.5 m high, and supported by a terrace (AA) may be part of a ballcourt incorporating Mound M as one end. If so, then it uses the large pyramid (I) as one of its sides. Another possibility is that it is a later structure, possibly Postclassic, since it is longer and narrower than buildings at most Classic sites in our study region.

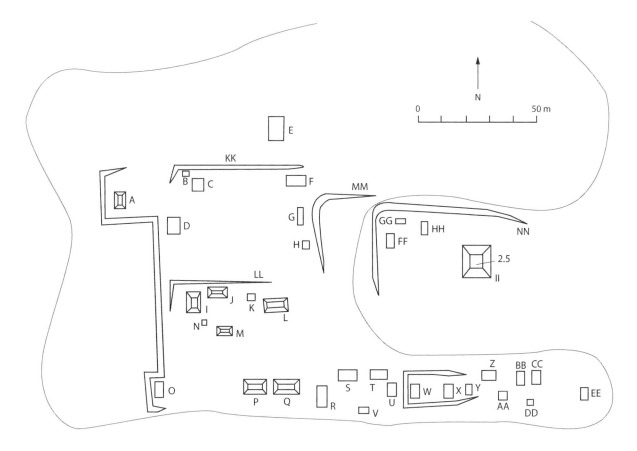

Figure 6.28. Site sketch of Tr-134, Santa Inéz 1.

The bulk of the residential zone is situated to the southeast of the ceremonial center. It consists of several house groups such as Mounds P and Q and U, V, and X. There may well be more isolated mounds such as Y which were not mapped during the reconnaissance.

References: de Montmollin 1989c:69-71, 239

TR-136 PASO AMATE (Figure 6.30)

Site Type: Ceremonial and habitation

Occupation: Late Preclassic, possible Protoclassic, Late Classic

Location and Setting: Tr-136 is located on the southern valley margin of the Río Santa Inés approximately 1 km west of where the river passes under the Pan-American Highway. Approximately 500 m to the east is located Tr-135. The vegetation in the vicinity is primarily grassy.

Environmental Stratum: Short Tree Savannah/ Thorn Woodland

Description: Paso Amate includes 24 ceremonial and house mounds scattered over an almost 400 m long band along the river. The largest mound at the site (F) is badly cut away, probably for land fill, but reached a height of 4 m. It is near the site center. To the west and north are a number of smaller platforms that were probably house mounds; however, they do not form clear patio groups. To the south of Mound F are more small mounds that appear to form clearer groupings, such as J, K, and Q, and R, T, and U. Smaller mounds associated with these house groups (i.e., K and S) may have been altars. Mound L is the second largest mound at the site and reaches a height of 2 m. It may have been the ceremonial focus for the southern group of houses at the site.

References: de Montmollin 1989c:234-235, 237

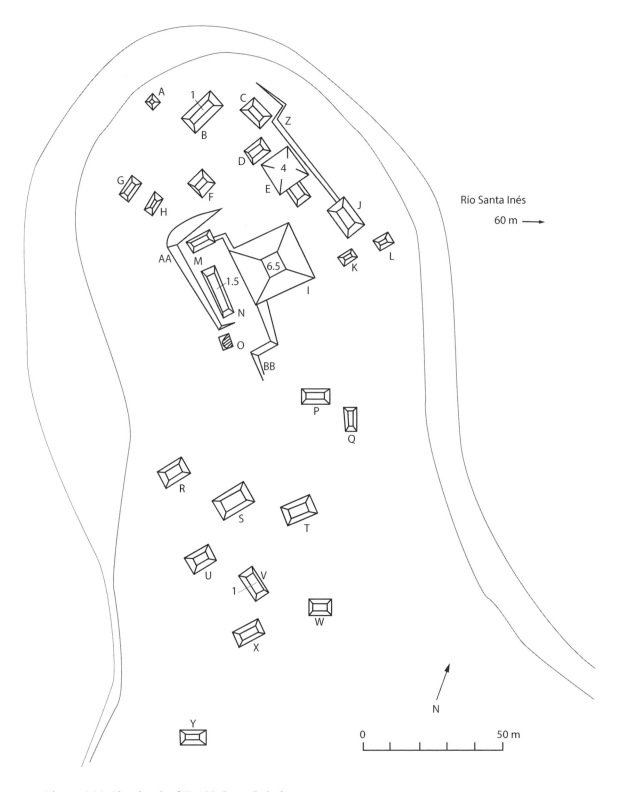

Figure 6.29. Site sketch of Tr-135, Santa Inéz 2.

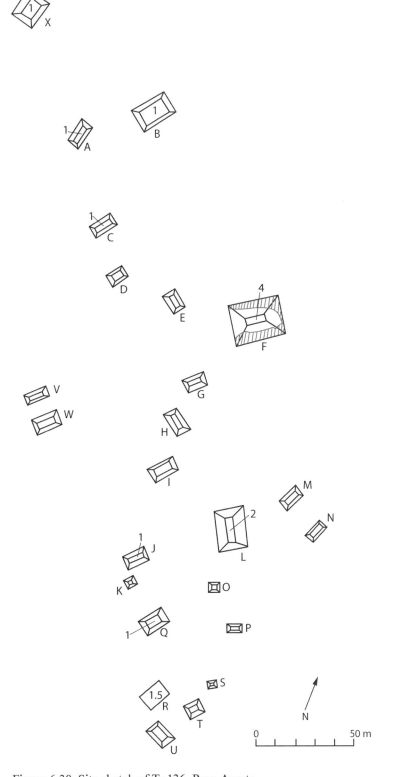

Figure 6.30. Site sketch of Tr-136, Paso Amate.

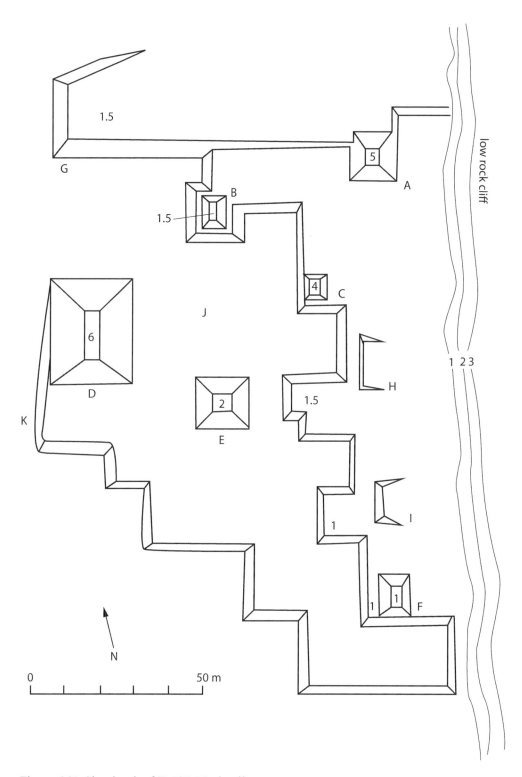

Figure 6.31. Site sketch of Tr-137, Mushquilar.

TR-137 MUSHQUILAR (Figure 6.31)

Site Type: Ceremonial and habitation

Ceramic Phase: Enub through Hun

Occupation: Middle Preclassic, Late Preclassic, Protoclassic

Location and Setting: Tr-137 is located approximately 4.5 km south of Colonia Chihuahua. The site is situated on a hillside with a seasonal stream flowing approximately 100 m north of the site. Also, a spring has been noted 200 m northwest of the site. Vegetation in the immediate vicinity consists mainly of pasture with trees sparsely covering the hills nearby.

Environmental Stratum: Short Tree Savannah/ Thorn Woodland

Description: Mushquilar has an interesting layout in that it is heavily terraced so as to form a number of low platforms over an area of approximately 2 ha. Although only the terraces and the larger mounds are sketched on the site map, there are a number of other habitation mounds west of the cliff that forms the eastern boundary of the site. The largest mound (D) is 25 by 30 m and 6 m high. It sits on Terrace K and forms the western edge of the large plaza (J). Mound E (2 m high), Mound B (1.5 m high), and Mound C (4 m high) outline the other three sides of the plaza. Another large mound (A), which is 5 m high, marks the northern edge of the ceremonial precinct. Two small terraces (H and I) may have been house platforms.

References: de Montmollin 1989c:212-213

TR-138 MUSHQUILAR SAN PEDRO (Figure 6.32)

Site Type: Ceremonial

Occupation: Protoclassic

Location and Setting: Tr-138 is located roughly 250 m southwest of Tr-137 and roughly 9.1 km south of Colonia Chihuahua. The site is situated in a small valley on the south side of a small seasonal stream. A dry stream is located approximately 200 m north of the site. Vegetation surrounding the site is primarily grassland, now used for pasture.

Environmental Stratum: Short Tree Savannah/ Thorn Woodland

Description: Only one mound was recorded during the reconnaissance. It is approximately 3 m high and has been partially quarried for rock fill. There are likely other smaller habitation mounds in the vicinity of this single pyramid.

References: de Montmollin 1989c:214-215

TR-139 SAN PEDRO JAMAI (Figure 6.33)

Site Type: Ceremonial and habitation

Occupation: possible Protoclassic, Late Classic

Location and Setting: Tr-139 is located approximately 4.5 km south and slightly west of Colonia Chihuahua and approximately 1 km east of Tenam Rosario (Tr-9). The site is situated in a small valley with a seasonal stream 50 m south of the site. Vegetation in the area of the site is primarily pasturage.

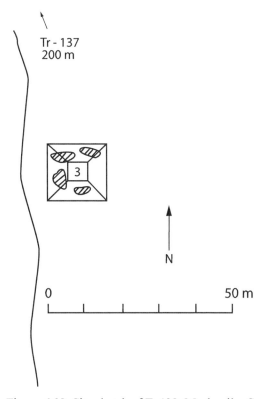

Figure 6.32. Site sketch of Tr-138, Mushquilar San Pedro.

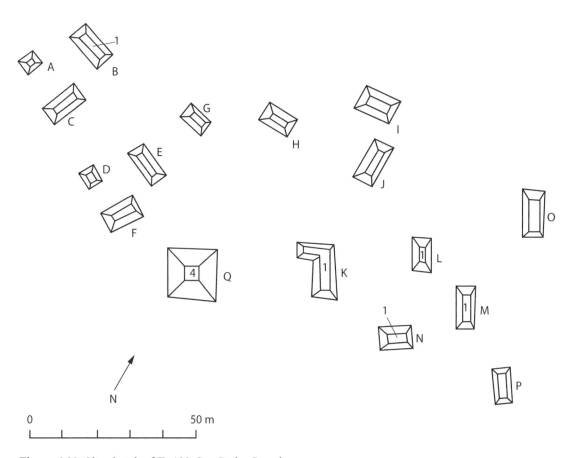

Figure 6.33. Site sketch of Tr-139, San Pedro Jamai.

Environmental Stratum: Short Tree Savannah/ Thorn Woodland

Description: San Pedro Jamai is a small habitation site with one ceremonial mound (Q) near its center. The 17 mounds lie over a zone approximately 180 m long and 80 m wide, and all but a few form distinct house groups. For example, Mounds A, B, and C surround a small patio. Some house mounds, such as Mound O, are relatively isolated. Mound K is directly opposite the pyramid and could have been a civic-ceremonial structure since it is L-shaped, unlike the other house mounds at the site. There were probably many more house mounds in the vicinity surrounding the ones we have recorded.

References: de Montmollin 1989c:210-212

TR-140 SAN PEDRO COLMENA 1
(Figure 6.34)

Site Type: Ceremonial and habitation

Occupation: Protoclassic, Early Classic, Late Classic

Location and Setting: Tr-140 is located approximately 5.75 km southwest of Colonia Chihuahua and 2.5 km east of the Pan-American Highway on a small dirt road to Rancho San Pedro. The site is situated in a small valley with no stream in the immediate vicinity. The site is cleared and under milpa cultivation, with trees on the surrounding hills.

Environmental Stratum: Short Tree Savannah/ Thorn Woodland

Description: San Pedro Colmena is a large habitation site with only one ceremonial structure (Mound PP). This small pyramid is 4 m high and sits towards the south end of the site. Most of the house mounds that were recorded sit in small patio groups of two or three structures. Some examples of these are Group A/B/C and Group F/G/H. Others are slightly more isolated, such as Mound L. Several of the houses have small walls connecting them, such as Mounds P and Q, while others simply have walls that connect with no other structures (e.g., Mounds O, S, and Y). We have noted on the map that there are a number of other mound groups to the northeast and east of the recorded mounds. Overall, the site covers more than 9 ha, but its exact boundaries are not known at this time.

References: de Montmollin 1989c:202-203

TR-141 SAN PEDRO COLMENA 2
(Figure 6.35)

Site Type: Habitation

Location and Setting: Tr-141 is located approximately 0.75 km east of the Pan-American Highway and 6.5 km southwest of Colonia Chihuahua. The site is situated on a low hill with grass and tree cover as the predominant vegetation. No water source is known in the immediate vicinity of the site.

Environmental Stratum: Short Tree Savannah/ Thorn Woodland

Description: Only nine mounds were recorded at this site. They form three house groups of three mounds each, separated from each other by 30 m in one case and 50 m in the other. One group (D and F) has a small square altar (E) between the two house platforms.

TR-142 EL ROSARIO (Figure 6.36)

Site Type: Habitation

Ceramic Phase: Mix

Occupation: Late Classic

Location and Setting: This site is located 500 m southeast of Tr-9 (Tenam Rosario) and 1.5 km east of Río Santa Inés. It is situated on the south side of Arroyo Rosario, which seasonally flows into Río Santa Inés. The whole site area is a gradual west-sloping alluvial fan that drains the hills to the east of the site. The zone is currently used mainly for pasturage so there is little tree cover. The arroyos, however, have a thicker cover of shrubby vegetation.

Environmental Stratum: Short Tree Savannah/ Thorn Woodland

Description: There are approximately 380 mounds of all sizes at this site covering an area of approximately 58 ha. The site was studied by Pierre Agrinier and Olivier de Montmollin during April and May of 1979 as part of the NWAF research of the Tenam Rosario (Tr-9) archaeological zone. More detailed reports review excavations and surface reconnaissance (Agrinier 1979; de Montmollin 1979), so the discussion here is limited.

There are six groups of habitation features defined by natural barrancas at the site. Ten habitation mounds and seven associated features from Group A were sampled by excavation. Five habitation mounds and an associated structure were excavated in Group E, and an additional two mounds from Group C and eight mounds in Group D were tested. Group A is the largest group in the site and although slightly isolated by barrancas, it is surrounded by the other five habitation groups. Group A is also the only one with much evidence of civic-ceremonial architecture. It has a small ballcourt and two 3 m tall temples mounds. Only Groups B and C also have 2-3 m temple mounds, and these are the most isolated from the main center in Group A. The house mounds in each of the six groups are arranged in domestic units of from one to three mounds, often around a patio and sometimes with a small structure on the open side of the patio (de Montmollin 1979: 84, 85).

Most of the domestic habitation units are tightly clustered, and almost all have roughly the same orientation from northeast to southwest. The site is very similar to Tr-29 (Los Cimientos) (Rivero 1987) in the types of structures present and their spatial organization. Both date to the same time period.

References: Agrinier 1979; de Montmollin 1989c: 81-87, fig. 46-52, 209

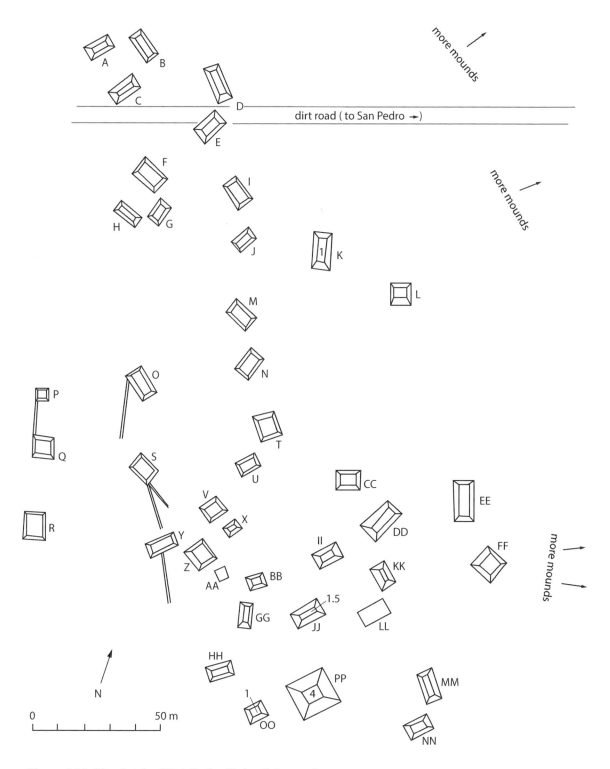

Figure 6.34. Site sketch of Tr-140, San Pedro Colmena 1.

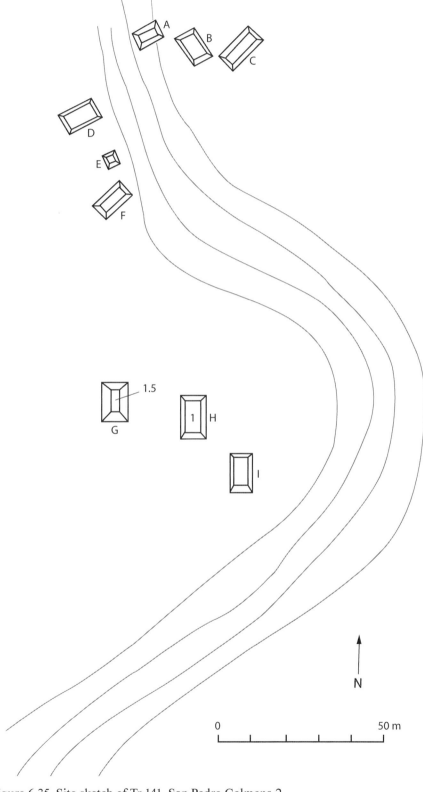

Figure 6.35. Site sketch of Tr-141, San Pedro Colmena 2.

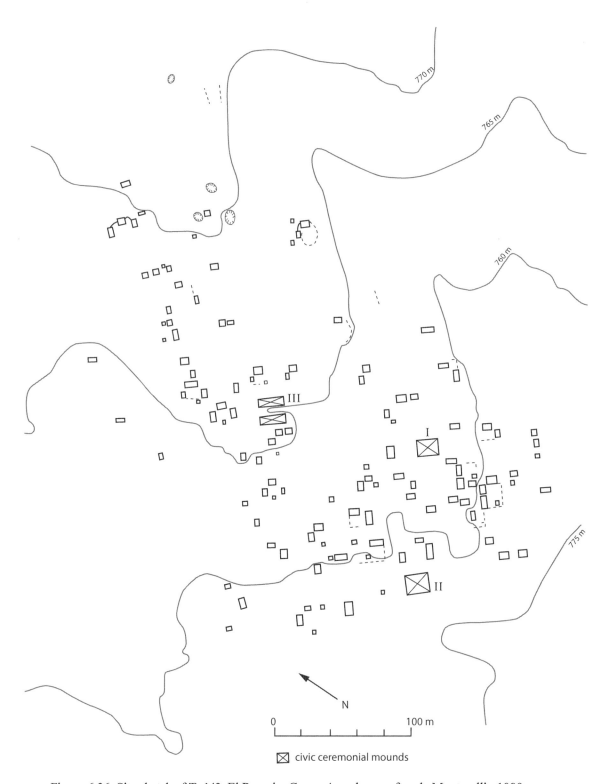

Figure 6.36. Site sketch of Tr-142, El Rosario, Group A; redrawn after de Montmollin 1989c.

TR-143 SAN PEDRO (Figure 6.37)

Site Type: Habitation

Occupation: possible Protoclassic, Late Classic

Location and Setting: Tr-143 is located 2.5 km east of the Pan-American Highway, 250 m southwest of Tr-142 (El Rosario). Colonia Chihuahua is approximately 4.5 km northeast of the site. It sits in a small valley with no source of water visible in the immediate vicinity. It has been used as milpa and pasturage.

Environmental Stratum: Short Tree Savannah/ Thorn Woodland

Description: This small site has five small mounds arranged in two groups. One group consists of a large house mound (C), which is 1 m high, and two smaller platforms that could be altars. Twenty meters south of this group are Mounds D and E that flank a small patio. There are likely more house mounds in the region surrounding the site.

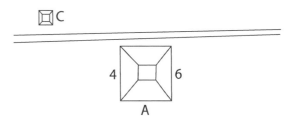

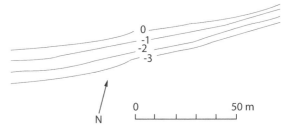

Figure 6.38. Site sketch of Tr-144.

TR-144 (Figure 6.38)

Site Type: Ceremonial and habitation

Location and Setting: Tr-144 is located approximately 1.25 km east of the Pan-American Highway and 5 km southeast of Colonia Chihuahua. The site is situated on a hilltop in an area of gently rolling hills. Río Santa Inés flows westward approximately 400 m north of the site. Vegetation in the vicinity of the site consists of grassland and trees. It is currently used as pasturage.

Environmental Stratum: Short Tree Savannah/ Thorn Woodland

Description: Tr-144 has only three mounds remaining, one of which is a large pyramid mound 25 m on a side. On the west side it is 4 m high and on the east it is 6 m high. To the northwest of this large mound are two smaller house platforms (B and C). They appear to be separate house groups. More house groups are likely to be found in the zone surrounding the site.

References: de Montmollin 1989c:205

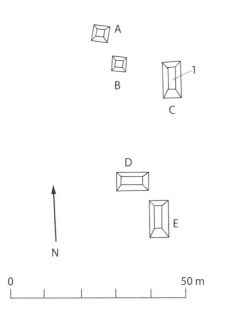

Figure 6.37. Site sketch of Tr-143, San Pedro.

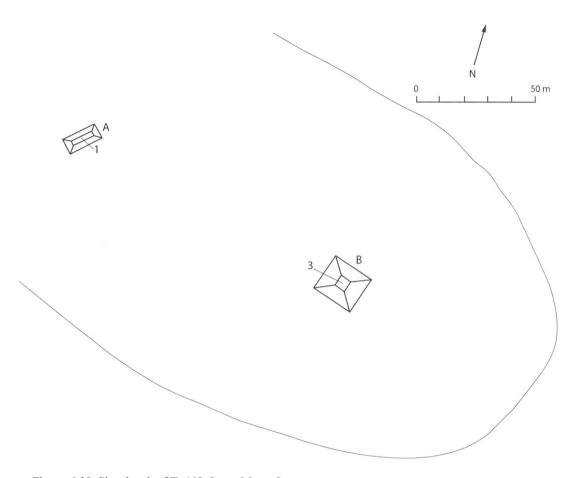

Figure 6.39. Site sketch of Tr-145, Santa Marta 2.

TR-145 SANTA MARTA 2 (Figure 6.39)

Site Type: Ceremonial

Occupation: Protoclassic, Middle Classic, Late Classic

Location and Setting: Tr-145 is located overlooking Río Santa Inés, 0.5 km east of where it passes under the Pan-American Highway. The site is situated on a low hill on the south side of the river. Vegetation surrounding the site consists primarily of grass used for pasturage. A modern house is located beside the smallest mound at the site.

Environmental Stratum: Short Tree Savannah/ Thorn Woodland

Description: There are only two mounds at the site. The largest (Mound B) is 18 by 15 m and 3 m high. Mound A is a smaller rectangular mound and only 1 m high. It is approximately 100 m north of Mound B. No other mounds were discovered during the reconnaissance.

References: de Montmollin 1989c:222-224

TR-146 (Figures 6.40-6.41)

Site Type: Ceremonial and habitation

Occupation: Early Classic, Late Classic, Postclassic

Location and Setting: Tr-146 is located 1 km west of the Pan-American Highway, 1 km southwest of its intersection with the dirt road to Colonia Francisco Javier Mújica and Colonia Los Limones. The site is situated in a small valley with cotton fields. A small stream passes approximately 300 m south of the site.

Environmental Stratum: Short Tree Savannah/ Thorn Woodland

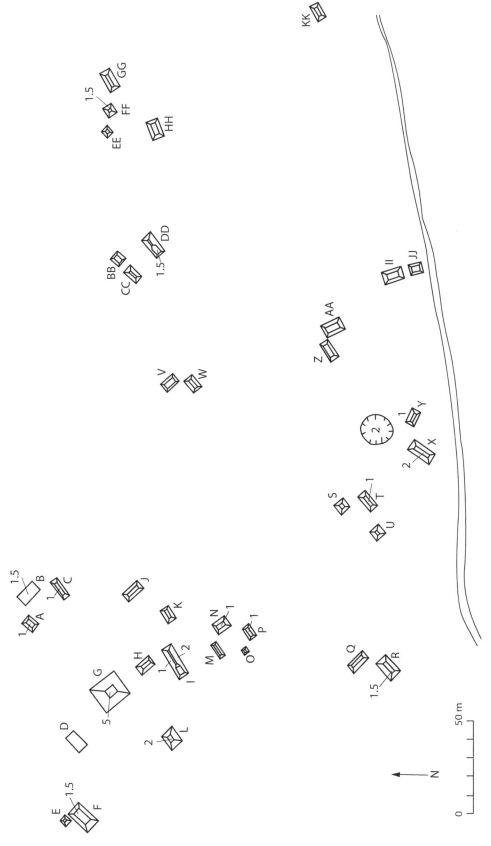

Figure 6.40. Site sketch of Tr-146.

Figure 6.41. Front and back views of ceramic molds from Tr-146.

Description: Tr-146 is a dispersed settlement with a small ceremonial center. The site map shows that there are approximately 15 house groups distributed in discreet aggregations over an area of about 450 by 220 m. The ceremonial center is defined principally by a small pyramidal mound (G) that reaches a height of 5 m. To the south of it is a small mound (L) and another elongated mound (I) that have a small platform extension. Combined with Mound H these structures form a plaza area. Most of the house groups contain only two platforms (e.g., Mounds Q and R), but some have three structures tightly arranged around a small patio (e.g., Mounds A, B, and C). Some house groups have small square platforms that could have been altars (e.g., O, E,

and EE). Only one structure is isolated (KK) and it sits at the eastern edge of the site.

The bulk of the settlement pattern appears to be characteristic of the Late Classic period. Any Postclassic occupation was probably ephemeral.

References: de Montmollin 1989c:73-76, 163-168; Lowe 1959:57-58

TR-147 (Figure 6.42)

Site Type: Habitation

Occupation: Late Classic

Location and Setting: Tr-147 is located 6 km east of Colonia Francisco Javier Mújica or 7 km on the dirt road leading northwest from that Colonia. The site is in an area of hilly terrain with dense grass as the principal vegetation. The site is now used as pasturage.

Environmental Stratum: Palm Forest

Description: Ten low platform mounds were recorded at this site, which apparently had no ceremonial structures. The mounds are probably house mounds and form groups of two or three. One house group (C/D) is partially cut by the Campana/Mújica road. Another group has two structures, one at which Mound H appears to be appended at right angles onto the other (G). The rest of the mounds are isolated from each other by between 25 and 80 m. There are probably more small mounds in the surrounding area that were either too low to see or whose foundation stones had been scavenged to build the recent stone corral nearby.

TR-148 SAN AGUSTÍN (Figure 6.43)

Site Type: Ceremonial and habitation

Occupation: Early Classic, Late Classic

Location and Setting: Tr-148 is located 2.5 km west of the Pan-American Highway and 2.2 km southwest of its intersection with the dirt road to Colonia Francisco Javier Mújica. The site is situated in a small valley with a stream passing 50 m to the north of the site. Vegetation surrounding the site consists primarily of grasses and trees.

Environmental Stratum: Tropical Deciduous Forest

Description: San Agustín was a dispersed settlement with one ceremonial focus at the southwest end of the site. The largest mound at the site (GG) is 6 m high and has a small altar facing it (FF). Nearby are small house groups, two of which have two platforms and one of which had three. Extending north for 300 m are

approximately seven additional house groups and one or two isolated platforms. One particularly large group (N-R) had five platforms. Another group (I and H) had a small square altar associated with it (J). Spacing between the house groups ranges between 30 and 50 m.

References: de Montmollin 1989c:158-161

TR-149 (Figure 6.44)

Site Type: Ceremonial and habitation

Occupation: Late Classic

Location and Setting: Tr-149 is located approximately 1.3 km west of the Pan-American Highway on the southwest side of the dirt road leading to Colonia Francisco Javier Mújica and Colonia Los Limones. The site is located on a low elongated ridge with no water source visible in the immediate vicinity. Vegetation around the site consists primarily of grasses and some trees left in the clearing. Land use is milpa.

Environmental Stratum: Tropical Deciduous Forest

Description: Tr-149 has a linear layout along the top of a low ridge. Many of the structures are built along the highest part of the ridge, but others are on shallow terraces on the hillside. The largest structure at the site is a small pyramidal mound (E) that is about 3 m high. Downslope from it are several small house platforms and terraces (A, B, D, F, and G) and a possible altar (C). Eighty meters to the northwest along the ridge are several additional house groups and one pyramid mound (P) reaching a height of 4 m. The houses on the site are quite tightly packed because of the restricted topography. Therefore, it is difficult to distinguish house groups; however, one (like Mounds U and T) has a small altar facing the house patio. One large mound (O) is extremely narrow for its length and has an extension appended onto it at right angles. Its slope is more characteristic of Late Postclassic constructions and indicates a possible re-occupation of the site during that period. Still, the sherds recovered were not diagnostic, so we cannot be sure of the date of occupation.

References: de Montmollin 1989c:155-157

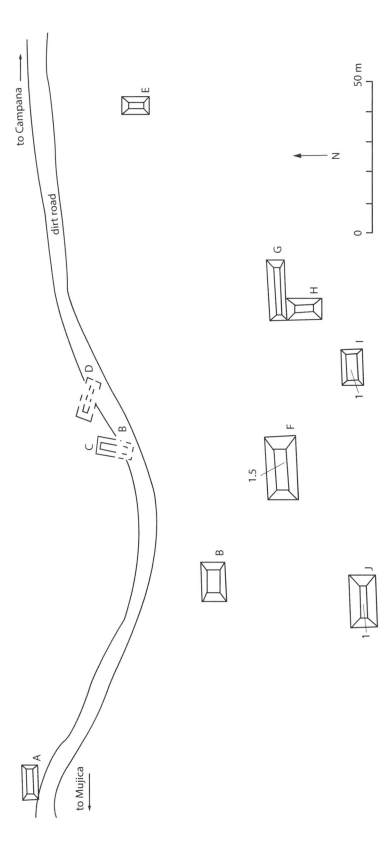

Figure 6.42. Site sketch of Tr-147.

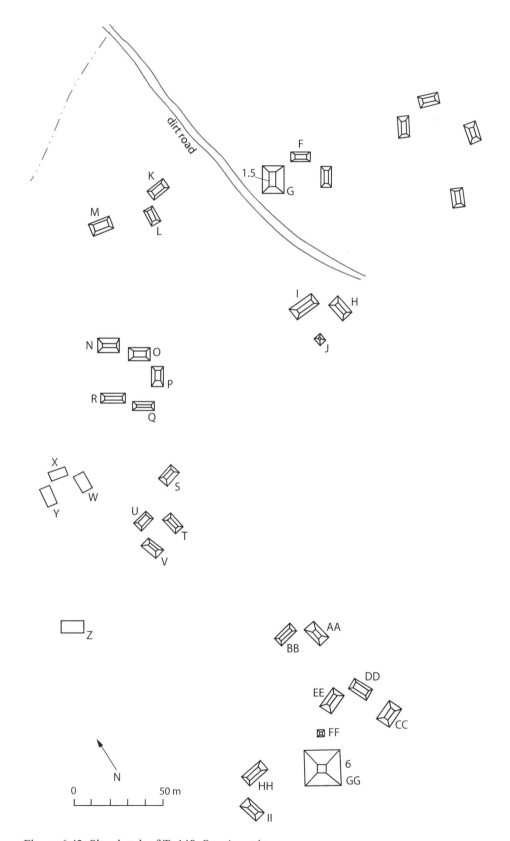

Figure 6.43. Site sketch of Tr-148, San Agustín.

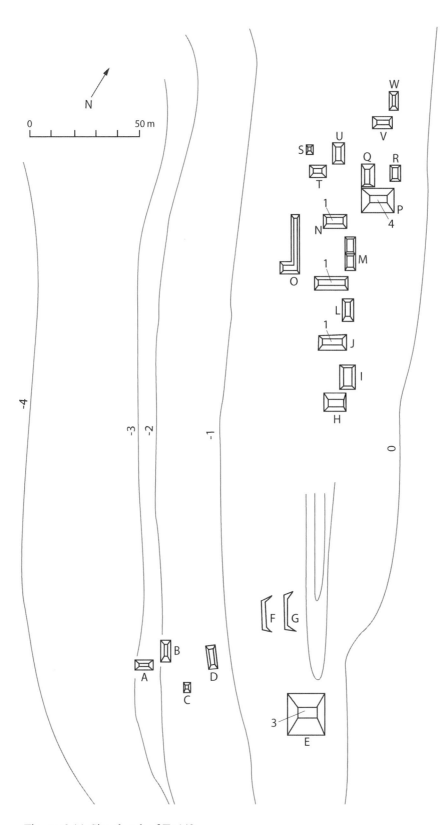

Figure 6.44. Site sketch of Tr-149.

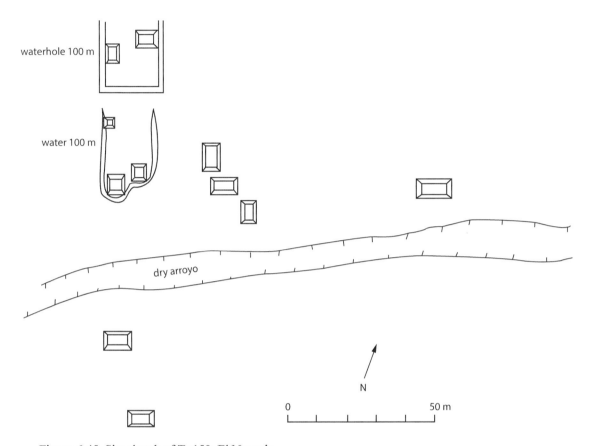

Figure 6.45. Site sketch of Tr-150, El Naranjo.

TR-150 EL NARANJO (Figure 6.45)

Site Type: Habitation

Occupation: Early Classic

Location and Setting: Tr-150 is located approximately 6.8 km east of Colonia Francisco Javier Mújica and 1 km northwest of the dirt road leading to the Colonia. The site is located in a small valley with a stream passing 400 m south of the site. Two waterholes are located within 100 m of the site and a dry arroyo bisects it. Vegetation is primarily for pasturage and consists of grass and some trees.

Environmental Stratum: Short Tree Savannah/ Thorn Woodland

Description: El Naranjo is a small habitation with only eleven house mounds recorded. The main group consists of eight mounds arranged in three separate house groups. Two of these

are situated on small terraces that provide level platforms. One group (A and B) is south of a small dry arroyo and isolated from the main group by about 50 m. There is one additional mound (C), a single structure 50 m to the east of the main group. More house platforms are probably located in the zone surrounding these.

TR-151 CHAPINGO (Figure 6.46)

Site Type: Ceremonial and habitation

Occupation: Late Classic

Location and Setting: Tr-151 is located approximately 7 km southwest of Colonia Chihuahua on the west side of the Pan-American Highway. The site is situated on a low hill in a hilly zone. The vegetation in the vicinity of the site is mainly milpa with occasional trees. Dense tree cover can be found approximately 0.5 km to the west.

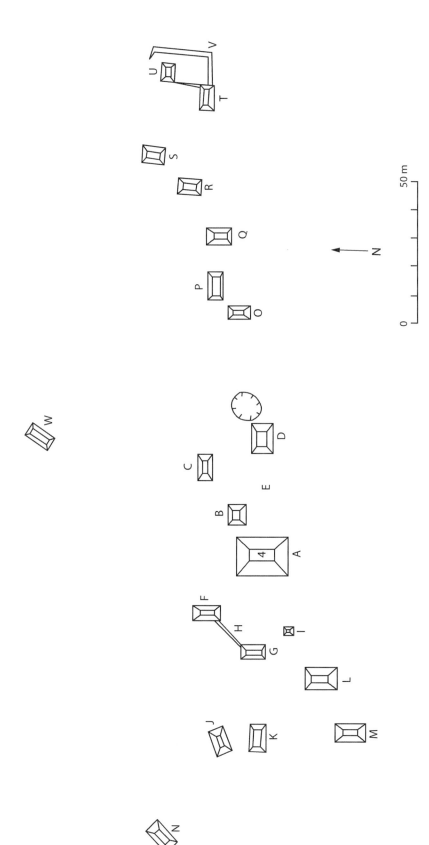

Figure 6.46. Site sketch of Tr-151, Chapingo.

Environmental Stratum: Tropical Deciduous Forest

Description: Tr-151 is a small nucleated linear settlement with one large temple platform, several low rectangular mounds, and some terracing. The maximum extent of the site measures approximately 280 by 130 m. The largest mound (A), measuring18 by 14 m and 4 m high, is located in a central position within the site. Immediately to the northeast is a small mound (B) that was probably associated with the temple platform. Mounds C and D may also have been associated, thus forming a plaza (E).

West of the ceremonial group, two mounds (F and G) are connected by a small wall (H). This pair, plus a small altar mound (I), may form a residential compound. Mounds J and K, L and M, and N were also probably residential compounds.

East of the central area, Groups O, P and Q, R and S, and Mounds T and U, interconnected by Terrace V, probably formed residential compounds. Finally, at the northern edge of the site, Mound W was also probably a residential structure.

This site appears to be a hamlet with mounds grouped into residential compounds having one to three structures each. The large temple platform (A), possibly in association with Mounds B to D, was probably the main civic-ceremonial center of the site. The orientation of the mounds is fairly regular suggesting most structures at the site may have been contemporaneous.

References: de Montmollin 1989c:242-244

TR-152 OJO DE AGUA (Figures 6.47-6.55)

Site Type: Ceremonial and habitation

Ceramic Phase: Dyosan, Foko, Hun, Ix, Kau, Lek, Mix

Occupation: Middle Preclassic, Late Preclassic, Protoclassic, Early Classic, Middle Classic, Late Classic, Postclassic

Location and Setting: Ojo de Agua is located around a small spring that forms the source of a small tributary stream of the Río Santa Inés. The spring is 3.5 km north of the river. The site is on the south side of a dirt road that runs west from the Pan-American Highway towards Colonia Francisco Javier Mújica. Today the site area is used as pasturage.

Environmental Stratum: Tropical Deciduous Forest-Riparian Forest

Description: The site is spread out over almost 400 ha, with 3 major foci of large-scale ceremonial construction. Group A in the north consists of the 3 tall pyramids (6.5, 9, and 10 m high) surrounding a raised and level plaza measuring 50 by 66 m, with a long axis oriented roughly east-west. These mounds were faced with travertine blocks. Southeast of Group A, Group B is dominated by a single 9 m earthen mound. Numerous house mounds and residence groups are located north and northeast of Groups A and B on upwardly sloping terrain.

Group C is located to the south of Groups A and B and is the largest of the civic-ceremonial precincts with dense construction located in an area of some 6 ha. There is a large central plaza flanked on the south side by a large elaborate acropolis. Another plaza fronts the acropolis on the south side. A third plaza is located to the north of the central plaza. A large I-shaped ballcourt lies northeast of the central plaza. Numerous residence groups continue east of Group C. The site also has numerous *chultunes* throughout.

The site map was done by Eduardo Martínez and field excavations were undertaken by Jorge Ceja Tenorio in 1976 and Doug Bryant and Gareth Lowe in 1980. A report of the excavations was published in 2008.

References: Bryant 1984, 2008

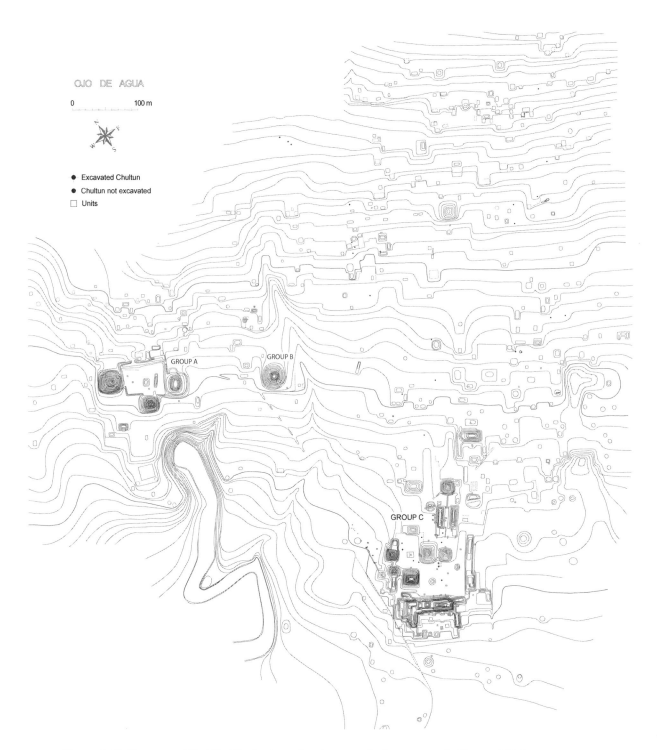

Figure 6.47. Site map of Tr-152, Ojo de Agua (see large-scale format map in Bryant 2008).

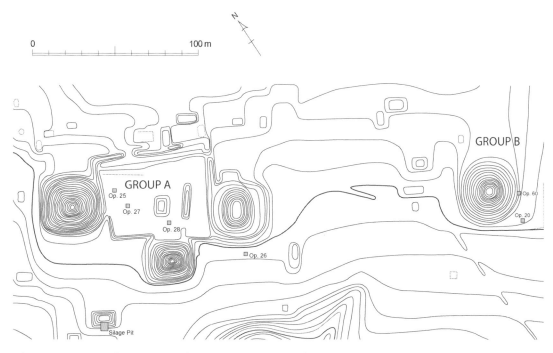

Figure 6.48. Map of Group A and Group B at Tr-152, Ojo de Agua.

Figure 6.49. Largest Mound in Group A at Tr-152, Ojo de Agua.

Figure 6.50. Primary Mound Group B at Tr-152, Ojo de Agua.

Figure 6.51. Ballcourt sculpture or marker from Ojo de Agua.

Figure 6.52. View of Tr-152, Ojo de Agua spring.

Figure 6.53. *Chultún* at Tr-152, Ojo de Agua.

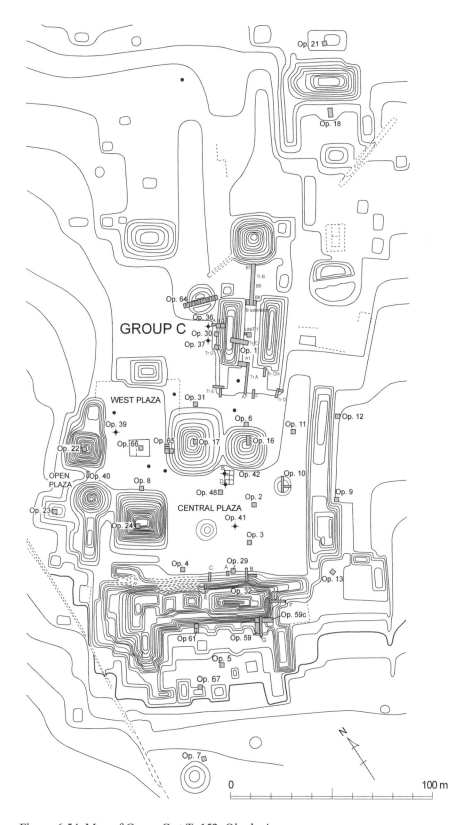

Figure 6.54. Map of Group C at Tr-152, Ojo de Agua.

Figure 6.55. Excavation at the acropolis, Tr-152, Ojo de Agua.

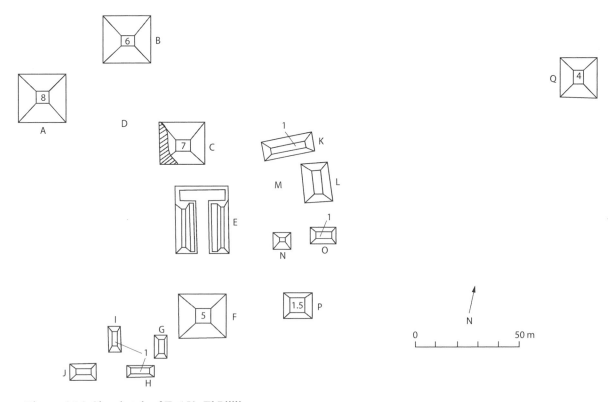

Figure 6.56. Site sketch of Tr-153, El Pijiji.

TR-153 EL PIJIJI (Figure 6.56)

Site Type: Ceremonial and habitation

Ceramic Phase: Enub, Guajil, Ix

Occupation: Middle Preclassic, Late Preclassic, Protoclassic

Location and Setting: El Pijiji is located circa 10.5 km east of Colonia Felipe Ángeles. The site is situated on a low hill, approximately 0.5 km southwest of the mouth of Río Santa Inés. A small stream flows 100 m from the site. The area surrounding the site is mainly under milpa cultivation with occasional trees.

Environmental Stratum: Tropical Deciduous Forest

Description: Tr-153 (El Pijiji) is a site with a large civic-ceremonial precinct and some possible evidence of habitation. Five large temple platforms, an I shaped ballcourt, and several low mounds of varying dimensions have been observed. The large mounds (A, B,

and C) dominate the northwestern sector of the site. These mounds, measuring 8 m, 6 m, and 7 m in height respectively, are arranged around an open plaza (D). South of Mound C is an I-shaped ballcourt with an enclosed northern end-zone. The two mounds of the ballcourt appear identical. South of the ballcourt is Mound F, which measures 5 m high.

In the southwestern corner are four low mounds (G and H, and I and J) that were probably elite residential compounds. East of the ceremonial group is another area of low mounds (K, L, N, and O) arranged around M, which were also probably elite residential compounds. The large size of Mounds K and L reinforces this interpretation. Mound P, measuring 1.5 m, may have had a residential function, or perhaps was functionally associated with the civic-ceremonial group.

Finally, at the northeastern edge of the site is an isolated temple platform (Q) measuring 4 m in height. This mound is separated from the other structures by approximately 120 m.

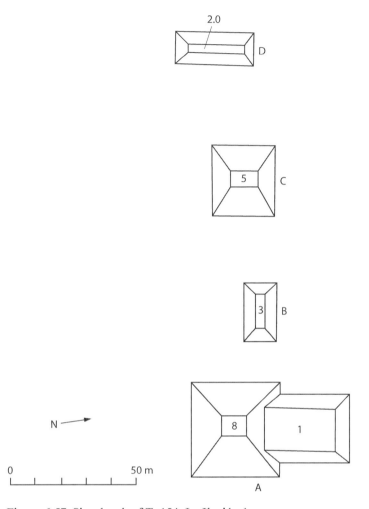

Figure 6.57. Site sketch of Tr-154, La Ilusión 1.

The layout of buildings in the central ceremonial group surrounding Plaza D suggests this group may have been constructed according to an ordered plan. The layout of the remaining structures, however, does not have a patterned appearance.

TR-154 LA ILUSIÓN 1 (Figure 6.57)

Site Type: Ceremonial (possible habitation)

Occupation: Protoclassic, Late Classic

Location and Setting: Tr-154 is located approximately 10.5 km east and slightly south of Colonia Felipe Ángeles near the headwaters of a side tributary of Río Ontela. The site is 3 km southeast of Ojo de Agua (Tr-152). It is situated in an area of low rolling hills. The vegetation surrounding the site consists of tree and bush cover.

Environmental Stratum: Tropical Deciduous Forest

Description: Tr-154 appears to be an isolated ceremonial center with possible elite residential occupation. Four very large ceremonial structures arranged in a linear pattern are concentrated in an area of 180 by 60 m. The distance between structures ranges from 15 to 30 m. The structures do not appear to be associated with a visible plaza area.

The largest mound visible is a double-tiered temple platform (A). The temple portion of this mound measures 8 m high and faces north over the lower tier, which measures 1 m high. Fifteen meters west of this is a long rectangular platform (B) measuring 3 m high. Another large temple platform (C), which measures 5 m high, is situated 25 m west of B. Finally, a long rectangular mound (D) measuring 2 m high is located 30 m west of C. The size and height of these mounds suggests that they are all ceremonial structures. The regular distribution of these mounds, aligned at intervals along an east-west axis, suggests they were a contemporary group, built according to an ordered plan. No habitation structures are visible. The complex may serve the civic-ceremonial needs of surrounding communities.

TR-155 LA ILUSIÓN 2 (Figure 6.58)

Site Type: Ceremonial and habitation

Occupation: Late Preclassic, Early Classic

Location and Setting: Tr-155 is located 10 km east and slightly south of Colonia Felipe Ángeles near a side tributary of Río Ontela. Approximately 3 km to the northeast is Ojo de Agua (Tr-152). The site is situated in an area of low rolling hills and ridges. The vegetation surrounding the site is mainly thick tree and brush cover.

Environmental Stratum: Tropical Deciduous Forest

Description: The site of Tr-155 (El Ilusión #2) has a large central civic-ceremonial sector and a possible habitation component. The main concentration of structures is located around a large plaza. Two more large temple platforms (Q and R) are isolated, one to the north and the other to the southwest of the main plaza.

The main ceremonial plaza group includes two large temple platforms (A and H), two lower temple platforms (E and I), one double pyramid (C), and several low mounds of various sizes. Some of the small low mounds (B, D, and J) located around the perimeter of the plaza probably had ceremonial functions associated with the larger temple platforms. The remaining low mounds (F and G, and M, L, and K) may have been residential structures occupied by people involved in the operation and maintenance of the ceremonial precinct. Mounds N and O, two very long, low rectangular

structures 1.5 m and 1 m in height, respectively, located immediately south of Mounds H and I may also have been residential structures, or perhaps had civic-ceremonial functions themselves.

The central group, arranged in an orderly manner around a large open plaza (P) may have been constructed according to a formal plan. The two outlying temple platforms (Q, on the northern edge and R at the southwestern edge) may have been contemporary with the main plaza group, or perhaps represent a different stage of construction.

TR-156 (Figure 6.59)

Site Type: Ceremonial and habitation

Occupation: late Middle Preclassic, Late Preclassic, Protoclassic, Late Classic

Location and Setting: Tr-156 is located 10.5 km east of Colonia Felipe Ángeles and 2.3 km northwest of Ojo de Agua (Tr-152). The site is situated on a hilltop in an area of rolling hills and ridges. The vegetation in the vicinity of the site is predominantly forest.

Environmental Stratum: Tropical Deciduous Forest

Description: Tr-156 is a nucleated residential settlement, with several ceremonial structures. The site appears to be divided into two general areas. A ceremonial area and probably elite residential groups are located upslope in the northern heavily terraced portion of the site. Downslope is the main concentration of habitation, with more ceremonial structures.

In the northern sector of the site a series of mounds of varying heights and dimensions are situated on a series of large terraces. The terraces appear to represent major artificial modification of the hillside, providing level ground and foundations for a large area of mound construction. The main ceremonial structures of this group are located on the east side of the terraced area, where more level ground is available. Mounds A and B, two platform mounds with frontal staircases, which measure 2 m and 3 m, respectively, in height are located on the lower level of the northern terrace

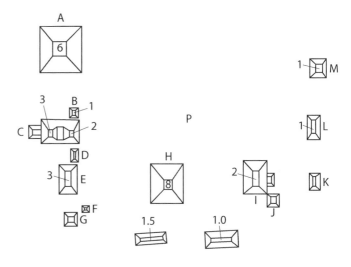

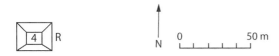

Figure 6.58. Site sketch of Tr-155, La Ilusión 2.

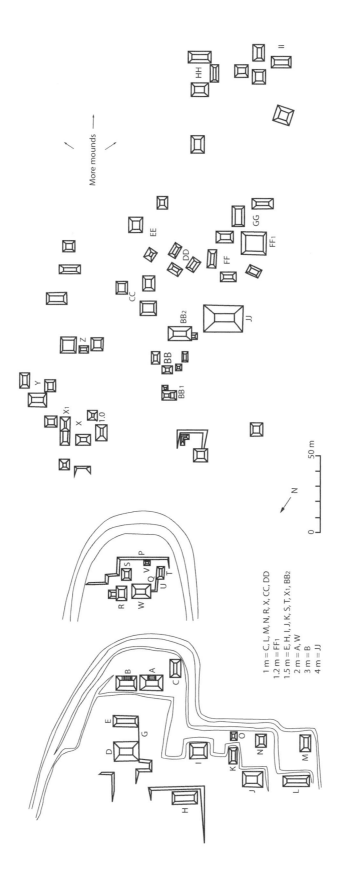

Figure 6.59. Site sketch of Tr-156.

system. Adjacent to these on the west is Mound C, a low mound probably associated with the ceremonial functions of A and B. Above these on the next terrace level is D, the largest mound in the northern group, measuring 4 m high. This is joined by a low rock alignment (G) to a lower platform (F). More small terraces above D may have housed more structures associated with the ceremonial buildings. On the western side of this terraced area, several rectangular mounds ranging in size from 1 to 1.5 m in height may have been elite residences.

South of this large terraced area is a smaller group built upon another terrace (P). This group consists of one large platform (Q) measuring 2 m high and a series of smaller mounds (R, S, T, and V) arranged around a patio (W). Mounds Q and T are connected by a wall (U). This compound may have been an elite residential compound, perhaps with some civic-ceremonial functions as well.

The bulk of the residential population is concentrated downslope of the terraced area (A). Residential structures appear to be arranged in clusters of mounds ranging in size from two to five or more structures (X, Y, and Z, and AA to II). Within this area, several irregular structures (X, BB, and FF) may have been ceremonial structures associated with individual residential groups. The largest ceremonial structure on the site (JJ), which measures 4 m high, is also located in the west-central section of the residential area. Finally, several isolated small mounds are scattered about this area that were probably also residential structures.

This site appears to represent a large settlement with both ceremonial and habitation structures. There appears to be a differentiation in size among the mounds, the largest non-ceremonial structures situated on the terraced slope and the majority of lower residential mounds in the downslope sector of the hill. Within the downslope area there appears to be a central ceremonial structure (JJ), as well as a series of smaller ceremonial structures associated with individual household groups.

The great extent of artificial land modification on the upslope terrace area suggests this was a contemporary unit built according to a formal plan; however, the downslope area does not appear to conform to a formal plan, suggesting that this area was constructed in stages.

Figure 6.60. View toward the Cuchumatan Mountains in Guatemala.

TR-157 LA LIBERTAD (Figures 6.60-6.62)

Site Type: Ceremonial and habitation

Ceramic Phase: Enub, Foko

Occupation: Middle Preclassic, possible Protoclassic; Late Classic, Postclassic

Location and Setting: La Libertad is located in the zone between the Ríos Lagartero and Dolores, 1 km west of the Guatemalan border. The site is in an area of flat open land alongside the rivers. The land is presently used as pasturage.

Environmental Stratum: Tropical Deciduous Forest

Description: The site presents significant investment in large platforms and pyramid, as well as notable mound alignments. The overall orientation is east of north. The site center is dominated by a large E-Group (Mounds 4 and 5), plaza, and acropolis. Mound 4, the cruciform mound, measures some 40 by 100 m and 3.5 m

in height. Mound 5 measures 58 m in diameter and 10.5 m in height. Balancing the E-Group is Mound 3 to the northeast. Mound 3 measures 60 m in diameter and some 10 m in height. With Mound 2, Mounds 3 and 4 define a large plaza area. Mound 2 is a large, elaborate acropolis. The platform base measures 170 by 98 m, including the adjacent Mound 6 on the north side, which creates an I-shaped ballcourt. Seven discrete superstructures (A-G) lie atop this massive platform.

To the north of this central core lies Mound 1, which measures 70 by 45 m with perhaps a graduated ramp or apron on its west side, and rises 8 m in height.

Two large bajo areas are found to the northeast and southwest sides of the site and were likely burrow pits and/or used for water storage.

The site is notable for its layout and alignments. The E-Group and Mound 3 "lie on a relative east-west axis 100 degrees east of north" (Miller 2014:39). Another series of mounds align

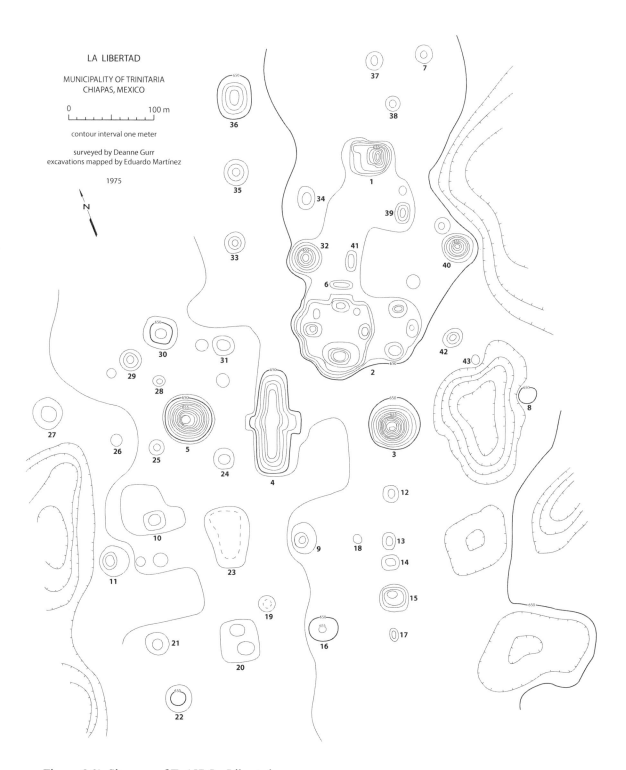

Figure 6.61. Site map of Tr-157, La Libertad.

Figure 6.62. View of Mound 3 prior to excavation, looking east from Mound 4 at Tr-157, La Libertad.

with Mound 3 to the south (12-15, 17), and yet another runs from the E-Group north (24, 31, 33, 35, 36).

Numerous house mounds and residence groups lie to the southwest of the ceremonial core.

The site was occupied in the Middle Preclassic Enub and Foko phases and then abandoned; Late Classic and Postclassic intrusive burials were found near the surface with no coeval occupation.

Mapping of the site was done by Susanna Ekholm, Deanne Gurr-Matheny, and Eduardo Martínez. Excavations were undertaken in 1975 by Tom Lee and more extensive work done in 1975-1976 by Don Miller, Glenna Nielsen, and Gareth Lowe (see Miller 2014 for report on the work).

References: Lee and Bryant 1996:62; Lowe 1959:61, figs. 32h, j, 64; Miller 2014

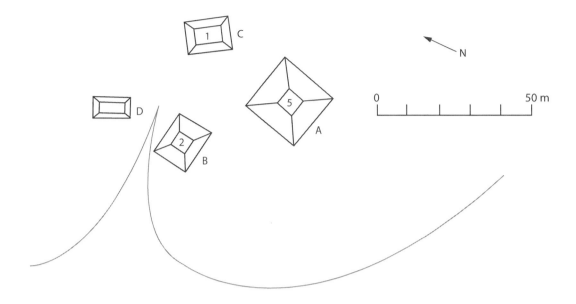

Figure 6.63. Site sketch of Tr-158, La Libertad Dolores.

TR-158 LA LIBERTAD DOLORES
(Figure 6.63)

Site Type: Ceremonial and habitation

Occupation: Protoclassic

Location and Setting: Tr-158 is located approximately 4.2 km east of Colonia Joaquín Miguel Gutiérrez and just 0.5 km southwest of La Libertad (Tr-157). The site is situated on the edge of a low hill just 0.5 km north of Río Dolores. It is in a low-lying zone near the confluence of the Ríos Dolores and Rincón Tigre, which flow from the Cuchumatan Mountains of Guatemala. Just 1.5 km downstream, Río Lagartero merges with other waters to form the Río San Gregorio. The vegetation in the area consists primarily of grasses with trees in arroyos around the site.

Environmental Stratum: Tropical Deciduous Forest

Description: The site of Tr-158 consists of a small group of structures situated close to the edge of a low hill. The structures are concentrated within an area of approximately 70 by 70 m. The structures include a 5 m pyramid (A) and a lower 2 m temple platform (B). In addition to these ceremonial structures, two low

rectangular mounds (C and F) may have been elite residences housing people involved in the operation and maintenance of the ceremonial needs of the surrounding communities.

TR-159 MANGO AMATE 2 (Figure 6.64)

Site Type: Ceremonial and habitation

Ceramic Phase: Enub, Foko

Occupation: Middle Preclassic

Location and Setting: Tr-159 is located 5.5 km northeast of Colonia Joaquín Miguel Gutiérrez. It is surrounded on the north, west, and southwest by Lagartero (Tr-99), Mango Amate (Tr-105), and La Libertad (Tr-157) respectively, each approximately 1.2 to 1.5 km from Tr-159. The site is situated in a low area on a low hill just 20 m south of a small stream also called the Mango Amate. The vegetation around the site is mainly grasses being used for pasture.

Environmental Stratum: Tropical Deciduous Forest

Description: Tr-159 consists of ceremonial structures as well as habitation structures. The structures appear to be distributed in two groups, one atop a low rise, and a second at the base of

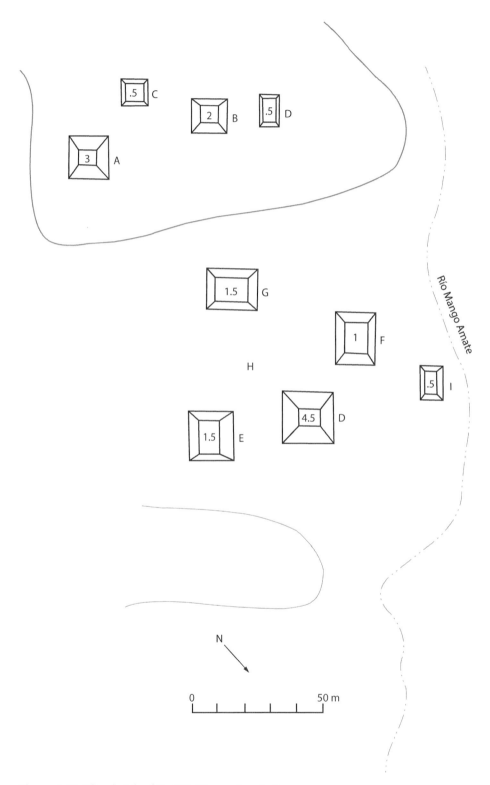

Figure 6.64. Site sketch of Tr-159, Mango Amate 2.

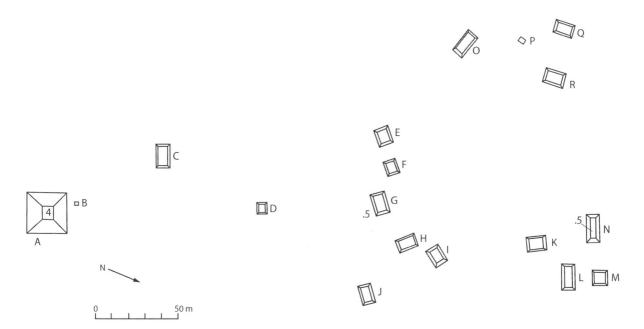

Figure 6.65. Site sketch of Tr-160, Dolores.

this rise. The largest structures are situated on the lower level.

The group of structures atop the low rise includes a 3 m temple platform (A) and a 2 m platform (B). In addition to the civic-ceremonial structures, two low mounds (C and D) probably functioned as residential structures.

At the base of the rise, five more structures are located. These include the largest structure on the site (Mound E), a 4.5 m pyramid. Flanking E are three large low mounds (E, F, and G) measuring 1.5 m, 1 m, and 1.5 m respectively, which together are arranged around a large open plaza area (H). A low mound (I) west of the plaza group may have functioned as a residential building.

These two groups of structures appear to represent civic-ceremonial occupation with a minor habitation component, probably associated with the ceremonial personnel.

TR-160 DOLORES (Figure 6.65)

Site Type: Ceremonial and habitation

Ceramic Phase: Mix, Tan

Occupation: Late Classic, Late Postclassic

Location and Setting: Tr-160 is located 4 km east and slightly south of Colonia Joaquín Miguel Gutiérrez south of Río Dolores. The site is situated on the valley floor east of Río Rincón Tigre. The vegetation surrounding the site is mainly grasses and isolated trees. The area is used for pasture.

Environmental Stratum: Tropical Deciduous Forest

Description: The site of Tr-160 consists of a small civic-ceremonial precinct and a series of low house mounds. The ceremonial structure (A) located in a slightly isolated position at the southern edge of the site is a 4 m pyramid. Immediately north of this pyramid is a very small rectangular feature (B) that probably functioned as an altar associated with the pyramid. The main concentration of habitation structures is located north of the ceremonial area within an area of approximately 160 by 150 m. Within this area are three small concentrations of house mounds (E to J, K to N, and O to R). Within these three concentrations probably six or more household compounds are represented. Finally, between the main habitation area and the ceremonial area to the south, two more low mounds (C and D) probably represent part of two separate house groups.

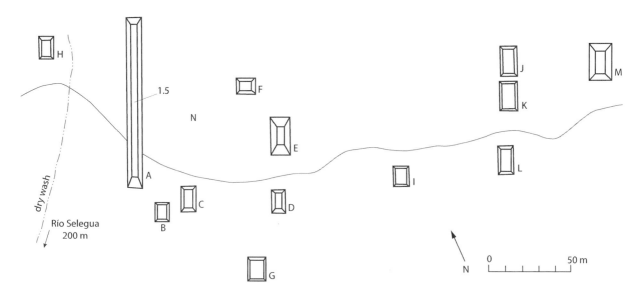

Figure 6.66. Site sketch of Tr-161, Dolores Puente.

TR-161 DOLORES PUENTE (Figure 6.66)

Site Type: Ceremonial and habitation

Ceramic Phase: Tan

Occupation: Protoclassic, Middle Classic, Late Postclassic

Location and Setting: Tr-161 is located 3.5 km east of Colonia Joaquín Miguel Gutiérrez, 200 m east of Río Rincón Tigre. The site is situated on the valley floor. The vegetation surrounding the site consists mainly of grassland used as pasture. A dry wash is located at the western side of the site.

Environmental Stratum: Tropical Deciduous Forest

Description: The site of Dolores Puente (Tr-161) consists of a sizable civic-ceremonial precinct, as well as a small number of habitation structures. The main concentration of ceremonial structures appears to be located in the western portion of the site. The site's western border is formed by a very long low mound measuring 10 m wide by 100 m long and 1.5 m high. Eighty meters west of Mound A, across a large open plaza area (N), is a temple platform (E) measuring 2 m in height. Several other smaller rectangular structures (B, C, D, and F) are also arranged around this large

plaza area. These latter may have served as elite residences or civic-ceremonial buildings, or perhaps both. Mound G, south of the plaza group, is a low mound, which was also probably a residential group. Mound H, west of the plaza group on the west side of the dry wash, was also probably a habitation.

East of the plaza group a series of low rectangular mounds (I, J, K, and L) were probably residential mounds. Mound M, at the eastern edge of the site, is a large structure measuring 14 by 23 m and 1.5 m high. This large structure may have been a temple platform or perhaps a large residence.

The orientation of the structures in the ceremonial group, either parallel or perpendicular to each other, suggests the complex was constructed according to a formal plan. The site appears to be a community with habitation and a substantial ceremonial precinct. Habitation is probably not limited to the visible mounds as there may be non-mounded habitations on the site.

References: Blake 2010:265, 267

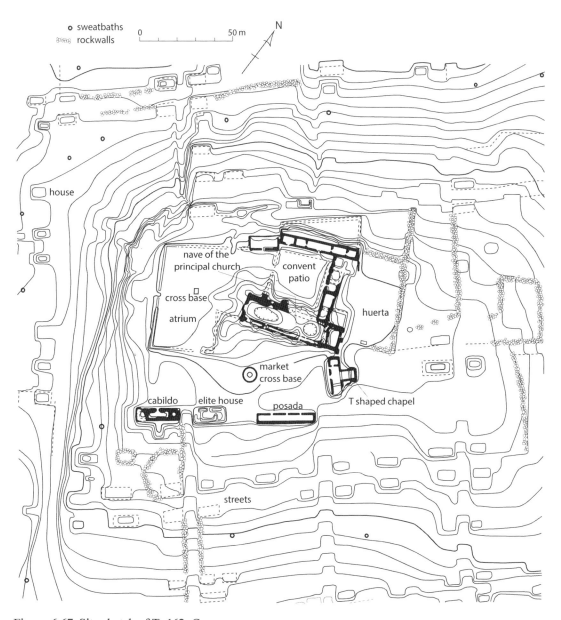

Figure 6.67. Site sketch of Tr-162, Coapa.

TR-162 COAPA (Figure 6.67)

Site Type: Ceremonial and habitation

Ceramic Phase: Ux

Occupation: Colonial

Location and Setting: Coapa was founded on a low hill a little over 1.1 km east of Río Ontela. The modern Colonia of Francisco Javier Mújica is 5 km west of the colonial site. The land is currently forested and used as a cattle range.

Environmental Stratum: Palm Forest-Tropical Deciduous Forest

Description: This was a Spanish-founded town in a location chosen for its lack of Pre-Columbian antecedents. The site has been laid out on a grid pattern. Architecture at the site core includes a large church-convent complex. Other features include stone walls, cross bases, quarries or barrow pits. Domestic residences are indicated by rectangles on the map and would consist of houses and patios, often with sweatbaths.

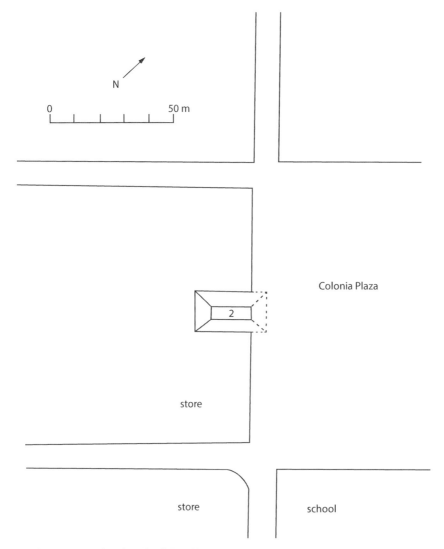

Figure 6.68. Site sketch of Tr-163.

Map of the site was done by Edudardo Martínez. Excavations were undertaken by Tom Lee and Sydney Markman in 1975-1976 (see Lee 1979a, 1979b).

References: Lee 1979a, 1979b, 1996; Markman 1984:244-248, 409-412, figs. 170-176

TR-163 (Figure 6.68)

Site Type: Habitation

Location and Setting: Tr-163 is located at the western edge of the central plaza of Colonia Rodolfo Figueroa. The site is situated on a low hill in an area of rolling hills and ridges. The land surrounding the site is being used for house compounds. Vegetation surrounding the Colonia is mainly milpa, grasses, and sparse tree cover.

Environmental Stratum: Fields or Pastures

Description: The visible portion of the site of Tr-163 consists of a single rectangular mound measuring approximately 28 by 15 m and 2 m high. This structure may have functioned either as a habitation or perhaps a small civic-ceremonial building. It is not possible to determine from surface evidence if the site was more extensive prior to the construction of the Colonia.

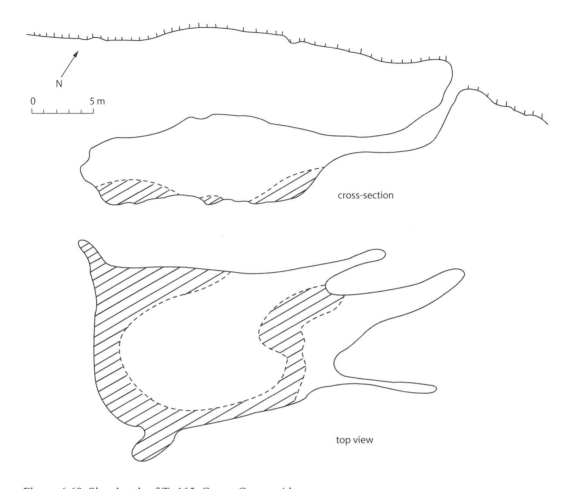

cross-section

top view

Figure 6.69. Site sketch of Tr-165, Cueva Campo Alegre.

TR-164 (see TR-116)

TR-165 CUEVA CAMPO ALEGRE
(Figure 6.69)

Site Type: Cave

Ceramic Phase: Tan

Occupation: Late Postclassic

Location and Setting: Tr-165 is located in the side of a high hill 5 km southwest of Colonia Rodolfo Figueroa. The site is located just 1 km south of the road leading from the Colonia to the Pan-American Highway and approximately 1.5 km west of Coneta (Tr-95). The area surrounding the site is characterized by rolling hills and ridges.

Environmental Stratum: Tropical Deciduous Forest

Description: Tr-165 is a small cave apparently used as an offering place. No occupation was visible on the surface. Vessels found in the cave were mostly three-loop handle water jars, one of which has a polychrome decoration in red and black on gray.

References: Lee and Bryant 1996:63

TR-166 CERRO BASH (no map)

Site Type: Ceremonial and habitation

Location and Setting: Tr-166 is located approximately 6 km southwest of Colonia Rodolfo Figueroa and approximately 4.3 km east of the point where the Pan-American Highway crosses Río San Gregorio. The site is situated in a hilly area on the southeast side of a gooseneck in Río San Lucas. The terrain around the site is densely covered with trees. Tr-167 is located 500 m from the Río San Lucas.

Environmental Stratum: Tropical Deciduous Forest-Riparian Forest

Description: No further details available.

TR-167 CERRO IGUANERO (Figure 6.70)

Site Type: Ceremonial and habitation

Occupation: Late Classic

Location and Setting: Tr-167 is located approximately 5.5 km southwest of Colonia Rodolfo Figueroa and 4.5 east and slightly north of the point where the Pan-American Highway crosses over Río San Gregorio. The site is situated on a knoll, in a large gooseneck of Río San Lucas. The site is bounded on three sides by Río San Lucas. The site is densely covered with trees and brush.

Environmental Stratum: Short Tree Savannah/ Thorn Woodland Riparian Forest

Description: Tr-167 is a nucleated hilltop settlement with evidence of ceremonial structures, habitations, and extensive terracing. The site covers the mesa and some habitations are visible on the slopes of the mesa, particularly in the southeastern area.

The densest concentration of occupation appears to be in the western half of the site where the mesa is widest. This also seems to be the main ceremonial area. The largest structure (A), a 3 m temple mound, is located in a central position in the western sector. Just 20 m from the western corner of Mound A is a small terrace (B) that may have supported a small altar structure associated with Mound A. Fifteen meters west of Mound A is an I-shaped

ballcourt. All of these structures are supported by a long terrace (D). At the eastern end of Terrace D is another low rectangular mound (E). South of Terrace D is a series of structures (F and G, I and J) that may have functioned as elite residences. A chultún (H) appears to be associated with the F/G pair. To the north and the west of the ceremonial group are two terrace and mound groups (L/M/N and O/P) that may also have been elite residences. Surrounding this central core area are several low mounds and wall foundation alignments, perhaps habitations, some of which are isolated and some of which appear to be arranged in compound groups.

In the eastern half of the site where the mesa narrows, the concentration of structures is less. The mesa is dominated by a large quadrangular terrace feature (NN) supporting three mounds (OO, PP, and QQ) and a small terrace (RR). The largest of the mounds (OO) measures 1.5 m high. The size of these structures and their apparent arrangement around a plaza (SS) suggests this compound was an elite residence or perhaps even had civic-ceremonial functions. Surrounding this terrace group on the west, south, and east sides are several small structures that appear to have been residences.

There does not appear to be any formal patterning to the arrangement of structures; rather, it probably grew by accretion. The location of terraces and probably also of structures likely a function of the natural contour of the site.

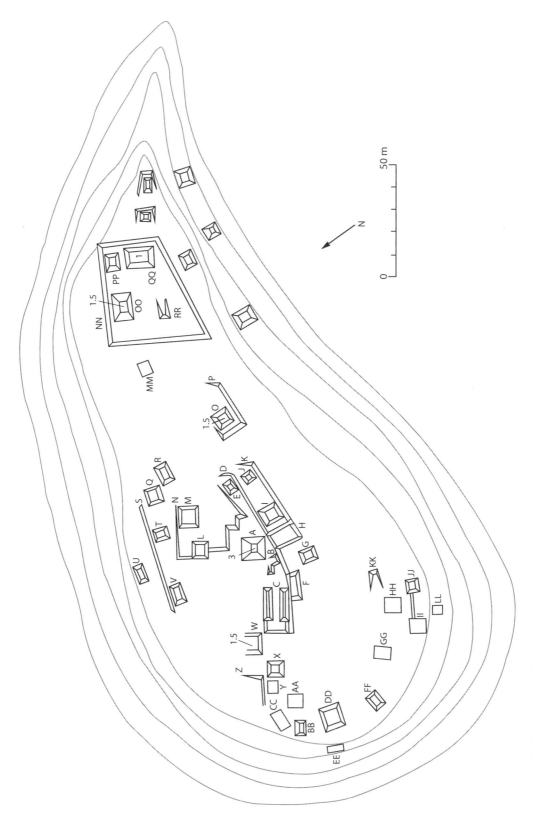

Figure 6.70. Site sketch of Tr-167, Cerro Iguanero.

Figure 6.71. Site sketch of Tr-168, Cueva Víbora.

TR-168 CUEVA VÍBORA/ CERRO VÍBORA
(no map, Figure 6.71)

Site Type: Ceremonial and habitation

Occupation: Late Postclassic

Location and Setting: The site of Cerro Víbora is located on a high hilltop overlooking Río San Lucas to the east about 7 km upstream from its confluence with Río Lagartero. It is 5 km south of Colonia Rodolfo Figueroa. The land is presently used as a cattle range.

Environmental Stratum: Fields or pastures

Description: Site consists of primary and simple platforms, as well as terraces. A cave is located in the site. Sketch map with further details is lost.

Excavations were undertaken by Tom Lee but not published.

References: Lee and Bryant 1996

Figure 6.72. Site sketch of Tr-169, Ojo de Agua 2.

TR-169 OJO DE AGUA 2 (Figure 6.72)

Site Type: Habitation

Location and Setting: Tr-169 is located roughly 3.5 km southwest of Colonia Rodolfo Figueroa on the east bank of Río San Lucas where the river margin begins to give way to hilly terrain. Vegetation in the site area consists of mainly grasses with some trees. Directly across the San Lucas, Tr-95 (Coneta) sits on the wide western margin of the river.

Environmental Stratum: Fields or pastures

Description: Tr-169 (is an isolated mound measuring 3 by 3.5 m and approximately 60 cm high. The road cuts close to the site and may have disturbed the mound. No other features noted. The mound was probably an isolated habitation site.

TR-170 (Figure 6.73)

Site Type: Ceremonial and habitation

Location and Setting: Tr-170 is located approximated 7 km east of Colonia Rodolfo Figueroa. The site itself is situated in a valley. Río Lagartero passes approximately 1 km south of the site. Land around the site is used mainly for corn agriculture.

Environmental Stratum: Short Tree Savannah/ Thorn Woodland

Description: Tr-170 appears to be an isolated ceremonial site with a few possible ceremonial structures. The site is divided into two groups, one on each side of the arroyo that cuts through the site.

The largest mound (A), which measures 6 m in height, is located on the east side of the arroyo. Just off the southeast corner of Mound A is a smaller mound (B) measuring 1.5 m in height. Mound B was probably also a civic-ceremonial building associated with A. To the north and south of this pair are three low rectangular mounds (C, D, and E), which may have been elite residences housing personnel associated with the ceremonial buildings.

On the western side of the arroyo, another three mounds (F, G, and H) are visible. The largest of these (Mound F), measuring 4 m high, is located between G and H. Mounds G and H, both 2 m high, may have been ceremonial structures as well.

TR-171 LA PAPAYA (Figure 6.74)

Site Type: Ceremonial and habitation

Occupation: Late Preclassic, Protoclassic

Location and Setting: Tr-171 is located roughly 6 km east of Colonia Rodolfo Figueroa. The site lies on a ridge jutting out of a large range of hills. Río Lagartero passes approximately 0.5 km south of the site. Land surrounding the site is under milpa cultivation, with trees on the mounds.

Environmental Stratum: Short Tree Savannah/ Thorn Woodland

Description: La Papaya appears to be a large ceremonial center with a small habitation component. The site is located in a hilly area with the main ceremonial precinct and some habitations sitting in a prominent place on a ridgetop, and a small concentration of habitations

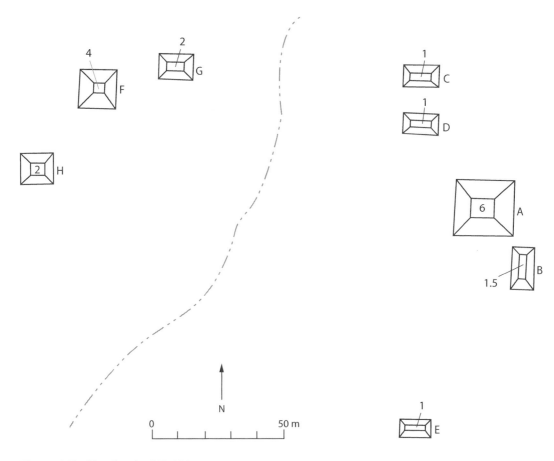

Figure 6.73. Site sketch of Tr-170.

on a low rise approximately 50 m west. The site includes large ceremonial mounds, low habitation mounds, and several terraces, both large and small.

In the main ceremonial precinct, two large platform mounds (A and B), 5 m and 4 m high respectively, three low mounds (C, D, and E), a plain stela (C), and one large rock-wall foundation alignment (F) are arranged around an open plaza (G). The largest mound (A) also functions as the south wall of an I-shaped ballcourt, with H acting as the north wall. A rock alignment (K) acts as the eastern end zone marker for the ballcourt. Finally, Mound J, a 4 m structure, overlooks the ballcourt on the north side. This entire complex is supported and interconnected by a series of terraces (K, L, M, N, and O). East of the ceremonial center are a series of small low mounds (P to S) and a small house terrace (T). These mounds probably represent one or two habitation components.

On a low rise to the west of the main ceremonial group, a series of low mounds and house terraces are situated. Mounds U, V, and west are arrayed around a common patio (X). These, along with Mound Y and Terrace Z, probably formed one or perhaps two habitation compounds. Northwest of this group is another terrace (A), which probably once functioned as a house terrace. Finally, southeast of the main habitation group is another habitation compound, enclosed by terrace BB.

The distribution of structures at Tr-171 appears to be partly a function of the contour of the local terrain, with the ceremonial group in an isolated and prominent position in the center, and habitations scattered around on high land. Still, the regular orientation of structures, particularly in the ceremonial group, arrayed at right angles around an open plaza, suggests this area was constructed according to a formal unified plan.

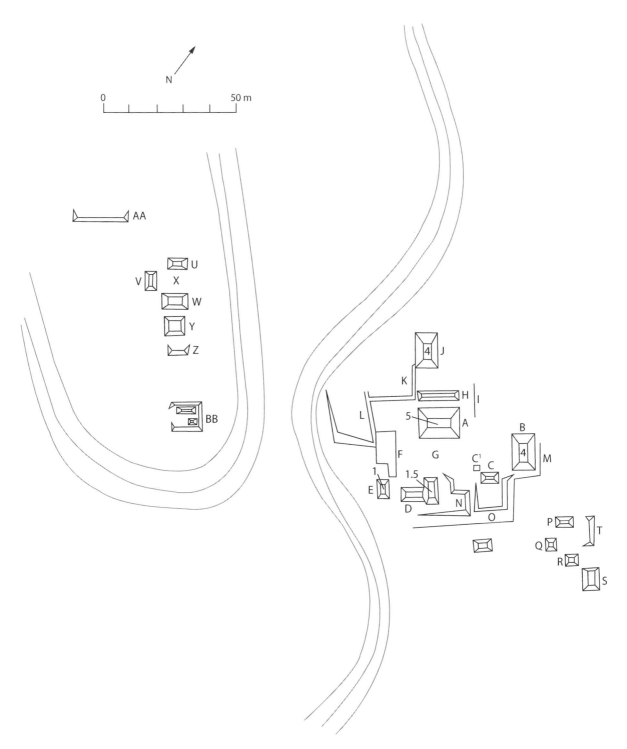

Figure 6.74. Site sketch of Tr-171, La Papaya.

Figure 6.75. View of Tr-172, Potrero Mango, looking north. Individuals on Mound 1 (center) are looking northeast toward the ballcourt.

TR-172 POTRERO MANGO
(Figures 6.75-6.78)

Site Type: Ceremonial and habitation

Occupation: Early Preclassic, Middle Preclassic, Late Preclassic, Protoclassic, Early Classic, Late Classic

Location and Setting: This site is located 3.5 km east of Colonia Joaquín Miguel Gutiérrez on a bench above the north side of Río Dolores and facing downstream to its confluence with Río Rincón Tigre. The site sits on a projecting bench 15 m above Río Dolores and occupies most of the available flat area. The land has been cleared for pasture and only a few trees remain on the site, which, under natural conditions, was probably heavily forested.

Environmental Stratum: Tropical Deciduous Forest

Description: On the east side of the site, there is a ceremonial group with two large mounds facing each other across a plaza 25 m long. The two large mounds are 4 m tall and were once probably pyramidal-shaped and are now rounded off. The north side of the plaza is formed by a 2 m tall mound that, although it is badly eroded, may have formed the southern half of a ballcourt. The other ballcourt mound is also badly eroded. There are six other low mounds that may have been residential platforms, scattered around the edge of the main ceremonial group.

On a knoll 10 m above and 80 m west of the main group is evidence of another residential group and an eroded 2 m mound. Only the large

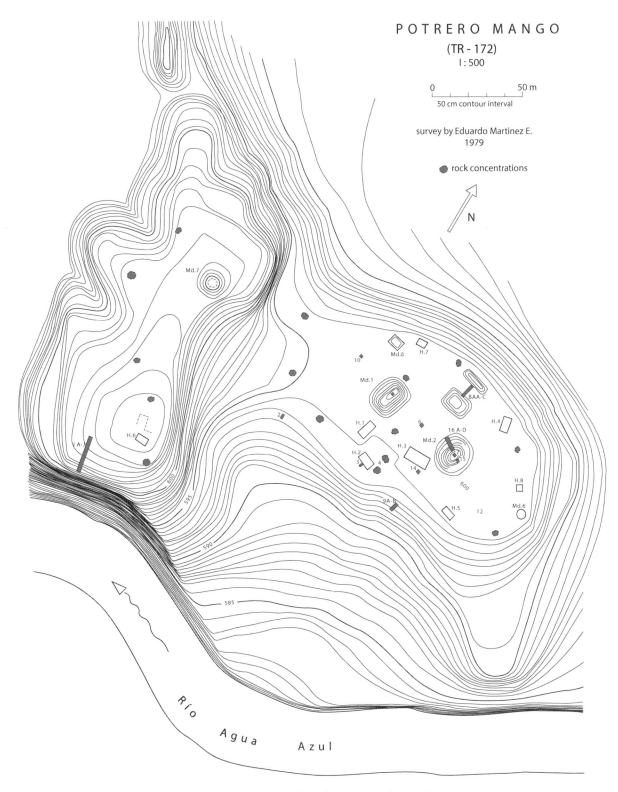

Figure 6.76. Site map of Tr-172, Potrero Mango, by Eduardo Martínez, 1979.

Figure 6.77. View of Tr-172, Potrero Mango.

Figure 6.78. View of Tr-172, Potrero Mango.

mounds in the main group are aligned with each other and their orientation is close to east-west. Other features at the site are ill-defined terraces backed with river cobbles.

The site was test excavated in 1977 by Don Miller and Gareth Lowe, along with several other sites, to determine the relationship between them and La Libertad (Tr-157), although an incorrect site number (Tr-122) was assigned in a recent publication of that report (Miller and Lowe 2014:213-219). Because two of the three test pits had Early Preclassic sherds in their deepest levels, it was decided to further test the site in a third field season (Lee 1980). A map of the site was made by Eduardo Martínez in 1979 and constituted the second field season.

References: Bryant and Clark 2005a:265-266; Lee 1980; Miller and Lowe 2014:213-219; Tejada 2000

TR-173 LAGUNA SECA (Figure 6.79)

Site Type: Ceremonial and habitation

Location and Setting: Tr-173 is located approximately 2.5 km west of Colonia Morelos and 2.5 km northeast of Colonia Ángel Albino Corzo. The site is situated on a low hill with a cañada passing 200 m from the site (location of cañada unspecified). Land in the vicinity is used primarily for milpa and pasture.

Environmental Stratum: Tropical Deciduous Forest

Description: Laguna Seca has a number of house platforms and terraces downslope from the main ceremonial center on the top of a low hill. The ceremonial precinct is a large terraced area (A) that forms a platform 50 by 70 m. On the north end of the platform sits Mound E, the largest structure at the site. It faces southwest towards two low, smaller, stone-faced platforms (C and D) that were probably altars. Mound B is a slightly smaller pyramid with the remnants of a stairway on its northeast side facing Mound E. There is also a small stairway leading from the platform or plaza (A) down to an open area that may have had more habitations. The main residential area consists of a series of well-defined terraces with some house groups

sitting on them (e.g., F and G; H and I). Farther downslope from these are a number of less well-defined terraces that probably supported low house platforms. Sixty meters east of the main group are two other house platforms (L and M). They are in the Terminal Classic style common at sites like El Rosario (Tr-12) (de Montmollin 1989c) and Los Cimientos (Tr-29) (Rivero 1987). Mound L has two low raised areas on it that may have been separate rooms.

A final group of mounds (N to Q) is located an additional 50 m east of Mound M. One of them appears to have been a small pyramid (N), while two others (O and P) are house mounds. Associated with this mound group is a semi-circular stone wall 10 m in diameter. This type of feature is common at other Terminal Classic sites in the study area.

TR-174 (Figure 6.80)

Site Type: Habitation

Occupation: Late Classic

Location and Setting: Tr-174 is located approximately 6.75 km northeast of Colonia Joaquín Miguel Gutiérrez and 7.5 km south of Colonia Rodolfo Figueroa. The site lies on the west bank of Río San Lucas, just 0.25 km north of its confluence with Río Lagartero. Vegetation surrounding the site consists mainly of grasses. Just 0.5 km north of this site are located Tr-70 and Tr-71, and 2 km southeast is Tr-99 (Lagartero).

Environmental Stratum: Tropical Deciduous Forest

Description: Tr-174 is a small nucleated settlement with evidence of three to five habitation compounds and one civic-ceremonial structure. The largest mound (A), which measures 1.5 m high and is located at the western edge of the site, may have been an elite residence or perhaps a civic-ceremonial structure. Mounds B and C at the top north edge of the site were probably a residential compound arranged around a patio (D). Another pair (E and F) in the southwest corner of the site is arranged around a patio (G). Mound A at the western edge was also

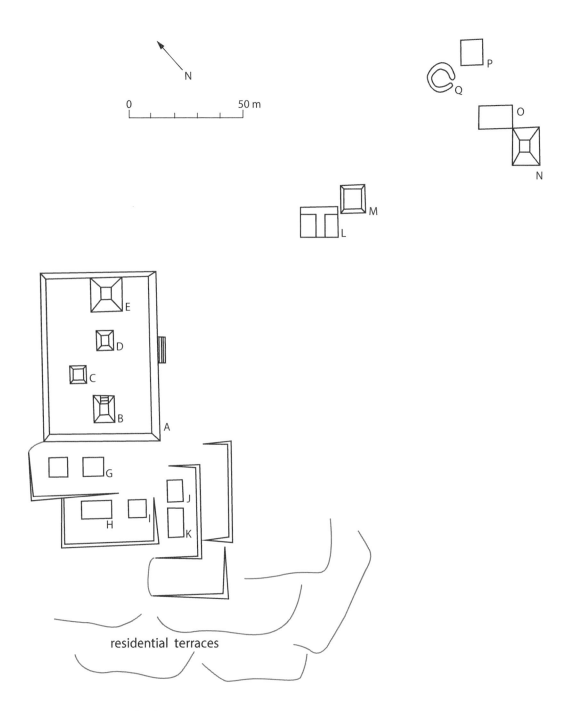

Figure 6.79. Site sketch of Tr-173, Laguna Seca.

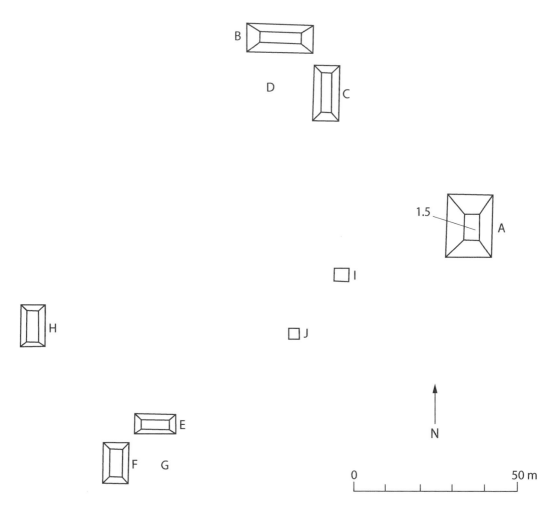

Figure 6.80. Site sketch of Tr-174.

probably a residential mound. Finally, there are two small, low mounds in the center of the site (I and J).

The site appears to be a small ceremonial site with a small residential settlement and a possible civic-ceremonial structure.

TR-175 (Figure 6.81)

Site Type: Ceremonial and habitation

Location and Setting: Tr-175 is approximately 4 km southwest of Colonia Chihuahua and 1 km east of the Pan-American Highway. It sits on a small hilltop 1 km northwest of Río Santa Inés. The zone is used for both maize farming and pasturage.

Environmental Stratum: Tropical Deciduous Forest

Description: Tr-175 is a small site with evidence of a civic-ceremonial structure, a habitation unit, and a large terrace feature. The civic-ceremonial structure (A) is a pyramid measuring 20 by 18 m and 4 m high. Approximately 25 m south of Mound A is a large terrace feature (B) measuring 60 m long. The terrace displays a large niche at the western edge that may have supported another structure, possibly associated with Mound A. Finally, approximately 55 m west of the terrace, a single low mound (C) is visible. This mound probably served as a habitation, perhaps housing personnel associated with the ceremonial structure. This site was likely a small ceremonial site, with a

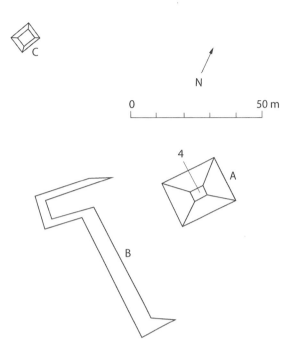

Figure 6.81. Site sketch of Tr-175.

small habitation component. At the time of the survey, the vegetation covering the site was chest-high, so there are probably many more house mounds surrounding the structures than have been mapped.

References: de Montmollin 1989c:157-158, 219-222

TR-176 EL ROSARIO 2 / EL MISTERIO
(no map)

Site Type: Habitation

Occupation: Late Classic

Location and Setting: Located in flat area between the Ríos Santa Inés and San Agustín, approximately 150 m northwest from the Santa Inés. Zone is used for milpa.

Environmental Stratum: Palm Forest

Description: Site consists of three low-lying mounds that appear to be residential platforms. Mounds are dispersed in a triangular formation roughly 100 m between them; other mounds may be present but plowed under.

References: de Montmollin 1989c:157-158

TR-177 (Figure 6.82)

Site Type: Ceremonial and habitation

Location and Setting: Tr-177 is located approximately 8.5 km west of the Pan-American Highway on the road leading to Colonia Francisco Javier Mújica and Colonia Los Limones. The site is situated on a low hill in an area of broken hilly terrain. Río Santa Inés passes 2.5 km south of the site. The site is presently located in a maize field.

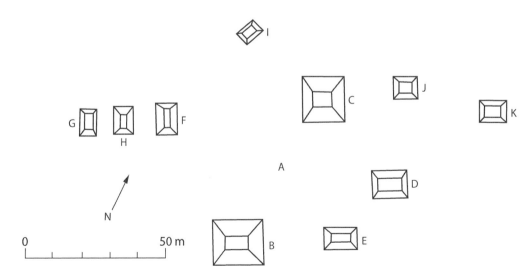

Figure 6.82. Site sketch of Tr-177.

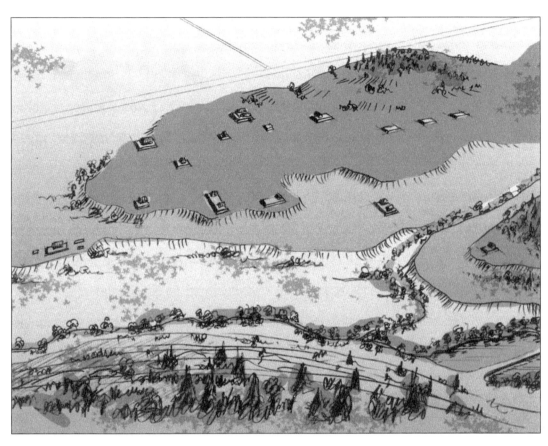

Figure 6.83. Recreation drawing of site Tr-178, Solferino/El Solferín by Ayax Moreno (Castellanos 2012b).

Environmental Stratum: Tropical Deciduous Forest

Description: The site of Tr-177 is a small ceremonial center with a small habitation component visible. The maximum extent of the site measures approximately 150 by 90 m. The visible structures appear to be roughly arrayed around a large central plaza (A). The largest structure (B) is a temple platform measuring 3 m high. North and kitty-corner across the plaza from B is another temple platform (C) measuring 2 m high. Surrounding the patio is a series of lower mounds (D, E, and F) that may have functioned as elite residences. Other lower mounds surrounding the ceremonial area (G to J) also probably functioned as residences.

The orderly arrangement of mounds around a plaza suggests this site was constructed according to a plan. The absence of other structures at Tr-177 suggests this small site may

have served as a ceremonial center for a non-resident population. A more likely possibility is that more house mounds surround the ceremonial precinct and that they were covered with vegetation at the time of the survey.

TR-178 SOLFERINO/ EL SOLFERÍN (Figures 6.83-6.84)

Site Type: Ceremonial and habitation

Occupation: late Middle Preclassic, Late Preclassic, Protoclassic, Early Classic, Middle Classic, Late Classic

Location and Setting: Tr-178 is located approximately 2.75 km north of La Trinitaria, just 250 m west of the Pan-American Highway on the edge of the Comitan Valley. The site was situated on a low hill with a small stream passing 100 m north of the site. Vegetation in the site area was not recorded.

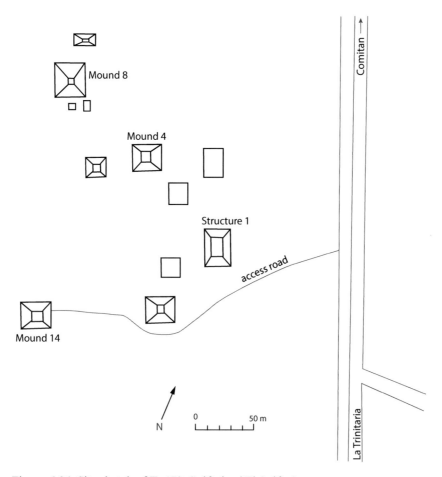

Figure 6.84. Site sketch of Tr-178, Solferino/ El Solferín.

Environmental Stratum: Pine/Oak Forest

Description: Tr-178 was a site with evidence of ceremonial and habitation occupation. Several mounds were noted, including four or five pyramids and two or three platform mounds.

References: Castellanos 2012a, 2012b; Lee 1989:272; Pina Chan 1961:54, Plano 1

TR-179 SAN FRANCISCO CAVE (no map)

Site Type: Ceremonial cave

Occupation: Late Postclassic, Modern

Location and Setting: Tr-179 is a cave site located just 0.5 km north of Colonia San Francisco Sarabia on the east side of the Pan-American Highway. The site is situated in a cliff at the end of a valley north of San Francisco Sarabia.

Environmental Stratum: Pine/Oak Forest

Description: Tr-179 is a large cave with evidence of prehistoric use. No structures were observed in the cave; however, ceramics were found and collected from four separate locations within it. The depth of occupation in the cave was noted as shallow, and the material conditions were poor. In modern times, the cave is used as a shrine, and a large fiesta is held on May 3rd to celebrate the feast day of Santa Cruz.

TR-180 (Figure 6.85)

Site Type: Ceremonial and habitation

Location and Setting: Tr-180 is located 3 km southwest of Colonia Rodolfo Figueroa on a hill overlooking Río San Lucas to the north. Vegetation in the vicinity is mainly brush thicket and grasses.

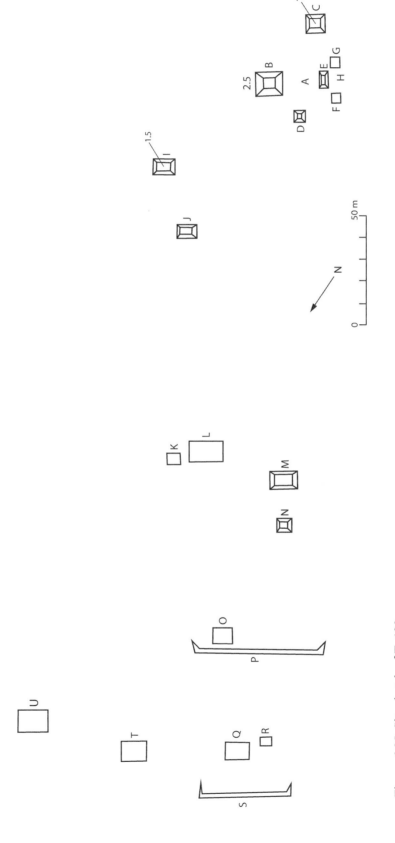

Figure 6.85. Site sketch of Tr-180.

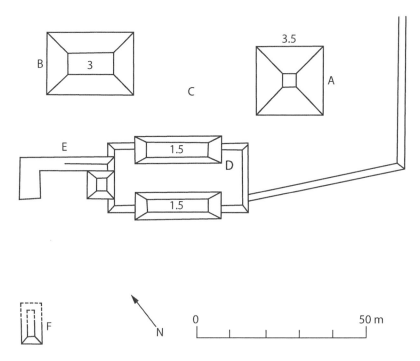

Figure 6.86. Site sketch of Tr-181.

Environmental Stratum: Tropical Deciduous Forest

Description: Tr-180 is a small settlement with evidence of ceremonial and residential occupation and some terracing. The site appears to be distributed in a linear pattern, lying northwest by southeast. The extent of the site measures approximately 350 by 150 m.

The ceremonial area is located in the southeast end of the site. This precinct appears to consist of several structures arrayed around a plaza (A). The largest structure (B) measures roughly 10 by 13 m and 2.5 m high. South of B is a lower mound (C) measuring 1 m high. On the opposite side of the plaza is another small mound (D). Mounds C and D may be associated with the ceremonial mound (B) or perhaps were residential mounds. Finally, Mound E is associated with two wall foundation alignments (F and G), all arrayed around a patio (H). The proximity of these to the main ceremonial mound suggests that it may have been an elite residential compound.

Scattered across the remaining expanse of the site to the northwest are a series of low mounds and rock-wall foundation alignments.

Many of these seem to be arrayed in groups of two (I and J, K and L, M and N, Q and R), suggesting they may have been residential compounds. The remaining mounds are more isolated (O, T, and U) and were also probably residential structures.

Two of the residential groups cut the northwestern edge of the site (O and Q, and R) and are supported by terraces (P and S).

This site was likely a small dispersed residential hamlet with a small civic-ceremonial precinct. The orderly arrangement of the structures in the ceremonial group around the plaza (A) suggests that this group was built as a planned complex.

TR-181 (Figure 6.86)

Site Type: Ceremonial and habitation

Location and Setting: Tr-181 is located 1.5 km north of Colonia Rodolfo Figueroa. The site is situated on a low hill on the west bank of Río San Lucas. Vegetation in the vicinity consists mainly of grasses and sparse trees.

Environmental Stratum: Short Tree Savannah/ Thorn Woodland

Description: Tr-181 is an isolated ceremonial complex with little evidence of habitation occupation. The main concentration of buildings lies within an area of 90 by 55 m. A single low mound is located circa 40 m west of the main concentration. The site, located on a low hill, is supported on the south side by a terrace wall. The ceremonial precinct includes a pyramid (A) measuring 20 by 20 m and 3.5 m high. Northwest of A across a large plaza (C) is a temple platform measuring 25 by 10 m and 2 m high. The southeast side of the plaza is bounded by an I-shaped ballcourt (D). The mounds of the ballcourt each measure 1.5 m high and are enclosed on both ends by a low rock end zone. Adjoining the northwest end zone of the ballcourt is a large, low, U-shaped structure facing in a southwestern direction. Finally, an isolated low mound (F) 20 m west of the ceremonial group was probably a habitation housing personnel associated with the ceremonial center.

This site was likely a small, isolated ceremonial center that probably served the surrounding population. The regular orientation of the structures with respect to each other and their arrangement around a large plaza suggest it was constructed as a planned complex.

TR-182 LOS AMANTES
(Figure 6.87)

Site Type: Habitation

Location and Setting: Tr-182 is located 3 km north of Colonia Rodolfo Figueroa on a low hill approximately 200 m west of Río San Lucas. Vegetation in the site vicinity consists mainly of grasses and scattered trees.

Environmental Stratum: Short Tree Savannah/ Thorn Woodland

Description: Tr-182 is a small nucleated habitation community with no evidence of ceremonial structures. The site, located on a low ridge, is concentrated within an area of approximately 190 by 100 m. The site consists of at least 18 structures, including rock-wall foundation alignments, as well as low mounds ranging in height from 0.25 to 1 m. Towards the northern edge of the site, two terraces are located that probably functioned as habitation terraces. The structures appear to be arranged in clusters ranging in size from 1 to 3 or 4 m. At the southern edge of the site, Mounds A to E probably represent two or more habitation compounds. North of this group, Mounds F, G, and H appear to be a compound arranged around a patio (I). A smaller structure (I) slightly downslope of this compound may have been an outbuilding associated with the F-H group. On the east side, Mounds K and L form an individual compound group. Mound H, supported by Terrace N, is also probably an individual group. Finally, at the northern tip of the site, Mounds O to T and Terrace U may have formed two to three habitation compounds.

There does not appear to be any formal patterning in the layout of the structures at the site. Rather, it is probably determined by the contour of the ridge on which the site is located. Nonetheless, within each compound or cluster, structures do seem to follow a regular orientation, either parallel or perpendicular to each other, suggesting the compounds were constructed according to a plan.

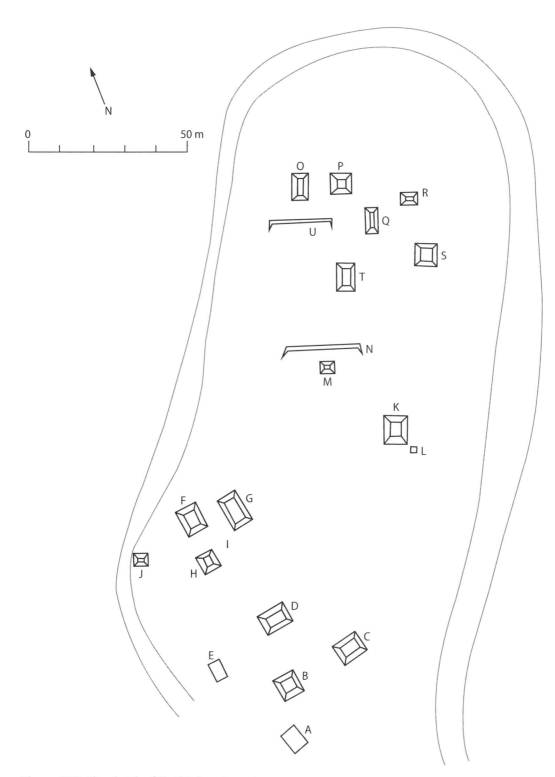

Figure 6.87. Site sketch of Tr-182, Los Amantes.

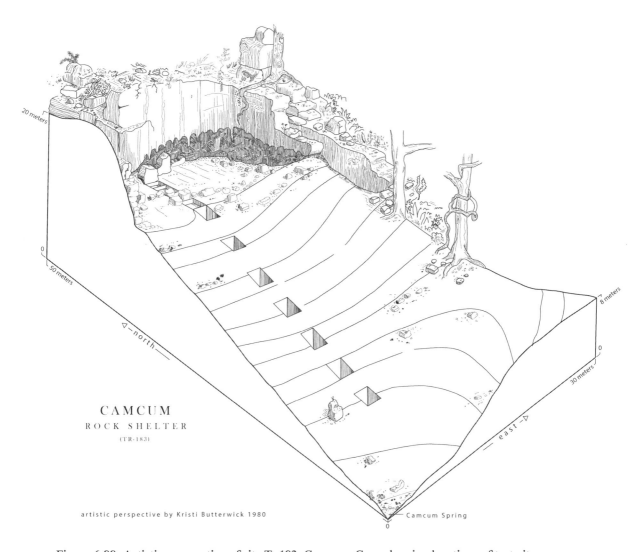

Figure 6.88. Artistic perspective of site Tr-183, Camcum Cave showing locations of test pits.

TR-183 CAMCUM CAVE
(Figures 6.88-6.91)

Site Type: Cave

Occupation: Archaic, Early Preclassic, Middle Preclassic, Late Preclassic, Protoclassic, Late Classic, Late Postclassic

Location and Setting: This rockshelter is situated in the side of a hill overlooking a large spring, which is the source of Río Camcum, a small tributary of Río Lagartero. The cliff and spring are remnants of an eroded cenote at the edge of the Camcum/Canajasté Valley. This cliff overlooks the site of Tr-189. At present, the cave is part of a cattle pasture-corral area used by residents of Colonia Las Delicias 4.5 km to the northwest.

Environmental Stratum: Tropical Deciduous Forest/Riparian Forest

Description: Camcum is a rockshelter that measures some 16.5 m in width and 11 m in depth, with a ceiling that ranges from 4.4 to 3.2 m in height.

The site was excavated in 1980 by Tom Lee and John Clark; a preliminary report has been published (Lee and Clark 1988)

References: Lee and Clark 1988

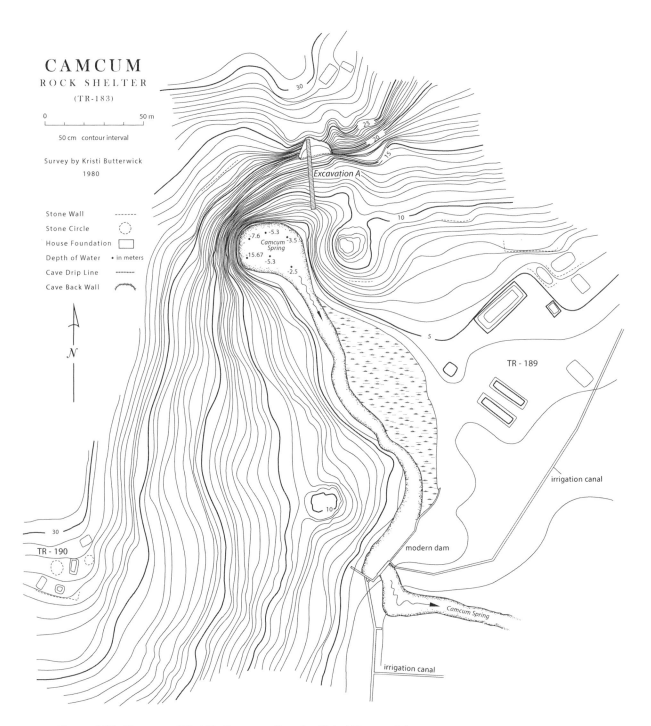

CAMCUM
ROCK SHELTER
(TR-183)

0 _____ 50 m

50 cm contour interval

Survey by Kristi Butterwick
1980

Stone Wall	- - - - - - -
Stone Circle	◌
House Foundation	▭
Depth of Water	• in meters
Cave Drip Line	••••••••••
Cave Back Wall	︿︿︿︿

N

Excavation A

Camcum
Spring

•-7.6   •-5.3
•-3.5
•-15.67
•-5.3
•-2.5

TR-189

irrigation canal

TR-190

modern dam

Camcum Spring

irrigation canal

Figure 6.89. Site map of Tr-183, Camcum Cave by Kristi Butterwick.

Figure 6.90. Largartero River coming out of Camcum spring.

Figure 6.91. View of site Tr-183, Camcum Cave looking north.

TR-184 (no map)

Site Type: Cave

Location and Setting: Tr-184 is located 3.5 km south of Colonia Rodolfo Figueroa. The site is situated on a hillside in a region of broken hilly terrain. No major water source is known for the immediate vicinity of the site; the Río San Lucas flows 3.5 km to the west, while Río Lagartero flows 3 km to the east. Vegetation at the site consists primarily of low deciduous forest.

Environmental Stratum: Tropical Deciduous Forest

Description: Tr-184 is a cave site located in the side of a hill.

TR-185 CUEVA DE LOS BANCOS DE COXOLAR (no map)

Site Type: Cave

Location and Setting: Tr-185 is located 1.5 km east of Colonia Ángel Albino Corzo. It is in a forested region south of the road connecting Colonia Ángel Albino Corzo and Colonia Morelos.

Environmental Stratum: Short Tree Savanna/ Thorn Woodland

Description: Tr-185 is a small cave that extends beneath the surface of a flat but rocky area. The cave's mouth is 1.5 m wide and opens into a large chamber a few meters below the surface. Inside the cave were a number of skeletal remains, ceramics, and some partially preserved wooden benches.

TR-186 SAN ANTONIO EL ZAPOTE (no map)

Site Type: Ceremonial and habitation

Occupation: Late Preclassic, Late Classic

Location and Setting: Tr-186 is located approximately 2 km east of the Pan-American Highway and 1 km north of the road to Colonia Rodolfo Figueroa. The site is located on a hilltop with grasses and low deciduous forest. It is currently used as a pasture. No water source is known in the immediate vicinity of the site.

Environmental Stratum: Tropical Deciduous Forest

Description: Tr-186 is a large, nucleated community with evidence of a large central ceremonial precinct, surrounded by several terraced habitation structures. The central ceremonial precinct includes seven larger structures, several of which (B to F) are arrayed around a large plaza (A). The southwestern boundary of the plaza is formed by a small closed ballcourt (F). Surrounding this central core on the north and east are three more large mounds (G, H, and I). On the western edge of the central core are two smaller structures (J and K).

Around the ceremonial core on all four sides is a series of well-preserved habitation terraces. The range of sizes of these structures is unknown. Most of the terraces support only one habitation structure (although some support two). The site map is schematic only and gives a general idea of the site layout.

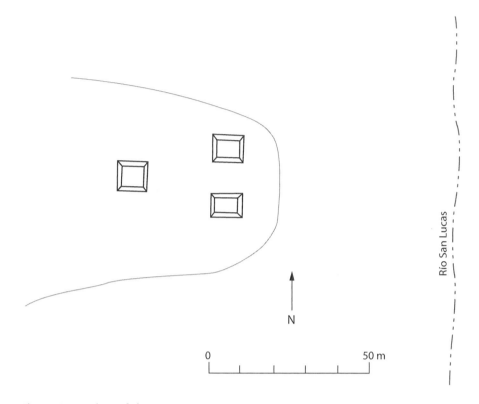

Figure 6.92. View of site Tr-187.

TR-187 (Figure 6.92)

Site Type: Habitation

Occupation: Late Classic

Location and Setting: Tr-187 is located 2.5 km north of Colonia Rodolfo Figueroa on the west bank of Río San Lucas. The area is primarily pasturage but some maize is also grown in the zone surrounding the site.

Environmental Stratum: Short Tree Savannah/ Thorn Woodland

Description: There are three habitation mounds recorded for this site, although more small mounds may be located in the immediate site zone. The three house platforms are on a small hill or ridge overlooking Río San Lucas. They are probably all part of the same house group.

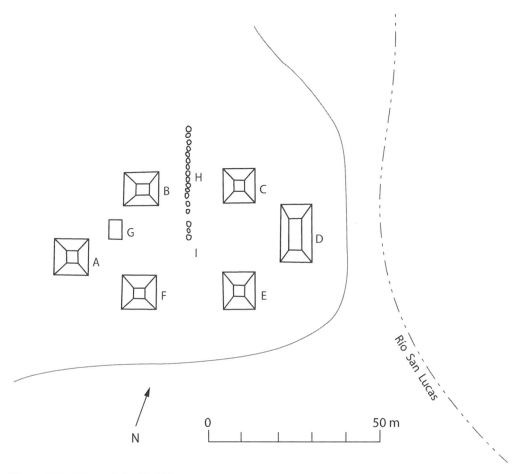

Figure 6.93. View of site Tr-188.

TR-188 MAZATLÁN
(Figure 6.93)

Site Type: Ceremonial and habitation

Occupation: Late Classic

Location and Setting: Tr-188 is located 2.25 km north of Colonia Rodolfo Figueroa on the west bank of Río San Lucas. Vegetation in the vicinity consists mainly of grasses with some palms.

Environmental Stratum: Short Tree Savannah/ Thorn Woodland

Description: The site of Tr-188 has evidence of several civic-ceremonial structures, as well as habitation mounds and terraces. The main ceremonial sector is concentrated on a bench above the river within an area of approximately 90 by 50 m. Within this area, six large structures were observed, arranged around a large open plaza area (I). Although the dimensions of the mounds are unknown, they were described as one primary pyramid, four small pyramids (A, B, C, E, and F), and one temple platform (D). Just off the northern corner of Mound A, a small mound was noted that probably functioned as an altar associated with the ceremonial structures. The large plaza (I) is partially divided in half by a long, low rock alignment (H). Finally, terraces with house platforms as well as terraces without evidence of structures have been noted, although these were not mapped or counted.

The regular arrangement of ceremonial structures around a large plaza suggests the ceremonial precinct was constructed according to an orderly plan.

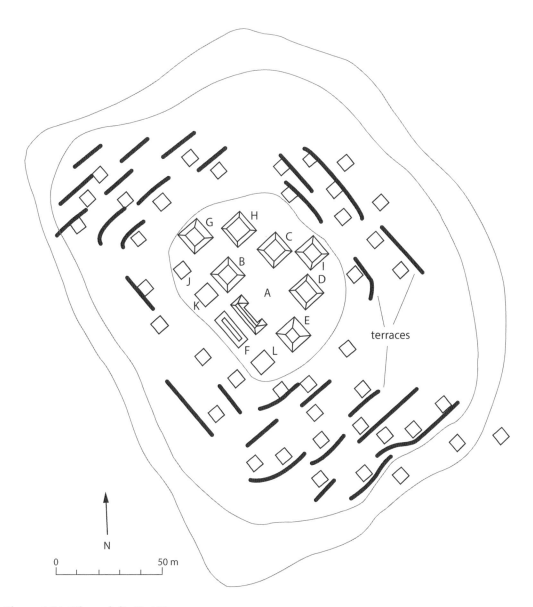

Figure 6.94. View of site Tr-189.

TR-189 (Figure 6.94)

Site Type: Ceremonial and habitation

Location and Setting: Tr-189 is located 4.25 km southeast of Colonia Las Delicias. The site is located in a valley near the head of the Río Camcum, which drains into Río Lagartero. A large rockshelter (Tr-183/Camcum Cave) is located a short distance upslope from this site (see Figure 6.89). The area is used for pasturage and milpa.

Environmental Stratum: Tropical Deciduous Forest, Riparian Forest

Description: The site of Tr-189 has evidence of ceremonial, as well as habitation occupation. Several types of architecture were noted. Structures included: pyramids of both primary and simple type, one open-sided ballcourt, primary and simple platform mounds, as well as habitation platforms.

TR-190 (Figure 6.95)

Site Type: Habitation

Occupation: Protoclassic, Late Classic

Location and Setting: Tr-190 is located 3.25 km southeast of Colonia Las Delicias. The site is situated on a low hill. Approximately 150 m east, a stream originates from a spring, flowing into Río Lagartero (see Figure 6.89). Vegetation in the vicinity consists of forest.

Environmental Stratum: Tropical Deciduous Forest

Description: The site lies on a slope; the part at the highest point has three mounds, three circular structures and two stone foundations. Further downslope, seven smaller mounds likely comprise two to three residential groups. The circular structures with openings may be ovens for burning cal or limestone.

TR-191 (no map)

Site Type: Ceremonial and habitation

Location and Setting: Tr-191 is located approximately 2.5 km southeast of Colonia Las Delicias, 0.75 km east of the Las Delicias road. The site is situated on a low hill in an area of broken hilly terrain. The vegetation in the vicinity consists primarily of deciduous forests with cleared patches used for pasture and milpa. The Camcum spring is nearby.

Environmental Stratum: Tropical Deciduous Forest

Description: Tr-191 has evidence of ceremonial and habitation occupation. Pyramids of both primary and simple type were observed. Habitation platforms were present and in some cases arranged around patios.

TR-192 CLIFF SITE (Figure 6.96)

Site Type: Ceremonial and habitation

Location and Setting: Tr-193 is located 2.5 km east and slightly south of Colonia Las Delicias. The site is situated on a high hill in an area of broken hilly terrain. Vegetation surrounding the site consists mainly of deciduous forests with clearings for pastures and milpas. A spring is located nearby.

Environmental Stratum: Tropical Deciduous Forest

Description: The fortified site of Tr-192 has evidence of ceremonial and habitation structures, as well as extensive terracing. The ceremonial structure A, a 2 m pyramid, is situated in a prominent position on the hilltop. Surrounding the pyramid is a very large U-shaped wall (B) measuring approximately 240 m long. The wall ranges in height from 1.5 to 3 m, and 1 to 1.5 m wide. The wall encloses an area of approximately 500 m². Pyramid A is the only structure visible within the walled area. On the south side of the wall a possible low entrance passage with a large boulder "lintel" was noted. A large terrace (D) measuring approximately 100 m long and 1.5 m high is located 25 m northwest of the walled ceremonial zone. No structures were visible on this terrace. Sixty meters downslope from Terrace D is another terrace (E), 130 m long and 1 m high. At the eastern end of this terrace is Mound F, measuring 1.5 m high. No other structures were visible on the terrace. Finally, south of Terrace E two small habitation terraces (G and H) were observed.

The site may have served as a defensive refuge in times of conflict. The lack of domestic structures may have resulted from such a function. Another possibility is that structures were perishable and built directly on the ground surface with no platform mounds to raise the floor.

TR-193 (no map)

Site Type: Habitation and agricultural terraces

Location and Setting: Tr-193 is located 4.5 km southeast of Colonia Las Delicias. The site is located in a small valley 200 m east of Río Camcum, which flows into Río Lagartero. The local terrain is broken and hilly. Vegetation in the site area consists of low sparse deciduous forest and grassland. The site is closed to Camcum (Tr-183) and Tr-189.

Environmental Stratum: Tropical Deciduous Forest

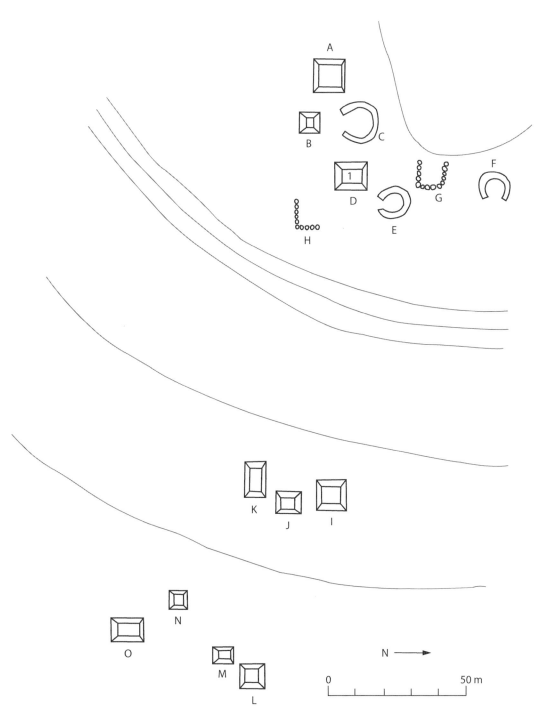

Figure 6.95. Site map of Tr-190.

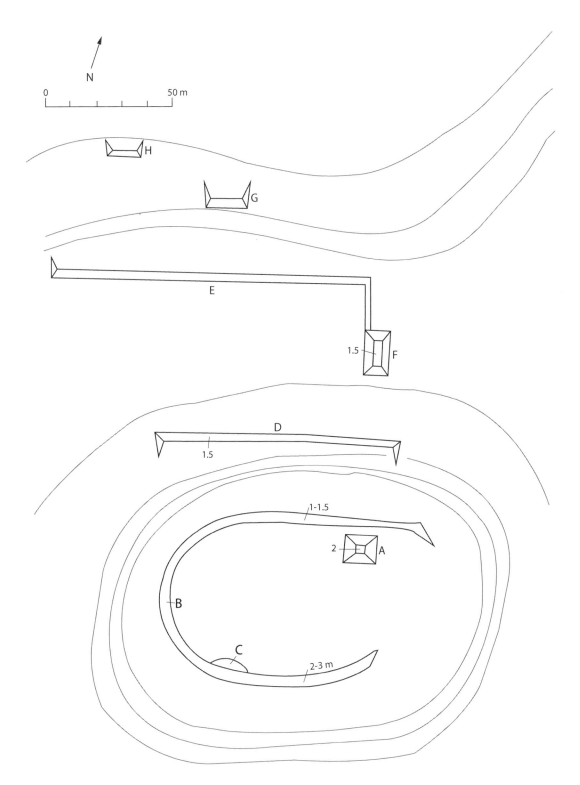

Figure 6.96. Site map of Tr-192, Cliff Site.

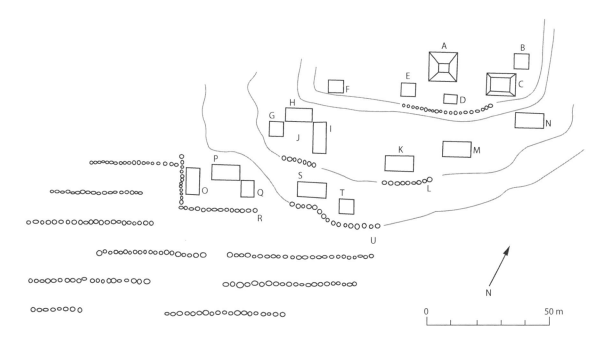

Figure 6.97. Site map of Tr-194, Barrio de la Cieneguilla.

Description: Tr-193 has some evidence of agricultural terraces. It is likely that these terraces served as habitation platforms since ceramics and lithics were found scattered over their surface. Its layout and the ephemeral nature of the habitation area fit well with a Late Preclassic pattern of occupation.

TR-194 BARRIO DE LA CIENEGUILLA
(Figure 6.97)

Site Type: Ceremonial and habitation

Location and Setting: Tr-194 is located 1.5 km west and slightly south of Colonia Morelos. The site is situated on a hilltop in an area of broken hilly terrain. The vegetation around the site consists mainly of low deciduous forest and grassland. No water source is known in the immediate vicinity of the site.

Environmental Stratum: Tropical Deciduous Forest

Description: Tr-194 is a nucleated hilltop settlement with ceremonial and habitation occupation. Mounded structures, rock-wall foundation alignments, and extensive habitation terraces are visible.

The main ceremonial precinct is located in a prominent position on the hilltop. This area, supported by a small terrace (C), includes a single medium-sized pyramid (A, height unknown), as well as a simple platform (B). In addition, on the hilltop, three small wall foundation alignments (D, E, and F), two of which are within 6 m of the pyramid, are visible. These may have served as elite residences housing religious personnel.

Downslope of the ceremonial area are several habitation terraces with the wall foundation of habitation structures. Groups G/ H/ I; O/ P/ Q; and S/ T appear to form complexes, each arranged around a common patio. Structures K/M/N may form individual households. Farther downslope are several more terraces with no visible structures. These were probably also habitation terraces.

TR-195 CUEVA FRACCIÓN LA GOMBRA
(no map)

Site Type: Ceremonial cave

Location and Setting: Tr-195 is located 4 km southeast of Colonia Las Delicias just 500 m east of the end of the dirt road from Las Delicias. The cave site is located on a high hill in an area of broken hilly terrain. Vegetation in the site area consists of low deciduous forest. A stream passes nearby.

Environmental Stratum: Tropical Deciduous Forest

Description: Tr-195 is a ceremonial cave with no evidence of habitation occupation. Lithics and ceramics were collected from the site.

TR-196 CUEVA CASIMIRA
(Figure 6.98)

Site Type: Cave

Occupation: Early Postclassic, Late Postclassic

Location and Setting: Tr-196 is located approximately 3 km southeast of Colonia Las Delicias just 500 m east of the dirt road leading from Las Delicias. The cave is situated on a high hill in an area of broken hilly terrain. Vegetation in the site area is primarily low deciduous forest. No water source is known in the immediate vicinity of the site.

Environmental Stratum: Tropical Deciduous Forest

Description: Tr-196 is a cave site with evidence of occupation at the mouth of the cave. Ceramics, lithics, and perishable materials were collected from the surface.

TR-197 CUEVA CALAVERA
(Figure 6.99)

Site Type: Ceremonial cave

Occupation: Late Postclassic

Location and Setting: Tr-197 is located approximately 1.75 km east of Colonia Las Delicias. The cave is situated in a cliff face overlooking the Camcum-Canajasté Valley, approximately 1 km from the Camcum spring.

Environmental Stratum: Tropical Deciduous Forest

Description: Tr-197 is a ceremonial cave that appears to have been used primarily for cremation burials. Three Late Postclassic

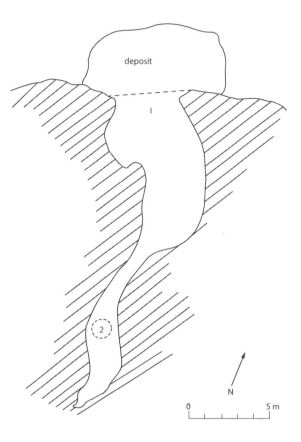

Figure 6.98. Site map of Tr-196, Cueva Casimira.

Chinautla style water jars with human cremations were found in a niche above the cave floor. The oldest jar held an individual with a mutilated tooth and 13 small pieces of gold. A fourth cremation was found broken on the floor below the niche. A human ossuary was found in another part of the site. Ceramics, lithics, and perishable materials were collected.

Site Type: Ceremonial cave

References: Lee and Clark 1988:31

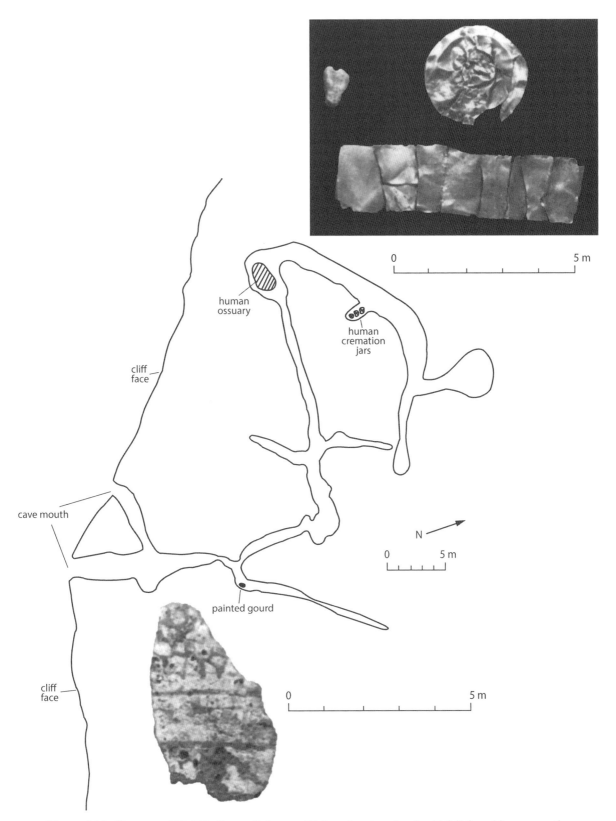

Figure 6.99. Site map of Tr-197, Cueva Calavera. Disk and rectangle of gold foil found in a cremation jar at the back of the cave and a fragment of painted gourd found near the entrance.

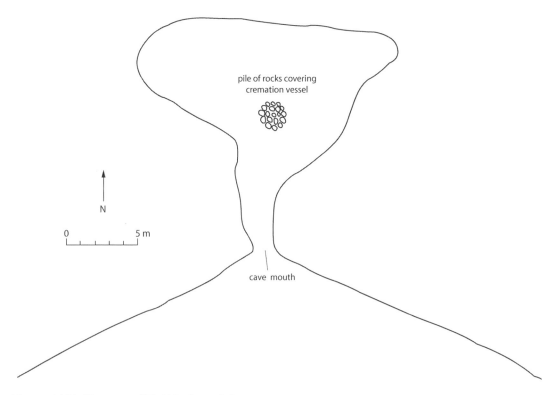

Figure 6.100. Site map of Tr-198, Cueva Masacuata

TR-198 CUEVA MASACUATA
(Figure 6.100)

Site Type: Ceremonial cave

Location and Setting: Tr-198 is located
1.8 km east of Colonia Las Delicias. The cave is
situated in a cliff face overlooking the Camcum-
Canajasté Valley, approximately 1 km from the
Camcum spring.

Environmental Stratum: Tropical Deciduous
Forest

Description: Tr-198 is a small ceremonial
cave site used as a repository for a single
cremation burial. A small pile of rocks was found
covering a ceramic vessel containing the human
cremation.

TR-199 CUEVA DE MURO (no map)

Site Type: Cave (possible ceremonial)

Location and Setting: Tr-199 is located
2 km east of Colonia Las Delicias. The cave is
situated on a high hill 500 m from the Camcum
spring. Vegetation in the area consists of tropical
deciduous forest, part of the Las Delicias forest
reserve.

Environmental Stratum: Tropical Deciduous
Forest

Description: Tr-199 is a cave in the side of a
high hill 27 m above the level of the valley floor.
The cave has not been visited, and it is unknown
if it contains evidence of human use.

Figure 6.101. Cave mouth opening Tr-200, Cueva Piñuela.

TR-200 CUEVA PIÑUELA
(no map, Figure 6.101)

Site Type: Ceremonial cave

Occupation: Postclassic

Location and Setting: Tr-200 is located 3 km southeast of Colonia Las Delicias on the north side of the dirt road coming from the Colonia. The cave is situated on a low hill, roughly 500 m from a spring. Vegetation in the area consists of tropical low deciduous forest.

Environmental Stratum: Tropical Deciduous Forest

Description: Tr-200 is a ceremonial cave that appears to have been used as a human cremation repository. Cord, mat, and textile fragments were collected from the cave, as well as ceramic and lithic materials. In addition to several cremation water jars, there were some possible mat bundle burials. Local informants said that a large petate (reed mat) came from the cave, but it was untraceable.

References: Lee and Clark 1988:31-33

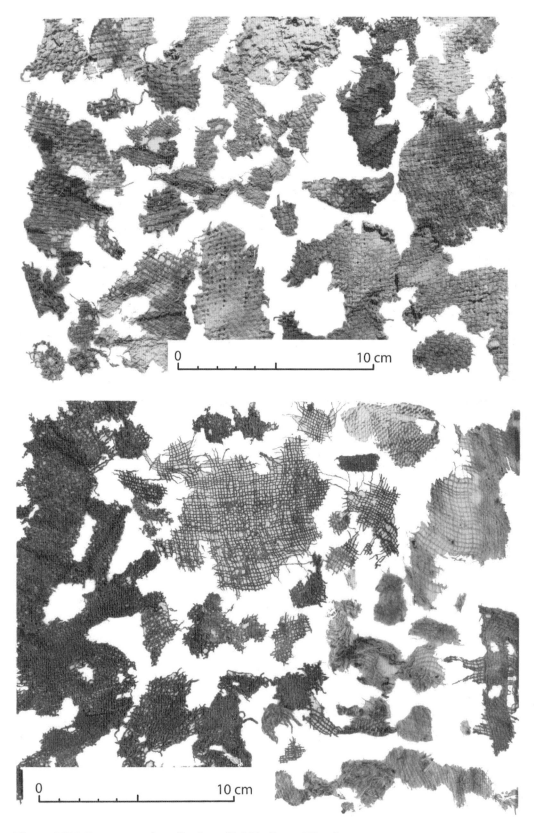

Figure 6.102. Fragments of textiles from Tr-200, Cueva Piñuela.

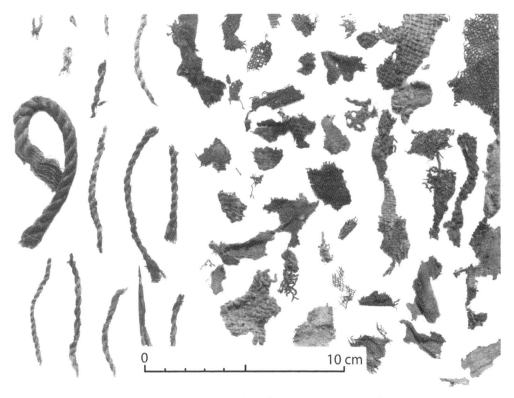

Figure 6.103. Fragments of textiles and cordage from Tr-200, Cueva Piñuela.

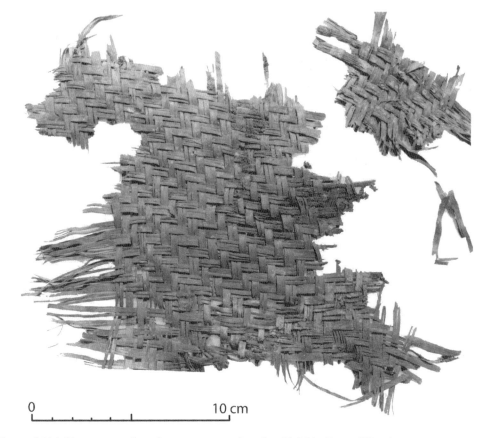

Figure 6.104. Fragments of reed mat or *petate* found at Tr-200, Cueva Piñuela.

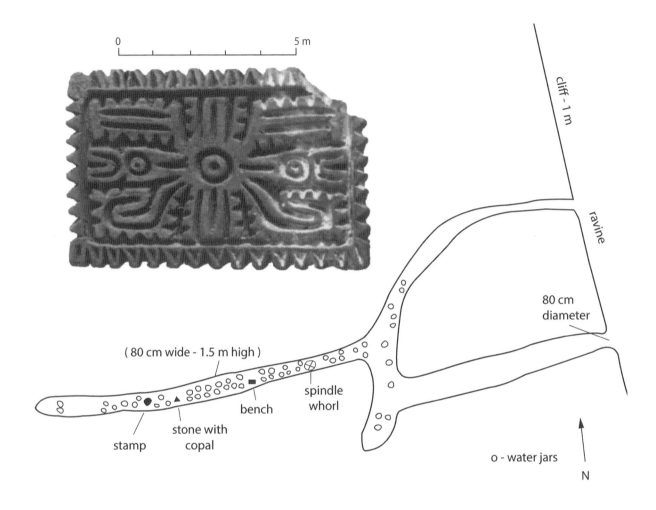

Figure 6.105. Site map of Tr-201, Cueva Pacal. Flat ceramic stamp with a hollow stem handle found in the cave.

TR-201 CUEVA PACAL (Figure 6.102)

Site Type: Ceremonial cave

Occupation: Late Postclassic

Location and Setting: Tr-201 is located approximately 1.8 km north of Colonia Las Delicias. The cave is situated in an area of broken hilly terrain. The vegetation consists mainly of low deciduous forest. No water source is recorded in the immediate vicinity of the site.

Environmental Stratum: Tropical Deciduous Forest

Description: Tr-201 is a small cave site used as a repository for human cremations. A spindle whorl with a monkey design, a pottery stamp depicting a two-headed bird, and a piece of wooden bench were recovered. Informants said jade beads and a copper ring had also been recovered. Lithic, ceramic, and perishable materials were collected from the site. The most remarkable aspect of the site is that dozens of whole and broken dull paint style water jars are located in the cave's deepest recesses.

References: Lee and Clark 1988:33

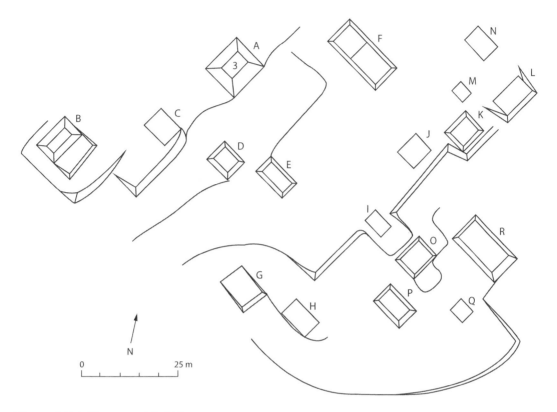

Figure 6.106. Site map of Tr-202.

TR-202 (Figure 6.103)

Site Type: Ceremonial and habitation

Occupation: Location and Setting: Tr-202 is located approximately 5.3 km east and slightly south of Colonia Las Delicias. The site is situated on a flat hilltop roughly 100 m northeast of a small stream which flows into Río Lagartero. Vegetation in the site area is mainly low deciduous forest and grassland. It is used for pasture.

Environmental Stratum: Tropical Deciduous Forest

Description: Tr-202 is a nucleated settlement with evidence of ceremonial structures, house mounds, and residential terraces. The ceremonial structures consisted of a small pyramid (A) and another pyramid (B) that had a small platform extension on its southeast side. These structures are situated at the highest point of the site. Downslope from them are located approximately five house groups. The largest group contained

Structures O, P, and R, with the possible Altar Platform Q. To its north was another large group (J, K, L, M, and N). Structure M may also have been a small altar platform.

The layout of the community as well as the shapes and sizes of the structures suggests a Late/Terminal Classic settlement in the study region.

TR-203 (no map)

Site Type: Ceremonial cave

Location and Setting: This cave is located at the foot of the cliffs overlooking the Camcum-Canajaste Valley. It is just south of Tr-204, 205, and 206.

Environmental Stratum: Tropical Deciduous Forest

Description: There were only a few scattered ceramics in the cave.

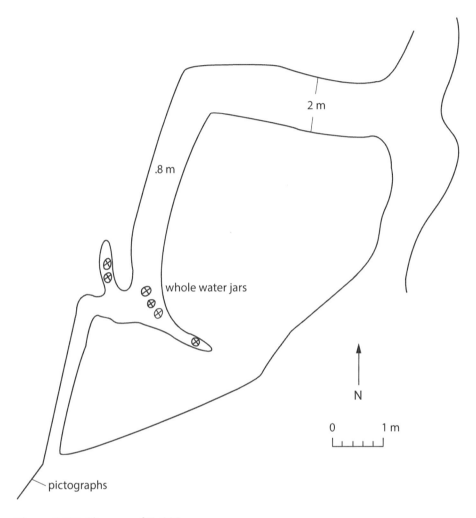

2 m

.8 m

whole water jars

N

0   1 m

pictographs

Figure 6.107. Site map of Tr-205.

TR-204 (no map)

Site Type: Ceremonial cave

Occupation: Late Postclassic

Location and Setting: Tr-204 is located 5.3 km east and slightly south of Colonia Las Delicias. The cave is situated in a cliff face on a low hill. A spring originates 500 m west of the site. Vegetation in the area consists of low deciduous forest.

Environmental Stratum: Tropical Deciduous Forest

Description: Tr-204 is a burial cave with human cremations and some crania. Six cremation

jars (some with lids), as well as crania were removed from the cave. Vessels were all the Late Postclassic three-loop-handle water jars of the dull paint style.

TR-205 (Figure 6.104)

Site Type: Ceremonial cave

Occupation: Late Postclassic

Location and Setting: This cave is located approximately 5.5 km southeast of Colonia Las Delicias. The cave is located in a cliff face formed by the collapse of an old cenote.

Environmental Stratum: Tropical Deciduous Forest

Description: Tr-205 is a cave site that was used as a repository for human cremations. The seven cremation vessels include three-loop-handle dull paint style water jars and ollas, several of which were sealed with lids. In addition, pictographs were noted on the cliff wall at the mouth of the cave. Access to the cave was quite difficult; the opening to the chambers is several meters above the bottom of the valley and less than a meter in diameter.

TR-206 (Figure 6.105)

Site Type: Cave/habitation

Location and Setting: This site is located about 5-6 km southeast of Colonia Las Delicias. It is in the same ecological zone as Tr-205. The cave is in a small valley formed by a collapsed cenote.

Environmental Stratum: Tropical Deciduous Forest

Description: This cave may have been used as a temporary habitation area. More likely, though, it was the location of ceremonial activity, judging from the pictographs. Artifacts on the surface included scattered ceramics and pieces of adobe. Pictographs were noted on the cliffs nearby the habitation area.

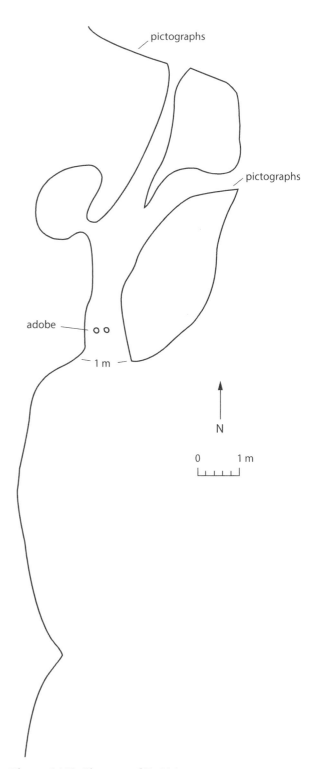

Figure 6.108. Site map of Tr-206.

CHAPTER 7

CONCLUSIONS

Mary E. Pye, John E. Clark, and Michael Blake

The extensive reconnaissance undertaken in the upper Grijalva River region resulted in the identification of over 300 sites, many of which were occupied for several centuries. As mentioned in the opening chapter, the 1973-1974 reconnaissance was not a systematic survey and did not check every square kilometer of space in the four municipalities and 3700 square kilometers represented in the sample area. Thus, we do not know what percentage of the total sites is represented by those reported here. The modus operandi of the reconnaissance was to take advantage of local knowledge and informant testimony to locate sites with obvious mounds and pyramids. The reconnaissance relied on the then current roads and trails to access different locales. The actual walk-abouts favored the low ground of cultivated valleys over the thorn-covered slopes of adjacent hills. This strategy for documenting known sites privileged those with monumental architecture over those indicated only by sherd scatters or stone alignments. Some small sites with a few house foundations and terraces are among the sites reported here, but this type of site is severely underrepresented in the sample, as revealed by later investigations. Given these limitations, our concluding assessments in this chapter of changes in settlement patterns per phase and overall population trends in the upper Grijalva region should be taken only as rough indicators rather than as hard facts. Systematic surveys in sections of the reconnoitered area subsequent to the 1973-1974 work demonstrate that Thomas Lee and his team did find the largest sites but only a minor percentage of the smallest sites.

To cite the most obvious case, Olivier de Montmollin's survey (1989a, 1989b, 1989c) of the Rosario Valley in 1983 revealed a significant difference in captured information between Lee's reconnaissance and de Montmollin's full-coverage survey. The Rosario Valley lies in the southwest corner of the region surveyed by Lee and reported here. De Montmollin's survey of this valley covered 52.65 km[2] and documented 213 sites. Of these, only 36 were located by Lee (cf. de Montmollin 1989b:3, Appendix 1) – 16.9 percent of all sites, or fewer than one in five. Most of the additional 177 sites found by de Montmollin in his full coverage survey were small clusters of stone foundations and terraces found on the slopes of hillsides. One should not get too distracted, however, by the low percentage of sites found in Lee's reconnaissance and reported here. Much depends on how individual sites were identified and delimited, their visibility, and access to these areas in a pickup in the 1970s. In terms of total hectares of occupation in the Rosario Valley, the sites found by Lee represent a third or more of the total occupation of the valley. The sites underrepresented in the original reconnaissance lie mostly on hill slopes in thorn forest. This is an environmental circumstance characteristic of the northern edge of the municipality of La Trinitaria in the transition zone between the upper Grijalva Valley and the adjacent Comitan Plateau to the north. This is to say that the disparity in the number of sites reported by Lee – and the actual number found later in the Rosario Valley – cannot be extrapolated to the total survey area. Different environmental circumstances are involved. Most of the sites in cultivated valleys were found in the reconnaissance, and the municipalities to the south of La Trinitaria are mostly flat land, thus a higher percentage of sites should have been found in these municipalities. It is well to point out that there is a southern piedmont zone even farther south that flanks the northern slope of the Sierra Madre Mountains. We have no independent check on the representation of sites found in this zone compared to their actual number. Nonetheless, we suspect the disparity between observed and actual is less on the southern flank because these slopes are generally much steeper, higher, and much less habitable than those to the north in the La Trinitaria municipality (see Lowe 1959).

The bias in Lee's reconnaissance revealed by de Montmollin also has a temporal dimension. Almost all the small sites he found on hillsides date to the Late and Terminal Classic period (de Montmollin 1989b, 1989c, 1995). As discussed in this chapter, most of the earlier settlements were on valley floors and close to rivers or streams. This pattern also is apparent in de Montmollin's findings. For example, he reports eight Late Preclassic sites with pyramids (de Montmollin1980b:20-21), which he argues represent a hierarchy of settlement. Of these, six were reported by Lee, or 75 percent. Lee's reconnaissance favored the discovery of Preclassic sites and by so doing disadvantaged the discovery of small Late Classic sites. Late Classic settlement in the upper Grijalva Valley is described and analyzed in detail in various publications by de Montmollin (1989a, 1989b, 1989c, 1995), but under his gaze earlier occupation was little more than a footnote and prelude to Late Classic developments. He lumped the first 2000 years of valley occupation into two periods to provide a very rough picture of antecedents. In contrast, in the following descriptions we deal with the evidence for all periods on a phase-by-phase basis, beginning with the earliest and proceeding chronologically to Colonial times.

PATTERNS OF SETTLEMENT IN THE UPPER GRIJALVA VALLEY

In the following sections we describe settlement patterns for the upper Grijalva Valley and then compare its demographic profile to those of other regions of the Chiapas interior. Accompanying maps show the locations of the sites with known occupation for each phase, along with sites that may have been occupied but for which the few artifacts found do not allow us to confirm the suspected occupation (Table 7.1), generally because the sherds in question are too small or too eroded for a secure identification of their type. It is worth noting that we take the presence of sherds at a site identified to a phase as evidence of occupation at that site for that phase but do not automatically

extrapolate the identified temporal periods to the age of mounds, ballcourts, or other cultural features recorded for the site. The identification of phases for a site is only as strong as the ceramic information available, and for most sites these are sherds collected during unsystematic survey. As is well appreciated, some phases are characterized by ceramic complexes that have more diagnostic traits than others, and with wares and modes that preserve better than others (see Bryant et al. 2005), hence, it is easier to identify these phases at sites than other phases. Indeed, those sites in the text with specific phase names had strong diagnostic ceramics associated with them; those sites with only the more general era marker, such as "Postclassic," indicate less surety. Sites listed as "possible" suggest an even lesser degree of certainty and are underlined in Table 7.1 and in italics in the period maps. Finally, some of the periods of low occupation discussed below (namely, the Middle Classic and Early Postclassic periods) may be underrepresented because of the more limited number of diagnostics characteristic of their ceramic assemblages.

As discussed in Chapter 1, a number of sites were excavated (see Table 1.2), some intensively, and information from the excavations offers key insights into the nature of occupation in the upper Grijalva River Valley for different periods of time. We have minimal information for the beginning and ending of pre-Hispanic human occupation in this region but excellent information for the Middle Preclassic and Late Classic periods.

LATE ARCHAIC PERIOD (2500-1900 BC) (FIGURE 7.1)

Only one site in the region of Lee's reconnaissance was determined to have had an Archaic occupation, but that was only after excavations were undertaken there in 1979-80 (Lee and Clark 1988). The site of Camcum (Tr-183) is a rockshelter located near Colonia Las Delicias. The rockshelter lies in a crag of a ridge overlooking the Camcum spring. This spring, probably the largest in the area, is the source for the Camcum River, which farther south joins the Lagartero River.

Camcum is a particularly attractive locale that offers freshwater, shelter, and food. The Camcum rockshelter is wide and shallow, but it is deep enough to offer shelter from the rain and a cramped living space for 10 to 20 people. The plentiful food source most close at hand is the freshwater snail, *xute* or *Pachychilus* sp., shells of which were found by the tens of thousands in the shell talus-midden spilling out of the mouth of the rockshelter. The thin, bottommost stratum of this midden lacked sherds but had chips of chert of various kinds. No carbon was obtained to date this stratum, but the immediate overlying layers with the oldest sherds was radiocarbon dated to the Early Formative period (Clark 1991:109). It is not certain that this aceramic level dates to the Late Archaic period, but if it does, it likely was at the very end of the period. There is no evidence of a cultural break in occupation between this midden layer and those that followed.

The Late Archaic is a poorly known period for Mesoamerica, although the state of Chiapas has more evidence of it than most regions (Clark and Cheetham 2002). Although Camcum is the only candidate for an Archaic site found thus far in the upper Grijalva Valley (Lee 1991), Archaic occupations have been documented in the highlands to the west around San Cristóbal de las Casas and Teopisca (García-Bárcena 1982; Guevara Sánchez 1981). More detailed information exists from excavations at the Santa Marta Rockshelter (Acosta 2008; García-Bárcena and Santamaría 1982; MacNeish and Peterson 1962), as well as from the Soconusco area of the Pacific Coast (Voorhies 1976, 2004, 2015). Camcum differs from these other Archaic sites in that it was visited and occupied off and on throughout the pre-Hispanic period.

LATO PERIOD (1700-1500 BC)
(FIGURE 7.2)

Excavations at Camcum (Tr-183) also uncovered ceramic evidence of Lato phase occupation in stratigraphic context. Sherds of this era were also found in mixed mound fill and midden at Portrero Mango (Tr-172), Entre Ríos (Tr-109), and Santa Marta Rosario (Tr-19). These were small numbers of sherds recovered from basal and mixed deposits, with the largest

sample being from Camcum (Clark 1991; Clark, Arroyo et al. 2005). Entre Ríos and Portrero Mango are both small ceremonial centers primarily dating to Preclassic and Protoclassic times. Both are proximate to the large Middle Preclassic center of La Libertad and lie on benches overlooking the Dolores River. Santa Marta Rosario was a Middle Preclassic civic-ceremonial center of some 3-5 ha in extent located in a bend of the Santa Inés River. West of these sites, in the Chicomuselo municipality, Ch-15 lies in a bend of the Chicomuselo River. Ch-15 consists of two small house platforms dating to the Late Classic period located on a bench above the river, but it was an eroding area on the hilltop 100 m from these platforms that revealed the Preclassic deposits. All of these sites had ready access to permanent and substantial freshwater. It should also be noted that these finds of early sites were uncovered either by excavation or erosion. Clearly, early settlement is not well represented on the surface; their underrepresentation is likely due to their concealment under later cultural and natural deposits.

OJALÁ PERIOD (1500-1300 BC)
(FIGURE 7.3)

The sites occupied during this phase mirror those of the preceding Lato phase. Again, ceramic samples are small, with the largest sample coming from Camcum. The Early Preclassic Lato and Ojalá phases remain poorly understood in terms of settlement patterns. The temporal distinctions of these Early Preclassic sites in the upper Grijalva are based on typological comparisons of survey ceramics with ceramics from Pacific Coast sites for which we have extensive, excavated samples (see Blake et al. 1995; Clark and Cheetham 2005; Lowe 1975). Phase names for early ceramic complexes in the upper Grijalva region were chosen to reflect similarities between ceramic assemblages by having them begin with the same letters. The Lato complex in the upper Grijalva region parallels the Locona complex of the Pacific Coast, and the Ojalá complex parallels the Ocós and Cherla complexes (Blake et al. 1995; Clark 1991; Clark, Arroyo et al. 2005). Lato phase sites

Table 7.1. Sites by phase and by municipality. Underlined numbers are sites that possibly date to that phase. The maximum site totals include the possible sites.

Phase	Trinitaria (Tr-)	Comalapa (Co-)	Chicomuselo (Ch-)	Bella Vista (BV-)	Max	Min
Archaic	183				1	1
Lato	19, 109, 172, 183		15		5	5
Ojalá	19, 109, 172, 183		15		5	5
Chacaj- IA	3, 19, <u>42</u>, 99, 109, 172, 183	4	15, <u>28</u>		10	8
Jocote- IB	19, 109, 172, 183		15, <u>28</u>		6	5
Chacte- IIA	19, 99, 109, 133, 172, 183	<u>13</u>	58		8	7
Dyosan- IIB	19, 99, 109, 133, 152, 172, 183		58		8	8
Enub- III	16, 19, 108, 114, 137, 153, 157, 159, 172, 183	6/25, 10, 14, 19, 60	31, <u>35</u>, 38, <u>40</u>, <u>41</u>, <u>54</u>, 58		22	18
Foko- IV	19, 38, 49, 90, 108, 114, 130, 137, 152, 156, 157, 159, 178, 183	10, 14, 22, 51, 60	<u>55</u>	3	21	20
Guajil- V	15, 19, 30, 37, 38, 47, 49, 80, 90, 108, 110, 113, 114, 116/164, <u>131</u>, 132, 133, 136, 137, 152, 153, 155, 156, 171, 172, 178, 183, 186	4, <u>6/25</u>, 8, 11, 15, 16, <u>21</u>, <u>22</u>, <u>24</u>, 51, 54, 59, <u>61</u>, 63, 69	<u>7</u>, <u>15</u>, 22, 23, <u>48</u>, 65		49	40
Hun- VI	10, 13, 19, 20, 21, <u>30</u>, 32, 38, 42, 43, 44, 45, 46, 47, 50, 55, 56, 58, 66, <u>67</u>, 68, 77, 79, 80, 81, 82, 83, 85, <u>87</u>, 90, 91, <u>97</u>, <u>98</u>, 99, 105, 108, 109, 110, 112, 114, 116/164, 118, 121, 122, 130, 132, 133, <u>136</u>, 137, 138, 140, <u>143</u>, 145, 152, 154, 156, <u>157</u>, 158, 161, 171, 172, 178, 183, 190	<u>6/25</u>, <u>7</u>, 8, 18, 66, 67	8, 33, 48, <u>54</u>, 57, 65	1, 3	78	67
Ix- VII	10, 13, 19, 20, 21, 32, 38, 42, 43, 44, 46, 50, 55, 56, 58, <u>67</u>, 68, 79, 81, 82, 83, 85, 91, 99, 105, 109, 112, 116/164, 118, 121, 122, 130, 138, <u>139</u>, 140, 145, 152, 153, 154, 158, 161, 171, 172, 183, 190	<u>7</u>, 8, 18, 59, 66, 67	8, 13, 19, 21, <u>29</u>, 31, 33, 48, 57, 65	1, 3	63	59
Kau- VIII	<u>2</u>, 8, 9, 24, 25, <u>38</u>, 42, 43, 44, 49, <u>54</u>, 55, 56, 84, 106, 130, 140, 146, 148, 150, 152, 153, 155, 172, 178, <u>187</u>	<u>12</u>, 58	8, <u>9</u>, 21, <u>50</u>, <u>57</u>, 58, 62	3	36	28
Lek- IX	4, 9, 25, 42, 44, 55, 84, 112, 145, 152, 161, 172, 178, 187	16, 59	<u>9</u>, 27		18	17

Phase	Trinitaria (Tr-)	Comalapa (Co-)	Chicomuselo (Ch-)	Bella Vista (BV-)	Max	Min
Mix- X	1, 2, 3, 4, 5, 6, 7, 8, 9, 11, 13, 15, 16, 17, 20, 21, 22, 24, 25, 27, 28, 29, 30, 31, 32, 33, 34, 35, 36, 37, 39, 40, 41, 42, 43, 44, 45, 46, 47, 48, 49, 50, 51, 52, 53, 54, 55, 56, 57, 58, 59, 60, 62, 63, 65, 66, 67, 68, 70, 73, 74, 75, 76, 77, 82, 83, 84, 85, 86, <u>87</u>, 88, 90, 91, 92, 93, 94, 96, 97, 98, 99, 104, 106, 107, 105, 108, 109, 110, 112, 113, 114, 115, 116/164, 118, 120, 121, 122, 125, 127, 128, 129, 130, 131, 134, 135, 136, 139, 140, 142, 143, 145, 146, 147, 148, 149, 151, 152, 154, 156, 157, 160, 167, 172, 174, 176, 178, 183, 186, 187, 188, 190	1, 2, <u>3</u>, 5, 6/25, 8, 9, 10, 12, 13, 14, 17, 18, 19, 20, 21, 22, 23, 26, 51, 52, 53, 55, 56, 58, 59, 60, 61, 62, 63, 65, 66, 67, 69	<u>3</u>, 4, 5, 7, 9, 10, 11, 13, 14, 15, 16, 19, 20, 21, 22, 26, 27, 28, 29, 30, 31, 32, 33, 36, 38, 40, 41, 42, <u>46</u>, 47, 48, 49, 50, 54, 57, 58, 61, 64	1, 3, 5, 6, 7, 8	208	204
Nichim- XI	1, 13, 24, 49, 51, 69, 94, 99, 105, 122, 157, 196	54, 59	9, 38		16	16
Tan- XII	9, 12, 13, 14, 21, 52, 55, 60, 68, 69, 73, 74, 75, 76, 81, 88, <u>92</u>, 94, 95, 99, <u>100</u>, 118, <u>121</u>, 128, 135, 146, 152, 157, 160, 161, 165, 168, 179, 183, 196, 197, 200, 201, 204, 205	1, 2, 3, 15, 16, 17, 54, 59, 62	8, 10, 14, 15, 19, 20, 25, 32, 33, 35, 37, 38, 54, 55, 56, 58, 59, 60, 61, 62, 63, 65	1, 3, 4, 5, 6, 7, 8	78	75
Colonial	95, 162	<u>1</u>, 3, 7, 15, 62, 64	1, 10, <u>63</u>		11	9
Historic			1, 10, 25, 43		4	4
NO DATE	18, 23, 26, 61, 64, 71, 72, 78, 89, 101, 102, 103, 111, 117, 119, 123, 124, 126, 141, 144, 163, 166, 169, 170, 173, 175, 177, 178, 180, 181, 182, 184, 185, 189, 191, 192, 193, 194, 195, 198, 199, 202, 203, 206	27, 57, 68	2, 6, 12, 17, 18, 24, 34, 39, 44, 45, 51, 52, 53, 66		61	61

Figure 7.1. Map of Archaic period site locations.

Figure 7.2. Map of Lato period site locations.

Figure 7.3. Map of Ojalá period site locations.

have also been reported for the Angostura region just downriver to the northwest (see Lowe 2007).

Lowe (1977, 2007) proposed that people from the Soconusco region of coastal Chiapas migrated into the Grijalva Valley and brought their ceramic technology with them. Based on historical linguistic studies, he argued that these earliest ceramic-using villagers of interior Chiapas were speakers of proto-Mixe-Zoque (Lowe 1977). He further assumed that coeval neighbors to the east in the Guatemalan highlands and to the north in the tropical lowlands spoke proto-Maya (see also, McQuown 1971; Vogt 1964). The story of the earliest pottery and villagers is complicated; their earliest roots may have been in Central America or South America (Lowe 1967, 1975; see also, Clark and Cheetham 2002; Clark and Gosser 1995; Clark and Knoll 2007). The earliest ceramics in highland Guatemala may also have come from the Pacific Coast. In the Antigua Valley of Guatemala the earliest ceramics uncovered at the sites of Rucal and Urias appear very similar to the Early Preclassic wares of El Balsamo located on the adjacent Pacific Coastal piedmont (Robinson and Pye 1997; Robinson et al. 2002).

CHACAJ PHASE (1300-1200 BC; CHIAPA IA) (FIGURE 7.4)

Early Preclassic settlement continued for the following phase at the sites of Camcum (Tr-183), Portrero Mango (Tr-172), Entre Ríos (Tr-109), Santa Marta Rosario (Tr-19), and Ch-15. Single diagnostic sherds were found at the marshy site of Lagartero (Tr-99), at Trapiche Viejo (Tr-3) located 400 m from the Santa Inés River (Clark, Arroyo et al. 2005:Table 2.3), and at Guadalupe Grijalva (Co-4) near the Blanco River. Chacaj material from the sites of Tr-3 and Co-4 was uncovered by intensive agricultural activities, again indicating that early occupations at sites in the region are present but buried. Chacaj phase sites were also reported in the Angostura Basin (Lowe 2007). The ceramic wares and forms of the Chacaj complex are similar to those of the Cuadros complex of the Pacific Coast (see, Blake et al. 1995; Clark, Arroyo et al. 2005).

Diagnostic sherds of this phase include a few Limon Incised and Calzadas Carved type examples recovered from Entre Ríos and Portrero Mango. These are types associated with the Gulf Coast site of San Lorenzo, Veracruz. The introduction of white-rim blackwares is also noted by the presence of a few Bano Black-and-white type sherds recovered from Camcum for the preceding Ojalá complex. The ceramics for the upper Grijalva region continue to show clear typological relationships with the Pacific Coast, including the presence of Gulf Coast imports (Clark, Arroyo et al. 2005). Survey in the Angostura Basin to the west of the upper Grijalva Valley uncovered Chacaj materials as well as Gulf Coast imports, and an occupation was noted for the site of Finca Acapulco (Lowe 2007:87-89).

JOCOTE PHASE (1200-1000 BC; CHIAPA IB) (FIGURE 7.5)

Settlement for this phase continued at sites that had previously seen Early Preclassic occupation (Tr-183, Tr-172, Tr-109, Tr-19, and Ch-15). No materials of this phase were reported for Tr-99, Tr-3, or Co-4, however, which had been occupied in the preceding Chacaj phase. Notably, more diagnostic sherds were recovered from this phase (n=522) than for the Chacaj phase (n=186), particularly at Entre Ríos (Tr-109) and Santa Marta Rosario (Tr-19) (Clark, Arroyo et al. 2005: tables 2.3, 2.4). The Jocote phase (200 years) was longer than the Chacaj phase (100 years), a difference that may explain the increase in diagnostic sherds present at key sites for this phase. The Jocote complex parallels the Jocotal complex of the Pacific Coast (Blake et al. 1995; Clark, Arroyo et al. 2005) and the Cotorra complex of Chiapa de Corzo (Clark and Cheetham 2005; Dixon 1959).

CHACTE PHASE (1000-850 BC; CHIAPA IIA) (FIGURE 7.6)

Evidence for occupation during this phase was found at the excavated sites of Camcum (Tr-183), Portrero Mango (Tr-172), and Santa Marta Rosario (Tr-19). No evidence for the phase was found at Ch-15, but traces were found at nearby Rancho Santa Teresa (Ch-58), a sherd scatter located adjacent to the Tachinula River. Also new was occupation at

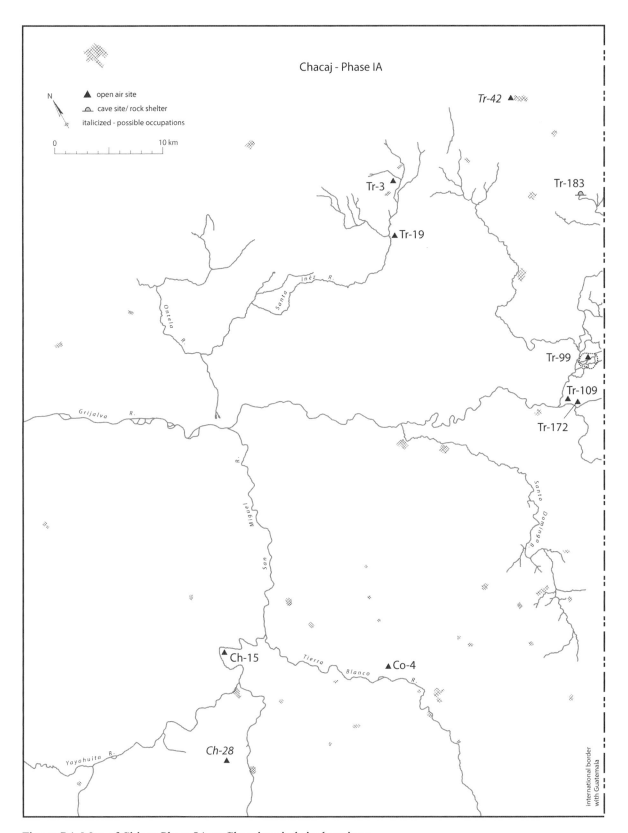

Figure 7.4. Map of Chiapa Phase IA or Chacaj period site locations.

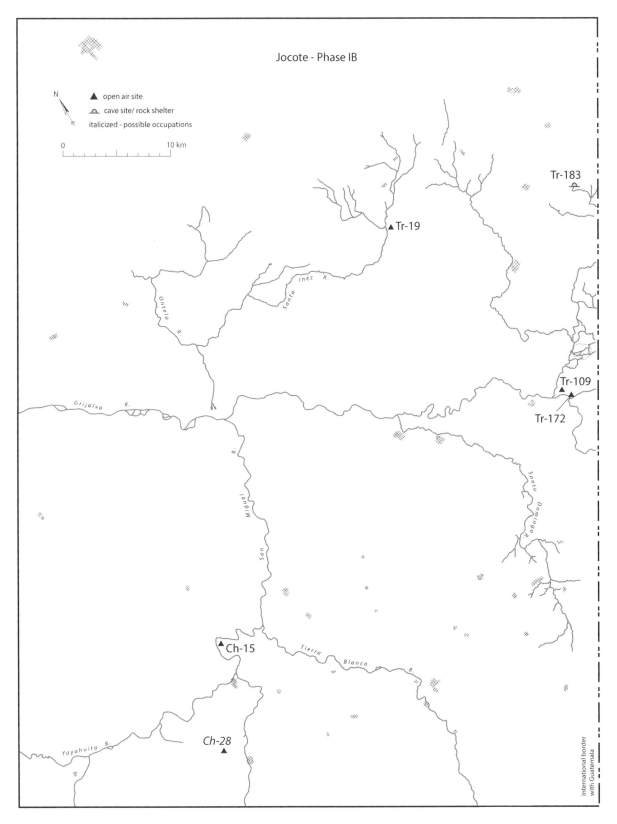

Figure 7.5. Map of Chiapa Phase IB or Jocote period site locations.

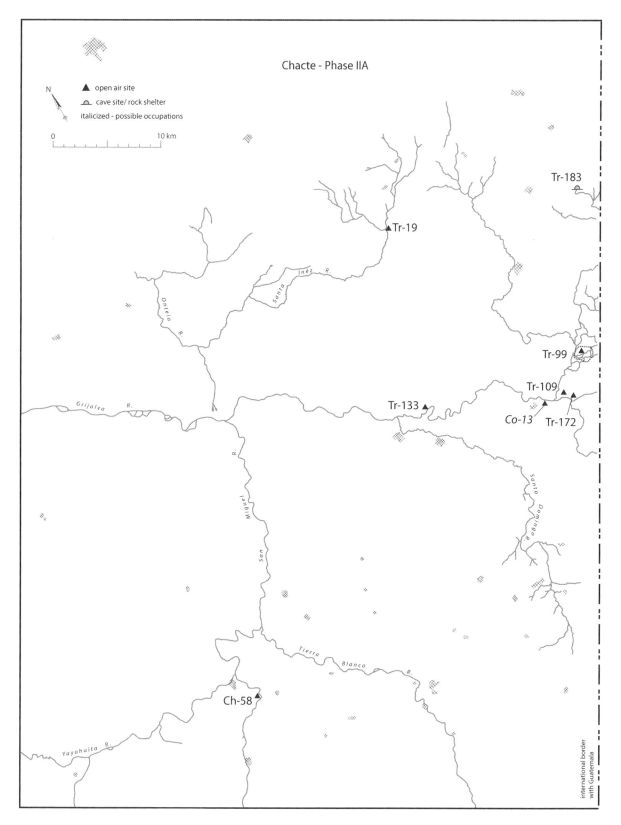

Figure 7.6. Map of Chiapa Phase IIA or Chacte period site locations.

Tr-133 on the San Gregorio River downstream from a cluster of occupied sites (Tr-109, Tr-172, and possibly Co-13) at the confluence of the Dolores and Lagartero Rivers, as well as at the site of Lagartero. The numbers of potsherds recovered from excavated sites are fewer than those of the previous Jocote period (Clark, Arroyo et al. 2005: tables 2.4 and 2.5). Most were found at Entre Ríos (Tr-109) and Santa Marta Rosario (Tr-19). Ceramic materials of the Chacte complex are similar to those of the Dili complex at Chiapa de Corzo (Dixon 1959) and the Conchas complex on the Pacific Coast (Clark and Cheetham 2005; Coe 1961; Love 2002).

The general continuity of settlement from Jocote to Chacte times in the upper Grijalva Valley, particularly for Entre Ríos and Santa Marta Rosario, contrasts markedly with settlement shifts in the Soconusco region and adjacent regions of coastal Guatemala. For example, the widespread occurrence of Jocotal sites in the Soconusco (coeval with Jocote) and in the El Mesak region of coastal Guatemala was followed by abandonment of these areas in the Conchas phase (coeval with Chacte). The single, greatest exception was a dramatic increase of Conchas occupation centered around the large ceremonial center of La Blanca in the Naranjo River Valley of coastal Guatemala and the adjacent area of Cuauhtemoc, Mexico (Love 2002; Rosenswig 2011). We argue that this new Naranjo Valley population was pulled in from surrounding areas (Clark 2001, 2016; Clark and Lowe 2013; Pye et al. 2011).

DYOSAN PHASE (850-750 BC; CHIAPA IIB) (FIGURE 7.7)

Dyosan phase occupation was noted at Camcum (Tr-183) and Santa Marta Rosario (Tr-19), as well as at Entre Ríos (Tr-109), Portrero Mango (Tr-172), and nearby Lagartero (Tr-99), thus marking continuity of settlement from the Chacte phase. Potsherds of this phase were also found at Ojo de Agua (Tr-152), a large, prominent Protoclassic and Classic period center located near a spring of the same name (Bryant 2008). None of the sites in the Chicomuselo subregion is known to have been occupied at this time.

As with the artifacts of the preceding Preclassic phases, the definition of Chiapa IIB types for the upper Grijalva Valley most closely follows those of the Soconusco sequence (Clark and Cheetham 2005). The definition of the coeval Duende complex from the coast has undergone various changes over the years, but the recent re-analysis and publication of Izapa work (Lowe et al. 2013), along with the recent re-evaluation of the survey ceramics of the Upper Grijalva River Basin Project by Clark, have led to more secure identifications of Dyosan phase sites in the upper Grijalva Valley.

ENUB PHASE (750-500 BC; CHIAPA III) (FIGURE 7.8)

This phase witnessed a dramatic increase in the number of sites in the survey region. Even if one adds up the sites dating to both the earlier Middle Preclassic phases (Chacte and Dyosan), only 8 sites and 1 possible one are known for the antecedent era. In contrast, for the Enub period there were at least 18 sites, and possibly 4 others. The Enub complex most closely parallels the Escalera complex downriver at Chiapa de Corzo rather than the Escalón complex of Izapa on the Pacific Coast (see Ekholm 1969; Lowe et al. 2013). This change in the direction of greatest cultural affinity is also true of the later ceramic complexes of the upper Grijalva region. This Middle Preclassic shift in shared ceramic complexes indicates greater contact with societies along the Grijalva River than with societies in the Soconusco region located over the Sierra Madre Mountains to the south.

A cluster of Enub phase sites was found near the confluence of the Dolores and Lagartero Rivers and just downstream along the San Gregorio River. The large center of La Libertad (Tr-157) anchored this cluster, suggesting that the smaller sites around it were satellite centers and hamlets and part of a three-tier settlement system. Test excavations were undertaken at La Libertad (Miller 2014), Mango Amate (Tr-159) (Paillés and Ávila 1987), and Tr-108 (Miller and Lowe 2014). La Libertad was the primary ceremonial center of the region during the Enub and Foko phases; it was the first of its kind in terms of size and labor investment. La Libertad extended over 45 ha and included numerous

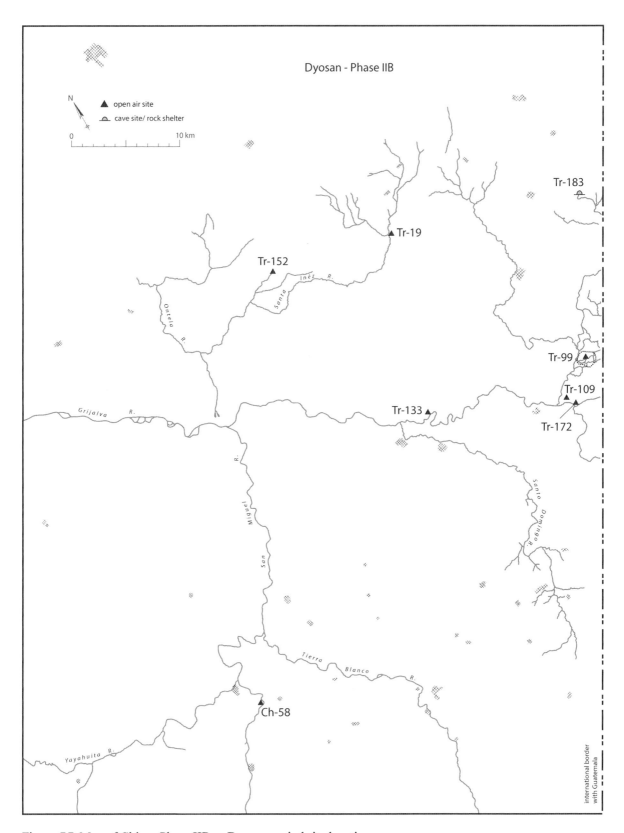

Figure 7.7. Map of Chiapa Phase IIB or Dyosan period site locations.

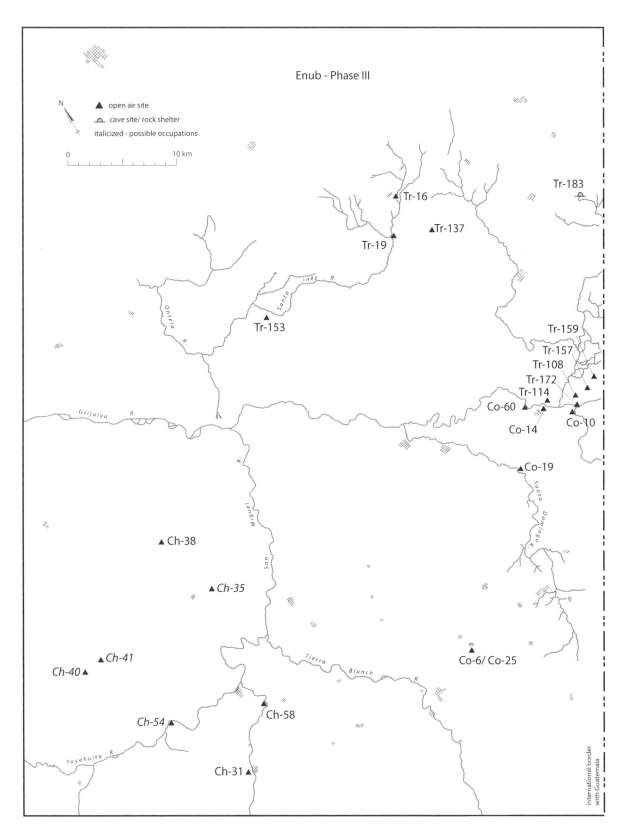

Figure 7.8. Map of Chiapa Phase III or Enub period site locations.

pyramid mounds, an E-Group, and a massive acropolis structure. Sites Tr-159, Tr-108, Tr-172, Tr-114, Co-60, Co-10, and Co-13 appear to have been smaller satellite ceremonial centers, although sites from Frontera Comalapa (Co) were unexcavated and multi-phase, hence it remains uncertain what was present at these sites in Enub times. From the excavated sites, mounds of the Enub phase and subsequent Foko phase are consistently earthen constructions, some very large and high, such as Mound 3 at La Libertad, which was some 60 m in diameter and 12 m in height when it was excavated in 1976 (Miller 2014:40-41).

Other sites with Enub phase occupation include Tr-178, Tr-19, Tr-137, and Tr-153. They were ceremonial centers that were occupied for several phases. Tr-19 (Santa Marta Rosario) and Tr-183 (Camcum) had occupation throughout the Preclassic era before Enub times. South of the San Gregorio/Grijalva River, three sites were identified with Enub material: Co-6/Co-25 and Ch-31 (both small habitation sites) and Ch-38 a multi-phase, extensive ceremonial center with pyramidal mounds. The remaining possible Enub sites in the Chicomuselo area are sherd scatters and small habitation sites.

FOKO PHASE (500-300 BC; CHIAPA IV) (FIGURE 7.9)

Settlement for the Foko phase was identified at 20 sites, with one additional possible locale. Nine of the Enub sites do not appear to have continued into Foko times, while 9 of the identified Foko sites appear to have lacked Enub occupation. These assessments could change with more intense collecting at these sites or placement of test excavations. Overall, the locations of late Middle Preclassic sites suggest a spreading out of population along rivers and streams. The satellite settlements around La Libertad (Tr-157) continued and included Tr-159, Tr-108, Tr-114, Co-14, Co-10, and Co-60. During this time, La Libertad appears to have been the regional center of a paramount chiefdom with at least a three-tier settlement hierarchy which included secondary centers and hamlets (Clark 1988). Clark and Lee (1984:264, fig. 11.8) considered Santa Marta Rosario (Tr-19) a secondary center to La Libertad during this phase. Santa Marta Rosario is about a tenth the

size of La Libertad in extent and monumentality. In contrast, de Montmollin (1989b:20) argued that Santa Marta Rosario was an independent center and the focal point of a local settlement system that included secondary and tertiary centers that had small pyramids. Elite burials at Santa Marta Rosario (Bathgate 1980) are comparable to those found at La Libertad (Miller 2014), perhaps indicative of the mutual independence of these communities within a broader shared cultural system.

Surprisingly, Foko phase artifacts were not found at Portrero Mango (Tr-172), Co-13, or Co-19. Foko sites lacking earlier Enub occupation occurred within a 20 km distance of La Libertad (at Co-51, Co-22, and Tr-90). Farther away, Tr-178 is a key site that was occupied continuously from the late Middle Preclassic up to the end of the Late Classic. Located at the edge of the La Trinitaria municipality, it lies in a strategic valley connecting the Central Highlands and the upper Grijalva region (Castellanos 2012a). Numerous sites were also found to the north of La Libertad, while farther south a small ceremonial center was found in the municipality of Bella Vista (BV-3), and other possible artifacts were found at a dense sherd scatter designated as Ch-55.

The fluorescence of La Libertad occurred during this period, as evident in extensive construction of earthen platforms and pyramids there and an increase in the size of the site. In addition, La Libertad was the easternmost of a group of large ceremonial centers of the Middle Preclassic period in Chiapas with ties to La Venta, Tabasco (Clark 2016). Referred to as "administrative centers" by Lowe (1977), these sites included Finca Acapulco and Chiapa de Corzo located downriver from La Libertad. People living at all these administrative centers shared ceramic styles and architectural configurations, such as E-groups, as well as elements of elite culture, such as burial practices (see, Bachand and Lowe 2011; Clark 2001, 2016; Clark and Hansen 2001; Lee and Clark 2016). These shared elements of cultural practices suggest that the upper Grijalva Valley, as represented by the La Libertad community, was part of an extensive political or social entity at this time (Clark 2016; Clark and Lee 1984, 2007; Lowe 1977).

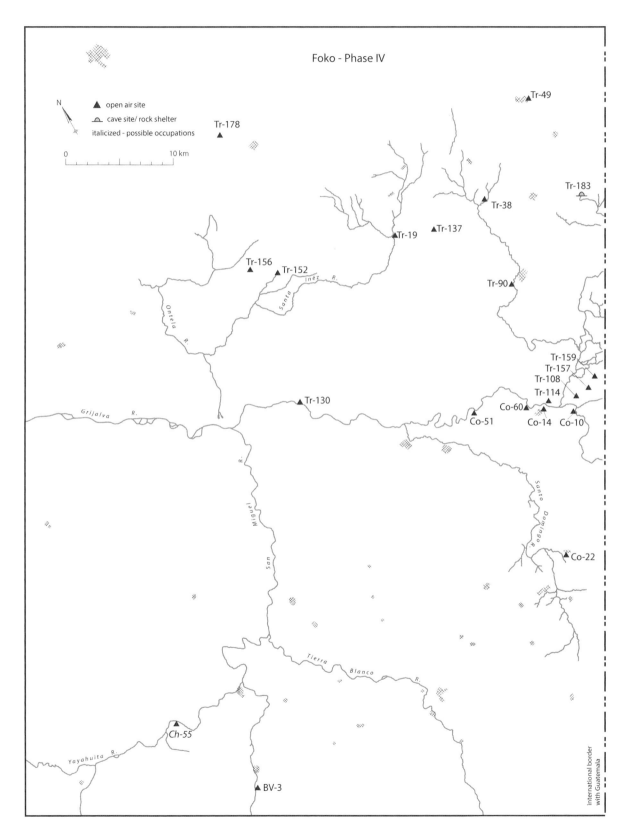

Figure 7.9. Map of Chiapa Phase IV or Foko period site locations.

GUAJIL PHASE (300-100 BC; CHIAPA V)
(FIGURE 7.10)

This is one of the more poorly known phases of the upper Grijalva Valley, but it was likely one of the most important. It represented a cultural inflection point and a change in culture and peoples. This phase saw significant changes in settlement, settlement patterns, and artifact assemblages. The number of identified sites increased to 40, with an additional 9 possible ones. The actual number of identified potsherds for Guajil phase sites, however, is minimal – one here, two there, and so on. While ceramic vessels of this phase show the continuation and development of some types from the previous Foko phase, there are fewer types currently identified for the Guajil complex. Notably, reddish-orange Mundet Red pottery was replaced by Sierra Red of the Maya Lowlands (Bryant and Clark 2005a). Other signal developments include the abandonment of La Libertad but not the secondary centers that ringed it. Overall, settlement continued to follow primary water ways, in particular in the area from the confluence of the San Gregorio and Santo Domingo Rivers west to the Guatemalan border and the confluence of the Dolores, Lagartero, and Selegua Rivers. New settlements were also founded south of the San Gregorio/ Grijalva River region constituted by the Frontera Comalapa and Chicomuselo municipalities.

The type site for the Guajil phase is Portrero Mango (Tr-172), a small site located near La Libertad (Clark, Arroyo et al. 2005). Presumably, when their community was disbanded some La Libertad inhabitants moved to nearby Portrero Mango, which had been occupied throughout the Preclassic period. It was never comparable in size, scale, or investment to La Libertad during that site's fluorescence in the Middle Preclassic period. Excavations at Portrero Mango recovered Guajil phase ceramics, although the sample of diagnostic sherds (n=772) is modest (Bryant and Clark 2005a: table 4.1). Another important site with a Late Preclassic component is Guajilar (Co-59), an impressive Late Classic site. Excavations there encountered Late Preclassic materials and structures in the southern half of

the site, most of them buried under Late Classic deposits (Lee 1976, 1978).

The nature of the Guajil phase as a key "transition" between the well-defined and thriving Middle Preclassic Enub and Foko phases and the later Protoclassic Hun and Ix phases makes it difficult to define. The key ceramic marker is Sierra Red pottery made with calcite temper, a ceramic type imported from the Maya Lowlands, perhaps by way of the Chiapas Highlands (Culbert 1965) and Comitan Plateau (Ball 1980). Imported Sierra Red pottery has been found at Ojo de Agua and Santa Marta Rosario. Imported vessels were perhaps the harbinger of, or initial marker of the appearance of, migrating peoples out of the Lowlands, perhaps propelled by the expansion of the El Mirador polity at the end of the Late Preclassic period (Bryant and Clark 1983; Clark and Hansen 2001; Clark et al. 2000; Clark and Pye 2011). While there was some continuation of ceramic types into the Guajil phase, there was minimal continuation of settlements. Only 6 sites out of 40 Guajil sites are known to have had been occupied during Foko times. Even including Enub sites, only an additional 3 sites had both Middle and Late Preclassic occupations. This temporal pattern suggests that the Maya cultural influence in the upper Grijalva region during the Late Preclassic resulted more from the movement of Mayas into the region than from trade or commerce with Lowland Maya peoples.

HUN PHASE (100 BC-AD 100; CHIAPA VI)
(FIGURE 7.11)

The early Protoclassic Hun phase witnessed an increase in the number of sites (67, with 11 more possible sites); most were located in the eastern half of the La Trinitaria municipality. There was an increase in the number of sites along the west end of the San Gregorio River, as well as a new focus of occupation in the Santa Inés River area and areas north of the confluence of the Dolores and Lagartero Rivers.

The far northwestern corner of La Trinitaria is where El Cerrito (Tr-42) was built on a flattened hilltop in the Morelos piedmont. The site had a commanding view of the small valley below. El Cerrito consists of three small pyramid

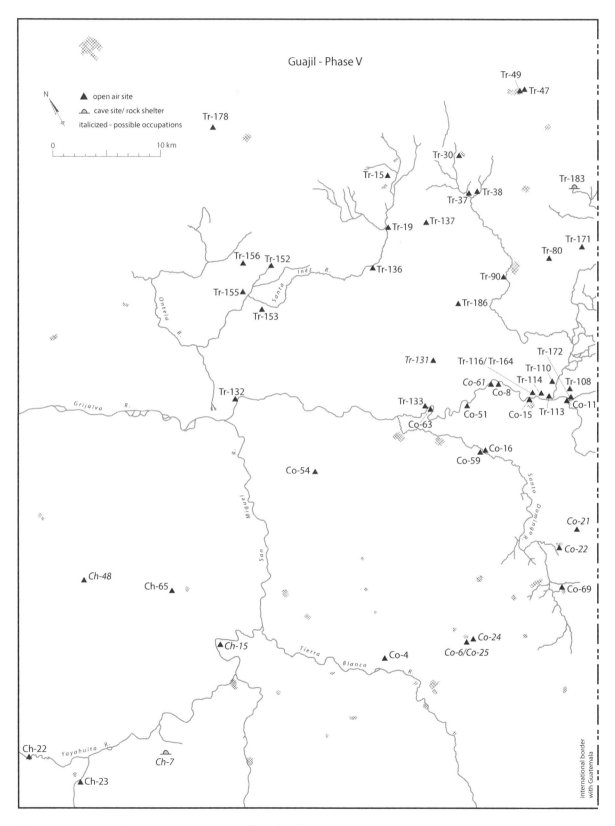

Figure 7.10. Map of Chiapa Phase V or Guajil period site locations.

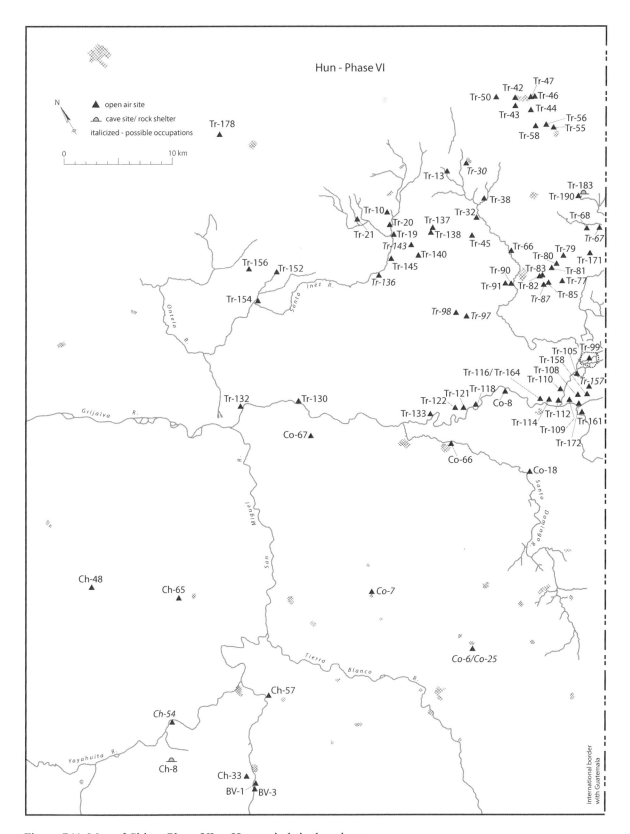

Figure 7.11. Map of Chiapa Phase VI or Hun period site locations.

mounds around a modest plaza and short-wall terraces on the descending slopes to the valley and a large spring and waterhole. Excavations in 1980 uncovered *chultunes* and housemounds and also determined that most of the site dates to the Hun phase. The site was initially identified as Late Preclassic (Bryant and Clark 1983; Clark and Lowe 1980); subsequent re-evaluation of the ceramics indicated a Protoclassic occupation. El Cerrito serves as the type site for the Hun phase in the upper Grijalva region (Clark, Lee et al. 2005:8). Eight more Protoclassic sites were found, in the Morelos Valley in addition to El Cerrito, but only one is known to have been occupied in the Late Preclassic period prior to the Hun phase. Most of these sites were new communities with different cultural practices.

To the southwest along the Santa Inés River is a cluster of 8-10 sites in the area around Santa Marta Rosario (Tr-19), of which 7-8 were also new settlements. Farther west, the site of Ojo de Agua (Tr-152) also had Hun and Ix phase occupations. Domestic midden material of the Hun and Ix phases was subsequently used as construction fill in Early Classic platforms, particularly on the northwest side of the Group C civic-ceremonial group (Bryant 2008:175-178). The full extent of the Protoclassic occupation at this site is unknown, however, because evidence for it lies buried beneath Early Classic and Late Classic occupations.

Still another cluster of new sites was created south of El Cerrito (Tr-42) and the Morelos Valley. These sites were located between the San Lucas and Lagartero Rivers (Tr-67 west to Tr-91). Of these 14 sites, 11 represented new occupations. Finally, 9 more sites were found scattered south of the Santo Domingo River in the Comalapa and Chicomuselo municipalities, a situation similar to that of the preceding Guajil phase. The focus of settlement, and especially new Hun phase settlement, was in the east and southeast areas of the survey region, a locale with a natural travel route to Chinkultic and routes from there that descend to the Maya cities of Tonina and Palenque on the northern edge of the Chiapas Central Highlands (Navarrete 1981).

The Hun phase ceramic complex consisted of some traditional types and forms as well as newly introduced wares "with a strong Maya cast" (Bryant and Clark 2005b:326). New pottery types included locally produced imitations of Sierra Red, San Felipe Brown, Escobal Red-on-buff, Flor Cream, and Polvero Black vessels. Close ceramic relationships are evident between the upper Grijalva Valley and the Chinkultic area at this time (Ball 1980:87-93). Strong Maya interaction or immigration into the upper Grijalva and east Chiapas area is indicated in the ceramics, but the antecedent Guajil ceramic complex was not completely replaced. Domestic wares continued to be made in the traditional, local style. We interpret all the evidence as indicating that some local Zoque populations remained in the subregions colonized by groups of Lowland Mayans (Bryant and Clark 2005b).

IX PHASE (AD 100-200; CHIAPA VII) (FIGURE 7.12)

The Ix ceramic complex has not been identified as a pristine assemblage at any single-component site. Rather, this complex was defined through comparative typology. Ix ceramic types are absence in the preceding Hun complex and following Kau complex, both better defined complexes (Bryant and Clark 2005b:327). There are just a few diagnostic Ix phase ceramic types; San Jacinto black pots are typically the key marker.

The sites identified with Ix phase occupation and diagnostic ceramics are the following: Ojo de Agua (Tr-152), Mango Amate (Tr-105), and Portrero Mango (Tr-172). A single San Jacinto Black bowl and some Sibak Mottled-incised (another marker) bowls were found with human burials at El Cerrito. The population at this site seems to have diminished at the beginning of the Ix phase (Bryant and Clark 2005b:348).

Given that this phase is relatively short and weakly defined, it is not surprising that the sites which are identified as having had Ix phase occupation overlap considerably with those with Hun phase occupation; 59 sites, with 4 more possible, were identified. In the municipality of La Trinitaria, only a single site (Tr-153) was identified as having an Ix phase occupation but

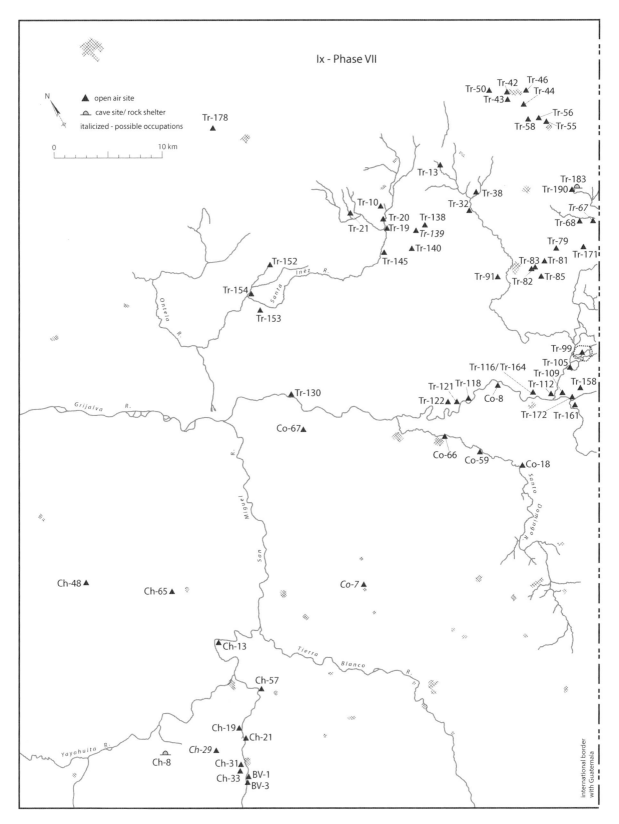

Figure 7.12. Map of Chiapa Phase VII or Ix period site locations.

lacking an earlier Hun occupation. Notably, the municipality of Chicomuselo had a cluster of Ix phase sites (n=8) along the Tachinula River, four of which lacked Hun phase occupation.

KAU PHASE (AD 200-500; CHIAPA VIII) (FIGURE 7.13)

This phase saw a significant reduction in the number of sites in the region (28, with 8 possible), and also the disappearance of occupation in key locales. In particular, settlement along the San Gregorio River, as well as along the Lagartero River, disappeared. Half of the Early Classic sites (n=13) represented a continuation of Protoclassic Ix phase occupations. A cluster of sites was present in the Morelos Valley, but the rest of the sites were scattered throughout the survey region.

A few new sites appeared around Ojo de Agua (Tr-152), which remained a thriving center during this time. Excavations there revealed an expansion of the center after the Protoclassic period; significant new construction focused on the Group C civic-ceremonial complex, which included the ballcourt. The other major site identified as having an Early Classic occupation is Tenam Rosario (Tr-9), an enormous fortified site located on the top of a small mesa. This Late Classic site covered over evidence of earlier occupation (Agrinier 1983; Clark, Lee et al. 2005). Given the number of sites in the upper Grijalva region excavated under the auspices of the NWAF, the absence of Early Classic materials at almost all sites is striking, particularly since Early Classic phase sites are numerous in the adjacent Central Highlands and Comitan Valley (Culbert 1965).

Ceramic markers of this phase are painted polychrome decoration and bowls with basal flanges. Incised decoration and highly polished monochrome slips, characteristic of the Preclassic period in the region, had disappeared by this time (Bryant 2005:398). The painted ceramics of the Kau period are simpler in design than those of their contemporaries in the Maya Lowlands; ceramic correspondences are also seen with the Chiapas Central Highlands (Culbert 1965).

LEK PHASE (AD 500-650; CHIAPA IX) (FIGURE 7.14)

The Middle Classic Lek phase is even more poorly represented in ceramic collections from the upper Grijalva than those of the preceding phase. The diagnostic sample is small (99 sherds and 12 whole vessels), the contexts from which they came are primarily ritual in nature, and the domestic wares that went along with them are unknown. This period is recognized by the evidence of Teotihuacan influence in the western half of Chiapas, but Teotihuacan-related artifacts are scarce in more eastern regions, i.e., the Angostura Basin, Comitan Valley, and Chiapas Central Highlands (Agrinier and Bryant 2005:412). Three sites of the upper Grijalva region have identified Lek phase artifacts and, hence, Lek phase occupation: Ojo de Agua (Tr-152), Tenam Rosario (Tr-9), and Lagartero (Tr-106). All three regional centers had both Early and Late Classic occupations. A Lek phase tomb and cache were found at Ojo de Agua, and another cache and burial of this phase were discovered at Tenam Rosario (Clark, Lee et al. 2005:10). Recent excavations at Lagartero recovered an early pyramid with talud-tablero facades somewhat like those from Teotihuacan (Sonia Rivero, personal communication to Clark, 2015).

Of the identified Lek sites (17, with one possible site), only one lacks an Early or Late Classic component: Dolores Puente (Tr-161), where a fragment of a Teotihuacan slab foot was recovered from the surface. Protoclassic and Late Postclassic ceramics were also found at this site. In his full-coverage survey of the Rosario Valley, de Montmollin (1989b, 1989c) did not find evidence of this period. He supposed there was a hiatus in occupation at this time. The absence of Middle Classic sites in the upper Grijalva region makes the population surge during the ensuing Late Classic period all the more remarkable.

MIX PHASE (AD 650-900; CHIAPA X) (FIGURE 7.15, 7.16)

The Late Classic was a period of fluorescence in the upper Grijalva region, as evident in the hundreds of sites and large

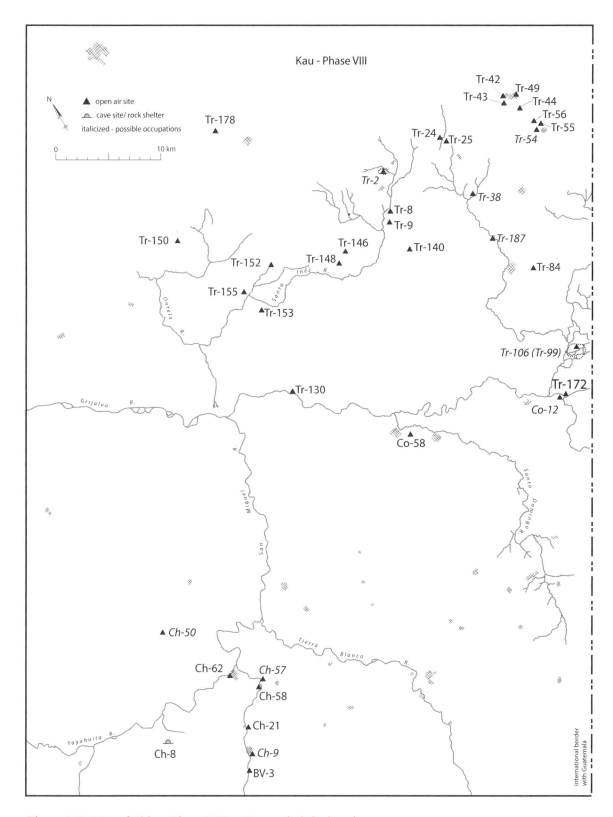

Figure 7.13. Map of Chiapa Phase VIII or Kau period site locations.

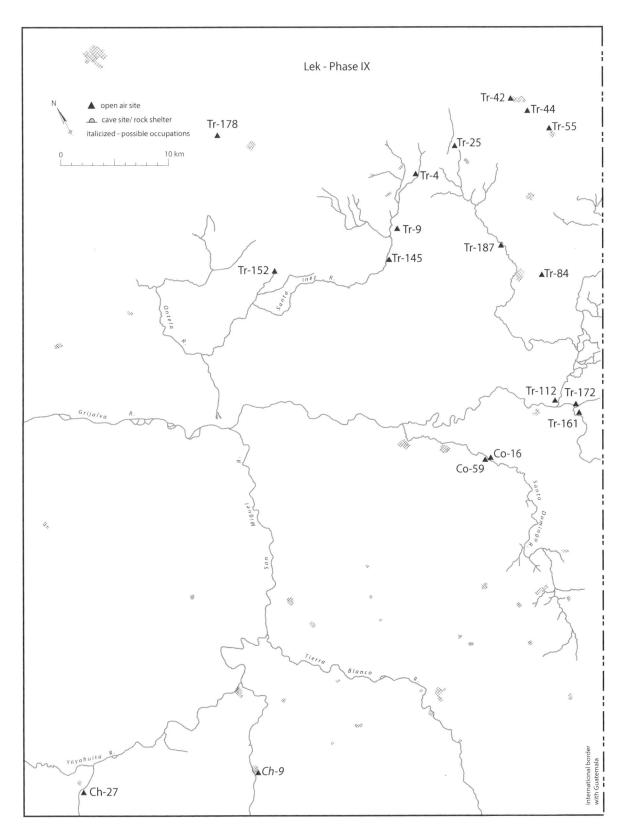

Figure 7.14. Map of Chiapa Phase IX or Lek period site locations.

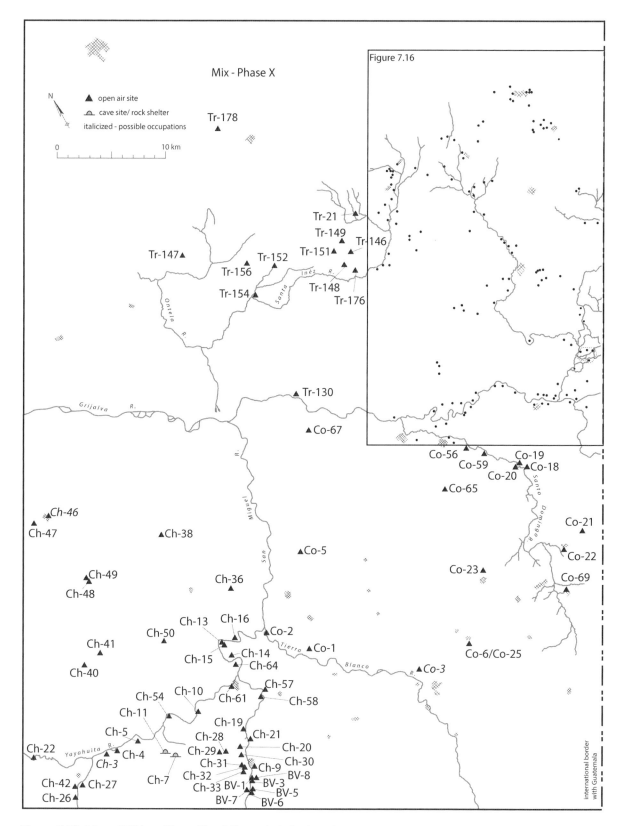

Figure 7.15. Map of Chiapa Phase X or Mix period site locations.

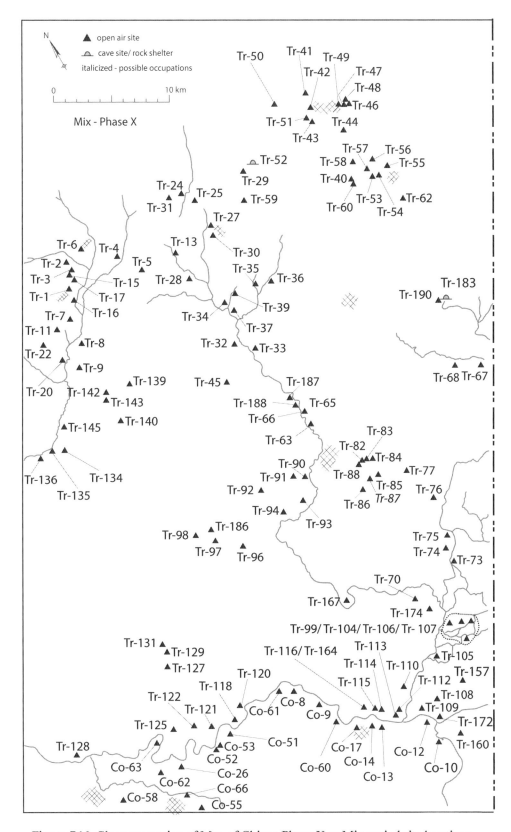

Figure 7.16. Close-up section of Map of Chiapa Phase X or Mix period site locations.

ceremonial centers found there so far. The Upper Grijalva River Basin Project documented at least 204 Late Classic site components, and several hundred more have been recorded since (e.g., Clark and Lowe 1980; de Montmollin 1989a, 1989b, 1989c, 1995; Rivero 1990). Overall, settlement was densely clustered along rivers and tributaries, but most new sites were in areas away from primary bodies of water, particularly in the municipality of Chicomuselo (e.g., Ch-46, Ch-47, Ch-38, Ch-48, Ch-49). Of those reported here for the 1973-74 reconnaissance, between 90-104 sites were first-time occupations – phenomenal new growth indicative of rapid population increase in this phase.

There were many large Late Classic centers, and many of these appear to have been capitals of small state societies (de Montmollin 1995). Extensive test excavations carried out at Lagartero, Tenam Rosario, Guajilar, and Ojo de Agua recovered ceramic vessels and potsherds that were used to define the Mix ceramic complex. Lagartero exhibits Late Classic occupation across much of its full extent, but Tr-99 is the sector where the ceremonial core was located. On this island at the site's southern end (Rivero 2001) are 170 mounds and 11 plazas. Tenam Rosario was built on a completely different kind of landscape. It is on a defendable hilltop, and its stone-faced pyramids, numerous plazas, and ballcourts spread over some 15 ha (Agrinier 1983). For its part, Guajilar has a Preclassic site arrangement, with its pyramids and plazas laid out in a line parallel to the Santo Domingo River. Its six tall and massive pyramidal mounds range from 7 to 17 m in height. Many were built over Preclassic mounds. Guajilar with is closely grouped mounds covers 16 ha (Lee 1978). Ojo de Agua, a thriving regional center from the Early Classic period, experienced another fluorescence in Late Classic times that included expansion of earlier platforms and new ceremonial construction. House mounds at the site are dispersed over 400 ha (Bryant 2008:10).

The Late Classic period was by far the period of maximum occupation in the upper Grijalva Valley. It appears clear that many of these people moved in from elsewhere into a region that had been virtually abandoned three

centuries earlier. The obvious source of many of these people would have been the Maya Lowlands (Adams 1961; Lowe 1959:15-18; Martínez 1987:251), which suffered a massive depopulation at this same period. We think all the upper Grijalva Valley was colonized by Maya speakers, likely representing several different dialectal groups. Shelley Wells (2015) argues that burial practices at different Late Classic centers showed marked differences. Based on stylistic similarities in their stone sculpture, Pierre Agrinier (1983) proposed that the people who built Tenam Rosario came from the Yaxchilan area of the Usumacinta. The situation at the time of the Spanish Conquest was that four or five different Maya groups (of different dialects) occupied the upper Grijalva Valley or upper tributaries region (Campbell 1988). This multilingual situation likely began during Protoclassic times; it certainly became more complex in Late Classic times. The region was heavily populated by the Late Classic period, but it was not a cultural unity. As mentioned, de Montmollin (1995) characterized it as divided among many small state societies. Many of these may have been of speakers of different Maya languages. Much more work needs to be done to determine cultural differences among these proposed polities.

Cultural practices that began in the Mix phase of the Late Classic period and continued into Postclassic times included secondary burial of human bones and burial of cremated human remains in large jars or small urns. Cremation and secondary burials are found at sites that had been vacated long before the time of burial. As previously noted, numerous shallow burials dating to the Late Classic and Postclassic periods were placed in the tops of Middle Preclassic mounds at La Libertad. These intrusive burials are typically in poor condition; their layouts suggest that the human remains were flexed or bundled and sometimes accompanied by identifiable ceramic vessels or metal artifacts (Miller 2014:71-166). By Late Classic times La Libertad would have been a relic site and perhaps a venerated shine. Cremation burials were sometimes accompanied with other kinds of artifacts, as reported for Guajilar (Bryant n.d.).

NICHIM PHASE (AD 900-1200; CHIAPA XI) (FIGURE 7.17)

The number of sites identified for this phase throughout the survey region represents a drastic reduction of occupation. Only 16 sites of this period are known. With two exceptions, all these Early Postclassic sites had Late Classic occupations. Analysis of the ceramics of these periods reveals the continuity of styles and modes. In fact, the continuities between Late Classic and Postclassic ceramics make it difficult to distinguish utilitarian pottery for these periods. This analytical problem may be a contributing factor to the lower numbers of sites identified for this period (Bryant, Lee et al. 2005); thus, we are not super-confident that the Early Postclassic period experienced the full demographic collapse the current numbers of sites appear to indicate. The key ceramic marker for this period in southern Mesoamerica is Plumbate pottery, but it was uncommon in the upper Grijalva region (Bryant, Lee et al. 2005). While the upper Grijalva did not suffer complete abandonment or collapse at this time, as did the southern Maya Lowlands, there clearly was a dramatic reduction in population. This population history contrasts with the thriving centers in the Central Highlands to the northwest and continued occupation on the adjacent Comitan Plateau around the center of Chinkultic (Ball 1980).

In the upper Grijalva Valley, the excavated sites of Los Encuentros, Guajilar, and Canajasté all had Early and Late Postclassic occupations, although the Canajasté occupation was likely late Nichim in date (Blake 2010:61). Guajilar, a primary center from Late Classic times, experienced a continuation of occupation into this period (Lee 1978). Los Encuentros was apparently first settled in the Late Classic but largely built during the Nichim phase, including the ceremonial center and southern end of the site (Lee and Bryant n.d.). The fact that the ceramic complex for this phase can be recognized at some sites supports the notion that the failure to detect it at others elsewhere in the region is not a recognition problem but evidence of depopulation.

TAN PHASE (AD 1200-1500; CHIAPA XII) (FIGURE 7.18)

According to our rough census of occupied sites per phase, the Late Postclassic period or Tan phase, saw a demographic rebound in the region, as indicated by 75 sites identified and another 3 possible sites. Site clusters were found around the confluence of the Dolores and Lagartero Rivers to the northeast, along the San Lucas River to the north, and along the San Gregorio to the west. A cluster of small habitational sites consisting of housemounds, some with small ceremonial components, was identified along the Yayahuita and Tachinula Rivers, almost half of which were new occupations in this phase. Areas that were not reoccupied after the Late Classic fluorescence include the Morelos Valley in the northeast corner of the survey region (only 2 sites in the Nichim period) and along the Santo Domingo River southwest of the confluence of the Dolores and San Gregorio Rivers. Diminished settlement was also noted along the Santa Inés River.

Other features of Late Postclassic occupation include secondary burials and cremation burials in small water jars; these have been found in abandoned sites such as La Libertad (Miller 2014:71-166) and in multi-phase sites such as Guajilar. Another noteworthy practice of this era was the ritual use of caves; fifteen with Late Postclassic remains have been identified. At least one of these caves had several hundred cremation jars (Lee and Clark 1988:28-33).

As mentioned above, the primary sites of Los Encuentros, Guajilar, and Canajasté all had Late Postclassic inhabitants. These three communities had very different physical configurations. Guajilar started as a Middle Preclassic ceremonial center, and its early linear layout was followed for the rest of its history through the Late Classic into Postclassic times. Some expansion and remodeling at the site occurred during Postclassic times, but overall it appears that Postclassic people continued living on the Late Classic site as it had been. In contrast, Los Encuentros was a dispersed ceremonial center with a main plaza and its defining mounds. Long, narrow "range" structures are present and are considered an

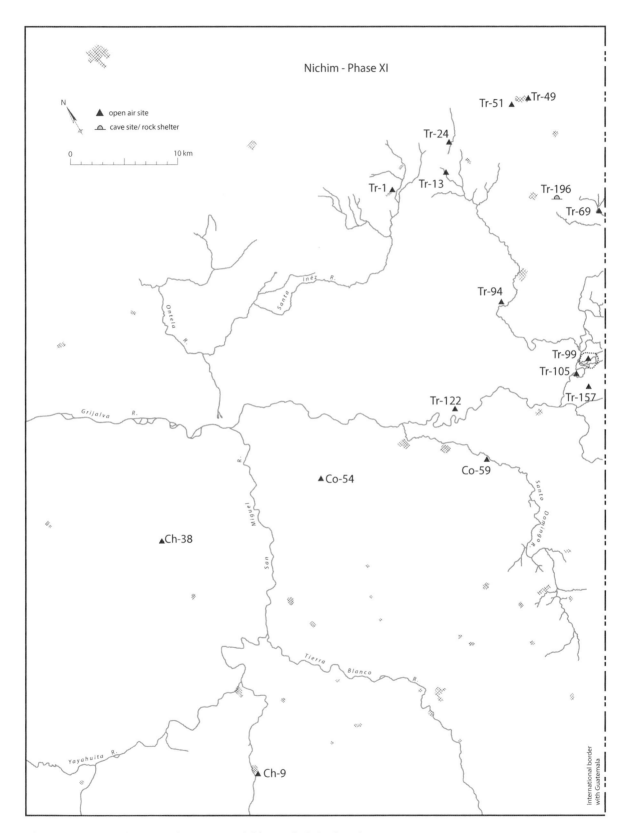

Figure 7.17. Map of Chiapa Phase XI or Nichim period site locations.

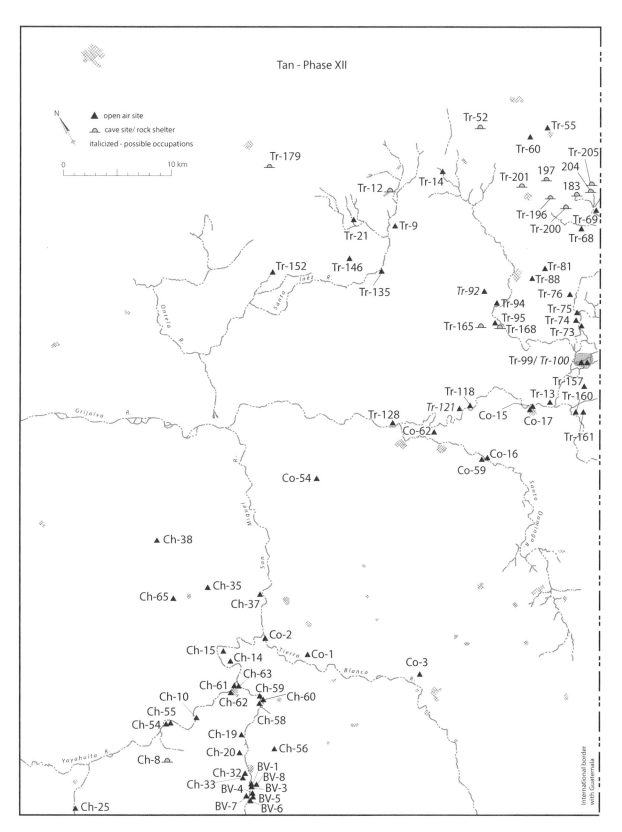

Figure 7.18. Map of Chiapa Phase XII or Tan period site locations.

architectural hallmark of the Postclassic period. Canajasté was primarily a Late Postclassic fortified site – well-planned and defensible. Located in a deep bend of the Lagartero River, Canajasté was bounded on three sides by water and on the fourth side by 2.5 m high stone wall (Blake 2010).

UX PHASE (AD 1500-1800; CHIAPA XIII) (FIGURE 7.19)

The impact of the Conquest and imposition of Spanish rule and religious administrative systems in this period is evident in the reduced number of sites found: 9, with another 2 possible. While some of the antecedent Late Postclassic sites would have continued into the Colonial period initially, the devastating epidemics that accompanied the early Spanish practice of *reducción* – centralizing native populations into Spanish settlements—rapidly depopulated the landscape.

The key Colonial period towns in the survey region were Coapa (Tr-162), Escuintenango (Co-64), and Aquespala (Co-15), which were all located along the Camino Real, the "royal road" that connected Mexico City, the capital of New Spain, with Antigua, the capital of the Capitanía General of Guatemala to the southeast (Lee 1998). The Colonial Coxoh Project, led by Lee and Sidney Markman (1977), focused on changes in material culture between the Late Postclassic and early Colonial periods in the upper Grijalva region. Excavations were undertaken at Postclassic Los Encuentros and its Colonial period neighbor, Coneta, to understand Coxoh Maya material lifeways during this dramatic transition (Lee 1979a, 1979b, 1985, 1996; Lee and Bryant 1988; Lee and Markman 1977, 1979; Markman 1984). Other Colonial settlements of the period were Pueblo Viejo (Ch-10), Cuxu (Co-3), Co-1, and possibly Utatlan in highland Guatemala; all were located southwest of the Camino Real (see Markman 1984).

HISTORIC SITES (POST-COLONIAL TO THE PRESENT) (FIGURE 7.20)

Although not considered within the scope of the survey project, a few post-Colonial period sites were recorded in the municipality of Chicomuselo. Two (Ch-1, Ch-25) appear to have been related to mining and processing of lead from surface veins in the area. Two other sites (Ch-10, Ch-43) may represent the remains of hacienda structures of the 19th century. The number of sites recorded for this period is clearly an underrepresentation. Many of the haciendas still in use date back a few centuries.

DEMOGRAPHIC TRENDS

Problems with extrapolating population from counted sites of surface surveys are well known, and many have been alluded to in preceding discussion. What we present here is only a rough measure based on the information collected in Lee's reconnaissance. We compare these data to similar information available for other parts of interior Chiapas to gauge the waxing and waning of settlements along most of the length of the Grijalva River. Comparative data are available for an extensive reconnaissance of western Chiapas (Peterson 2014) and a salvage survey from the Malpaso region of the middle Grijalva River just to the north (Lee et al. 2015). For Figure 7.21 we consolidated both of these studies to represent "western" Chiapas on this graph. The data from the upper Grijalva Valley are depicted in the same graph as "eastern" Chiapas. Information for the intervening area of "central" Chiapas comes from an analysis of three salvage projects by Alejandro Martínez (1987).

As evident in the three demographic profiles (Fig. 7.21), all three regions of the Central Depression of Chiapas experienced somewhat similar population trends, as gauged over broad regions and crudely assessed by the number of identified site components per phase. Maximal population occurred during the Late Classic period throughout interior Chiapas. This observation is certainly true of the upper Grijalva Valley. As remarked above, Lee's survey systematically underrepresented Late Classic sites because many of them where on lands that today are agriculturally marginal and highly unpleasant to walk through, and these lands appear to have been marginal for agriculture for most of prehistory. The Late Classic peak shown in Figure 7.21 for eastern Chiapas would be two to four times as

Figure 7.19. Map of Colonial or Ux period site locations.

Figure 7.20. Map of Historic period (post-Colonial to the present) site locations.

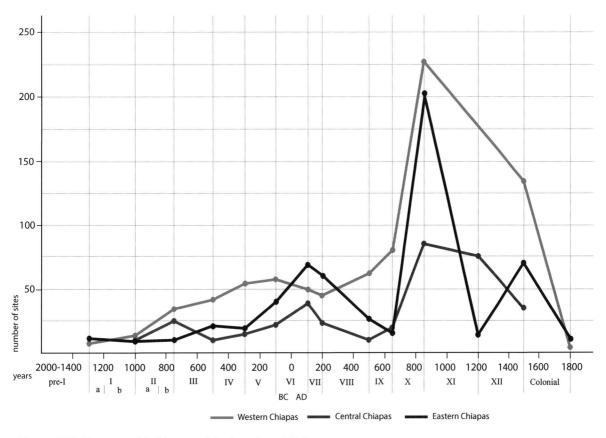

Figure 7.21. Demographic history of the interior of Chiapas.

high as shown if we added those found by de Montmollin and made adjustments for site sizes. Occupation of marginal lands may have been the logical consequence of the population explosion and pressure characteristic of the Late Classic period. Alternatively, the presence of sites in these locations may be indicative of a period of greater rainfall and, hence, of an expansion of lands suitable for rainfall agriculture about AD 800-1000. Whether the settlement of the numerous hillsides in the La Trinitaria municipality was cause or effect has yet to be determined. It was likely partly both. The overall trends for different sectors of Chiapas, however, indicate that the population surge in the upper Grijalva region in Late Classic times was not a consequence of local environmental conditions or weather.

As apparent on the settlement maps provided in this chapter, occupation for different periods distributed itself unequally across subareas. Lumping all the data together for purposes of presentation homogenizes the data and covers over what may have been significant differences by sub-regions. As apparent in Figure 7.21, for example, another period of peak occupation – at least compared to what came before – was in the Late Preclassic-Protoclassic era. This peak is evident for eastern and central Chiapas but not for western Chiapas. We attribute much of the increase for the Protoclassic period to the movement of Maya peoples from the lowlands to the north into the Chiapas Highlands, Comitan Plateau, and upper Grijalva Valley. Lowland Maya peoples do not appear to have moved into western Chiapas (Clark 2016). It is worth noting that Protoclassic sites of the central and eastern sectors of the Grijalva River Valley represented different cultures, as evident in significant differences in their ceramic wares. In the upper Grijalva, Protoclassic sites are characterized by monochrome red vessels that clearly derived from wares from the Maya Lowlands. In contrast, Protoclassic sites along the Grijalva River just to the west and downriver (i.e., Angostura region) were characterized by polished and incised black vessels more akin to ceramic wares from the central highlands of Guatemala (see, Brockington 1967; Bryant and Clark 2005b; Lowe 1977, 1978; Martínez 1978). These sites clearly belonged to two very different ceramic spheres and were made and used by peoples of different cultural affiliations.

It would be appropriate to monitor demographic trends by sub-regions that shared the same material culture signatures, but that is a task for another day. The data reported here from Lee's reconnaissance need to be blended with the more complete information collected by de Montmollin to reconstruct a more nuanced picture of demographic trends in the upper Grijalva Valley. It would also be well to translate all the data and scraps of data into estimates of the total number of hectares occupied per century rather than raw counts of sites per phase. A site with two house foundations should not be given equal demographic weight as one with 200 or 2000 such foundations, as has been done in Figure 7.21. New data obtained in recent projects from central Chiapas also need to be factored in. We doubt these new data will affect the overall character of the population peaks and valleys, but surely they will change their magnitudes for different eras. At the moment, the data show a slow and steady population increase in all regions of interior Chiapas, beginning in Early Preclassic times. Depending on the region, population appears to have peaked during the Protoclassic and to have been followed by a precipitous population decline for the Early and Middle Classic interval. This population trend was also true of the Pacific Coast area of Chiapas (Clark and Lowe 2013). Western Chiapas is an exception to the Early Classic collapse. But most of the sites represented on the graph are cave sites with Early Classic ceramic offerings rather than habitation sites. This latter kind of site is infrequent in western Chiapas as well (Clark 2014).

The Postclassic period represented another period of demographic decline following a population maximum. As mentioned for the upper Grijalva Valley, we are still not totally confident that Late Classic utilitarian wares did not persist into Postclassic times, hence we caution that the dramatic decline in population for Postclassic times shown in Figure 7.21 could entail or be based on a recognition problem. This caveat, however, only applies to the beginning of the Postclassic period and for determining the chronological boundary between periods. Late Postclassic ceramics are easy to recognize and pick out from Late Classic wares. The low frequency of Late Postclassic sites in the upper Grijalva Valley is clear evidence of a dramatic reduction of population from Late Classic times. What remains in doubt is whether this was the population nadir of steady decline or whether the Late Postclassic population represented a rebound from an even more massive, and earlier, population crash similar to that of Early Classic times. The data from central and western Chiapas show an incremental decline from Late Classic times to the end of the Postclassic. Some of this gradualism could be due to how potsherds available for surface sites there were analyzed – particularly fragments of Plumbate pottery. This ceramic type bridges the Late Classic to Postclassic transition. Different investigators may have characterized these sherds differently for different surveys, and this analytical inconsistency could explain some of the differences of estimated population for different sectors of interior Chiapas displayed in Figure 7.21.

We lack good information for post-Conquest sites and population. There is no question that the upper Grijalva region suffered a major population decline, with some Colonial towns being abandoned soon after they were founded (Lee and Bryant 1988). Our summary population chart only shows relative magnitudes. For the Late Classic period, de Montmollin (1989c:40) estimates that the 53 km² of the Rosario Valley were home to about 20,000 people. The greater region at that time would have accommodated well over 100,000 souls. We imagine that the Protoclassic period population would have been well below half of this high population mark.

SOME CONCLUDING THOUGHTS

Within the broad Isthmian geographic block, we have seen that the great Grijalva River trench and its basins formed a major natural route between north and south. Despite its two impassable canyons and rugged terrain and rapids, the extensive Grijalva system truly connected southern Veracruz and Tabasco with the highlands of Guatemala. (Lowe 2007:65)

This posthumous observation by Gareth Lowe succinctly captures the cultural importance of the Central Depression of Chiapas in Mesoamerican prehistory and is apropos for concluding our study of the easternmost sector of that system. Lowe came by his knowledge the hard way. In 1956 he was the first to undertake systematic survey by jeep, cayuco, and on foot of the upper basin of the Grijalva River or upper tributaries region (Lowe 1959). While not offering the tropical climate of the Pacific Coastal plain to the south or of the Maya Lowlands to the north, or of the better-watered areas of the Comitan Plateau and adjacent Guatemala Highlands, the many rivers, tributaries and natural springs of the upper Grijalva region did provide year-round permanent water and resources in what was otherwise a semi-arid environment. Nonetheless, "the variable path of the river through numerous shallows and constricted canyons prevented the development of extensive riverine communication … [and] encouraged the development of regionalism which is reflected in a variety of archaeological patterns" (Lowe 1959:21). These limitations of the Grijalva River system contrast with the extensive system of mangroves and estuaries seen along the Pacific Coast, which afforded canoe transportation and broader regional connections and developments over a stretch of 1000 kilometers (Navarrete 1978, 1988; Pye et al. 2011).

Still, despite the difficulties of travel along the Grijalva River, it was the major conduit of the region in pre-Hispanic times, and connections with central and western Chiapas are clearly demonstrated in shared ceramic traditions (Bryant et al 2005; Clark and Cheetham 2005), movement of obsidian products

(Clark and Lee 2007), and other relationships seen at distinct moments in prehistory, such as Middle Preclassic site layouts and shared elite burial practices from La Libertad on the Guatemala border to La Venta, Tabasco (Clark 2016). Communication routes connecting the Central Depression to other parts of Chiapas and to the rest of Mesoamerica have been explored elsewhere (see Lee and Navarrete 1978). The Central Depression, constituted largely by the Grijalva River Valley, and the Pacific Coast were two parallel and key communication routes connecting Central America to central Mexico in prehistory. The Pacific Coast was likely the easier route, particularly by canoe, but only in the dry season. It was a beastly route during the rainy season and virtually impassable. Traveling through the always drier Chiapas interior would have been a better option for any needed rainy season travel or commerce. The Spanish built the Camino Real through central Chiapas for sound and practical reasons. Other factors, such as politics, access to resources (e.g., obsidian), or local geographic conditions would have impacted which routes were used and when (Pye and Gutierrez 2007).

From ethnohistoric sources, it is known that Zoques of western Chiapas and of the middle Grijalva River region around Quechula, as well as Maya groups from the Central Highlands, were renown traders during the Late Postclassic and Conquest periods (Clark and Lee 2007; Clark et al. 2015; Lee and Navarrete 1978; Sahagún 1959:21-22). Unfortunately, there is little such information available for the upper Grijalva region. By virtue of its location, however, the upper Grijalva basin would clearly have been part of major crossroads in Mesoamerica (Clark and Lee 2007; Navarrete 2001).

The outlines of key moments and developments in Chiapas prehistory are highlighted in the findings of the Upper Grijalva River Basin Project. The project explored a virtually unknown region 3,700 km² in extent and mapped out and traced its prehistory from the beginnings of agrarian village life about 1800 BC to just past the Spanish Conquest. Few projects have undertaken such a herculean task in Mesoamerica; the best examples of such systematic survey and excavation work are the Valley of Oaxaca project (see, Flannery and Marcus 1983; Marcus and Flannery 1996) and the Basin of Mexico project (Sanders et al. 1979). The work done to date in the upper Grijalva Valley (delimitation of and description of its ceramic sequence, settlement pattern study, and site excavations) offers a framework for future research on culture history and processes in the region and adds to the growing body of knowledge on the importance of Chiapas in Mesoamerican prehistory.

REFERENCES CITED

–Letter from Thomas A. Lee Jr., to Gareth W. Lowe, March 24, 1972

–Letter from Gareth W. Lowe to Thomas A. Lee Jr., April 7, 1972

–Letter from Gareth W. Lowe to Thomas A. Lee Jr., January 4, 1973

Correspondence, Gareth W. Lowe Papers, L. Tom Perry Special Collections, Harold B. Lee Library, Brigham Young University, Provo.

–Report to the New World Archaeological Foundation Board by Gareth W. Lowe and Thomas A. Lee, July, 1973

–Reports to the NWAF Board, Gareth W. Lowe Papers, L. Tom Perry Special Collections, Harold B. Lee Library, Brigham Young University, Provo.

ACOSTA OCHOA, GUILLERMO
2008   *La cueva de Santa Marta y los cazadores-recolectores del Pleistoceno Final-Holoceno Temprano en las regiones tropicales de México.* Unpublished Ph.d. thesis, Instituto de Investigaciones Antropológicas, UNAM, Mexico.

ADAMS, ROBERT M.
1961   Changing Patterns of Territorial Organization in the Central Highlands of Chiapas. *American Antiquity* 26:341-360.

AGRINIER, PIERRE
1969   Dos tumbas tardías y otros descubrimientos en Chinkultic. *Boletín del INAH* 35:21-28.

1979a   Informe de trabajo efectuado en las zonas arqueológicas de Tenam Rosario y El Rosario, municipio de La Trinitaria, Chiapas, México. Report submitted to the Instituto de Antropología e Historia, Mexico.

1979b   Late Classic Elite vs. Non-Elite Domestic Varieties from the Tenam Rosario Zone. Paper presented at the XLIII International Congress of Americanists, Vancouver.

1983   Tenam Rosario: Una posible relocalización del Clásico Tardío Terminal maya desde el Usumacinta. In *Homenaje a Frans Blom: Antropología e historia de los mixe-zoques y mayas*, edited by Lorenzo Ochoa and Thomas A. Lee Jr., pp.241-254. BYU and UNAM, Mexico

1984   Densidad de población contemporánea y del Clásico Tardío Terminal en el valle de Santa Inés-Rosario, Chiapas. In *Investigaciones arqueológicas en el área maya, XVII Mesa Redonda (1981)*, vol. 1, pp. 423-430. Sociedad Mexicana de Antropología, San Cristóbal de las Casas.

1991   The Ballcourts of Southern Chiapas, Mexico. In *The Mesoamerican Ballgame*, edited by Vernon Scarborough and David Wilcox, pp. 175-194. University of Arizona Press, Tucson.

1993   El juego de pelota prehispánico en el valle El Rosario, municipio de Trinitaria, Chiapas. Antropología, In *Historia e imaginativa: Homenaje a Eduardo Martínez Espinosa*, edited by Carlos Navarrete and Carlos Álvarez, pp. 127-132. Gobierno del Estado de Chiapas and Instituto Chiapaneca de Cultura, Tuxtla Gutiérrez.

n.d.   Preliminary Investigations of the Rosario Valley, Chiapas, Mexico. In The Upper Grijalva Basin Maya Project Report on Field Work, 1975-1976, edited by Gareth Lowe. Manuscript on file, Fundación Arqueológica Nuevo Mundo, San Cristóbal de las Casas, 1976.

AGRINIER, PIERRE, AND DOUGLAS D. BRYANT
2005   Middle Classic Ceramics. In *Ceramic Sequence of the Upper Grijalva Region,*

Chiapas, Mexico, part 2, edited by Douglas D. Bryant, John E. Clark, and David Cheetham, pp. 401-413. Papers of the New World Archaeological Foundation, No. 67. BYU, Provo.

ÁLVAREZ ASOMOZA, CARLOS
2000   *El patrón de asentamiento en Las Margaritas, Chiapas*. UNAM, Mexico.

ANDREWS V, E. WYLLYS, AND NORMAN HAMMOND
1990   Redefinition of the Swasey Phase at Cuello, Belize. *American Antiquity* 55(3):570-584.

BACHAND, BRUCE, AND LYNNETH S. LOWE
2012   Chiapa de Corzo's Mound 11 Tomb and the Middle Formative Olmec. In *Arqueología reciente de Chiapas: Contribuciones del encuentro celebrado en el 60° Aniversario de la Fundación Arqueológica Nuevo Mundo*, edited by Lynneth S. Lowe and Mary E. Pye, pp. 45-68. Papers of the New World Archaeological Foundation, No. 72. BYU, Provo.

BALL, JOSEPH W.
1980   *The Archaeological Ceramics of Chinkultic, Chiapas, Mexico*. Papers of the New World Archaeological Foundation, No. 43. BYU, Provo.

BASAURI, CARLOS
1931   *Tojolabales, tzeltales y mayas: Breves apuntes sobre antropología, etnografía y lingüística*. Talleres Gráficos de la Nación, Mexico.

BATHGATE, DAVID
1980   *Cultural-Ecological Adaptation at Santa Marta(Tr-19): A Preclassic Village in the Upper Grijalva Basin, Chiapas, Mexico*. Unpublished MA thesis. Dept. of Anthropology, BYU, Provo.

n.d.   Mound 3 Excavations at Tenam Rosario. Unpublished manuscript on file with the Fundación Arqueológica Nuevo Mundo, San Cristóbal de las Casas, 1978.

BEARD, J. S.
1944   Climax Vegetation in Tropical America. *Ecology* 25(2):127-158.

BECQUELIN, PIERRE, AND CLAUDE F. BAUDEZ
1982   *Tonina, une cité maya du Chiapas (Mexique), Tomes II-III*. Mission Archéologique et Ethnologique Française au Mexique, Mexico.

BLAKE, MICHAEL
1986   Canajasté: Una ciudad-estado maya en transición. In *Anuario*, 1:119-157. Instituto de Estudios Indígenas, UNACH, San Cristóbal de las Casas.

2010   *Colonization, Warfare, and Exchange at the Postclassic Maya Site of Canajasté, Chiapas, Mexico*. Papers of the New World Archaeological Foundation, No. 70. BYU, Provo.

BLAKE, MICHAEL, JOHN E. CLARK, BARBARA VOORHIES, GEORGE MICHAELS, MICHAL W. LOVE, MARY E. PYE, ARTHUR A. DEMAREST, AND BARBARA ARROYO
1995   Radiocarbon Chronology for the Late Archaic and Formative Periods on the Pacific Coast of Southeast Mesoamerica. *Ancient Mesoamerica* 6:161-183.

BLOM, FRANS FERDINAND, AND GERTRUDE DUBY
1955-57 *La selva lacandona*. 2 vols. Editorial Cultural, Mexico.

BORHEGYI, STEPHAN F.
1965   Settlement Patterns of the Guatemalan Highlands. In *Handbook of Middle American Indians*, vol. 2, edited by Gordon R. Willey, pp. 59-74. University of Texas, Austin.

BORGSTEDE, GREGORY
2004   *Ethnicity and Archaeology in the Western Maya Highlands, Guatemala*. Unpublished Ph.D. dissertation in anthropology, University of Pennsylvania, Philadelphia.

BREEDLOVE, DENNIS E.
1973   The Phytogeography and Vegetation of

Chiapas (Mexico). In *Vegetation and Vegetational History of Northern Latin America*, edited by Alan Graham, pp. 149-165. Elsevier Scientific, Amsterdam

BROCKINGTON, DONALD L.
1967   *The Ceramic History of Santa Rosa, Chiapas, Mexico*. Papers of the New World Archaeological Foundation, No. 23. BYU, Provo.

BRYANT, DOUGLAS D.
1984   The Early Classic Period at Ojo de Agua, Chiapas, Mexico. In *Investigaciones arqueológicas en el área maya, XVII Mesa Redonda (1981)*, vol. 1, pp. 391-398. Sociedad Mexicana de Antropología, San Cristóbal de las Casas.

2005   Early Classic Ceramics. In *Ceramic Sequence of the Upper Grijalva Region, Chiapas, Mexico*, Part 2, edited by Douglas D. Bryant, John E. Clark, and David Cheetham, pp. 353-399. Papers of the New World Archaeological Foundation, No. 67. BYU, Provo.

2008   *Excavations at Ojo de Agua, an Early Classic Maya Site in the Upper Grijalva Basin, Chiapas, Mexico*. Papers of the New World Archaeological Foundation, No. 69. BYU, Provo.

n.d.   Preliminary notes and interpretations from fieldwork at Guajilar, Chiapas. Manuscript on file at New World Archaeological Foundation, San Cristóbal de las Casas, 1978.

BRYANT, DOUGLAS D., AND JOHN E. CLARK
1983   Los primeros mayas precolumbinos de la cuenca superior del río Grijalva. In *Homenaje a Frans Blom: Antropología e historia de los mixe-zoques y mayas*, edited by Lorenzo Ochoa and Thomas A. Lee Jr., pp. 223-239. BYU and UNAM, Mexico.

2005a   Late Preclassic Ceramics. In *Ceramic Sequence of the Upper Grijalva Region, Chiapas, Mexico*, Part 1, edited by Douglas D. Bryant, John E. Clark, and David Cheetham, pp. 265-282. Papers of the New World Archaeological Foundation, No. 67. BYU, Provo.

2005b   Protoclassic Ceramics. In *Ceramic Sequence of the Upper Grijalva Region, Chiapas, Mexico*, Part 1, edited by Douglas D. Bryant, John E. Clark, and David Cheetham, pp. 283-349. Papers of the New World Archaeological Foundation, No. 67. BYU, Provo.

BRYANT, DOUGLAS DONNE, JOHN E. CLARK, AND DAVID CHEETHAM (EDITORS)
2005   *Ceramic Sequence of the Upper Grijalva Region, Chiapas, Mexico*. 2 vols. Papers of the New World Archaeological Foundation, No. 67. BYU, Provo.

BRYANT, DOUGLAS DONNE, THOMAS A. LEE JR., AND MICHAEL BLAKE
2005   Postclassic Ceramics. In *Ceramic Sequence of the Upper Grijalva Region, Chiapas, Mexico*, Part 2, edited by Douglas D. Bryant, John E. Clark, and David Cheetham, pp. 549-625. Papers of the New World Archaeological Foundation, No. 67. BYU, Provo.

CAMPBELL, LYLE, AND BRANT GARDNER
1988   Coxoh. In *The Linguistics of Southeast Chiapas, Mexico*, by Lyle Campbell, pp. 315-338. Papers of the New World Archaeological Foundation, No. 50. BYU, Provo.

CASTELLANOS, MAYARI
2012a   La cerámica de El Solferín, Chiapas. In *Arqueología reciente de Chiapas: Contribuciones del encuentro celebrado en el 60° Aniversario de la Fundación Arqueológica Nuevo Mundo*, edited by Lynneth S. Lowe and Mary E. Pye, pp. 127-133. Papers of the New World Archaeological Foundation, No. 72. BYU, Provo.

2012b   *Tipología cerámica de Solferín, Chiapas*. Licenciatura thesis, Department of Anthropology, Universidad de las Américas, Puebla.

CIUDAD REAL, ANTONIO DE
1993   *Tratado curioso y doctor de las grandezas de la Nueva España*. 2 vols. UNAM, Mexico.

CLARK, JOHN E.
1988   *The Lithic Artifacts of La Libertad, Chiapas, Mexico. An Economic Perspective*. Papers of the New World Archaeological Foundation, No. 52. BYU, Provo.

1991   La fase Lato de la cuenca superior del río Grijalva: Implicaciones por el despliegue de la cultura mokaya. In *Primer Foro de Arqueología de Chiapas*, pp. 107-110. Gobierno del estado de Chiapas, CONECULTA, and Instituto Chiapaneca de Cultura, Tuxtla Gutiérrez.

2001   Ciudades tempranas olmecas. In *Reconstruyendo la ciudad maya: El urbanismo en las sociedades antiguas*, edited by Andrés Ciudad Ruiz, María J. Iglesias Ponce de León, María Del C. Martínez Martínez, pp. 183-210. Sociedad Española de Estudios Maya, Madrid.

2014   Notes on Culture History. In *A Brief Reconnasissan of Three Chiapas Municipalities*, by Fredrick A. Peterson, pp. 217-240. Papers of the New World Archaeological Foundation, No. 77. BYU, Provo.

2016   Western Kingdoms of the Middle Preclassic. In *Early Maya States*, edited by Robert Sharer and Loa Traxler, pp. 123-224. University Museum, Philadelphia.

CLARK, JOHN E., BARBARA ARROYO, AND DAVID CHEETHAM
2005   Early Preclassic and Early Middle Preclassic Ceramics. In *Ceramic Sequence of the Upper Grijalva Region, Chiapas, Mexico*, Part 1, edited by Douglas D. Bryant, John E. Clark, and David Cheetham, pp. 21-139. Papers of the New World Archaeological Foundation, No. 67. BYU, Provo

CLARK, JOHN E., AND DAVID CHEETHAM
2002   Mesoamerica's tribal foundations. In *The Archaeology of Tribal Societies*, William Parkinson, ed., pp. 278-339. International Monographs in Prehistory, Ann Arbor. ed., pp. 278-339.

2005   Cerámica del Formativo de Chiapas. In *La producción alfarera en el México Antiguo I*, edited by Beatriz Leonor Merino Carrión and Ángel García Cook, pp. 285-433. INAH, México.

CLARK, JOHN E., AND DENNIS GOSSER
1995   Reinventing America's First Pottery. In *The Emergence of Pottery: Technology and Innovation in Ancient Socities*, edited by William K. Barnett and John W. Hoopes, pp. 209-221. Smithsonian Institution, Washington, DC.

CLARK, JOHN E., AND RICHARD D. HANSEN
2001   The Architecture of Early Kingship: Comparative Perspectives on the Origins of the Maya Royal Court. In *Royal Courts of the Ancient Maya, Vol. 2: Data and Case Studies*, edited by Takeshi Inomata and Stephen D. Houston, pp.1-45. Westview, NY.

CLARK, JOHN E., RICHARD D. HANSEN, AND TOMÁS PÉREZ SUÁREZ
2000   La zona maya en el Preclásico. In *Historia antiguo de México, Vol. 1: El historia antiguo, sus áreas culturales, las orígenes y el horizonte Preclásico*, edited by Linda Manzanilla and Leonardo López Luján, pp.437-510. INAH, Mexico.

CLARK, JOHN E., AND MICHELLE KNOLL
2005   The American Formative Revisited. In *Gulf Coast Archaeology: The Southeastern U.S. and Mexico*, edited by Nancy White, pp. 281-303. University Press of Florida, Gainesville.

CLARK, JOHN E., AND THOMAS A. LEE JR.
1984   Formative Obsidian Exchange and the Emergence of Public Economies in Chiapas, Mexico. In *Trade and*

Exchange in Early Mesoamerica, edited by Kenneth Hirth, pp. 235-274. University of New Mexico Press, Albuquerque.

2007 The Changing Role of Obsidian Exchange in Central Chiapas. In *Archaeology, Art, and Ethnogenesis in Mesoamerican Prehistory: Papers in Honor of Gareth W. Lowe,* edited by Lynneth S. Lowe and Mary E. Pye, pp.109-139. Papers of the New World Archaeological Foundation, No. 68. BYU, Provo.

CLARK, JOHN E., THOMAS A. LEE JR., AND DOUGLAS DONNE BRYANT
2005 Introducing the Grijalva Maya Project. In *Ceramic Sequence of the Upper Grijalva Region, Chiapas, Mexico, Part 1,* edited by Douglas D. Bryant, John E. Clark, and David Cheetham, pp. 1-20. Papers of the New World Archaeological Foundation, No. 67. BYU, Provo.

CLARK, JOHN E., AND GARETH W. LOWE
2013 Izapa History. In *Middle and Late Preclassic Izapa: Ceramic Complexes and History,* by Gareth W. Lowe, Susanna M. Ekholm, and John E. Clark. Papers of the New World Archaeological Foundation, No. 73. BYU, Provo.

CLARK, JOHN E., GARETH W. LOWE, AND THOMAS A. LEE JR.
2015 The Malpaso Project and Zoque Prehistory. In *Reconnaissance and Excavations in the Malpaso Basin, Chiapas, Mexico,* edited by Thomas A. Lee Jr, Carlos Navarrete, and John E. Clark, pp. 171-224. Papers of the New World Archaeological Foundation, No. 78. BYU, Provo.

CLARK, JOHN E., AND RONALD W. LOWE
1980 Investigaciones arqueológicas en la región de Morelos, municipio de Trinitaria, Chiapas, Mexico. Report submitted to the Instituto Nacional de Antropología e Historia, Mexico.

CLARK, JOHN E., AND MARY E. PYE
2011 Revisiting the Mixe-Zoque: A Brief History of the Preclassic Peoples of Chiapas. In *The Southern Maya in the Late Preclassic,* edited by Michael Love and Jonathan Kaplan, pp. 25-45. University Press of Colorado, Boulder.

CLARK, JOHN E., MARIO TEJADA BOUSCAYROL, DONALDO CASTILLO VÁLDEZ, DAVID CHEETHAM, DEIRDRE NUTTAL, AND BEATRIZ BALCÁRCEL
2001 Prospección arqueológica de la cuenca superior del río Grijalva en Huehuetenango, Guatemala. Informe final de la Temporada 1999. Report submitted to the Instituto de Antropología e Historia, Guatemala.

COE, MICHAEL D.
1961 *La Victoria: An Early Site on the Pacific Coast of Guatemala.* Papers of the Peabody Museum, Harvard University, No. 53. Cambridge, Mass.

CULBERT, T. PATRICK
1965 *The Ceramic History of the Central Highlands of Chiapas, Mexico.* Papers of the New World Archaeological Foundation, No. 19. BYU, Provo.

DE MONTMOLLIN, OLIVIER
1979 Informe de las excavaciones realizadas en El Rosario (Tr-42). Report submitted to the Instituto Nacional de Antropología e Historia, Mexico.

1988 Tenam Rosario - A Political Microcosm. *American Anthropologist* 53:351-370.

1989a *The Archaeology of Political Structure.* Cambridge University Press, Cambridge.

1989b Land Tenure and Politics in the Late/Terminal Classic Rosario Valley, Chiapas, Mexico. *Journal of Anthropological Research* 45(3): 293-314.

1989c *Settlement Survey in the Rosario Valley, Chiapas, Mexico.* Papers of the New World Archaeological Foundation, No. 57. BYU, Provo.

1992 Patrones fronterizos de los reinos mayas del Clásico en los altos tributarios del río Grijalva. *Arqueología* 7(ene-jun): 57-67.

1995 *Settlement and Politics in Three Late Classic Maya Polities.* Prehistory Press, Madison.

1997 A Regional Study of Classic Maya Ballcourts from the Upper Grijalva Basin, Chiapas, Mexico. *Ancient Mesoamerica* 8:23-42.

2014 Comparing Ritual Life in Different Households from a Classic (AD 600-900) Maya Community. In *Arqueología reciente de Chiapas: Contribuciones del encuentro celebrado en el 60° Aniversario de la Fundación Arqueológica Nuevo Mundo,* edited by Lynneth S. Lowe and Mary E. Pye, pp. 69-86. Papers of the New World Archaeological Foundation, No. 72. BYU, Provo.

DIXON, KEITH A.
1959 *Ceramics from Two Preclassic Periods at Chiapa de Corzo, Chiapas, Mexico.* Papers of the New World Archaeological Foundation, No. 5. BYU, Provo.

DUTTON, BERTHA P.
1943 *Excavations at Tajumulco, Guatemala.* University of New Mexico, Albuquerque.

EKHOLM, SUSANNA M.
1969 *Mound 30a and the Early Preclassic Sequence of Izapa, Chiapas, Mexico.* Papers of the New World Archaeological Foundation, No. 25. Brigham Young University, Provo.

1977 The Necropolis Aspect of the Southwestern Maya Site of Lagartero, Chiapas. Paper presented at the Annual Meeting of the Society for American Archaeology, New Orleans.

1979a The Lagartero Figurines. In *Maya Archaeology and Ethnohistory,* edited by Norman Hammond and Gordon R. Willey, pp. 172-186. University of Texas Press, Austin.

1979b The Significance of an Extraordinary Maya Ceremonial Refuse Deposit at Lagartero. In *Actes du XLIIe Congrè International des Americanistes; Congrès du Centenaire, 2-9 septembre 1976,* Vol. 8, edited by Andrés Marcel d'Ans, Arnaud Castel and Georgette Soustelle, pp. 147-159. Societé des Americanistes, París.

1984 Cerámica maya policroma anómala de Lagartero, Chiapas. In *Investigaciones recientes en el área maya, XVII Mesa Redonda de la Sociedad Mexicana de Antropología (1981),* Tomo 2, pp. 371-378. Sociedad Mexicana de Antropología, San Cristóbal de las Casas.

1985 Lagartero Ceramic Pendants. In *Fourth Palenque Round Table, 1980,* edited by Elizabeth P. Benson, pp. 211-219. Precolumbian Art Research Institute, San Francisco.

1990 Una ceremonia maya del fin de ciclo: El gran basurero ceremonial de Lagartero, Chiapas. In *La época Clásica: Nuevos hallazgos, nuevas ideas,* edited by Amalia Cardós de Méndez, pp. 455-468. INAH, México.

EKHOLM, SUSANNA M., AND EDUARDO MARTÍNEZ
1983 Lagartero: Una situación única de los mayas de la cuenca superior del Grijalva. In *Arqueología e historia de los mixe-zoques y mayas: Homenaje a Frans Blom,* edited by Lorenzo Ochoa and Thomas A. Lee Jr., pp. 255-270. UNAM and BYU, México.

FLANNERY, KENT V., AND JOYCE C. MARCUS
1983 *The Cloud People: Divergent Evolution of the Zapotec and Mixtec Civilizations.* Academic Press, New York.

GARCÍA-BÁRCENA, JOAQUÍN
1982 *El precerámico de Aguacatenango, Chiapas, México.* INAH, Mexico.

GARCÍA-BÁRCENA, JOAQUÍN, AND DIANA
SANTAMARÍA
1982   *La cueva de Santa Marta,*
        Ocozocoautla, Chiapas: Estratigrafía,
        cronología y cerámica. INAH, Mexico.

GARCÍA-COOK, ÁNGEL, JESÚS MORA, AND PATRICIO
DÁVILA
1970   Informe general de la primera fase de
        los trabajos de salvamento arquelógico
        en el vaso de la presa de la Angostura.
        Report submitted to the Instituto
        Nacional de Antropología e Historia,
        Mexico.

GOLDMAN, EDWARD ALPHONSO
1951   *Biological Investigations in Mexico.*
        Miscellaneous Collections, Vol. 115.
        Smithsonian Institution, Washington,
        DC.

GOLDMAN, EDWARD ALPHONSO, AND R. T. MOORE
1946   The Biotic Provinces of Mexico.
        Journal of Mammalogy 26:347-360.

GÓMEZ-POMPA, ARTURO
1965   La vegetación de México. *Boletín de*
        Sociedad Botánica de México 29:76-
        120.

GONZÁLEZ QUINTERO, LAURO
1974   Tipo de vegetación de México. In El
        escenario geográfico, pp. 111-120.
        INAH, Mexico.

GUEVARA SÁNCHEZ, ARTURO
1981   *Los talleres líticos de Aguacatenango,*
        Chiapas. INAH, Mexico.

GURR, DEANNE M.
1988   *The Northwest Plaza Burials*
        of Lagartero, Chiapas, Mexico.
        Unpublished Ph.D. dissertation, Dept.
        Of Anthropology, University of Utah,
        Salt Lake City.

GUSSINYER, JORDI
1972   Rescate arqueológico la presa de
        la Angostura (primera temporada).
        Boletín del INAH, época II, 1:3-14.

HAMMOND, NORMAN, S. DONAGHEY, RANIER
BERGER, S. DE ATLEY, V. R. SWITSUR, AND A. P.
WARD
1977   Maya Formative Phase Radiocarbon
        Dates from Belize. *Nature* 267:608-610.

HELBIG, KARL
1964   *La cuenca superior del río Grijalva:*
        Un estudio regional de Chiapas.
        Sureste de México. Instituto de
        Ciencias y Artes de Chiapas, Tuxtla
        Gutiérrez.

KAUFMAN, TERRENCE S.
1971   Materiales lingüisticos para el studio
        de las relaciones internas y externas
        de la familia de idiomas mayanos.
        In *Desarollo cultural de los mayas,*
        2nd edition, edited by Evon Z. Vogt
        and Alberto Ruz Lhullier, pp. 81-36.
        UNAM, Mexico.

LALÓ JACINTO, GABRIEL, AND MARÍA DE LA LUZ
AGUILAR
1993   El Proyecto Arqueológico Tenam
        Puente. In *Cuarto Foro de Arqueología*
        de Chiapas, pp. 151-162. Gobierno
        del Estado de Chiapas and Instituto
        Chiapaneco de Cultura, Tuxtla
        Gutiérrez.

LEE, THOMAS A. JR.
1974a   The Middle Grijalva Chronology and
        Ceramic Relationships: A Preliminary
        Report. In *Mesoamerican Archaeology:*
        New Approaches, edited by Norman
        Hammond, pp.1-20. University of Texas
        Press, Austin.

1974b   *Mound 4 Excavations at San Isidro,*
        Chiapas, Mexico. Papers of the New
        World Archaeological Foundation, No.
        34. BYU, Provo.

1975   The Uppermost Grijalva Basin:
        A Preliminary Report of a New
        Archaeological Project. In *Balance*
        y perspectiva de la antropología
        de Mesoamérica y del norte de
        México, XIII Mesa Redonda, vol. 2:
        Arqueología, pp. 35-47. Sociedad
        Mexicana de Antropología, Mexico.

1976   A Preliminary Report of the First Phase of Excavations at Guajilar, Chiapas. Report submitted to INAH, Mexico.

1978   Informe Preliminar de la 2a Temporada de Campo, Febrero-Junio, 1978, del Proyecto de la Zona Guajilar-Niagara. Report submitted to INAH, Mexico.

1979a   Coapa, Chiapas: A Sixteenth-Century Coxoh Maya Village on the Camino Real. In *Maya Archaeology and Ethnohistory*, edited by Norman Hammond and Gordon R. Willey, pp. 208-222. University of Texas Press, Austin and London.

1979b   Early Colonial Coxoh Maya Syncretism in Chiapas, Mexico. *Estudios de Cultura Maya* XII: 93-109.

1980   Tercera Temporada de Campo en Portrero Mango (Tr-172) Rancho Entre Ríos, Municipio Trinitaria, Chiapas. Preliminary report submitted to the Instituto Nacional de Antropología e Historia, Mexico.

1984   Investigaciones arqueológicas recientes del clásico, postclásico y colonial maya en Chiapas: resumen e implicaciones. In *Investigaciones arqueológicas en el área maya, XVII Mesa Redonda (1981)*, vol. 1, pp.113-130. Sociedad Mexicana de Antropología, San Cristóbal de las Casas.

1985   Ramifications of the Colonial Coxoh Maya Household Group. In *Estudios del reino de Guatemala: Homenaje al Professor S. D. Markman*, edited by Duncan Kinkead, pp. 61-76. Escuela de Estudios Hispano-americanos de Sevilla, Seville.

1989   La arqueología de los Altos de Chiapas: Un estudio contextual. *Mesoamérica* 18:257-293.

1991   Los cazadores-recolectores y agricultores tempranos en el Alto Grijalva. In *Primer Foro de Arqueología de Chiapas*, pp. 131-138. Gobierno del Estado de Chiapas,

CONECULTA, and Instituto Chiapaneco de Cultura, Tuxtla Gutiérrez.

1994   Las relaciones extra-regionales del complejo cerámico Nichim de Guajilar, Chiapas. In *Anuario 1993: Instituto Chiapaneco de Cultura*, pp. 270-289. Gobierno del Estado de Chiapas and Instituto Chiapaneco de Cultura, Ocozocoautla de Espinosa, Chiapas.

1996   Sincretismo coxóh: Resistencia maya colonial en la cuenca superior del río Grijalva. In *Quinto Foro de Arqueología de Chiapas*, pp. 175-190. Gobierno del Estado de Chiapas and UNICACH, Tuxtla Gutiérrez.

1998   Veredas, caminos reales y vías fluviales: Rutas antiguas de comunicación en Chiapas. In *Rutas de intercambio en Mesoamérica: III Coloquio Pedro Bosch-Gimpera*, edited by Evelyn C. Rattray, pp. 239-359. UNAM, Mexico.

LEE, THOMAS A. JR., AND DOUGLAS D. BRYANT
1988   The Colonial Coxoh Maya. In *Ethnoarchaeology among the Highland Maya of Chiapas*, Mexico, edited by Thomas A. Lee Jr. and Bryan Hayden, pp. 5-106. Papers of the New World Archaeological Foundation, No. 56. BYU, Provo.

1996   Patrones domesticas del periodo Postclásio Tardío de la cuenca superior del río Grijalva. In *Quinto Foro de Arqueología de Chiapas*, pp. 53-68. Gobierno del Estado de Chiapas and UNICACH, Tuxtla Gutiérrez.

n.d.   A Preliminary Report of Archaeological Investigations at Los Encuentros, Chiapas (TR-94). Manuscript on file in the NWAF office, BYU, Provo, 1977.

LEE, THOMAS A. JR., AND JOHN E. CLARK
1988   Oro, tela y xute: Investigaciones arqueológicas en la región Camcum, Colonia Las Delicisas, Chiapas. *Arqueología* 4: 7-46.

2016   *Chiapa de Corzo, Mound 17: Comparative Analysis of a Salvage Excavation*. Papers of the New World Archaeological Foundation, No. 80. BYU, Provo,

LEE, THOMAS A. JR., AND SIDNEY MARKMAN
1977   The Coxoh Colonial Project and Coneta, Chiapas, Mexico. A Provincial Maya Village under the Spanish Conquest. *Historical Archaeology* 11:56-66.

1979   Coxoh Maya Acculturation in Colonial Chiapas: A Necrotic Archaeological-Ethnohistorical Model. *Actes du XLII Congrés International des Américanistes* 8: 57-66. Congrés du Centenaire, Paris.

LEE, THOMAS A. JR., AND CARLOS NAVARRETE (EDS.)
1978   *Mesoamerican Communication Routes and Cultural Contact*. Papers of the New World Archaeological Foundation, No. 40. BYU, Provo.

LEE, THOMAS A. JR., CARLOS NAVARRETE, AND JOHN E. CLARK
2015   *Reconnaissance and Excavations in the Malpaso Basin, Chiapas, Mexico*. Papers of the New World Archaeological Foundation, No. 78. BYU, Provo.

LEOPOLD, A. S.
1950   Vegetation Zones of Mexico. *Ecology* 31:507-518.

LOVE, MICHAEL
2002   *Early Complex Society in Pacifica Guatemala: Settlements and Chronology of the Río Naranjo, Guatemala*. Papers of New World Archaeological Foundation, No. 66. BYU, Provo

LOWE, GARETH W.
1959   *Archaeological Exploration of the Upper Grijalva River, Chiapas, Mexico*. Papers of the New World Archaeological Foundation, No. 2. Orinda.

1967   Discussion. In *Altamira and Padre Piedra, Early Preclassic Sites in Chiapas,* by Dee Green and Gareth Lowe, pp. 53-79. Papers of New World Archaeological Foundation, No. 20. BYU, Provo.

1975   *The Early Preclassic Barra Phase of Altamira, Chiapas: A Review with New Data*. Papers of New World Archaeological Foundation, No. 38. BYU, Provo.

1977   The Mixe-Zoque as Competing Neighbors of the Early Lowland Maya. In *The Origins of Maya Civilization*, R. E. W. Adams, ed., pp. 197-248. University of New Mexico Press, Albuquerque.

1978   Eastern Mesoamerica. In *Chronologies in New World Archaeology*, edited by R. E. Taylor and C. W. Meighan, pp. 331-393. Academic Press, New York.

2007   Early Formative Chiapas: The Beginnings of Civilization in the Central Depression of Chiapas. In *Archaeology, Art, and Ethnogenesis in Mesoamerican Prehistory: Papers in Honor of Gareth W. Lowe*, edited by Lynneth S. Lowe and Mary E. Pye, pp. 63-108. Papers of the New World Archaeological Foundation, No. 68. BYU, Provo.

LOWE, GARETH W., SUSANNA M. EKHOLM, JOHN E. CLARK
2013   *Middle and Late Preclassic Izapa: Ceramic Complexes and History*. Papers of the New World Archaeological Foundation, No. 73. BYU, Provo.

LOWE, LYNNETH S., AND CARLOS ÁLVAREZ ASOMOZA
2007   Recent Explorations at the Postclassic Site of Los Cimientos de las Margaritas. In *Archaeology, Art, and Ethnogenesis in Mesoamerican Prehistory: Papers in Honor of Gareth W. Lowe*, edited by Lynneth S. Lowe

and Mary E. Pye, pp. 321-336. Papers
of the New World Archaeological
Foundation, No. 68. BYU, Provo.

MacNeish, Richard S., and Frederick Peterson
1962   *The Santa Marta Rockshelter,
Ocozocoautla, Chiapas, Mexico.* Papers
of the New World Archaeological
Foundation, No. 14. BYU, Provo.

Marcus, Joyce, and Kent V. Flannery
1996   *Zapotec Civilization: How Urban
Society Evolved in Mexico's Oaxaca
Valley.* Thames and Hudson, London.

Markman, Sydney David
1984   *Architecture and Urbanization in
Colonial Chiapas, Mexico.* Memoirs
153. American Philosophical Society,
Philadelphia.

Marquina, Ignacio
1939   *Atlas arqueológico de la República
Mexicana.* INAH, México.

Martínez M., Alejandro
1976   Distribución de la población
prehispánica en el vaso de la presa
de La Angostura, Chiapas. *XIV Mesa
Redonda de la Sociedad Mexicana de
Antropología,* Vol. 1:181-190.

1978   *Don Martín, Chiapas: Inferencias
económico-sociales de una comunidad
arqueológica.* Licenciatura thesis,
Escuela Nacional de Antropología e
Historia. Mexico.

1987   Notas sobre los sistemas de
asentamiento en el centro de Chiapas.
*Memorias del Primer Coloquio
Internacional de Mayistas,* pp. 245-257.

Matheny, Ray T., and Deanne L. Gurr
1979   Ancient Hydraulic Techniques in the
Chiapas Highlands. *American Scientist*
67(4):441-449.

McQuown, Norman
1971   Los orígenes y la diferenciación de
los mayas según se infiere del estudio
comparativo de las lenguas mayas. In
Desarollo cultural de los mayas, edited

by Evon Z. Vogt and Alberto Ruz
Lhullier, pp. 49-78. UNAM, Mexico.

Miller, Donald E.
2014   *Excavations at La Libertad, a Middle
Formative Ceremonial Center in
Chiapas, Mexico.* Papers of the New
World Archaeological Foundation,
No. 64. BYU, Provo.

Miller, Donald E., and Gareth W. Lowe
2014   Appendix 1: Test Excavations on the
La Libertad-Entre Ríos Peninsula.
In *Excavations at La Libertad, a
Middle Formative Ceremonial Center
in Chiapas, Mexico,* by Donald E.
Miller. Papers of the New World
Archaeological Foundation, No. 64.
BYU, Provo.

Miranda, Faustino
1952   *La vegetación de Chiapas.* Gobierno
del Estado de Chiapas, Tuxtla
Gutiérrez.

1975   *La vegetación de Chiapas.* 2nd edition.
Gobierno del Estado de Chiapas, Tuxtla
Gutiérrez.

Miranda, Faustino, and Efraím Hernández
1963   Los tipos de vegetación de México y
su clasificación. *Sociedad Botánica de
Mexico* 28:29-179. Escuela Nacional de
Agricultura, Mexico.

Mülleried, Friedrich (Federico) K. G.
1957   *La geología de Chiapas.* Gobierno del
Estado de Chiapas, Tuxtla Gutiérrez.

Navarrete, Carlos
1966   *The Chiapanec History and
Culture.* Papers of the New World
Archaeological Foundation, No. 21.
BYU, Provo.

1975   Chinkultic (Chiapas): Trabajos
realizados en 1975. *Boletín del INAH,*
época II, 19:11-22.

1976   Chinkultic (Chiapas): Trabajos
realizados en 1976. *Boletín del INAH,*
época II, 19:43-58.

1978a   The Prehispanic System of
Communications between Chiapas
and Tabasco. In *Mesoamerican
Communication Routes and Cultural
Contacts*, edited by Thomas A.
Lee Jr. and Carlos Navarrete, pp.
75-106. Papers of the New World
Archaeological Foundation, No. 40.
BYU, Provo.

1978b   *Un reconocimiento de la Sierra Madre
de Chiapa: Apuntes de un diario de
campo.* Centro de Estudios Maya,
UNAM, Mexico.

1981   Las rutas de comunicación prehispánica
en los Altos Cuchumatanes. Un
proyecto arqueológico y etnohistórico.
In *Los legítimos hombres:
Aproximación antropológico al grupo
Tojolabal,* Vol. 1, edited by Mario
Humberto Ruz, pp. 75-88. UNAM,
Mexico.

1984   *Guía para el estudio de los
monumentos esculpidos de Chinkultic,
Chiapas.* Centro de Estudios Mayas.
UNAM, Mexico.

1998   La navegación en la costa de Chiapas.
Arqueología 6(33):32-39.

1999   Algunas representaciones iconográficas
en Chinkultic, Chiapas. *Anales de la
Academia de Geografía e Historia de
Guatemala* 74. Guatemala.

2001   Arqueología de los altos orientales
de Chiapas. *Arqueología Mexicana*
9(50):32-37.

2007   El complejo escénico en Chinkultic,
Chiapas. In *XX Simposio de
Investigaciones Arqueológicas en
Guatemala*, edited by Juan Pedro
Laporte, Héctor Mejía and Barbara
Arroyo, pp. 801-812. Ministerio
de Cultura y Deportes, IDAEH,
Asociación Tikal, Fundación
Arqueológica Nuevo Mundo,
Guatemala.

NAVARRETE, CARLOS, AND ROCÍO HERNÁNDEZ
JUÁREZ
2002   Variaciones interpretativas sobre el
juego de pelota de Chinkultic, Chiapas.
Anales de Antropología 36:11-41.

NELSON, FRED W., AND JOHN E. CLARK
1998   Obsidian Production and Exchange
in Eastern Mesoamerica. In *Rutas
de intercambio en Mesoamérica: III
Coloquio, Pedro Bosch Gimpera*,
edited by Evelyn Rattray, pp. 277-333.
UNAM, Mexico.

PAILLÉS, MARICRUZ, AND RAÚL ÁVILA LÓPEZ
1987   Mango Amate, algunas inferencias
arqueológicas durante el Protoclásico
en la cuenca superior del río Grijalva,
Chiapas. *Revista Mexicana de Estudios
Antropológicas* 33(2):343-356.

PENNINGTON, T. D., AND J. SAURKHÁN
1968   *Árboles tropicales de México: Manual
para la identificación de principales
especies.* Instituto Nacional de
Antropología e Historia, Mexico.

PETERSON, FREDRICK
1968   *A Brief Reconnaissance of Three
Chiapas Municipalities.* Papers of the
New World Archaeological Foundation,
No. 77. BYU, Provo.

PIÑA CHÁN, ROMÁN
1961   Reconocimientos arqueológicos en el
estado de Chiapas. In *Los mayas del
sur y sus relaciones con los nahuas
meridionales, VII Mesa Redonda*,
pp. 53-62. Sociedad Mexicana de
Antropología, San Cristóbal de las
Casas.

PLASCENCIA-VARGAS, HÉCTOR, MARIO GONZÁLEZ-
ESPINOSA, NEPTALÍ RAMIREZ-MARCIAL, DAVID
ÁLVAREZ-SOLIS, AND KARIM MUSÁLEM-
CASTILLEJOS
2014   Características físico-bióticas de la
cuenca del río Grijalva. In *Montañas,
pueblos y agua. Dimensiones y
realidades de la cuenca Grijalva*,
edited by Mario González-Espinosa
and Marie Claude Brunel Manse,
pp. 29-72. El Colegio de la Frontera
Sur, and Juan Pablos Editor, Mexico.

PYE, MARY E., AND GERARDO GUTIÉRREZ
2007   The Pacific Coast Trade Route
        of Mesoamerica: Iconographic
        Connections between Guatemala
        and Guerrero. In *Archaeology, Art,
        and Ethnogenesis in Mesoamerican
        Prehistory: Papers in Honor of Gareth
        W. Lowe*, edited by Lynneth S. Lowe
        and Mary E. Pye, pp.229-245. Papers
        of the New World Archaeological
        Foundation, No. 68. BYU, Provo.

PYE, MARY E., JOHN HODGSON, AND JOHN E.
CLARK
2011   Jocotal Settlement Patterns, Salt
        Production, and Pacific Coast
        Interactions. In *Early Mesoamerican
        Social Transformations: Archaic and
        Formative Lifeways in the Soconusco
        Region*, edited by Richard Lesure,
        pp. 217-241. University of California,
        Berkeley and Los Angeles.

RIVERO TORRES, SONIA
1978   Los Cimientos: Análisis del patrón de
        asentamiento por localización espacial.
        Estudios de Cultura Maya XI: 113-121.

1983   *Late Classic Rural Settlement
        Patterns in the San Gregorio Region,
        Chiapas, Mexico.* Unpublished Ph.D.
        dissertation, Faculty of Archaeology,
        Cambridge University, Cambridge.

1987   *Los Cimientos, Chiapas, México: A
        Late Classic Maya Community.* Papers
        of the New World Archaeological
        Foundation, No. 51. BYU, Provo.

1990   *Patrón de asentamiento rural en la
        región de San Gregorio, Chiapas, para
        el Clásico Tardío.* INAH, Mexico.

1994   Patrón de asentamiento en la cuenca
        superior del río Grijalva. In *Cuarto
        Foro de Arqueología de Chiapas*,
        pp. 163-192. Gobierno del Estado de
        Chiapas y Instituto Chiapaneca de
        Cultura, Tuxtla Gutiérrez.

1996   El juego de pelota del sitio de
        Lagartero, Chiapas. In *Quinto Foro
        de Arqueología de Chiapas*, pp. 39-
        52. Gobierno del Estado de Chiapas,

        UNICACH, Centro de Estudios
        Superiores de México y Centro
        América, Tuxtla Gutiérrez.

1997   La cerámica y lítica de Lagartero,
        Chiapas, procedente de El Limonar,
        Unidad 1. In *Homenaje al profesor
        César A. Sáenz*, coordinated by Ángel
        García Cook, et al., pp. 201-250. INAH,
        Mexico.

1999   Montículo 1 del sitio arqueológico
        Lagartero, Municipio La Trinitaria,
        Chiapas. *Mexicon* XXI:58-61.

2001   Lagartero and its Environs (Chiapas,
        Mexico). In *Archaeology of Ancient
        Mexico and Central America, an
        Encyclopedia*, edited by Susan T. Evans
        and David L. Webster, p. 392. Garland
        Publishing, Inc., NY and London.

2002   *Figurillas antropomorfas y zoomorfas
        del juego de pelota de Lagartero,
        Chiapas.* UNICACH. Tuxtla Gutiérrez.

2003   Cuatro vasos policromos de Lagartero,
        Chiapas. *Arqueología*, 2nd época, 29:
        162-166.

2006   Lagartero. In *Mayas, zoques y otras
        culturas: El sureste mexicano, Chiapas*,
        p. 32. Ciudades prehispánicas, estudio y
        reconstrucción, núm 2. CONACULTA,
        INAH y Grupo AZABACHE, Mexico.

2007a   La cerámica del Clásico Terminal y el
        Posclásico Temprano en el estado de
        Chiapas. In *La producción alfarera
        en el México Antiguo IV*, edited by
        Beatriz Leonor Merino Carrión and
        Ángel García Cook, pp. 15-56. INAH,
        Mexico.

2007b   El sitio arqueológico de Lagartero,
        Chiapas. *Liminar: Estudios sociales y
        humanísticos* Año 5, 5: 183-194. Tuxtla
        Gutiérrez. http://liminar.cesmeca.
        mx/index.php/r1/article/view/242/224
        (accessed November 10, 2015)

RIVERO TORRES, SONIA, T. CALLIGANO, DOLORES
TENORIO, AND M. JIMÉNEZ REYES
2008   Characterization of archaeological
        obsidians from Lagartero, Chiapas,

by PIXE. *Journal of Archaeological Science* 35(12):3168-3171.

RIVERO TORRES AND DOLORES TENORIO
2005   Artefactos líticos de Montículo num. 5 de Lagartero, Chiapas. *Arqueología* 35(ene-abril):166-182. 3168-3171.

ROBINSON, EUGENIA J., PAT M. FERRELL, KITTY F. EMERY, DOROTHY E. FREIDEL, AND GEOFFREY BRASWELL
2002   Preclassic Settlement and Geomorphology in the Highlands of Guatemala: Excavations at Urias, Valley of Antigua. In *Incidents of Archaeology in Central America and Yucatan: Essays in Honor of Edwin M. Shook*, edited by Michael Love, Marion Popenoe de Hatch, and Héctor Escobedo, pp. 251-276. University Press of America, Lanham.

ROBINSON, EUGENIA J., AND MARY E. PYE
1997   Investigaciones en Rucal, Sacatepéquez: Hallazgos de una ocupación Formativo Medio del altiplano de Guatemala. In *X Simposio de Investigaciones Arqueológicas en Guatemala, 1996*, edited by Juan Pedro Laporte and Héctor L. Escobedo, pp. 478-487. Museo Nacional de Antropologia, Guatemala.

ROSENSWIG, ROBERT M.
2011   An Early Mesoamerican Archipelago. In *Early Mesoamerican Social Transformations: Archaic and Formative Lifeways in the Soconusco Region*, edited by Richard Lesure, pp. 242-271. University of California, Berkeley and Los Angeles.

SAHAGÚN, BERNARDINO DE
1959   *Florentine Codex: A General History of the Things of New Spain. Vol. 9: The Merchants*. Translations with notes and illustrations by Arthur J. O. Anderson and Charles E. Dibble. School of American Research and University of Utah Press, Santa Fe and Salt Lake City.

SANDERS, WILLIAM T.
1961   *Ceramic Stratigraphy at Santa Cruz, Chiapas, Mexico*. Papers of the New World Archaeological Foundation, No. 13. BYU, Provo.

WILLIAM T. SANDERS, JEFFREY R. PARSONS, AND ROBERT S. SANTLEY
1979   *The Basin of Mexico: Ecological Processes in the Evolution of a Civilization*. Academic Press, New York.

SHARER, ROBERT J., AND DAVID W. SEDAT
1987   *Archaeological Investigations in the Northern Maya Highlands, Guatemala: Interaction and the Development of Maya Civilization*. University Museum, Mon. 59. University of Pennsylvania, Philadelphia.

SHOOK, EDWIN M.
1956   *An Archaeological Reconnaissance in Chiapas, Mexico*. New World Archaeological Foundation, Publication 1, pp. 20-37. Orinda.

TEJADA, MARIO, JOHN CLARK, AND BEATRIZ BALCÁRCEL
2000   Exploraciones arqueológicas de la cuenca superior del río Grijalva en Huehuetenango, Guatemala. In *XIII Simposio de Investigaciones Arqueológicas en Guatemala, 1999*, edited by Juan Pedro Laporte, Héctor Escobedo, Bárbara Arroyo, and A.C. de Suasnávar, pp. 705-717. Museo Nacional de Arqueología y Etnología, Guatemala. http://www.asociaciontikal.com/pdf/56.99_-_Mario_Tejada.pdf (accessed May 22, 2016)

TENORIO CASTILLEJOS, DOLORES, JOSEFINA BAUTISTA MARTÍNEZ, AND SONIA RIVERO TORRES
2012   Los entierros de la Pirámide No.2 de Lagartero, Chiapas. In *Arqueología reciente de Chiapas: Contribuciones del encuentro celebrado en el 60° Aniversario de la Fundación*

Arqueológica Nuevo Mundo, edited by Lynneth S. Lowe and Mary E. Pye, pp.101-112. Papers of the New World Archaeological Foundation, No. 72. BYU, Provo.

VOGT, EVON Z.
1964   The Genetic Model and Maya Cultural Development. In *Desarollo cultural de los mayas*, edited by Evon Z. Vogt and Alberto Ruz Lhullier, pp. 9-48. UNAM, Mexico.

1971   The Genetic Model and Maya Cultural Development. In *Desarollo cultural de los mayas*, edited by Evon Z. Vogt and Alberto Ruz Lhullier, pp. 9-48. UNAM, Mexico. (reprint)

VOORHIES, BARBARA
1976   *The Chantuto People: An Archaic Period Society of the Chiapas Littoral, Mexico*. Papers of the New World Archaeological Society, Number 41, BYU, Provo.

2004   *Coastal Collectors in the Holocene: The Chantuto People of Southwest Mexico*. University Press of Florida, Gainesville.

2015   *An Archaic Mexican Shellmound and Its Entombed Floors*. UCLA Cotsen Institute of Archaeology Press, Los Angeles.

n.d.   Vegetation Formations of the Upper Grijalva Basin, Chiapas, Mexico. Unpublished manuscript on file, San Cristóbal de las Casas, Chiapas, 1981.

WAGNER, PHILIP L.
2015   Natural Vegetation of Middle America. *Handbook of Middle American Indians, Vol. 1: Natural Environments and Early Cultures*, edited by Robert C. West, pp. 216-264. University of Texas Press, Austin.

WELLS, SHELLEY
2015   *Grave Matters: A Presentation and Comparative Analysis of the Late*

Classic Burials from Guajilar, Chiapas, Mexico. unpublished MA thesis, Department of Anthropology, BYU, Provo.

WEST, ROBERT C.
1964   Surface Configuration and Associated Geology of Middle America. In *Handbook of Middle American Indians, Vol. 1: Natural Environments and Early Cultures*, edited by Robert C. West, pp. 33-83. University of Texas Press, Austin.

WHITE, JAMES MURRAY
1976   *The Cultural Sequence at Chicomucelo, Chiapas*. Unpublished MA dissertation. Department of Archaeology, Simon Fraser University, Burnaby, British Columbia.

WILLEY, GORDON R.
1970   The Real Xe Ceramics of Seibal, Peten, Guatemala. In *Monographs and Papers in Maya Archaeology*, edited by William R. Bullard, pp.315-356. Memoirs of the Peabody Museum of Archaeology and Ethnology, Vol. 61. Harvard University, Cambridge.

1973   *The Altar de Sacrificios Excavations: General Summary and Conclusions*. Papers of the Peabody Museum of Archaeology and Ethnology, Vol. 64. Harvard University, Cambridge.

Willey, Gordon R., William R. Bullard, John B. Glass, and James C. Gifford
1965   *Prehistoric Maya Settlements in the Belize Valley*. Papers of the Peabody Museum of Anthropology and Ethnology, Vol. LIV. Harvard University, Cambridge.

WOODBURY, RICHARD B.
1953   *The Ruins of Zaculeu, Guatemala*. 2 vols. United Fruit Company, New York.